ATTACK POLITICS

STUDIES IN GOVERNMENT AND PUBLIC POLICY

ATTACK POLITICS
NEGATIVITY IN
PRESIDENTIAL
CAMPAIGNS SINCE 1960

Emmett H. Buell Jr. and Lee Sigelman

University Press of Kansas

© 2008 by the University Press of Kansas

Published by the University Press of Kansas (Lawrence, Kansas 66045), which was
organized by the Kansas Board of Regents and is operated and funded by Emporia State
University, Fort Hays State University, Kansas State University, Pittsburg State University,
the University of Kansas, and Wichita State University

Library of Congress Cataloging-in-Publication Data

Buell, Emmett H.
    Attack politics : negativity in presidential campaigns since 1960 / Emmett H. Buell Jr.
and Lee Sigelman.
        p.   cm. — (Studies in government and public policy)
    Includes bibliographical references.
    ISBN 978-0-7006-1561-2 (cloth : alk. paper)
    1. Presidents—United States—Election—History. 2. Political campaigns—United
States—History. 3. Political candidates—United States—History. I. Sigelman, Lee. II. Title.
    JK524.B785 2008
    324.7097309′045—dc22   2007050289

British Library Cataloguing-in-Publication Data is available.

Printed in the United States of America
10 9 8 7 6 5 4 3 2 1

The paper used in this publication is recycled and contains 50 percent postconsumer waste.
It is acid free and meets the minimum requirements of the American National Standard
for Permanence of Paper for Printed Library Materials Z39.48–1992.

ONTENTS

PREFACE AND ACKNOWLEDGMENTS

On Friday, October 29, 2004, approximately 20,000 Bush supporters filled the Nationwide Arena in Columbus, Ohio, to the rafters. Thousands stood in line for two hours or more before the doors opened, and many others took their places over the next two hours, before the arrival of President Bush, First Lady Laura Bush, and California governor Arnold Schwarzenegger. A high school band and an African American singing group provided musical entertainment, followed by Republican officeholders, including Representative Deborah Pryce, who spoke of Ohio's importance in the upcoming election. Bush's opponent, Senator John Kerry, also appeared, not in the flesh but as a dour flip-flopper on gigantic screens suspended from the ceiling. Uninterrupted by Republican commentary, the video consisted entirely of Kerry making contradictory pronouncements on Saddam Hussein's weapons of mass destruction and the Iraq War. Repeat showings occurred every half hour. When the presidential party finally arrived, thousands shouted, cheered, and waved a variety of banners and signs for fifteen minutes or more. This outpouring of affection visibly moved Bush and his exhausted wife.[1]

Bush then delivered a campaign speech so traditionally structured that a time-traveled Lord James Bryce could have followed it without difficulty. Indeed, this famous observer of American politics of the late nineteenth and early twentieth centuries might have noticed that the more things changed in campaign discourse, the more they stayed the same. Lines such as "We love campaigning in your state" and "Ohio is a wonderful place" have tripped from the lips of presidential candidates for a century or more. Similarly, expressions of gratitude to campaign workers, exhortations to the party faithful to turn out the vote, and assurances that victory is around the corner have been staples of candidate rhetoric since it became proper for presidential candidates to appeal directly for votes. Thus Bush trod a well-worn path when he asked his supporters for more than just their votes: "I'm here to ask you to get your friends and neighbors to go to the polls. Turn out our fellow Republicans, fine independents, and discerning Democrats. Four days to go, and we're counting on your help. There's no doubt in my mind, with your help, we will carry Ohio again and win a great victory on Tuesday."[2]

The methods that Bush used when blistering Kerry on that October night would not have surprised Bryce, who knew a thing or two about negativity in American presidential campaigns. True, Bush's references to September 11, the Iraq War, Social Security, health care, partial birth abortion, and the "sanctity of marriage" might have puzzled him; and he would not have understood the references to Ronald Reagan, Ted Kennedy, and the first George Bush. Still, Bryce would have recognized fear arousal for what it is when Bush warned that a Kerry victory would result in a federal tax hike of $2,000 for the average American family. No stranger to the ridiculing of opponents or to assaults on their integrity, Bryce would have recognized both manifestations in this volley by Bush:

> You might remember the most famous quote of the 2004 campaign. When asked about his vote on the $87 billion, Senator Kerry said, "I actually did vote for the $87 billion, before I voted against it." [Audience boos.] Now, I haven't—I haven't spent a lot of time in Columbus, but I doubt we're going to find many people here who talk that way. [Audience laughs.] He's given several explanations since about his $87 billion vote. Perhaps the most illustrative one of them all was when he said the whole thing was a complicated matter. [Audience laughs.]

Similarly, Bryce would have been alert to the old tactic of casting the contest as a choice between poor and sound judgment. Bush often hit that note in Columbus, as in the following thrust at Kerry:

> My opponent said that September the 11th did not change him much at all. September the 11th changed me a lot.

Likewise Bryce would have understood a line of attack that combined labeling of an opponent's leadership and positions with other tactics already mentioned:

> During the last twenty years, in key moments of challenge and decision for America, Senator Kerry has chosen the position of weakness and indecision. With that record, he stands in opposition, not just to me, but to the great tradition of the Democratic Party. The party of Franklin Roosevelt, the party of Harry Truman, the party of John Kennedy is rightly remembered for confidence and resolve in times of war and hours of crisis. Senator Kerry has turned his back on "pay any price" and "bear any burden," and he's replaced these commitments with "wait and see" and "cut and run."

In short, the kind of event that the Ohio Republicans staged in Columbus has been a primary forum for negative campaigning since the emergence of the two-party system. Similarly, the partisan pamphlet still figures in the negativity of twenty-first-century campaigns, as do the speeches of surrogates for presidential candidates; candidate press conferences and interviews; press releases and campaign statements; and more recently, nationally televised debates.[3] Our study begins with the Kennedy-Nixon contest of 1960, when TV attack ads played a minor role at best, and it ends with the 2004 race, by which time the Internet was maturing as a powerful medium of attack politics. The prospect of simultaneously measuring attack propensities on the Internet as well as in the TV ads, candidate speeches, presidential debates, press releases, and other venues that constitute the totality of negative campaigning in each presidential contest dwarfs even our massive undertaking. Accordingly, we make no claim to having covered every source of campaign attacks. Still, we offer a breadth and depth of coverage seldom found in the scholarly or popular literature on negative campaigning.

This book was long in the making, and we are indebted to many who helped or encouraged us along the way. Fred Woodward expressed interest in the project some years ago and patiently awaited the manuscript. It was a joy to work with Susan Schott, Susan McRory, and others at the University Press of Kansas. We must acknowledge the essential contribution of our two coding assistants, Warren Gunnels and Adam Crowther, both Buell students and Denison University graduates. Emmett Buell owes a debt to the late Nelson W. Polsby, whose generosity enabled him to spend a most productive sabbatical at the Institute of Governmental Studies (IGS), University of California–Berkeley, where much of the coding for this book took place. Buell also wishes to express appreciation to Charles Morris and David Anderson, former Denison provosts, as well as to Associate Provost Keith Boone, for their crucial support in obtaining sabbatical leave, Robert C. Good fellowships, and a merit leave to complete this massive undertaking. Buell also thanks Clarke Wilhelm, Denison professor of history (retired), for his careful critiques of early chapter drafts. Cheryl Johnson, instructional technologist for the Modern Languages Department at Denison, generously guided Buell through the thicket of Excel chartmaking. Aaron Bestic cheerfully and competently met Buell's every Internet request, and Denison students Nathan Dailey and Chris Penny helpfully pointed up typos and other mistakes in drafts of the manuscript. Lee Sigelman hereby records his amazement at and gratitude for Emmett Buell's willingness and ability to suspend virtually every other form of human activity save racquetball over the course of several years for the sake of spending untold thousands of hours poring over back issues of the *New York Times*. Finally, both of us are grateful to James W. Ceaser and the other prepublication reviewer for the University Press of Kansas for their constructive suggestions about how the manuscript could be improved.

ATTACK POLITICS

1. Negativity and Presidential Campaigns

Our objective in this book is to provide a detailed and systematic analysis of negativity in every presidential campaign from 1960 to 2004. In Chapters 2 through 8, we describe the electoral context in each race that circumscribed the strategic options of some contestants while permitting greater flexibility for their opponents. We further measure the propensity of each side to attack the other (or others in three-way races), ascertain whether each side acted in accordance with the predictions and suggestions of those who have constructed analytical models of negative campaigning, and determine the degree to which the competing tickets joined battle on the same topics or issues. We also examine the attack behavior of presidential and vice-presidential candidates as well as the degree to which they themselves came under attack. Similarly, we look at attacks by sitting presidents not seeking reelection, former presidents lured out of retirement and onto the campaign trail, party officials, members of Congress, and various others. In Chapter 8, we weave these strands together into a general fabric, addressing whether the propensity to attack has increased consistently since 1960 and the specific ways in which campaigns have become more (and less) negative. Here, we set forth our concept of negativity, stipulate how we measured it, and relate our research design to the substantial literature on negative campaigning.

THE CONCEPT OF NEGATIVE CAMPAIGNING

Have presidential campaigns become more negative since 1960? Many scholars suggest that they have, and by way of evidence, some have pointed to a rise in attack advertising since the 1970s.[1] Moreover, the advent of shorter ads is said to have increased the frequency of negative messages, as has the emergence of cable television and the Internet.[2] Passage of the Bipartisan Campaign Reform Act (BCRA) opened the floodgates to new groups bent on attacking presidential candidates in 2004, and the measure doubtless will figure importantly in future races.[3] Some old media of attack politics have recently come back into their own, most notably Michael Moore's resurrection of "documentary" film as a visceral medium of campaign attacks.[4] Similarly, the outpouring of books that assailed a particular candidate in 2004 probably exceeded the total of such works in all previous

1

presidential campaigns going back to 1960.[5] Owing to these developments—as well as to the increased overlap between presidential nominating politics and postconvention campaigning—one can argue plausibly that conventional wisdom about when to go negative has changed as well. Stephen Ansolabehere and Shanto Iyengar, for instance, maintain that candidates dare not hold back for fear "that the opposition will throw the first punch" or because "they will appear weak if they don't respond in kind."[6] Moreover, because attacks usually beget counterattacks, campaigners see voters as less likely to blame just one side for going negative.[7]

Still, the accumulated weight of all this evidence and conjecture does not lead to the conclusion that the next presidential campaign will always be more negative than the last one. Looking at campaigns of the late twentieth century, for example, Darrell West uncovered evidence that Americans perceived the two most recent races as less negative than the previous one, the donnybrook of 1988. "When asked whether the 1988 race had been more positive, more negative, or about the same as past presidential campaigns," West reported, "48 percent of the respondents said it had been more negative. But 1988 was the high point in terms of voter views about negativity. In 1992, 36 percent felt that the presidential race was more negative than past contests. In 1996, just 11 percent believed that the race had been more negative than in the past."[8] The Pew Research Center for the People and the Press has asked a similar question in its polls since 1992. In 2004, to take one example, 72 percent of the Pew respondents said that there had been more "mudslinging" in that year's campaign than in previous races (much more than in 2000 and 1996 and slightly more than in 1992).[9] Such findings must be viewed with skepticism because different respondents doubtless had different races in mind when asked about past contests. Similarly, individual definitions of negative campaigning surely varied as well. Further, these understandings may have varied according to age, party loyalty, interest in politics, and a host of other factors that influence political behavior.

Most analysts draw a clear distinction between negative and positive campaigning. Negativity invariably means taking the fight to an electoral opponent—attacking "the other candidate personally, the issues for which the other candidate stands, or the party of the other candidate."[10] Along the same lines, William Mayer described how negative campaigning focuses on "the weaknesses and faults of the opposition; the mistakes they have made, the flaws in their character or performance, the bad policies they would pursue."[11] By contrast, positive campaigning usually (but not invariably) "dwells on the candidate's own strengths and merits."[12] Thus, Richard Lau and Gerald Pomper characterized positive campaigning as talking about one's own accomplishments and qualifications, "just the opposite" of criticizing an opponent's accomplishments and qualifications.[13] To these formulations, we add that presidential candidates typically get plenty of help from others in their party or otherwise of like mind when going negative. The cast of characters generally includes running mates, a former president, governors, members of Congress, party officials, campaign aides, and celebrities (see our discussion under "Basic Questions" later in this chapter).

As Lau and Pomper noted, "negative campaigning has a bad reputation."[14] That is indeed true, but analysts differ on what to make of it. By some accounts, terms such as *negative* and *mudslinging* are pejorative and should be replaced with more neutral words, such as *attack* and *criticism*. Some scholars decry personal attacks while granting the legitimacy of policy disagreements. A few call for drawing the line between attacks that are true or false, fair or unfair, relevant or irrelevant to governance.[15]

For the most part, such concerns have not influenced this study. We use *negative campaigning* and *negativity* as synonyms for *attacking* or *criticizing* electoral opponents and their policies. We restrict the use of terms such as *smear* and *mudslinging* to the making of "wild, unsubstantiated charges" of a personal nature.[16] We dismiss as fatuous the sort of claim made by James A. Baker III that personal attacks constitute negative campaigning whereas attacks on a candidate's record do not,[17] and we agree with Kathleen Hall Jamieson that "accuracy has not characterized policy attacks any more than personal ones."[18] Like John Geer, we do not attempt to determine the fairness, validity, accuracy, relevance, or appropriateness of every campaign attack.[19] Other things being equal, credible charges pack a bigger punch than patent falsehoods,[20] but the difficulty of determining degrees of untruth in many, if not most, instances is insuperable.[21] The same holds true of efforts to determine the fairness of attacks (assuming that fairness can be distinguished from accuracy). Further, we have reason to doubt that positive messages provide more accurate information about a candidate's accomplishments, issue stands, or personal life than do the opposition's attacks.[22]

Similarly, we regard the counterattack as no less an expression of negativity than the attack that likely provoked it. The fact that a counterattack follows an attack should be of no consequence if one's purpose is to measure campaign negativity. Accordingly, a counterattack should not be consigned to a separate class of campaign messages labeled as "defenses."[23] Moreover, trying to determine whether an exchange began or ended with a particular attack may involve one in a pointless search for first causes. In part, this is so because counterattacks often alter the content of exchanges. "If your opponent calls you a liar," an old axiom holds, "do not deny it; just call him a thief."[24] And of course, in an age when "rapid response" has become the norm, the difference between attacks and counterattacks has become even more difficult to determine.[25]

Although, as noted earlier, most analysts adhere to roughly the same concept of negative campaigning, no such consensus exists on how best to measure negativity. This is no less true of attacks that appear in print than of those aired on television. Attack ads on television, however, have gotten the lion's share of attention.

Even when drawing ads from the same archive, researchers have reached different conclusions about the prevalence of negativity in the same campaigns. Given differences in units of analysis and sampling designs, it could not be otherwise.

Consider a plethora of studies of presidential campaign ads of the late twentieth century. West found that the proportion of negative ads rose spectacularly from 1960 to 1968, fell off dramatically in the seventies, reached a new high in 1988, and then declined sharply in 1992 and 1996. Linda Lee Kaid and Anne Johnston reported that negativity jumped markedly in 1964, declined dramatically in 1968, increased slightly in 1972, fell off slightly in 1976, increased moderately in 1980, and remained nearly constant through 1988. Kaid also found that negative advertising broke all previous records in 1996. Jamieson and others associated with the Annenberg School's Campaign Discourse Mapping Project (CDMP) determined that the proportion of attack ads increased during the sixties but at a less dramatic pace than maintained by West. The CDMP findings closely paralleled those of Kaid and Johnston for the campaigns of 1968–1976 but differed greatly for those of 1988–1996. Separate analyses by William Benoit and John Geer agreed that negativity surged from 1960 to 1964, fell off in 1968, and continued rising and falling until 1988, which marked the beginning of a steady increase extending through 1996. Geer reported a falloff for 2000 and projected that the percentage of negative appeals would reach a new high in 2004. In short, using different units of analysis and different methods of ad selection, leading studies of attack ads rated the negativity of some of the same campaigns quite differently.[26]

The rest of this chapter sets out our approach to capturing the complexity of presidential campaigning. We call attention to metaphors of warfare and other acts of violence in the argot of negative campaigning. Such terminology underscores a more general point that electioneering is a form of civic combat. We make the case for a precise measurement of negativity, assert the need for systematic comparison across more than one campaign, and point up the importance of selecting one unit of analysis rather than another. After describing the rest of our research design, we discuss two concepts that guided our research: the rational formulation of campaign strategy in varying electoral contexts and the idea that presidential tickets stress issues that work to their advantage while avoiding those that do not.

THE LANGUAGE OF CIVIC COMBAT

Although democracies rely on a free, fair, and peaceful process of elections to determine who governs, campaigns typically are described in ways suggestive of warfare.[27] Consider some of the many metaphors of military origin that have long dominated campaign discourse, beginning with campaign itself. Verbs regularly borrowed from the battlefield include attack, target, invade, nuke, and finish off. One hears count-less references to air wars and ground wars, strategies, skirmishes, strongholds, en-emy camps, troops on the ground, battleground states, and war rooms. Ground zero came into vogue even before the terrorist attacks of September 11, 2001. Rhetorically at least, presidential aspirants also dodge bullets, take no prisoners, dig in, or otherwise prepare for trench warfare. Occasionally, someone strings such terms together in memorable fashion, as did Pat Buchanan immediately after winning the New Hamp-shire primary in 1996: "Mount up everybody and ride to the sound of the guns."[28]

Pugilistic metaphors also show up in campaign accounts. Candidates put a premium on figurative fisticuffs, whether putting on the gloves or taking them off. Those of a populist persuasion make much use of the verb *to fight,* as when Al Gore vowed to fight for the middle class in 2000. It was by design that Robert M. La Follette Sr. billed himself as "Fighting Bob" in 1924.[29] Candidates also *come out swinging,* go *toe to toe,* and *pummel* one another, all the while demonstrating their ability to take as well as duck, deflect, or throw a *punch.* Journalists often frame presidential debates as prizefights in which one candidate's only hope is to try for a *knockout.* Some never *lay a glove* on an opponent; others suffer *body blows,* perhaps going *down for the count.* Few are content to *shadowbox,* and even fewer admit to *throwing in the towel.*[30]

NEGATIVITY INTEGRAL TO CAMPAIGNING

No one disputes that negativity has long been a part of presidential campaigning. Even in 1789, when George Washington faced no organized opposition, Pennsyl-vania Federalists warned voters of a plot to choose presidential electors hostile to him.[31] Both sides in the first contested election of 1796 painted a grim picture of what would happen if they lost. Similar admonitions enlivened the 1800 rematch between John Adams and Thomas Jefferson, a race colored by Federalist pros-ecutions of political opponents under the Sedition Act. One Jefferson supporter warned fellow Republicans that the reelection of Adams would mean "chains, dungeons, transportation, and perhaps the gibbet." If Jefferson prevailed, a Con-necticut Federalist declared, "murder, robbery, rape, adultery, and incest will be openly taught and practiced, the air will be rent with cries of distress, the soil will be soaked with blood, and the nation black with crimes."[32]

Personal assaults on the dignity and character of candidates have been staples of presidential campaigns from the beginning. In 1800, for example, supporters of Jefferson called Adams a monarchist and accused him of turning his back on re-publicanism. Federalists branded Jefferson a "howling atheist" and questioned his courage during the Revolution, claming that he had fled like a jackrabbit when the

British raided Charlottesville in 1781.[33] Accused of murder and other crimes, Andrew Jackson cried out against the abuse heaped not only upon himself but also on family members: "Mrs. Jackson is not spared, and my pious Mother, nearly fifty years in the tomb, and who, from her cradle to her death, had not a speck upon her character, has been ... held to public scorn as a prostitute who intermarried with a negro ... and my eldest brother sold as a slave in Carolina."[34] Abraham Lincoln's opponents whispered that he, too, was the son of a slave woman, a rumor floated in conjunction with another one asserting that his administration meant to foster miscegenation as well as emancipation.[35] *Harper's Weekly* listed a score of epithets hurled against him in 1864, including "Despot," "Buffoon," "Monster," and "Butcher."[36] Republicans countered by disputing the loyalty of General George B. McClellan, the Democratic nominee.[37]

Sexual innuendo often figured in the rough-and-tumble of nineteenth-century electioneering. Republican mudslingers imputed homosexuality to James Buchanan in 1856 and played the same card against Samuel Tilden in 1876. Similarly, Republicans spread rumors in 1880 that Winfield Scott Hancock wore a corset and, four years later, that Grover Cleveland had fathered an illegitimate child. Cleveland supporters hit back by insisting that the Republican nominee, James G. Blaine, had a similar blot on his ledger. One Democratic newspaper even accused Blaine of being overly fond of fellow Republicans: "But this thing of his kissing men—of pressing his bearded lips upon bearded lips—is too aggressive!"[38] The atmosphere of American campaigns, Lord Bryce wrote, was "thick with charges, defences, recriminations, 'till the voter knows not what to believe."[39]

Although sorely provoked, presidential candidates of the nineteenth century generally adhered to a powerful, if unwritten, code that militated against them making their own case on the campaign trail. This taboo against "cadging," or directly soliciting votes, had obvious consequences for going negative. Surrogates made the case against the opposing party while standard-bearers remained seemingly aloof. Behind the scenes, however, some nominees formulated strategy and/or wrote correspondence intended for publication in friendly newspapers.[40]

By the end of the century, however, the attack role of nonincumbent candidates for president had become more transparent. William Jennings Bryan stumped tirelessly in his 1896 bid to defeat William McKinley, and he may well have used the occasion to inaugurate the "trickle-down" argument that countless Democrats since have uttered against the economy under Republicans. Confinement to the front porch in 1920 did not prevent Warren G. Harding from accusing Franklin D. Roosevelt (FDR), the Democratic nominee for vice president, of having uttered "the most shocking assertion that ever emanated from a responsible member of the government of the United States." Nor did it stop Governor James Cox, Roosevelt's running mate, from avowing that "every traitor in America will vote tomorrow for Warren G. Harding!"[41]

Eventually, even incumbent presidents felt free to lash out publicly at challengers. Sorely provoked by the Democrats, Herbert Hoover dropped the pose that an economic emergency required his presence in Washington and hit the campaign trail. In the process, he traveled 10,000 miles, delivered ten major speeches, and spoke informally on many other occasions. In 1940, supposedly preoccupied with the outbreak of war in Europe, FDR could not resist responding to the "deliberate falsifications and misrepresentations" uttered by Republicans.[42]

The 1948 campaign lives on as the leading example of what can happen when a candidate refuses to join battle with a shrill opponent. Heavily favored in the polls, Governor Thomas E. Dewey of New York acted as if he were the incumbent instead of the beleaguered Harry Truman. Although committed to a whistle-stop effort the equal of Truman's, Dewey made a point of passing up countless opportunities to criticize the president. His ebullient running mate, Governor Earl Warren of California, followed the same course and thereby rendered the Republican effort even more soporific. Possibly, Dewey pulled his punches to change his image from slugger in 1944 to statesman in 1948.[43] He may also have held back for fear of jeopardizing his lead, which, as we will discuss, may well have been a rational strategy for one far ahead in the polls. (If so, Dewey refused to adjust once it became clear that his support was slumping.) Or he may not have wanted to anger Democrats unhappy with Truman but still loyal to their party.[44]

In any case, Truman presented himself as the underdog and proceeded to give the Republicans "hell" in speech after speech.[45] He finally provoked a response from Dewey by claiming that Communists and Fascists alike hoped for a Republican victory. (Earlier, Dewey had drawn an obvious contrast with the Democrats by vowing that his administration would not hire Communists and fellow travelers.) Because he refused to single Truman out, Dewey's rebuke lacked much of a punch: "*They* have scattered reckless abuse along the entire right of way coast to coast, and now, I am sorry to say, reached a new low in mudslinging. This is the kind of campaign I refuse to wage."[46]

For all of the aspersions cast on negative campaigning and despite the many ailments of the body politic attributed to it, many a scholar has acknowledged its valuable contribution to free elections. Glen W. Richardson extolled it as "one of democracy's most cherished expressive freedoms."[47] Mayer argued that such criticism provides essential information for casting an informed vote.[48] Similarly, Geer argued that the practice of democracy requires candidates to go negative, for otherwise, the costs or benefits of electing one of them would not come out.[49] Likewise, Kathleen Hall Jamieson, Paul Waldman, and Susan Sherr viewed campaign negativity as "a legitimate and important part of differentiating one candidate's biography and positions from another's."[50]

ANECDOTAL AND SINGLE-CASE STUDIES OF NEGATIVITY

The anecdotal literature on presidential campaigns teems with assertions that a particular contest grossly exceeded the limits of fair play and honest disagreement. In a rare comparison of numerous campaigns, Bruce Felknor maintained that only six of the forty-one presidential races up to 1948 had been "spectacularly dirty": those of 1828, 1864, 1876, 1884, 1928, and 1940. Six others—those of 1796, 1800, 1916, 1932, 1936, and 1944—"contained substantial elements of viciousness and unfairness" but did not qualify as "real mud baths." As Felknor saw it, campaigns from 1952 to 1964 had given rise to unfounded charges of treason and disloyalty, as well as to the "shrill and frenzied denunciation" of presidential candidates on a "wholesale basis."[51] Precisely how he arrived at these designations is unclear. But as his own account revealed, similar charges had been aired as early as 1796.

Most other works of this type focus on just one presidential contest. Consider a nineteenth-century account of the 1840 race that condemned Martin Van Buren for unleashing "the most slander, vituperation, and abuse" known to Americans up to that point.[52] One history of Lincoln's 1864 race quoted James Gordon Bennett on the quality of campaign discourse: "Never were . . . frauds so plentiful, fabrications so numerous, delusions so popular, humbugs so transparent and falsehoods so generally circulated."[53] In 1928, a scholar has noted, "the American people reached into the muck at the bottom of the well, pulling up primordial hate from those murky places we hope never see light, turning a man's bid for the White House into one of the most revolting spectacles in the nation's history."[54] Appalled by Richard Nixon's savaging of Adlai Stevenson, Stephen Ambrose contended that 1952 should go down in history as one of America's "bitterest" races for the White House.[55] Academics and pundits upset by so much emphasis on Willie Horton and flag salutes condemned the 1988 race as among the meanest and most vapid contests in modern times.[56] More recently, pundit E. J. Dionne wrote that 2000 was "the most bitterly contested presidential election in 124 years."[57] In sum, anecdotal accounts by definition fall far short of providing a framework for precise and systematic comparison of campaign negativity.

COMPARATIVE STUDIES OF NEGATIVE CAMPAIGN ADS

Some other studies have measured negative campaigning in two or more contests. Nearly all of this research (twenty of twenty-seven studies surveyed by Jamieson, Waldman, and Sherr) focused on televised attack ads.[58]

One bone of contention has to do with the unit of analysis. When analyzing the content of television spots, numerous researchers have categorized *entire ads* as either positive or negative.[59] This approach is unsatisfactory because some ads contain positive as well as negative content. Some researchers have attempted to get around the problem by classifying any ad mentioning the sponsor's opponent as negative and by coding any ad that focuses entirely on the sponsor as positive.[60] This approach cannot accommodate an ad saying no more than Candidate X favors a tax cut that Candidate Y opposes. Nor can it accommodate an ad declaring that both candidates favor the same tax cut.

Other researchers classify ads according to their dominant focus even though they sometimes neglect to specify how to determine dominance. This approach labels ads directed mainly at the sponsor's opponent as negative and categorizes ads chiefly about the sponsor as positive.[61] West, for example, classified an ad as negative when "at least 50 percent of the presentation challenged an opposing campaigner in terms of policy positions or personal qualities." However, if the ad contained "unflattering or pejorative comments made about the opponent's domestic performance," this alone sufficed to earn it a negative label.[62]

Yet another approach is to classify entire ads as comparative, negative, or positive.[63] Under this scheme, an ad that acclaims the feats of Candidate X while disparaging those of Candidate Y is coded as comparative rather than negative. This decision rule not only masks the ad's negativity but also ignores the fact that such contrasts almost always diminish, if not demean, the opposing candidate.[64]

Problems of this type can be avoided by utilizing the statement or appeal as the unit of analysis rather than the entire ad. Geer, for instance, determined that a fair number of appeals in ads classified as "negative" were positive, that a smaller number of attacks came out of ads labeled as "positive," and that 41 percent of all appeals in "contrast" ads were negative.[65] In addition to refining the specification of negativity, changing the unit of analysis also allows researchers to compare appeals in television spots with appeals found in speeches, press releases, debate transcripts, and other venues of campaign communication.[66]

Still another area of methodological dispute has to do with sampling, that is, whether spots selected for analysis constitute a representative sample of the universe of campaign ads made for television. Researchers have generally sampled from archives at the University of Oklahoma or the University of Pennsylvania, where the collections, though large, are neither complete nor identical.[67] Moreover, scholars focusing on the same elections and working at the same archive often draw quite different samples.[68]

The fact that some ads never show up on television screens further complicates the issue of representativeness, as does variation in the length of spots actually aired. Sampling from the Oklahoma collection, Geer analyzed 757 ads from the presidential campaigns of 1960–1996. Because he did not know where and how often these ads were shown, he weighted them equally. Jamieson and her colleagues made a good case for taking account of the number of airings when gauging negativity, so that a spot run only once or twice is not weighted the same as a frequently aired ad.[69]

West employed a weighting scheme of sorts to select only "prominent" ads, or those he deemed "noteworthy, entertaining, flamboyant, or effective," for analysis. Yet, as other contributors to this literature have pointed out, a nonrandom choice of so-called prominent ads overstates the prevalence of negativity in campaign advertising and misreads some election years. While acknowledging that he had not sampled randomly, West maintained that prominent ads deserved notice and lesser ones did not.[70]

In sum, a methodological thicket has grown up around the subject of negative campaigning. Although almost everyone accepts that negative campaigning means criticizing or attacking a rival candidate, slate, or party during a contest for elected office, no such consensus holds when the same researchers measure the prevalence of negativity in particular campaigns. The preoccupation with television ads has not precluded considerable variation in the findings of studies focused exclusively on such spots. Researchers studying the same campaigns have employed different units of analysis, approached the weighting issue differently, and used a variety of sampling methods when drawing from incomplete archives.

NEGATIVE CAMPAIGNING EFFECTS

Much of the research reviewed thus far has focused on the consequences of campaign attacks. By some accounts, negativity harms the political process by turning off voters and depressing turnout, but other researchers have found just the opposite. Similar differences show up regarding negativity's effect, if any, on distrust of politicians and disdain for politics. A systematic analysis of such effects lies beyond the purpose of this study.[71] Rather, we focus on determining the prevalence of negativity in a variety of electoral contexts. To be sure, we comment on apparent linkages of attack patterns to poll standings and campaign events, but we do so in the realization that other factors may have influenced our findings. In analyzing the 1968 race, for instance, we suggest that Hubert Humphrey owed his belated comeback to several developments, such as his speech in Salt Lake City (widely understood as a deviation from administration policy on the war in Vietnam), organized labor's drive to discredit George Wallace in battleground states, and media reaction to the relatively benign view that General Curtis LeMay (Wallace's running mate) expressed about nuclear fallout. This is not to deny that other developments also contributed to the rise in Humphrey's ratings and a corresponding drop in Wallace's.

BASIC QUESTIONS

In what follows, we try to draw upon the strengths while avoiding the weaknesses of the two main types of research on negative campaigning that have preceded our study. The value of anecdotal and single-case studies lies in their highlighting of key developments, as well as in providing a rich and in-depth account of a campaign's ebb and flow. However, such studies either lack broadly applicable generalizations about the phenomena of interest or offer selective and subjective generalizations lacking in academic rigor. At the same time, comparative (that is, multiple-election) studies have typically sacrificed depth for breadth by treating each campaign as a data point in a time series. Though worthwhile, such research has been challenged on conceptual and methodological grounds. In this book, we offer up-close-and-personal accounts of negative campaigning, and beyond that, we make use of theoretical accounts and models of strategy in negative campaigning across twelve presidential contests. On the one hand, we have immersed ourselves in journalistic and historical accounts of presidential campaigns, as well as in candidate biographies and documentary materials, to supplement the huge supply of news items in the *New York Times*. On the other hand, we have executed a research design that married a rich and enormous data set to careful measurement and well-documented analysis.

The basic questions that structured our data collection were: who attacked whom, how frequently, on what issues, in what ways, and at what point in the campaign? Let us examine each question in depth.

Who Attacked Whom?

To answer this question, we devised twenty-three categories of attackers with an identical list of targets. Thus, a party's presidential nominee could be the only target as well as the sole maker of an attack. As we shall see, presidential candidates typically make a large share of their party's attacks and are just as likely to be targeted by their opponents. We also examined the roles of vice-presidential candidates as both attackers and targets.[72] Other solo sources and targets of attack on our list were: an incumbent president not seeking election, a sitting vice president who is not a candidate for president or reelection, a former president, a former vice president not running for president, a national campaign official or spokesperson (such as a party chair, campaign manager, or communications director), a current or former member of Congress (or a candidate for a House or Senate seat), a current or former member of the administration (such as a cabinet secretary), a state or local official or party functionary, a spouse or other member of the presidential nominee's family, a member of the vice-presidential nominee's family, a celebrity (such as an actor or author) backing a presidential candidate, a group supporting a presidential candidate, and a newspaper editorial (mentioned in a news item) endorsing a presidential candidate. We also classified multiple attackers and targets such as both members of the ticket, the nominee and a sitting president, and three or more from the preceding list.

How Frequently?

The frequency of attacks is critical to our basic measure of negativity, the "attack propensity score." To gauge the relative negativity of each campaign—as well as the negativity of parties, candidates, surrogates, and other sources of campaign statements in a presidential contest—we calculated a straightforward measure that divided the number of attack statements by total campaign statements. Scores ranged from 0 (indicating a complete absence of attacks) to 1.00 (indicating that every statement contained an attack). This measure allowed us to determine the negativity of the contest overall and of each side, as well as the attack propensities of specific campaigners, such as presidential candidates and their running mates.

On What Issues?

To answer this question, we devised an elaborate code encompassing forty-eight topics of varying breadth (see Table 1.1).[73] Some issues, such as "class conflict," have long figured in campaign discourse. Thus, William McKinley took this line in his speech accepting the 1896 Republican nomination: "All attempt to array class against class, the classes against the masses, section against section, labor against capital, poor against rich, or interest against interest, is in the highest degree reprehensible."[74] Others, such as affirmative action and gay rights, are of more recent vintage.

In What Ways?

This question speaks to the variety of attack methods that show up in published reports. Fear arousal is one such method, and it is used to paint a grim future if the other side wins. Other methods are ridicule or humor at the opponent's expense, guilt by association or pejorative labeling, apposition (unfavorable comparison of the opponent with the sponsoring candidate), and accusing the opposition of lying or being inconsistent (see Table 1.2).[75]

At What Point in the Campaign?

Because we noted the date of every attack, we are able to track variations in the incidence of attacks at different points during the campaign. Dividing each

Table 1.1. Attack Topics

Opponent attacked but topic not explicit in news item

Credibility, trustworthiness, candor, integrity, or substance of opponent not specific to any issue listed below

Derogatory remark or epithet (e.g., "Bozo") not specific to issues

Vote wasted on opponent

Campaign finances, questionable contributions or spending, trying to buy the election

Opponent's unwillingness to debate, all other debate issues

Opponent's state of mind, sanity, mental health

Age, physical condition, appearance of opponent

Opponent indifferent or unaware of problems in a state or region, dismissive of state or region (e.g., a northerner who looks down his nose at the South)

Social status or social class of opponent (e.g., born with a silver spoon in mouth)

Opponent's youthful excesses and indiscretions other than sexual (e.g., alcohol abuse, cheating on exams)

Opponent's failure as a spouse or parent, sexual morality, marital infidelity

Opponent's personal or family finances, business dealings, tax records

All matters pertaining to voting issues

Corruption, violation of public trust, abuse of power

Comments on opponent's leadership

Opponent's understanding or indifference to public opinion, needs of voters

Dirty campaigning, appealing to fear, trying to scare voters (not to be confused with fear arousal method)

Opponent's resort to class conflict, dividing rather than uniting nation along class lines

Opponent's Americanism, patriotism, loyalty, military service record

Opponent's partisanship and/or ideology

All matters pertaining to the federal courts

Power of national government, national powers versus state powers, federalism

All crime-related issues not specific to race, gun control, drugs, penal policy

Racial issues, affirmative action, race riots, criminality linked to race

Religion, school prayer

Abortion and women's causes, family leave, comparable worth, women in the military, sexism, feminism, affirmative action for women

"Hot-button" social issues: gays, AIDS, pornography, obscenity

Immigration issues

Poverty and welfare when not race specific, Aid to Families with Dependent Children, food stamps, public housing for poor, welfare fraud, urban problems

Table 1.1. Attack Topics (*continued*)

Social Security, Medicare, veterans' benefits, infant mortality, childcare

Labor laws, labor unions, working conditions, strikes, minimum wage, plant closings, job training

Agricultural policy, grain embargoes, farm subsidies

Educational policy when not race specific, aid for public and religious schools, testing

Energy and environmental issues such as conservation, Superfund, logging, offshore drilling, energy fees and taxes, wetlands, solar power, strategic oil reserve, national parks

Taxes, spending, deficits, national debt, budget deficits and surpluses

Unemployment, recession, economic inequities

Declining productivity, profits, competitiveness of particular industries or sectors except agriculture, industrial policy proposals

Inflation, high cost of living, wage-price controls, rents, interest rates

Housing starts, mortgages, other housing policy issues except public housing

Stagflation or the "misery index"

More-generalized attacks pertaining to "bad" economy, residual category for domestic economic concerns

Residual domestic but noneconomic issues

Trade and international economic concerns, most-favored-nation status

Foreign aid excluding military assistance

All attacks pertaining to war and national defense, specific wars, the Cold War, arms sales, intelligence gathering, defense budgets, selective service, military alliances

More-generalized attacks on foreign policy leadership when not specific to the three categories just listed

Iranian hostage issue of 1980 campaign

Relations with particular nations other than military or Cold War adversaries

campaign into weeks facilitates such an analysis and enables us to isolate associations between campaign events, changes in the polls, and attack propensities.

UNIT OF ANALYSIS

The campaign statement serves as our unit of analysis. Whether conveyed in a clause, sentence, paragraph, or multiple paragraphs, a statement speaks to one particular issue. Every statement focuses on some aspect of the campaign, and we have classified as negative those statements that expressly or implicitly criticize a rival ticket or party.[76] We coded all other campaign statements as nonattacks. Only

Table 1.2. Examples of Attack Methods

Fear Arousal: Jimmy Carter attacking Ronald Reagan in 1980: "I think it would be a bad thing for our country if Governor Reagan is elected. I don't know what he would do in the White House, but his opposition to the SALT II treaty, his opposition to Medicare, his opposition to many of the programs that are important like the minimum wage or unemployment compensation, his call for the interjection of American military forces into place after place around the world, indicates to me that he would not be a good president or a good man to trust with the affairs of this nation in the future." (Terrence Smith, "Carter Asserts Reagan Presidency Would Be 'Bad Thing' for Country," *New York Times*, October 11, 1980, A8.)

Ridicule: Walter Mondale in 1984 exploiting a Reagan statement that a ballistic missile could be recalled after launching: "Two years into this administration the President said submarine ballistic missiles are recallable. Think about that for a minute. You fire missiles, they come out of the submarine hole, go through the water, go into the air for several thousand miles and then you decided not to fire them. So they're stopped. Like a movie rolling backward, the missile backs up, goes down through the water and back into the submarine hole." (Jane Perlez, "Mondale Questions Reagan's Ability to Understand Nuclear Arms," *New York Times*, October 16, 1984, A24.)

Labeling or Guilt by Association: George Bush's use of the "L word" against Michael Dukakis in 1988: "I would hate to be my opponent, the man who doesn't like the big L word. . . . We used the L word and he kept talking about it. I'm not the one who said, 'I am a progressive liberal governor of Massachusetts.' And I'm not the one who said, 'I am a card-carrying member of the ACLU.'" ("The Basic Speech/George Bush," *New York Times*, October 24, 1988, B5.)

Apposition: Al Gore contrasting his plans for economic prosperity with those of George W. Bush in 2000: "What will we do with our prosperity? Well, I want to put it to work for you, the hard-working families of this country and make sure that you get your fair share of the pie. . . . [Bush] has a different view. He wants to change the very best things about the economic course we're on. He wants to go back." (Kevin Sack, "In Strategy Shift, Gore Ads Question Bush's Capability," *New York Times*, November 3, 2000, A1.)

Lying or Inconsistency: Bill Clinton assailing George H. W. Bush in 1992: "You've got a president who will say anything to be elected. . . . I mean this guy's been out there for two months making up charges about me, deliberately falsifying my plan. . . . And if you're totally shameless and somebody tells you you're not telling the truth, and you keep on doing it anyway, which is what Bush does, it's hard for the American people to know what to make of it." ("In Their Own Words," *New York Times*, October 30, 1992, A10.)

some of the latter type constitute "acclaims," or positive claims about the character or accomplishments of the sponsoring candidate or party. Other nonattacks contain positive or neutral remarks about opposing candidates and campaign advisers. A more common form of nonattack statement pertains to the horse race, which is often discussed in mechanical fashion without assailing the opposition. Related to the horse race and also fairly common, some statements take a dim view not of an opposing candidate or ticket but of one's own candidate or party. For instance, party leaders sometimes lament the poll standings, gaffes, and debate performances of their own candidates. Such criticisms count as nonattack statements in our analysis because they do not take aim at the other party.

DATABASE

Our database consists of campaign statements extracted via a systematic coding procedure from every news item published in the *New York Times* about the presidential campaigns of 1960 to 2004. To make our cut, an item had to make explicit mention of the presidential race during an observation period that started on Labor Day and extended through election day.[77] In addition to news stories, we also coded shorter news notes; analysis pieces found in the news section; and the complete or partial texts of press releases, campaign ads on radio and television, and campaign speeches.[78] All told, we extracted 17,124 campaign statements from 10,686 news items (see Table 1.3).

Two trained coders working independently of one another coded the *New York Times* items used in this research. One or the other of them coded the great majority of items, but in order to assess reliability, we designated 280 items in nine of the races for both to code. At least one attack was reported in each of these items, and sometimes as many as eleven were. For each attack identified in a given item, the coder recorded the identity of the attacker(s) (using a 21-category classification scheme); the identity of the target(s) of the attack (using the same 21 categories); the setting (using an 18-category scheme); the topic of the attack (using a 48-category code); and whether an attack employed blame, ridicule, labeling, apposition, and/or charges of lying (coded as a series of binaries). Across all the attacks that were double-coded in this way, the two coders assigned exactly the same code 94.5 percent of the time—an impressive result, especially in light of the intricacy of our classifications.

The agreement percentage between coders, however, can be misleading. If, for example, the question was whether some rare event was or was not reported in an item, two untrained coders could achieve high agreement simply by checking "did not occur" every time. If, however, the event occurred frequently, the coders would have had to know what they were doing, paying close attention to content in order to achieve a high level of agreement. Therefore, statisticians have devised reliability coefficients that go beyond simple agreement percentages. A standard reliability coefficient, kappa, corrects the intercoder agreement percentage for the percentage that would be expected based purely on chance.[79] Thus defined, kappa would equal 0 if the coders agreed exactly as often as would have been expected by

Table 1.3. News Items and Campaign Statements, 1960–2004

Presidential Contest	News Items	Campaign Statements
1960	1,585	2,072
1964	1,123	1,330
1968	1,409	1,719
1972	848	1,011
1976	684	964
1980	947	1,662
1984	861	1,499
1988	773	1,454
1992	821	1,637
1996	594	1,011
2000	641	1,575
2004	400	1,190
Totals	10,686	17,124

Source: *New York Times* news items, Labor Day to election day of each presidential campaign.

chance, and it would approach 1.0 as agreement between the coders progressively improved upon chance.

Across all 280 double-coded items, kappa averaged .79, a positive and very encouraging result. It reached especially high levels for our classifications of attackers, targets, and settings, averaging .89 in such instances. For more judgmental coding, such as the use of specific methods of attacking, it averaged .78. Although kappa was lower for the double coding of attack topics (.68), reflecting the challenges of applying a 48-category classification scheme, it was still well within acceptable bounds. In general, the high percentages of agreement accompanied by the impressive kappa coefficients provide strong evidence of the reliability of the coding for this project.

Now, why did we pick the *New York Times*? The *Times* is generally recognized as the closest thing to a newspaper of national record in the United States, and it is likewise seen as a standard-setter for other news organizations. It is true that leading newspapers generally have given more coverage to negative rather than positive ads on television,[80] but the same can be said of every other media outlet that considers conflict more newsworthy than substance. Indeed, the *Times* offers more substance on candidate stands than that provided by nightly news reports or thirty-second spots. Moreover, what shows up on the small screen hardly represents all of what happens during a campaign. In 1960, for instance, Kennedy and Nixon uttered more than half of all their campaign statements while speaking at rallies and other public gatherings. They also delivered ninety-nine formal speeches, participated in the first presidential debates ever, hosted news conferences, and gave interviews to selected reporters. Meanwhile, their aides wrote candidate statements, position papers, and the like.[81]

Surrogate campaigners have always figured importantly in presidential contests. Some, such as members of Congress, governors, and campaign spokespersons, show up regularly in network news reports. Others, including local celebrities, state party officials, and congressional challengers, stand a better chance of getting noticed in the *Times*, especially when expressing opinions that no presidential nominee would utter in public. At a 1992 Republican rally, for example, an ultimately unsuccessful candidate for Congress branded Bill Clinton "a rebellious, philandering, fornicating, adulterating liar."[82]

Similarly, most presidential contests unleash a flood of flyers, pamphlets, and direct mailings. Although massive, most of this effort escapes notice on the nightly news. In 2004, to cite one example, America Coming Together sent out 23 million pieces of mail attacking George Bush. Similarly, the Swift Boat Vets reinforced their TV offensive with direct mail. The National Rifle Association ridiculed John Kerry in a memorable mailer that depicted an "austere French poodle" outfitted in a Kerry campaign sweater. "That dog don't hunt," the text declared.[83]

Of course, not everything said and done during a campaign shows up in the pages of the *Times*. Accordingly, we make no claim to have coded every instance of negative campaigning in the presidential contests of 1960–2004.[84] Like every other study of negative campaigning, ours is source dependent. Moreover, like all news organizations, the *Times* reports only that news it deems "fit to print."[85] Still, it offers a wealth of campaign coverage seldom matched by its competitors, and it rates at the top of the pecking order of American news outlets.

We freely acknowledge that the conventions of political reporting have changed since 1960, owing largely to television's replacement of newspapers as the main source of news for most Americans. News organizations supposedly have responded to the television challenge by focusing more on candidate personalities than ever before,[86] while making less of an effort to be objective.[87] The media are said to have fixated on strategy and the horse race so much that they fail to spot gross distortions in policy statements.[88] Supposedly, candidates have become more guarded in their relationships with the press, a phenomenon that one account traces back to the McCarthy era, when reporters resented having to report charges they regarded as dubious.[89] Other accounts maintain that a new era of press cynicism (and power over the electoral process) arose out of the reaction to presidential disinformation about Vietnam and Watergate.[90]

Still, we should not forget that print personages of the nineteenth and early twentieth centuries such as Horace Greeley, William Randolph Hearst, and Robert R. McCormick knew a thing or two about the power of the press. For most of American history, editorial policy influenced political reporting. A 1936 analysis discovered that editorial endorsements had a lot to do with the space allocated to coverage of presidential candidates. If impartiality meant approximately equal treatment of the candidates, this study concluded, "few newspapers could claim impartiality."[91] Today, we suspect that a similar study of the *Times* likely would find much less of a correlation between editorial endorsement and print lines per candidate. We further suspect that game plans and other aspects of the horse race have figured in news accounts of presidential campaigns since Washington's day. As for cynicism, the "ink-stained wretches" of the press have always been viewed as uncommonly jaded, especially in their dealings with candidates and officeholders.

ELECTORAL CONTEXT

The negative campaigning literature reflects a general recognition that electoral context influences the decisions of candidates to go negative. Seemingly, competitors in very close races are less likely to adopt different strategies than candidates in contests where circumstances overwhelmingly favor one side. Although not all candidates act in accordance with their poll standings, we have good reason to expect less negativity from clear front-runners in two-candidate races than from their opponents. The closer the contest, however, the less obvious is the strategy on either side. The following classification captures the range of two-party scenarios:[92]

- "Runaway" campaigns (analyzed in Chapter 2) occurred in 1964, 1972, and 1984, when favored tickets enjoyed a huge and remarkably consistent lead from Labor Day to election day.
- "Somewhat competitive" races (Chapter 3) took place in 1988, 1992, and 1996, when one ticket consistently led the other, albeit sometimes by a slender margin.
- "Comeback" contests (Chapter 4) occurred in 1968 and 1976, when a seemingly hopeless opponent eventually caught up with the favorite.
- Very close races or "dead heats" occurred in 1960 and 1980 (Chapters 5 and 6) as well as in 2000 and 2004 (Chapter 7), when the difference between leading and trailing was, for the most part, negligible. Indeed, in three of the four contests, the lead changed hands one or more times between Labor Day and election day.

Even though our labels reflect the fluctuating fortunes of candidates before election day, each says something about the expected outcome. To nobody's surprise, every runaway ended in a landslide for the long-anticipated winner. Although expected winners also prevailed in all of the somewhat competitive races, only in 1988 did the victor garner a majority of the popular vote. As for comeback races, Nixon in 1968 eked out one of the narrowest pluralities of the popular vote, and Jimmy Carter in 1976 won a much smaller majority than expected of a candidate who started with such a big lead. Two of the dead heats resulted in "runner-up presidents," that is, presidents who won a majority of electoral votes while losing the popular vote. Kennedy almost certainly finished behind Nixon in the 1960 popular vote,[93] and no one disputes that Al Gore led Bush in 2000 by roughly half a million votes. Conversely, the Republican landslide in 1980 came as a shock to most who followed that dead heat closely.[94] Gallup's final preelection poll in 2004 showed Bush and Kerry tied at 49 percent.[95] Bush defeated Kerry 51 to 48 percent in the popular vote and narrowly prevailed in the Electoral College.

Table 1.4 summarizes this distribution of popular and electoral votes between the Democrats and Republicans for all twelve elections. On average, runaway winners garnered 60.2 percent of the popular vote and 94.9 percent of the electoral vote. The popular vote averaged 48.5 percent for winners of the somewhat competitive races, offset by a mean 72.8 percent in the Electoral College. Victors in comeback races averaged only 46.7 percent of the popular vote but picked up just over 58 percent of the presidential electors. Dead heat winners averaged about 49 percent of the popular vote (depending on how one allocates the popular votes in Alabama that were cast for electors pledged to support Senator Harry F. Byrd but were mistakenly counted for Kennedy). The Electoral College haul for dead heat winners came to 63.1 percent (53.8 percent if one omits the Ronald Reagan landslide of 1980).

With varying importance, third-party and independent candidates have figured in all twelve elections in our study. For the most part, however, minor-party candidates exerted no discernible influence on the race or its outcome. Most joined the fray without hope of accomplishing anything more than promoting a cause. The great majority represented the ideological fringe, and most expected to win no more than a fraction of a percent in the popular vote. No third-party or independent candidate since 1960 has won any electoral votes except George Wallace in 1968. Still, since 1960, presidential ballots in two or more states have regularly listed the Socialist Workers Party, the Prohibition Party, and the Libertarian Party (since 1972). The Socialist Labor, Natural Law, and Communist Parties also have contested a number of these elections. It also is worth noting that the number of minor and independent candidates running for president quadrupled between 1960 and 2000 (see Table 1.5).

Of the 116 candidacies summarized in Table 1.5, only 5 seriously distracted one or both of the major parties: George Wallace in 1968 (with 13.5 percent of the popular vote and 8.5 percent of the electoral vote), John Anderson in 1980 (6.6 percent of the popular vote), H. Ross Perot in 1992 (18.9 percent of the popular vote), Perot again in 1996 (8.4 percent of the 1996 popular vote), and Ralph Nader

Table 1.4. Presidential Election Outcomes, 1960–2004

Year	Campaign Type	Winner (party)	Popular Vote (%)	Loser (party)	Popular Vote (%)	Winner's Electoral Vote (%)
1960	Dead heat	Kennedy (D)	49.7	Nixon (R)	49.5	58.0
1964	Runaway	Johnson (D)	61.1	Goldwater (R)	38.5	90.3
1968	Comeback	Nixon (R)	43.4	Humphrey (D)	42.7	61.2
1972	Runaway	Nixon (R)	60.7	McGovern (D)	37.5	96.8
1976	Comeback	Carter (D)	50.1	Ford (R)	48.0	55.2
1980	Dead heat	Reagan (R)	50.7	Carter (D)	41.0	90.9
1984	Runaway	Reagan (R)	58.8	Mondale (D)	40.6	97.6
1988	Somewhat competitive	G. Bush (R)	53.4	Dukakis (D)	45.6	79.2
1992	Somewhat competitive	Clinton (D)	43.0	G. Bush (R)	37.4	68.7
1996	Somewhat competitive	Clinton (D)	49.2	Dole (R)	40.7	70.4
2000	Dead heat	G. W. Bush (R)	47.9	Gore (D)	48.4	50.4
2004	Dead heat	G. W. Bush (R)	50.7	Kerry (D)	48.3	53.1

Notes: Popular vote entries are percentages of the total, not only two-party vote. Kennedy's lead over Nixon in 1960 is not correct because the Associated Press added votes for anti-Kennedy Democratic electors in Alabama to votes cast for Democratic electors pledged to Kennedy.

Source: *Guide to U.S. Elections*, vol. I, 5th ed. (Washington, DC: Congressional Quarterly Press, 2005).

in 2000 (2.7 percent of the popular vote).[96] Nader belongs on this list because, by most accounts, he took enough votes away from Gore in Florida and New Hampshire to elect Bush.[97]

THE SKAPERDAS-GROFMAN MODEL

For more insight into the dynamics of two- and three-way races, we turn to Stergios Skaperdas and Bernard Grofman's formal model of electoral strategy.[98] This model posits that presidential candidates have a more accurate understanding of how well they are doing during the campaign than how they will do on election day. It assumes that some voters pick a candidate early, whereas others require more time to decide, and it further assumes positive campaigning appeals more to undecided voters—who want to learn about the candidates—than to voters already committed to a candidate. Hearing only positive messages from both sides in a two-party race, undecided voters eventually will divide their support evenly between the contestants. Positive campaigning, then, drains the pool of undecideds. Negative campaigning increases indecision among voters by sowing dissonance and

Table 1.5. Vote for Minor-Party Candidates and Independents in Presidential Elections of 1960–2004

Year	Candidates	Share of Popular Vote			Electoral Vote %
		Combined %	Highest %	Lowest %	
1960	3	.19	.06	.07	0
1964	4	.15	.06	.01	0
1968	6	13.75	13.53	.01	8.5
1972	9	1.70	1.40	<.01	0
1976	11	1.88	.93	.01	0
1980	11	8.14	6.61	.01	0
1984	12	.33	.08	<.01	0
1988	11	.20	.05	<.01	0
1992	14	19.22	18.86	<.01	0
1996	13	9.89	8.40	<.01	0
2000	13	3.72	2.74	<.01	0
2004	9	.94	.38	<.01	0

Notes: This table includes only candidates appearing on the ballot in two or more states. Wallace won 13.5 percent of the popular vote and 8.5 percent of the electoral vote in 1968; Anderson garnered 6.6 percent of the popular vote in 1980; Perot won 18.9 percent of the popular vote in 1992 and 8.4 percent in 1996; Nader got 2.7 percent in 2000 compared with 0.38 percent in 2004.

Sources: Steven J. Rosenstone, Roy L. Behr, and Edward J. Lazarus, *Third Parties in America*, 2nd ed. rev. (Princeton, NJ: Princeton University Press, 1984), app. A; J. David Gillespie, *Politics at the Periphery: Third Parties in Two-Party America* (Columbia: University of South Carolina Press, 1993); *Presidential Elections 1789–1996* (Washington, DC: Congressional Quarterly Press, 1997), 136–138; Federal Election Commission, "2000 Presidential Popular Vote Summary for All Candidates on At Least One State Ballot," available at www.fec.gov/pubrec/fe2000. *Ballot Access News* is the source of 2004 data.

creating doubt among supporters of the targeted candidate. The side that attacks, however, risks disillusioning its supporters to the point of pushing some of them into the undecided column. Accordingly, a rational candidate assesses the potential costs as well as the likely benefits of going negative before taking any action.[99]

How, then, can one's own support be maximized while minimizing that of an opponent? The Skaperdas-Grofman model assumes that a candidate will be less inclined to go negative when the risk outweighs likely benefits. Skaperdas and Grofman's leading propositions for two-candidate competitions are as follows:

- A front-runner who enjoys an initially sufficient lead over the trailing candidate will not engage in negative campaigning.
- If a candidate's initial support is sufficiently low, that candidate may put all of his or her effort into negative campaigning.
- If both candidates engage in positive as well as negative campaigning, the initial leader engages in more positive and less negative campaigning than the trailer.

- If the number of undecided voters increases, both candidates increase positive campaigning.
- The front-runner always reduces positive campaigning when the harm of negative campaigning to the trailing candidate increases.
- The trailing candidate also reduces positive campaigning when the harm of negative campaigning to the front-runner increases—unless the front-runner is so far ahead that further attacks are pointless.

As previously noted, five of the twelve presidential campaigns from 1960 to 2004 attracted independent or third-party candidates of consequence. Skaperdas and Grofman incorporate such candidacies in two models. The first takes account of a so-called spoiler who, despite the label, threatens neither of the top two candidates. Rather, concerned only about his or her own support, the spoiler wages an entirely positive campaign regardless of what the top two candidates say or do.[100] By waging a wholly positive campaign, the spoiler helps reduce the pool of undecided voters, a process expedited further by the reluctance of the top two candidates to attack the spoiler. Some voters end their indecision by supporting the spoiler. As the number of undecideds dwindles, negativity on the part of the top two candidates increases. The front-runner always wages a less negative and more positive campaign than the runner-up. In short, this model resembles the two-candidate formulation "with the difference that some currently undecided voters will go to a third candidate."[101]

We view the spoiler more conventionally—as one who runs last in a three-candidate race, seemingly has little chance of winning, and appears bent on preventing one of the top two candidates from winning.[102] Eugene McCarthy's feeble effort to hurt Jimmy Carter in 1976 met all three conditions: "Spoiling the difference between Carter and Ford would be a very slight burden of conscience," McCarthy told one reporter. "I am quite willing to bear that."[103] Seldom slow to recognize such threats, intended victims respond in a variety of predictable ways both before and after the spoiler gets into the race.

Skaperdas and Grofman formulated a second model of three-way competition, in which the third-ranked candidate joins the runner-up in attacking the front-runner. This proposition arose partly from the game-theory paradox that the best shooter in a three-way gunfight has the least chance of surviving because the others try to take him or her out before aiming at each other. Skaperdas and Grofman noted that the analogy falls short in winner-take-all elections because the weakest candidate (that is, the worst shooter) has the least chance of winning.[104] In their model, each candidate attacks only the stronger of the two rivals. Thus, the front-runner assails the runner-up, the runner-up blasts the front-runner, and the candidate in last place lambastes the front-runner. In 1992, however, Perot attacked runner-up Bush more than front-runner Clinton, thereby contradicting the model. Perot's behavior led Skaperdas and Grofman to consider adding a term that takes account of a candidate's vulnerability to attacks.[105]

In sum, except for their concept of a spoiler candidacy, Skaperdas and Grofman have given us some useful predictions for analyzing actual presidential campaigns. They are: (1) going negative can backfire on the attacker;[106] (2) the front-runner should wage a more positive and less negative campaign than the runner-up; (3) negativity on the part of the runner-up against the front-runner should fall off once defeat appears certain; and (4) each candidate in a three-way race should always attack the strongest rival—that is, neither of the top two should go after the lowest-ranked candidate, and the candidate in third place should assail the front-runner instead of the runner-up.

ISSUE OWNERSHIP OR CONVERGENCE?

Few generalizations about presidential campaigning have been in circulation longer than the claim that parties play up some issues while avoiding others. V. O. Key advanced this idea as early as 1964: "Campaigners, as they avoid or parry charges, naturally place emphasis on what they regard as their strong points; likewise they say little about the weaker elements in their record or program. The opposition follows a like policy of speaking endlessly of the popular features of what it has to offer and of minimizing mention of the less attractive aspects. In consequence the issues seem never to be joined in campaign oratory."[107]

In their study of twenty-three democracies, Ian Budge and Dennis Fairlie pointed up issues showcased by "socialist/reformist" parties of the Left and by "conservative/bourgeois" parties of the Right. Selective emphasis leads to ownership in their account: "One would not normally associate a left-wing party with upholding traditional religious and moral standards. This results in playing such questions down, thus ceding 'ownership' of the issue to the right while emphasizing those appeals which the right cannot make."[108] Looking at the Democratic and Republican platforms of 1920–1972, Budge and Fairlie found that Republicans had staked out eight of fourteen topics, such as civil order and defense. Similarly, Democrats had locked onto several more, including social and economic equality. Still other issues were too "erratic" for either side to possess.[109]

John Petrocik followed the same trail, collecting evidence of selective emphasis and finding party ownership in a study of fourteen issues in the presidential campaigns of 1952–1988.[110] More recently, he, William Benoit, and Glenn Hansen analyzed candidates' acceptance speeches and television commercials in the campaigns of 1952–2000.[111] The latter analysis concluded that the Democrats owned "social welfare and intergroup relations" whereas the Republicans had cornered the market on taxes, government spending, and the size of government. Like Budge and Fairlie, Petrocik classified some so-called performance issues (such as the conduct of public officials and economic vicissitudes) as too mercurial to confer a lasting advantage on either party.[112]

Adam Simon formalized the issue-ownership thesis, postulating that a presidential campaign naturally gravitates toward some problems and away from others. Motivated by the desire to win, each side selects particular campaign themes for the purpose of purveying an optimal message mix of issues that will enhance its prospects. "Dialogue," or convergence on the same issues, should never occur, in his account, because "no themes can work to the advantage of both candidates."[113]

Contrary findings, however, have led other exponents of the issue-ownership thesis to step back from such claims. "The actual state of the world," Budge and Fairlie conceded, may force convergence on a few issues.[114] Petrocik, Benoit, and Hansen elaborated upon this point: "A party can lose an advantage on a constituency-based issue when major shifts occur in the party coalitions. Short-term circumstances can change the advantage on performance issues. . . . Candidates or parties can even lose control of their issues. . . . A candidate who is especially well-liked can be viewed as able to handle a problem that is not usually an issue strength of his (or her) party."[115] Indeed, Petrocik and his colleagues found repeated instances of Democrats addressing Republican issues more frequently than their own. Except for George W. Bush in 2000, Republican candidates generally emphasized Republican issues.[116]

The issue-ownership thesis has come under attack from other political scientists. John Aldrich and John Griffin found that both sides in the 2000 campaign had framed their issue agendas in ways consistent with the concerns of undecided and independent voters. That is, the competing tickets relied largely on issues they did not own. Because party loyalists went along with the new priorities, most voters converged in their understanding of which issues were most important, "even if the means to address these problems remained a matter of dispute."[117] Interestingly, Aldrich and Griffin sought to expand the concept of issue ownership even as they chipped away at its foundation. Issue ownership, in their view, need not be exclusive to one party or the other; indeed, ownership can be joint. Further, even independent and undecided voters own some issues (such as education and health care in 2000).[118]

Similarly, David Damore found enough evidence of thematic "trespassing" in the campaigns of 1976–1996 to cast doubt on issue ownership.[119] In 1984, for example, 34 percent of all the issue appeals in Walter Mondale's TV ads addressed issues supposedly "owned" by the Grand Old Party (GOP). Like Petrocik, Benoit, and

Hansen, Damore argued that Democrats had to campaign on Republican themes because so many "Democratic" issues no longer resonated with most voters. To appear credible on Republican themes, however, Democrats needed to forgo attacks on Republicans.[120]

At this point, we should state our differences with the issue-ownership thesis. Despite clear evidence that parties stress some issues more than others, selective emphasis need not lead to the degree of possession implied by the term *ownership*. Multiple findings that candidates abandoned their party's issues have wreaked havoc with the ownership thesis, as have Aldrich and Griffin's effort to improve it. Their suggestion that both parties can "own" the same issue at the same time does away with Petrocik's notion of possession. Joint "ownership" means nothing more than that both parties feel free (or are forced by electoral circumstances) to stress the importance of the same issue. Likewise, the notion that independent voters "own" an issue means only that such voters view said issue as important. It is also important to note that selective emphasis hardly precludes convergence (that is, both sides opposing one another on the same issue). Elsewhere, we have offered our initial findings on this question,[121] and we have more to say more about convergence in the chapters that follow.

We also need to point up the fundamental difference between our concept of convergence and that set out in Anthony Downs's seminal application of economic theory to democratic elections.[122] Downs began by postulating an electoral system in which both candidates and voters act in accordance with precisely calculated estimates of utility. Parties in this model "formulate policies in order to win elections, rather than win elections in order to formulate policies."[123] Seeking votes from an electorate that is overwhelmingly concentrated at the middle of the political spectrum, both parties eliminate almost every trace of policy difference by taking *identical* positions on nearly every issue. Convergence in our formulation occurs when both sides take *conflicting* positions on most issues, thereby illuminating their differences.

SUMMARY

We have made our case for a concept of negativity and operationally defined it, proclaimed our commitment to a systematic comparison of many campaigns across time, stipulated our unit of analysis, and described our database. In the following chapters, we determine the overall negativity of every presidential contest from 1960 to 2004, as well as the negativity of each side and the attack propensities of presidential candidates, their running mates, and other campaigners. Our study provides answers to the following questions: who attacked whom, how frequently, on what issues, in what ways, and at what point in the campaign? We apply the predictions and suggestions of the Skaperdas-Grofman model to campaigns waged in a variety of electoral contexts. And we determine the degree to which the parties converged on the same topics and issues. To enrich the analysis, we compare our findings with previously published accounts of these campaigns, including firsthand accounts by candidates and their confidants.

2. The Runaway Races of 1964, 1972, and 1984

As expected, prohibitively favored incumbents won lopsided victories over hapless challengers in the runaway contests of 1964, 1972, and 1984. The electoral situation in such a race is obvious to nearly everyone who takes part in the campaign or follows it closely.[1] In the two-party version, one ticket consistently leads by a huge margin in the polls, and nothing attempted by the other side appreciably narrows the gap. The advantage that Richard Nixon maintained over George McGovern (see Figure 2.1) illustrates how little candidate standings change during a runaway contest.[2]

PLIGHT OF THE UNDERDOG

The 1964 Republicans

Senator Barry M. Goldwater of Arizona harbored no illusions about upsetting President Lyndon B. Johnson (LBJ), yet he ran anyway to facilitate a conservative takeover of the GOP.[3] First, however, he had to win the Republican nomination. Although beaten in half of the contested primaries, Goldwater prevailed in the nonprimary states, defeated Nelson Rockefeller in the key California primary, and showed up at the San Francisco convention as the presumptive nominee. Liberal Republicans such as Rockefeller, William Scranton, and George Romney—all big-state governors—as well as Senators Hugh Scott and Jacob Javits failed in eleventh-hour attempts to moderate the platform and to block the nomination.[4] A defiant Goldwater chose William E. Miller, the fiercely conservative congressman from upstate New York, as his running mate. Goldwater also wrote the liberals off in his acceptance speech: "Anyone who joins us in all sincerity we welcome. Those who do not care for our cause we don't expect to enter our ranks in any case." A witness to these proceedings, Richard Nixon later wrote that half of the delegates had cheered Goldwater's words, while "the other half sat in stunned silence: they had just been read out of the Goldwater campaign and out of the party."[5] Adding insult to injury, Goldwater delivered the fateful lines that would haunt the rest of his campaign: "I would remind you that extremism in the defense of liberty is no vice. And let me remind you also that moderation in the pursuit of justice is no virtue." At that point, Senator Kenneth Keating and many others in the New York delegation walked out in protest.[6] Millions of normally Republican voters would follow their example on election day.

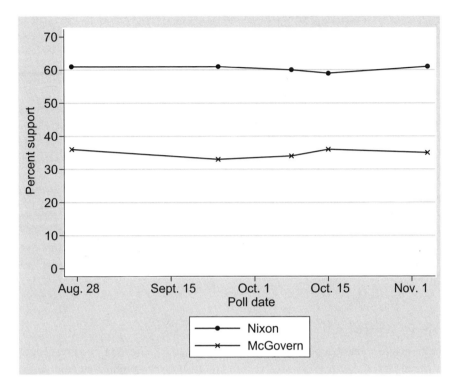

Figure 2.1 The runaway race of 1972
Source: The Gallup Poll: Public Opinion 1972 (Wilmington, DE: Scholarly Resources, 1973).

With little hope of carrying Rockefeller's New York, Scranton's Pennsylvania, or Romney's Michigan, Goldwater strategists looked elsewhere for an electoral majority. They came up with a plan to sweep the Mountain West, the Great Plains, and the South, while eking out narrow victories in Johnson's home state of Texas, as well as in California, Ohio, Indiana, and Illinois.[7] Everything depended on the emergence of a hitherto hidden majority of whites committed to the struggle against communism, suspicious of the United Nations, appalled by the civil rights movement, distrustful of big government, worried about crime and civil unrest, and outraged by changing standards of morality.[8]

Long of like mind on such issues, Goldwater offered such voters a "choice rather than an echo." He had taken a tough line against the Kremlin in a 1960 book,[9] and in the Senate he had voted against a treaty banning atmospheric testing of nuclear weapons. "If it means political suicide to vote for my country and against this treaty," he proclaimed, "then I commit it gladly."[10] He also voted against the 1964 Civil Rights Act, albeit reluctantly. "If my vote is misconstrued," he told his Senate colleagues, "let it be, and let me suffer the consequences."[11] Other stands, such as his support for privatizing Social Security and selling the Tennessee Valley Authority, lent credibility to Democratic characterizations of him as extreme.

Rather than awakening a silent majority, Goldwater's nomination drove a significant number of Republicans to vote for Lyndon Johnson. An Opinion Research Corporation poll revealed in mid-September that only 35 percent of all *Republicans* saw Goldwater as more likely to keep the peace than Johnson. Goldwater fared even worse on Social Security, on which he trailed Johnson by 23 to 41 percent.[12] The situation in one must-win state after another looked grim as well, leading Goldwater to admit that defeat was certain unless the picture changed dramatically by mid-October. When the ides of October arrived with no sign of improvement, he acknowledged the obvious.[13] On election day, Goldwater carried only Arizona and five states in the Deep South for a total of fifty-two electoral votes, garnering only 38.5 percent of the popular vote.[14] According to Gallup, one out of every five Republican voters defected to Johnson, who also got 56 percent of the independent vote.[15]

The 1972 Democrats

Although Senator George McGovern of South Dakota clung to hopes of upsetting Richard Nixon, few Democrats gave him any chance of winning.[16] He had nearly caught up with Nixon earlier in the year, but July polls showed him running twenty-three points behind. Much of this decline can be attributed to the Eagleton affair.

By a process of elimination, McGovern had settled on Senator Tom Eagleton as his running mate, hoping that the Missouri Catholic would strengthen the ticket. However, only hours after the offer had been accepted, rumors began circulating that Eagleton had undergone multiple treatments for depression. A press frenzy followed, and under enormous pressure from fellow Democrats, the *New York Times*, and other leading publications, McGovern dumped Eagleton. His efforts to find a replacement met with refusals from at least six prominent Democrats before Sargent Shriver (experienced in a variety of government posts but perhaps best known for marrying a Kennedy) agreed to join the ticket.[17] All accounts agree that the Eagleton affair took a heavy toll of McGovern's support.[18] According to his campaign manager, Gary Hart, "Anything that took place thereafter was anticlimactic and politically inconsequential in terms of the final result of the election."[19] McGovern likewise conceded that the episode had inflicted "nearly irreparable damage" on his candidacy.[20]

Yet, as McGovern also admitted, his problems hardly began with Eagleton, and they hardly ended with the choice of Shriver.[21] Having played a major role in changing his party's rules of delegate selection following the 1968 convention, he had aroused the enmity of party bosses whose power had been diminished by reform. Already angered by issues of race, gender, and youth quotas, Mayor Richard J. Daley of Chicago blamed McGovernites when the 1972 convention refused to seat his delegates.[22] No old lion roared more fiercely than the president of the American Federation of Labor and Congress of Industrial Organizations (AFL-CIO), George Meany. Like Daley, he inveighed against "the convention that nominated the candidate who chaired the commission that made up the rules that governed the selection of the delegates who selected the candidate."[23] Meany soon took his revenge by denying McGovern the AFL-CIO endorsement. He engineered a similar repudiation by the steelworkers, and he probably influenced nine other union presidents to declare McGovern "wholly unacceptable" before throwing their support to Nixon.[24]

McGovern had also run afoul of Lyndon Johnson and other hawks on the war in Vietnam. LBJ made no secret of his feelings, telling visitors to his Texas ranch that McGovern was "crazy as hell" on the war. Johnson smiled on John Connally's formation of Democrats for Nixon, ultimately the sponsor of a lethal TV ad against McGovern, and he advised Nixon on how to beat McGovern.[25]

Postconvention polls indicated the potential for a massive defection of ethnic and working-class Democrats to Nixon. "Our primary and perhaps only chance to win," McGovern advisers warned in one memorandum, "will lie in reclaiming those millions of traditional Democrats who are now undecided or leaning to Nixon."[26] A *New York Times*–Yankelovich poll showed Nixon leading by three percentage points among *Democrats*.[27] Similar portents of disaster surfaced in the internal polls taken by Pat Caddell. One uncovered widespread doubts about McGovern's competence, and another showed that the ratio of positive to negative assessments was 1:3 (a complete reversal of his pre-Eagleton numbers). The same poll indicated a 35 percent decline in his support since July.[28] Reflecting on the doubts about his competence and steadiness, McGovern wrote that he "was never to escape that prism. By Labor Day I was beginning a long uphill climb from even farther down than I had been a month before in the midst of the Eagleton crisis."[29]

McGovern's advisers expected to lose the popular vote yet hoped to eke out a bare majority in the Electoral College. Seeing no chance of winning anywhere in the South, McGovern decided to go all out in the "traditionally Democratic Northern states and on the Pacific Coast."[30] According to Hart, the plan was to carry California, New York, Illinois, Pennsylvania, and New Jersey for a total of 158 electoral votes. Texas or Ohio, supplemented by Massachusetts, Minnesota, and Wisconsin, would bring another 60 votes. Victories in Maryland, Connecticut, West Virginia, Iowa, Oregon, Hawaii, Rhode Island, South Dakota, Alaska, and the District of Columbia would yield 60 more, for a grand total of 278.[31]

The improbability of this strategy soon became clear as the campaign unfolded. Still, McGovern hoped to pull off an upset like Harry Truman's comeback in 1948. He believed that the voters would turn to him "if they could be made to understand the implications of Watergate, the hard truth about Vietnam, the stark facts of economic injustice."[32] However, as McGovern later acknowledged, his passion for ending the war had backfired: "The more I reflected on the costs of Vietnam in lives and scarce resources, the more I wanted to cry out to the American people. But the more I cried out, the more strident my public statements sounded. My very anguish may have pushed voters in the other direction—toward the apparently cool man in the White House who insisted that he was heading steadily for 'peace with honor.'"[33]

On election day, McGovern carried only Massachusetts and the District of Columbia, garnering a mere 17 votes in the Electoral College and ending up with 37.5 percent of the popular vote. One of every three Democrats who cast a presidential ballot voted for Nixon. McGovern lost nearly half of all voters who belonged to union families, as well as 69 percent of the independent vote.[34]

The 1984 Democrats

Former vice president Walter Mondale undoubtedly realized that he stood little chance of upsetting Ronald Reagan. His rivals in the primaries had painted him as a tool of the special interests, as well as a purveyor of stale ideas, and exit polls indicated that he had lost the white vote to Gary Hart.[35] A brief surge against Reagan had evaporated by July, and a poll just before the San Francisco convention showed him trailing by fourteen points. This poll also suggested that the public doubted Mondale's capacity to lead and that they gave Reagan credit for the economic recovery.[36]

As Democrats assembled in San Francisco for their national convention, various factions in the party brought much-publicized pressure to bear on the nominee apparent. In so doing, they likely hurt Mondale's standing in Middle America. The National Organization for Women (NOW) demanded that Mondale put a woman on the ticket and threatened a floor fight if he did not.[37] Jesse Jackson demanded that Mondale show him "respect" for having garnered so many black votes in the primaries. Mondale, however, had to take account of the ill will that Jackson aroused among Jews in particular and whites in general. In any case, Jackson and Hart made no secret of how they rated Mondale's chances, and each used the convention to launch his 1988 bid for the nomination. Gays and lesbians paraded in an ostentatious show of their strength. Meanwhile, journalist William Greider searched in vain for just one delegate willing to predict a Mondale victory in November.[38]

Desperate to turn the corner, Mondale agreed to changes in the 1988 rules that would benefit Hart and Jackson. He stumbled, however, by trying to replace Democratic National Committee (DNC) chairman Charles T. Manatt with the tarnished Bert Lance.[39] Mondale not only lost this tussle but also renewed the doubts about his leadership abilities. He did make history by putting Representative Geraldine Ferraro of New York on the ticket, but the euphoria over her selection soon gave way to controversies over her abortion views, her husband's tax returns, and his business dealings, issues that plagued Ferraro for the rest of the campaign.[40]

The most serious tax problem for Mondale, however, was one of his own making. In a calculated decision to attack Reagan on the deficit, he called for higher taxes: "Let's tell the truth," he declared in his acceptance speech. "Mr. Reagan will raise taxes, and so will I. He won't tell you. I just did."[41]

Mondale's tax hike seemed heaven sent to Republicans desperate for a wedge issue, and Reagan instantly realized its potential. "We will not be satisfied until all Americans understand that they are welcome with us and belong with us," he proclaimed on Labor Day.[42] A CBS/New York Times poll showed him leading even among those registered voters who disagreed with his policies. The same poll showed that Mondale was in trouble with nominally Democratic groups.[43] On October 25, Manatt conceded that Mondale had fallen behind Reagan in forty-six states.[44] The same poll estimated Mondale support at 40 percent of likely voters, with only 5 percent undecided.[45]

On election day, Mondale carried only his home state of Minnesota and the District of Columbia, for a total of thirteen votes in the Electoral College, the worst drubbing for a major-party candidate since 1936.[46] At the polls, one-third of the Democrats voted Republican, as did 48 percent of union family members and two-thirds of the independents. Mondale received 40.6 percent of the popular vote, marginally higher than McGovern's and Goldwater's totals.[47]

In sum, the odds for each of these underdogs appeared well nigh insuperable after Labor Day. With every poll signaling disaster, each seemingly had little to lose by going negative. If so inclined, their favored opponents were better positioned to wage mostly positive campaigns than any other presidential candidates of the late twentieth century.

ATTACKERS

The core insight of the Skaperdas-Grofman model is that candidate strategy in a two-way race depends on who is ahead and by how much. Although the leading candidate in a runaway race has little incentive to attack, the underdog has little hope of winning without going negative. It follows that the trailing side should wage a much more negative campaign than the favored side. When we say that one "side" attacked the other, we really mean that a variety of individuals spoke

Table 2.1. Negativity in Runaway Races

Campaign Week	1964 Democrats	1964 Republicans	1972 Democrats	1972 Republicans	1984 Democrats	1984 Republicans
1	.671	.766	.681	.526	.662	.333
2	.633	.627	.620	.625	.494	.347
3	.603	.537	.500	.451	.678	.468
4	.679	.740	.792	.440	.769	.377
5	.698	.670	.690	.641	.792	.406
6	.458	.647	.712	.613	.732	.474
7	.533	.741	.803	.571	.681	.524
8	.513	.616	.851	.409	.679	.465
9	.667	.383	.676	.296	.512	.517
Overall	.593	.654	.699	.489	.665	.443
N	661	662	622	374	859	621

Notes: Each side's weekly attack propensity score was computed as a proportion of all of its campaign statements for the week in question. Our observation period began on Labor Day and ended on election day. The 1964 period started on September 17 and ended on November 3, the 1972 period began on September 4 and ended on November 7, and the 1984 period commenced on September 3 and ended on November 6. Each week extended from Monday to Sunday except for the final one; week nine varied in length from two days in 1964 to nine days in 1972 and 1984.

against the other party, whether solo or in concert with others. Accordingly, we report attack propensity scores not only for the presidential nominees but also for their running mates as well as for the "side" (combining all of the party's voices as one). We begin with the latter measure.

Overall Attack Propensities

Our expectation that the trailing side in a runaway race should have waged a much more negative campaign than the leading side held up nicely in 1972 and 1984 but not as well in 1964. Weekly scores for each side in 1964 showed that the favored Democrats gave more than they got from the Republicans in four of the nine weeks (see Table 2.1). This is not to say that the Republicans let up on the Democrats, whom they blasted in more than two-thirds of their campaign statements in weeks one, four, five, and seven. Regarding overall scores for nine weeks, the Democrats attacked the Republicans in slightly more than 59 percent of all their campaign statements, which was not much different from the Republican figure of 65 percent.

The campaigns of 1972 and 1984 looked a lot more like what Skaperdas and Grofman had in mind. In both contests, the prohibitively favored Republicans exhibited much less negativity than the underdog Democrats. Total attack propensity scores for Republican tickets came to 49 percent in 1972 and 44 percent in 1984, as compared with 70 percent for Democrats in 1972 and nearly 67 percent in 1984. Weekly breakdowns of these campaigns show that Democratic negativity levels topped 70 percent four times in 1972 and three times in 1984.

Solo Attacks by Presidential Nominees

Focusing on the solo statements of competing nominees, we found strong support for the Skaperdas-Grofman prediction in all three races. Goldwater attacked the Democrats in 69 percent of his statements, compared with 43 percent of Johnson's statements that took aim at Republicans. The result was a substantial difference of twenty-six points in the expected direction. Likewise, McGovern assailed the Republicans in 79 percent of his solo statements, compared with 29 percent of Nixon's statements attacking Democrats, a whopping difference of fifty points. Similarly, Mondale blasted Republicans in 79 percent of his solo statements, thereby surpassing Reagan's score by thirty-one points.

Solo Attacks by Vice-Presidential Nominees

Although the Skaperdas-Grofman model makes no mention of vice-presidential candidates, we nonetheless expected to find that they also differed dramatically in terms of the propensity to attack. Instead, we found only modest differences, on the order of about ten percentage points, albeit in the right direction. Miller railed against Democrats in 82 percent of his statements, and Humphrey flayed Republicans in 72 percent of his. Similarly, Shriver (66 percent negative) ran up a somewhat higher score than Agnew (54 percent) in 1972, and Ferraro surpassed Bush, 54 to 44 percent.

All Other Campaigners

Until the twentieth century, most presidential nominees relied on members of Congress, state party officials, and other surrogates to fight their battles. The rise of presidential candidates as negative campaigners, however, did not end the importance of surrogates. Rather, conventional wisdom holds that a prohibitively favored candidate such as Johnson should let others do the dirty work. At first, Johnson did restrain himself while Humphrey and myriad other Democrats lit into his opponent. At one point, Goldwater even complained about Johnson's unwillingness to make his own case: "Instead, he sends forth his curious crew of camp followers to speak for him. Some are socialistic radicals like his running mate, Hubert Horatio. Some are bosses of big cities, big unions, and big business. Some are bureaucratic lackeys. Some are even buildings. We keep hearing that the White House announces or that the Pentagon says such-and-such. The Pentagon talks so much that I've suggested that it be given a name, like Peter Pentagon."[48]

Surrogates took on even greater attack responsibilities on Nixon's behalf. "Only after McGovern was nominated," Nixon later wrote, "did I accept the fact that I was virtually assured of reelection without having to wage much of a campaign. It was clear that the less I did, the better I would do."[49] We found that Nixon made fewer campaign statements than any other presidential nominee in these runaway races. Meanwhile, Agnew and a legion of others went after McGovern. The surrogate list included every cabinet secretary, as well as members of Congress, governors, and mayors.[50]

We expected to find that underdog candidates delivered a higher proportion of their side's attacks than was true of their favored opponents. This clearly happened in 1964 and 1972. Counting only solo statements, Goldwater made 41 percent of all Republican attacks, whereas Johnson accounted for only 22 percent of Democratic attacks, a nineteen-point difference. An even bigger disparity showed up in 1972, when McGovern made 48 percent of all the attacks for his side, and Nixon accounted for only 13 percent of the Republican attacks. In 1984, however, the difference narrowed to nine percentage points (Mondale at 52 percent; Reagan at 43 percent).

Consistent with the Skaperdas-Grofman model, we anticipated that surrogates helping trailing tickets would outattack supporters of leading tickets. Instead, our combined measure of surrogate attack propensities yielded no one pattern. In 1964 and 1972, surrogates on the losing side scored slightly higher than their counterparts on the winning side, but Reagan surrogates outattacked Mondale supporters in 1984.

In sum, although the Skaperdas-Grofman model held up for presidential candidates speaking solo, it had less relevance for understanding the attack roles of vice-presidential candidates and none whatever for surrogates.

TARGETS

Only statements aimed at the other party qualified as attacks in our study.[51] The lineup of possible targets corresponds exactly to our list of potential attackers. For instance, an attack by the presidential nominee of one party may be aimed at just one target or several. We found that each side went after the other party's presidential nominee more frequently than any other target. Most of these attacks singled the nominee out, but many others included him in a more general blast at the opposing party. Our "nominee targeted" scores in Table 2.2 summarize the degree to which each side took aim at the other's standard-bearer. Indeed, the scores exceeded 80 percent in thirteen of eighteen cases. Goldwater and McGovern ended up in the crosshairs far more than Johnson and Nixon. In 1964, to take one case, 86 percent of all Democratic attacks targeted Goldwater, as did 83 percent of Johnson's attacks and 93 percent of Humphrey's. Conversely, 56 percent of all Republican attacks targeted Johnson, as did 59 percent of Goldwater's solo attacks and 56 percent of Miller's. Even so, the favored Reagan showed up as the most frequently targeted of all six nominees. Nearly 88 percent of the 1984 Democratic attacks fell on him, as did 94 percent of Mondale's attacks and 84 percent of Ferraro's.

These findings indicate that a nominee's standing had less to do with targeting than his vulnerability, real or imagined. The Democrats pounced on Goldwater because he so willingly played the part of right-wing extremist. Democrats lined up to assail the dangerous radical and make themselves look good. Owing to Goldwater's stands, his candidacy invited a divide-and-conquer response, whereby the Johnson camp sought to drive a wedge between the Republican nominee and moderate Republicans. Helped immeasurably by McGovern's shrill message on Vietnam, the Republicans made serious inroads into the Democratic base. The reasoning behind Mondale's decision to concentrate on the popular Reagan is less apparent. We cannot say whether he acted out of personal disdain, a desire to appear decisive, sheer desperation, some other motivation, or some combination of these factors.[52]

OWNERSHIP OR CONVERGENCE?

We turn now to questions of issue ownership and convergence. Recall the prediction of the ownership thesis that one side will avoid an issue "owned" by the other. However, as pointed out in Chapter 1, researchers with varying perspectives on ownership have documented myriad instances in which both sides addressed the same issues. Such findings suggest that convergence is more common than avoidance, especially on important issues. We can get at the convergence issue by answering the following question: what topics did each side emphasize most in these runaway campaigns? For present purposes, let us consider each side's top-ten topics, as determined by total campaign (attack and nonattack) statements about each (see Table 2.3).

We found that both sides generally addressed the same topics and, further, that they often attached roughly the same importance to these concerns. Let us look at each runaway race.

In 1964, both sides placed a higher priority on military and defense issues than any other set of concerns. The next most important topic for Democratic and Republican campaigners alike pertained to liberalism-conservatism issues. Likewise, both sides addressed campaign-related concerns, leadership questions, race-related issues, foreign policy problems, and the meaning of Americanism. It is

Table 2.2. Targeting of Attacks in Runaway Races

	1964 Democratic Targeting of Republicans	1964 Republican Targeting of Democrats	1972 Democratic Targeting of Republicans	1972 Republican Targeting of Democrats	1984 Democratic Targeting of Republicans	1984 Republican Targeting of Democrats
Targets of all attacks						
Presidential nominee	338	244	325	154	499	223
Other targets	55	190	110	29	70	52
N attacks	393	434	435	183	569	275
Nominee targeted	.860	.562	.747	.841	.877	.811
Solo attacks of presidential nominee	Johnson	Goldwater	McGovern	Nixon	Mondale	Reagan
Presidential nominee	72	105	162	20	277	102
Other targets	15	73	48	3	19	16
N attacks	87	178	210	23	296	118
Nominee targeted	.828	.590	.771	.870	.936	.864
Solo attacks of vice-presidential nominee	Humphrey	Miller	Shriver	Agnew	Ferraro	Bush
Presidential nominee	90	57	47	36	63	51
Other targets	7	44	7	2	12	10
N attacks	97	101	54	38	75	61
Nominee targeted	.928	.564	.870	.947	.840	.836

Note: Some attacks on presidential candidates also targeted others of the same party.

Table 2.3. Topics Most Emphasized in Runaway Races

1964 Democrats	1964 Republicans	1972 Democrats	1972 Republicans	1984 Democrats	1984 Republicans
Military/defense (111)	Military/defense (120)	Campaign (103)	Military/defense (73)	Military/defense (169)	U.S. economy (118)
Ideology/party (83)	Ideology/party (90)	Military/defense (96)	Corruption/power (48)	Campaign (107)	Military/defense (105)
Leadership (71)	Campaign (82)	Domestic economy (70)	Leadership (41)	Domestic economy (90)	Campaign (76)
Campaign (68)	Leadership (60)	Corruption/power (47)	Domestic economy (40)	Leadership (79)	Leadership (37)
Social/health programs (47)	Corruption/power (49)	Leadership (41)	Campaign (38)	Social/health programs (70)	Ideology/party (37)
Race (46)	Race (38)	Social/health programs (41)	Social/health programs (17)	Women's rights (42)	Religion (30)
Domestic economy (32)	Patriotism (32)	Ideology/party (35)	Race (15)	Religion (40)	Social/health programs (27)
Foreign policy (27)	Foreign policy (30)	Foreign policy (20)	Ideology/party (14)	Ideology/party (39)	Women's rights (26)
Farm policy (22)	Personal morality (29)	Campaign finance (19)	Crime (14)	Foreign policy (37)	Foreign policy (25)
Patriotism (20)	Social/health programs (23)	Labor (19)	Patriotism (13)	Education (23); race (23)	Personal comments (25)

Notes: Each topic listed according to its number of campaign statements, in parentheses. The top-ten topics of the Democrats accounted for 80 percent of all Democratic campaign statements in 1964, 79 percent in 1972, and 81 percent in 1984. The Republicans' top ten accounted for 83 percent of total Republican statements in 1964, 84 percent in 1972, and 81 percent in 1984.

true that Democrats stressed social policies much more than Republicans, and Republicans dwelled on patriotism more than Democrats. Even so, social policies showed up among the Republican top ten, and patriotism similarly made the Democratic cut. In short, not only did both sides address eight of the same topics, they also resembled one another in degree of emphasis.

In 1972, both sides emphasized the same seven topics though they exhibited less agreement on their relative importance. Republican campaigners emphasized military and defense issues more than any other, and the Democrats made slightly more of campaign issues than war and defense budgets. The war, however, became McGovern's signature issue. Interestingly, in this first year of the Watergate scandal, Republicans dedicated a larger proportion of their statements to corruption and abuse of power than the Democrats did (even though the actual number of statements was nearly identical for both sides). The economy figured prominently in both agendas, as did leadership, social policies, and ideology. Three topics stressed by Democrats—foreign policy, campaign finance, and labor issues—did not show up as Republican priorities. Similarly, Democrats said little about race, crime, and patriotism.

Both sides converged on nine of the same topics in 1984 while exhibiting a similar sense of priorities. Thus, defense and military issues emerged as the topic most emphasized by Democrats and as second in importance to Republicans. Although Republicans stressed economic issues more than any others, Democrats devoted more statements to defense and campaign matters. Leadership came in fourth on both lists, and foreign policy placed ninth. Both sides also addressed social policies, abortion and other "women's issues," religion, and ideology.

Thus, convergence emerged as the dominant pattern of campaign discourse in every runaway campaign.[53] This pattern lends support to our argument that selective emphasis hardly prevents both sides from addressing the same concerns. Rather, it appears that selective emphasis results in convergence more often than not. Note that five topics invariably figured in the leading concerns of both sides—military and defense, ideology, leadership, social policies, and campaign concerns—and that two others (the economy and foreign policy) appeared in five of the six lists.

TOPICS OF ATTACKS

We turn now to the question of which topics each side used to attack the other. To explore this ground, we must extract attack statements from the totality of campaign statements in each contest. That done, we examine the ten topics most utilized by each side in every runaway race (see Table 2.4). Nearly every topic listed in the previous table reappeared in this one (counting "dirty campaign," the negative side of the "campaign" coin). As before, convergence emerged as the dominant pattern, with both sides clashing on eight of the same topics in each campaign. In 1964, for example, both sides willingly fought one another over military and defense issues, their ideological differences, leadership qualities of their respective nominees, patriotism, race-related issues, foreign policy, social policies, and the economy.

METHODS OF ATTACK

We kept track of five methods when coding campaign attacks. As detailed in Chapter 1, they were fear arousal, ridicule, guilt by association (or labeling), apposition, and charges of lying or being inconsistent. Table 2.5 reveals the tactics employed by presidential nominees, vice-presidential candidates, and all attackers.

Presidential Candidates

Every presidential nominee except Goldwater made more use of fear arousal than any other method. Goldwater relied most on labeling, as in his repeated references to "Light Bulb Lyndon" and his "curious crew." Nixon made the most use of apposition and, as best we could determine, avoided making charges of lying or resorting to ridicule. Mondale hurled accusations of dishonesty more frequently than any other presidential candidate, and Reagan showed up as the most humorous candidate.

Vice-Presidential Candidates

Miller, Bush, Shriver, and Ferraro closely resembled their running mates in their choice of attack methods. Humphrey, Miller, and Agnew resorted to labeling more than any other method. Humphrey, for one, seldom missed an opportunity to brand Goldwater as a radical and right-winger. Similarly, Agnew routinely painted McGovern as the dupe of Hanoi. Unlike Nixon, Agnew displayed a sense of humor when on the campaign trail, although it soured when turned against McGovern. Ferraro stood out among the vice-presidential candidates for accusing Reagan of lying or inconsistency.

All Attackers

Our findings regarding the methods used by all of the attackers suggest that the tactics of surrogates basically supplemented those utilized by the presidential and vice-presidential candidates. In 1964, for instance, Goldwater's surrogates appear

Table 2.4. Leading Attack Topics in Runaway Races

1964 Democrats	1964 Republicans	1972 Democrats	1972 Republicans	1984 Democrats	1984 Republicans
Military/defense (83)	Military/defense (90)	Military/defense (71)	Military/defense (38)	Military/defense (134)	Domestic economy (79)
Ideology/party (68)	Ideology/party (48)	Dirty campaign (59)	Leadership (29)	Domestic economy (70)	Military/defense (45)
Leadership (41)	Corruption, abuse of power (48)	Domestic economy (57)	Domestic economy (18)	Social/health programs (66)	Ideology/party (29)
Race (30)	Leadership (40)	Corruption, abuse of power (35)	Dirty campaign (17)	Leadership (62)	Leadership (18)
Social/health programs (29)	Patriotism/war record (28)	Social/health programs (35)	Social/health programs (13)	Ideology/party (32)	Personal slurs (18)
Dirty campaign (19)	Foreign policy (26)	Leadership (29)	Ideology/party (12)	Foreign policy (31)	Religion (13)
Farm policy (18)	Race (21)	Ideology/party (18)	Corruption, abuse of power (8)	Religion (28)	Women's issues (12)
Foreign policy (16)	Personal morality (20)	Labor (14)	Patriotism/war record (7)	Women's issues (23)	Social/health programs (10)
Domestic economy (15)	Social/health programs (17)	Campaign finance (14)	Race (6)	Race (17)	Dirty campaign (8)
Patriotism/war record (10)	Domestic economy (13)	Foreign policy (13)	Foreign policy (5)	Energy/environment (17)	Foreign policy (7)

Notes: The top-ten attack topics of the Democrats accounted for 84 percent of all Democratic attacks in 1964, 79 percent in 1972, and 85 percent in 1984; corresponding percentages for the Republican top ten were 81 in 1964, 84 in 1972, and 87 in 1984.

Table 2.5. Attack Methods in Runaway Races

	Presidential Candidate (solo)	Vice-Presidential Candidate (solo)	All Attackers
1964 Democrats			
Fear arousal	.540	.495	.461
Ridicule	.034	.155	.081
Labeling	.448	.660	.514
Apposition	.368	.454	.275
Dishonesty	.080	.124	.122
1964 Republicans			
Fear arousal	.421	.436	.403
Ridicule	.062	.079	.053
Labeling	.657	.634	.631
Apposition	.213	.248	.207
Dishonesty	.129	.218	.173
1972 Democrats			
Fear arousal	.629	.667	.602
Ridicule	.033	.111	.046
Labeling	.533	.500	.529
Apposition	.271	.185	.221
Dishonesty	.267	.259	.278
1972 Republicans			
Fear arousal	.522	.447	.481
Ridicule	.000	.184	.049
Labeling	.435	.737	.536
Apposition	.478	.184	.213
Dishonesty	.000	.368	.235
1984 Democrats			
Fear arousal	.584	.587	.561
Ridicule	.111	.107	.111
Labeling	.368	.413	.360
Apposition	.291	.320	.269
Dishonesty	.311	.413	.295
1984 Republicans			
Fear arousal	.576	.426	.455
Ridicule	.203	.115	.138
Labeling	.500	.410	.447
Apposition	.373	.344	.387
Dishonesty	.220	.328	.244

Note: Entries are percentages of attacks employing a particular method, e.g., President Johnson used fear arousal in 54 percent of his attacks on Republican targets.

to have followed his lead in their choice of attack methods. Similar patterns show up between McGovern and all Democratic attackers in 1972, Mondale and Democratic attackers in 1984, and Reagan and Republican attackers in 1984.

Further scrutiny of Table 2.5 reveals that Democrats resorted to fear arousal more frequently than Republicans, that underdog campaigners in these races (with Agnew as a notable exception) played the dishonesty card more often than their opposite numbers, and that favored candidates relied more on apposition than underdogs did in 1964 and 1984.[54]

Because our code could accommodate the use of more than one attack method, we were curious to see if candidate standing correlated with the number of attack methods utilized. When we looked at the number used by opposing sides, however, sixty-four of the seventy-two means computed for this analysis fell below two methods per attack. Evidently, therefore, standing has little or nothing to do with the choice or number of attack methods. In any case, we never intended to measure degrees of negativity according to the number of methods employed; indeed, this is not possible because the methods differ qualitatively. It follows that one or two methods of attack need not signify less negativity than four or five. Much depends on the particular topic and the context in which the attack occurred. In wartime, for example, calling the president a murderer or likening him to Hitler probably packs more of an emotional punch than a peacetime assault on the incumbent's handling of the economy that attributes hard times to his policies, ridicules his explanation of how the slump began, labels him as Herbert Hoover II, and accuses him of dissembling about who would gain most from his tax cut.

ECHOES FROM THE CAMPAIGN TRAIL

Let us move beyond our findings to examples of how the contestants clashed on the same topics. We begin with the 1964 exchange on ideology and party tradition, turn next to the 1972 debate over military and defense issues, and conclude with the 1984 clash on economic issues.

The 1964 Exchange on Ideology

Both sides set out to do ideological battle in 1964. For his part, Goldwater saw the campaign as an opportunity to awaken Americans to the dangers of surrendering too much power to the national government. When Johnson failed to mention individual freedom when extolling the Great Society on Labor Day, Goldwater likened his vision to that of a Soviet bureaucrat.[55] In North Carolina, he denounced the Johnson administration for setting up government as "the master, not the servant of the people" and for operating a bureaucracy that regarded citizens merely as nameless numbers: "We want to give the government of this nation back to the people of this nation," he avowed. "An administration that understands, rather than one that tried to wreck the balances of constitutional power, can do the job."[56] In Milwaukee, Wisconsin, he assailed liberal Democrats as monarchists, absolutists, and fascists, and in Lubbock, Texas, he called Johnson a "radical liberal" with socialistic tendencies.[57]

Republican campaigners pounced on Humphrey's association with the liberal group Americans for Democratic Action (ADA). Goldwater took up the cry, calling Humphrey "the most prominent, left-wing, ADA radical in this country" and warning that he and others of his ilk would lead the United States "into the swampland of collectivism."[58] Similarly, Miller denounced Humphrey as "a founder of the Americans for Democratic Action, a secret-membership organization which preaches a philosophy of foreign, socialistic totalitarianism."[59] Republican National Committee (RNC) chairman Dean Burch decried "the offbeat and dangerous policies of the ADA, which Hubert Humphrey helped to found and served as vice chairman."[60] On the stump for Goldwater, Richard Nixon urged voters not to follow a "very dedicated radical" down the road to socialism.[61]

Goldwater's admittedly ideological candidacy exposed him to ideological attacks from Democrats. No Democrat saw this opening more clearly than President Johnson, who later wrote that Goldwater had given him a golden opportunity to claim the center.[62] "Let's just make it a general rule never to refer to Goldwater as a Republican," LBJ instructed his running mate. "A lot of Republicans in this country ought to be Democrats, but we've never given them a chance to come in. This is the best opportunity we're ever going to get."[63]

Times accounts confirm that LBJ stayed on message: "Americans are faced with a concerted bid for power by factions which oppose all that both parties have supported," the president told a gathering of electrical workers on September 24. "It is a choice between the center and the fringe, between the responsible mainstream of American experience and the reckless and rejected extremes of American life."[64] "One of our great parties," he informed New Englanders, "has been captured by a faction of men who stand outside the whole range of common agreement and common principles which have brought us to the summit of success."[65] He hit the same note in New Jersey: "The two-party system dangles by a slim thread when the faction that controls one party wants to repudiate the policies that have built our progress step by step over 30 years. I do not believe that responsible Republicans are going to let control of their party rest for very long with men who want to repeal the present and veto the future."[66]

As instructed, Humphrey painted Goldwater as too extreme for most Republicans. In New Mexico, he asserted that "large numbers of Eisenhower Republicans,

Scranton Republicans, Rockefeller Republicans—that is, solid, constructive, middle-of-the-road Republicans—cannot bring themselves to vote for Goldwater. They are putting country above party, principles above politics."[67] "Senator Goldwater fails to realize that the exercise of freedom is related to opportunity," Humphrey proclaimed in Indiana. "The essential role of a government of the people is to provide the opportunity for freedom. Mr. Goldwater's freedom is the freedom to be uneducated, to be sick, to be hungry, to be unemployed."[68] Goldwater, he declared in Kentucky, saw government as "a kind of foreign agent."[69] In Chattanooga, Tennessee, he linked Goldwater to the ultraconservative John Birch Society: "We don't need the radicals of the right, or the radicals of the left, or the playmates of the Birchers."[70] And in Virginia, he accused "the Goldwater party" of lining up with the "lunatic fringe of American politics."[71]

Other Democrats invoked totalitarian images when flaying the Republican nominee and his followers. Perhaps unaware of Goldwater's Jewish ancestry, George Meany likened the senator to Hitler: Nobody had paid much attention to Hitler at first, he pointed out, but "suddenly the crackpot took over."[72] Likewise, Mayor Robert Wagner of New York City lashed out at "homegrown fascists" supporting Goldwater.[73] Senator J. William Fulbright, however, saw "Goldwaterism" as more akin to Stalinism.[74]

The 1972 Exchange on Military and Defense

McGovern frequently accused the administration of sacrificing American lives to prop up a detestable regime in Saigon. "Never again," he vowed in Minneapolis, "will we send the precious young blood of this country to try and bail out a corrupt dictatorship 10,000 miles away."[75] He returned to this theme several weeks later in Baltimore, asserting that not one more American life should be expended, and again during a televised address on October 10.[76]

McGovern also accused President Nixon, Secretary Melvin Laird, and the Pentagon of blocking the early return of American prisoners of war (POWs).[77] The issue took on new meaning when Hanoi offered to free three pilots as a goodwill gesture—but only if the U.S. military played no part in their return. When administration officials denounced this gesture as a propaganda stunt, McGovern blasted the White House for not complying with Hanoi's conditions.[78] The Democratic nominee later attacked Nixon for not telling the truth about American POWs: "The truth is that each day this war continues is just one more day that our prisoners remain in their cells."[79]

McGovern also characterized U.S. bombing policy as barbaric in several speeches. "We've counted bodies so long that somehow they don't seem to count anymore," he told a gathering of financial contributors in Philadelphia.[80] It was around this time that McGovern likened the bombing of Vietnamese targets to Hitler's bombing of Europe.[81] The Democratic nominee invoked a shocking and by then familiar image during a speech on ending U.S. participation in the war: "The reality of this war is seen in the news photo of the little South Vietnamese girl, Kim, fleeing in terror from her bombed out school. She has torn off her flaming clothes and she is running naked into the lens of that camera. How can we rest with the grim knowledge that the burning napalm that splashed over Kim and countless thousands of other children was dropped in the name of America?"[82] Appearing at the University of Minnesota, he produced a tape recording by a supposedly distraught Vietnam veteran who sobbed while describing the effects of napalm on human flesh.[83] And as this uneven contest ended, he called Nixon's bombing of Vietnam "the most evil thing ever done by any American president."[84]

Worried that Henry Kissinger might reach an agreement with Hanoi before voters went to the polls, McGovern took various steps to minimize the effect that such news would have on his candidacy. First, he reminded voters of Nixon's so-called secret plan to end the war in 1968. That plan remained a secret, he acidly noted, to the 20,000 Americans who had been killed in action since Nixon took office. Second, he recalled Nixon's 1968 declaration that "those who have had a chance for four years and could not produce peace should not be given another chance." And third, he argued that the war could have been ended four years earlier on the same terms likely to be obtained by Kissinger.[85]

Thus primed, McGovern quickly responded to Kissinger's peace-is-at-hand declaration on October 26: "Why, Mr. Nixon, did you take another four more years to put an end to this tragic war? What did either we or the rest of the world gain by the killing of another 20,000 young Americans these past four years? What did we get from the terrible, unprecedented bombardment that has gone on these last four years—bombardment and artillery attacks that we are told have either killed or maimed or driven out of their homes some six million people, most of them in South Vietnam?"[86] A few days later, when Nixon announced that peace was not yet at hand, McGovern denounced his "cruel political deception."[87] On November 4, he implored voters not to "let this man trick you once again into believing that he stands for peace, when he's a man who makes war."[88] The following day, he again cried out against "one of the cruelest frauds ever perpetrated on the American people."[89]

Shriver attacked Nixon's Vietnam policy with particular bitterness, no doubt sustained by memories of the 1968 peace conference in Paris that he suspected Nixon had torpedoed.[90] Responding to Kissinger's announcement only five days before the election, Shriver reiterated McGovern's argument: "The question, I think, that Americans have to ask is this: Was four years' additional expenditure of money and blood worth the terms we have agreed to today? My answer is: No." "If that is peace with honor," he said of the Kissinger plan in San Francisco, "I'd like to know what surrender is."[91] After Nixon announced that peace was not quite at hand, Shriver lashed out: "There's no military victory for the people who sought military victory, no cease fire, no guaranteed future for South Vietnam, no decisive end to United States involvement, no democratic regime in South Vietnam, no sign of a Vietnamese surrender in the North. No matter what you want, Nixon has failed to deliver."[92]

Nixon rightly understood that most issues pertaining to the war worked against McGovern. "The opinion polls," he later wrote, "confirmed my own intuition that, in terms of voter support, my handling of the war was generally viewed as a positive issue for me and a negative one for McGovern, who was perceived as weak and favoring surrender."[93] Nixon accordingly ordered Agnew and all other Republican campaigners to zero in on the McGovernites, while avoiding general attacks on "the Democrats" and going all out to win the independent vote.[94]

Consistent with this strategy, Nixon chose to engage McGovern on the issue of granting amnesty to draft evaders. Even before Labor Day, he had contrasted his stand on this problem with McGovern's position. Contrary to what "the other side" thought, he contended, draft dodgers had broken the law and had to pay the penalty.[95] He repeated this line in unscheduled remarks to a Washington meeting of the National League of Families of American Prisoners.[96] Later, while praising Americans who had fought in previous wars, he inveighed against the "small minority" that "has tried to glorify the few who have refused to serve."[97]

Vice President Agnew took a harder line, criticizing McGovern for "parroting the propaganda of the North Vietnamese" and for remaining indifferent to the deaths of "hundreds of thousands" of South Vietnamese at the hands of the enemy.[98] Agnew also decried the "myopic isolationism" behind McGovern's willingness to abandon South Vietnam to a cruel fate.[99] McGovern's "defeatist philosophy," he told a South Dakota audience, was "very popular in certain segments of North Vietnamese society."[100] Agnew pounced when McGovern claimed the right to renegotiate any Nixon pact with Hanoi. "The Senator's position borders on the incredible," he declared. "After ten years of blood, sweat, and tears, the United States is closer than ever before to an honorable peace for which so much national sacrifice has been made. Yet Mr. McGovern says that he would renegotiate that honorable peace, betray our Vietnamese ally, and agree to an American surrender."[101]

Other Republicans joined the fray. Secretary of Defense Melvin Laird took strong issue with McGovern's charge that the administration had delayed a POW release for political reasons: "It is a despicable act of a presidential candidate to make himself a spokesman for the enemy."[102] When McGovern set out a plan for a quick withdrawal of U.S. forces, Republicans orchestrated a response, beginning with Laird, who said that this proposal amounted to nothing less than "unconditional surrender." Senator Hugh Scott complained of McGovern's readiness to render "our allies helpless before an advancing enemy," and after calling McGovern "unreal," House Minority Leader Gerald Ford denounced this "formula for a Communist takeover."[103]

During the Democratic primaries, McGovern had proposed $30 billion in defense cuts. Pushed by opponents to explain how he would preserve national security after big reductions in personnel and weapon systems, he proposed to rely chiefly on a nuclear deterrent. Republicans took these ideas to task during the fall campaign. Speaking in St. Louis, Agnew claimed that McGovern was bent on rendering the U.S. military incapable of fighting a conventional war.[104] Laird took a similar line: "Senator McGovern doesn't just want to return to neo-isolationist fortress America, he wants to dismantle the fortress."[105] Nixon claimed that McGovern's cuts would "massively increase the danger of aggression around the world."[106] By then, John Connally's group, Democrats for Nixon, had televised the campaign's most memorable attack ad. While a giant hand swept a board clear of toy soldiers, planes, and ships, the voice-under solemnly ticked off McGovern's proposed reductions of conventional force levels and weapons systems.[107]

The 1984 Exchange on the Economy

According to the *Times*, the Democratic plan of attack called for an offensive on two fronts—"war and peace" and the domestic economy.[108] Reagan's team proved more than willing to fight both battles. Ultimately, the Democrats made more of military and defense matters than economic issues, and the Republicans homed in on Mondale's pledge to raise taxes. The Reagan camp frequently reminded voters of just how high inflation had risen during the Carter-Mondale years. Reagan also made a point of contrasting his optimistic view of the future with Mondale's gloom.

Mondale launched his fall campaign with a flurry of attacks blaming Reagan for the deficit and decrying the lack of "fairness" in his tax cuts. "Let's tell the truth," the former vice president exclaimed in Wisconsin. "Mr. Reagan has piled up the worst deficit in world history and is running on a platform that will double it. . . . Whoever is elected, this budget must be squeezed and revenues restored. . . . I refuse to make your family pay more so that millionaires can pay less."[109] His biggest difference with the president on taxes, Mondale asserted in California, was Reagan's favoring of the rich over average Americans. Indeed, this inequity made him "mad," "angry," and "damned mad."[110] On September 10, Mondale unveiled "the economic centerpiece" of his presidential campaign, a six-year plan to trim the deficit by $177 billion, with $85 billion in tax increases and spending cuts totaling $105 billion. He used this occasion to demand a response from Reagan:

"Enough is enough, Mr. President. You can't hide your red ink with blue smoke and mirrors."[111] "You can run but you can't hide," he taunted Reagan the next day in Chicago.[112] Speaking in Peoria, Illinois, Mondale accused Reagan of avoiding "the most important domestic issue of our time, namely, how's he going to get those deficits down." The Reagan deficit, he claimed, had cost thousands of jobs at a local tractor plant. Peorians, he urged, should "pick a president who hurts when you hurt."[113]

For all of the fervor conveyed in these attacks, Mondale soon realized that his combination of tax hikes and spending cuts did not resonate with most voters. On October 3, the *Times* reported that bad poll numbers had impelled a Democratic shift of emphasis to issues of war and peace.[114] Figure 2.2 lends support to this interpretation by showing a falloff in the frequency of Democratic attacks on economic issues after week two and a corresponding rise in attacks on military and defense issues. (The latter fastened on Reagan's response to the bombing of the U.S. embassy in Beirut and the lack of arms-control negotiations with the Soviets.) Criticisms of Reagan's tax and deficit policies rose again in week five but soon subsided.[115] A final spasm of economic attacks (coinciding with a drop in military/defense attacks) probably resulted because of a late barrage of Republican criticism on Mondale's deficit-reduction plan.

Reagan pounced on Mondale's vow to increase taxes, realizing that it made his depiction of the Democratic candidate as "another classic tax-and-spend liberal" all the more credible.[116] In the event, he succeeded in converting the tax issue into a powerful valence issue.[117] Reagan also worked at persuading voters that they had fared better with him in the White House than under the Carter-Mondale administration. Figure 2.2 shows that Republicans kept up a rolling barrage on economic issues for the first six weeks of the fall campaign before unleashing an all-out bombardment at the end.

On Labor Day, an ebullient Reagan reminded Californians of inflation under Carter, expressed his predilection for "high tech not high taxes," and disputed charges that he favored the rich at the expense of others.[118] At a rare press conference, he dismissed Mondale's deficit-reduction package as nothing more than "a tax-increase plan," maintaining that his own budget proposals showed the way to reduce deficits.[119] Campaigning upstate in New York, he contrasted his vision with that of statist Democrats: "We see an America where every day is the Fourth of July and they see an America where every day is April Fifteenth."[120] Americans had worked too hard to achieve the current level of economic growth, he declaimed in New Jersey, "to let anybody destroy it with a massive tax and spending scheme."[121] By that point, the president had taken to asking his audiences whether anyone wished to "go back to the days of economic stagnation and a heavier and heavier tax burden." Clearly enjoying himself in Brownsville, Texas, Reagan joked that the

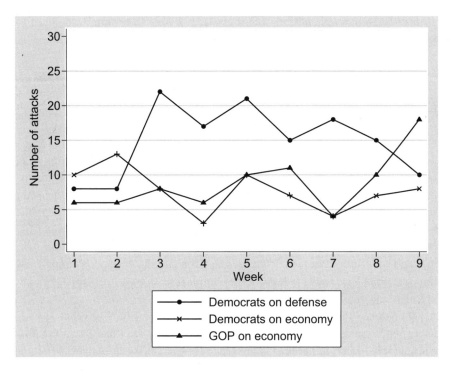

Figure 2.2 Attacks on defense and the economy, by party, 1984

Mondale campaign song was "Deep in the Heart of Taxes."[122] On October 13, he characterized his opponent's deficit-reduction package as "the lemon you got rid of four years ago."[123] In Dixie, he challenged Mondale's vision as offering "such dreary mediocrity—endless tax increases on those who dream of better days."[124] "If I could find a way to dress up as his tax program," he chortled at Ohio State University, "I could scare the devil out of people on Halloween."[125] As the campaign moved into the final week, he spoke repeatedly of the "Mondale mortgage," as well as the Carter-Mondale record of "torpor, timidity, and taxes."[126]

Ferraro and Bush echoed their running mates on the economy. Ferraro, of course, had to overcome unwanted coverage of her husband's tax returns. She soldiered on all the same, pitching Mondale's fairness theme in places such as Memphis: "If you are making over $100,000, this administration gave you enough tax cuts to buy a new car. But if you're a teacher in Memphis, you didn't even get enough to buy a hubcap."[127] In Illinois, she accused Reagan of concealing the deep budget cuts he planned to inflict on the poor.[128] Meanwhile, Bush kept up a steady attack on Mondale's deficit-reduction package, charging that it would increase unemployment and strangle economic growth.[129] In Ohio, for example, he railed against the Democratic notion of fairness "as if it's selfish to want to hold on to some of the rewards of your own labor and not have your paychecks taken away by escalating taxes."[130]

CONCLUSION

Consistent with the Skaperdas-Grofman model, Goldwater, McGovern, and Mondale fought ferociously against prohibitively favored opponents. Speaking solo, favored nominees waged a less negative campaign in every instance. Other campaigners, however, did not behave as predicted. Vice-presidential candidates on underdog tickets ran up modestly higher attack scores than their opposite numbers, whereas surrogates exhibited no one pattern for all three races. Overall attack scores for each side revealed much greater negativity by the trailing side in 1972 and 1984 but not in 1964. It makes sense, then, to determine who exactly did the attacking if one wants to fathom the complexities of negative campaigning in presidential elections.

On balance, the Skaperdas-Grofman model shed some light on what actually happened in these runaway campaigns, and the issue-ownership thesis provided considerably less illumination. Convergence emerged as the dominant pattern in these contests, not avoidance. Underdogs remained true to their convictions even when they knew the cause was lost.

3. The Somewhat Competitive Races of 1988, 1992, and 1996

The "somewhat competitive" races of 1988, 1992, and 1996 exhibited greater complexity than the runaways described in the previous chapter. As before, the expected winner prevailed—but not by as big a margin as in the runaway contests.[1] No independent or third-party candidate of consequence emerged during any of the runaways, but H. Ross Perot played a big part in one of the somewhat competitive contests and a lesser role in another.

STRATEGIC ENVIRONMENTS

The 1988 Race

Vice President George Bush came out of the Republican convention with a lead over Governor Michael Dukakis that varied some but never vanished.[2] Bush won the election with 53 percent of the popular vote and 426 of the 538 electoral votes.[3] This outcome represented a stunning reversal of fortunes from the spring of 1988, when polls showed Dukakis far ahead (see Figure 3.1). To comprehend the fall campaign, one must understand how Bush managed to overtake Dukakis in the summer.

The story of Bush's recovery began in May 1988, when the vice president met with top campaign consultants at his family home in Kennebunkport, Maine. The March and April polls had shown Dukakis far ahead, and Bush's advisers worried that the extra bounce Dukakis would get from the Democratic convention could put the race out of reach. Polls indicated that voters seemed to know a lot more about Bush than Dukakis, and the more they knew, they less they liked. The vice president had been tarred with the brush of the Iran-Contra scandal; his title as the nation's drug czar did not impress; Republican conservatives had repeatedly called him a "wimp"; and despite a lengthy residence and political career in Texas, he came across as an effete Brahmin. Dukakis, by contrast, was terra incognita for most voters. He got some credit for engineering the so-called Massachusetts Miracle that had revived the Bay State's economy. Voters also liked what they heard about his frugal lifestyle. Yet few outside Massachusetts knew where he stood on

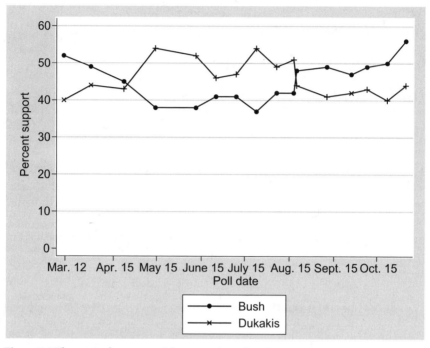

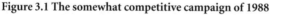

Figure 3.1 The somewhat competitive campaign of 1988
Note: The trial heats matched Dukakis against Bush until August 21, after which they matched Dukakis-Bentsen against Bush-Quayle.
Source: *The Gallup Poll: Public Opinion 1988* (Wilmington, DE: Scholarly Resources, 1989).

taxes, national defense, capital punishment, prisoner furloughs, and requiring pupils in public schools to recite the Pledge of Allegiance. At the Kennebunkport session, Bush agreed with his advisers that Dukakis had to be defined as a tax-and-spend, proabortion, antigun liberal who was weak on defense, soft on crime, and opposed to flag saluting.[4] Lee Atwater, Bush's youthful campaign manager, already had outlined the rudiments of such a strategy on an index card.[5]

At first, Bush had balked at such recommendations, but he came around after viewing tapes of New Jersey focus groups.[6] Most of the participants were white, Catholic, and middle class. They had voted for Reagan in 1984 but now leaned toward Dukakis. Minds changed, however, when the moderator asked numerous questions that were damaging to Dukakis. Did they know that he, as governor, had vetoed a bill requiring public school students to recite the Pledge of Allegiance? Did they know that he opposed the death penalty, even for kingpins in the drug trade? Did they know that he objected to prayer in the public schools? And did they know that he stood by a policy of giving weekend passes to murderers and other violent felons not yet eligible for parole? Visibly recoiling from these revelations, at least half of the participants endorsed Bush.[7] Thus convinced, Bush agreed to play a major role in a June offensive against Dukakis.

Although the Dukakis organization had won acclaim during the Democratic primaries, it performed poorly after the nomination had been secured. Paralysis brought on by turf wars and competing egos stifled the response to Republican attacks. Dukakis bore the principal responsibility for this costly lapse. Rather than hit the campaign trail right after the Democratic convention, he remained in Massachusetts and attended to gubernatorial responsibilities. He also skipped strategy sessions, rarely visited campaign headquarters, and appeared unresponsive when worried party figures visited. Insinuations of clinical depression surfaced in the *Washington Times*, *Boston Globe*, and *New York Times*, and they made the front page when President Reagan jokingly referred to Dukakis as an "invalid." The resulting media frenzy forced Dukakis to make his entire medical history public. His records and his categorical denials plus an apology from Reagan put an end to the episode but not before Dukakis had dropped in the polls.[8]

"If your slate is blank," Christine Black and Thomas Oliphant wrote in their postmortem on the Dukakis candidacy, "you either write on it at once or you can be certain your opponent will do the job for you."[9] The comparison of net favorable ratings (percent positive minus percent negative) for each man shown in Figure 3.2 indicates that the Bush strategy worked, even though Bush's image suffered in the process. Dukakis got his convention bounce, but he was never again to lead after the Republican convention.

The fall campaign witnessed a barrage of Republican attack ads consistent with Atwater's battle plan. Much of this effort painted Dukakis as being weak on crime. Conservative groups not officially part of the Bush-Quayle effort played up a prison furlough for the infamous Willie Horton that went badly wrong.[10] The official Republican version soon followed, and although it never mentioned Horton, it, too, packed a wicked punch. In the latter ad, actors costumed as convicts moved in and out of a prison via a revolving door as the voice-under ticked off the putative consequences of giving weekend passes to violent criminals. Later Republican spots ridiculed Dukakis's credentials as an environmentalist, lampooned his views on national defense, and skewered him as a tax-and-spend liberal.

Overmatched in the air war, Democrats counted on Dukakis's superior debating skills to put them back in contention. Yet Bush more or less held his own in their first encounter, and an ailing Dukakis indisputably lost the second debate.[11] Dan Quayle's dismal performance against Lloyd Bentsen in the vice-presidential showdown had slight effect on Bush's standings in the Gallup Poll.

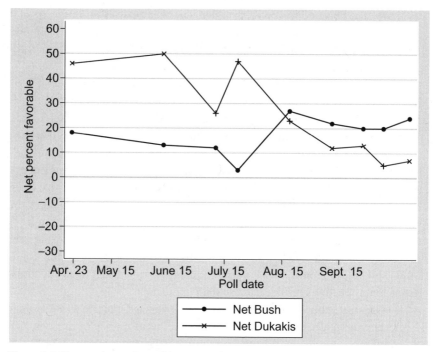

Figure 3.2 Changes in net favorable rating of Bush and Dukakis
Source: The Gallup Poll: Public Opinion 1988 (Wilmington, DE: Scholarly Resources, 1989).

The 1992 Race

On election day, George H. W. Bush became the fifth and last president of the twentieth century to be denied a second term.[12] In a three-way race roiled by H. Ross Perot's independent candidacy, Bush garnered 37 percent of the popular vote, compared with Bill Clinton's 43 percent and Perot's nearly 19 percent. Thus, Bush ended up with a smaller percentage of the vote than Herbert Hoover received in 1932, and Clinton won with the smallest plurality of any first-term president except for Abraham Lincoln and Woodrow Wilson.[13] Even though he carried no state, Perot garnered the biggest vote share of any independent or third-party candidate except for former presidents Theodore Roosevelt and Millard Fillmore. Clinton dominated in the Electoral College, with 370 votes to 168 for Bush and nil for Perot.[14]

Of the many problems plaguing Bush during his term in the Oval Office, two deserve particular mention. The first ironically resulted from a Republican policy success: the collapse of the Soviet Union and an end to the Cold War. The downside for Republicans in general and Bush in particular was that they lost the advantage on military and defense issues that had worked so well against the Democrats in 1972, 1984, and 1988. The end of the Cold War also removed an important impediment to Democratic unity. The second problem consisted of a worse-than-expected recession underscored by layoffs at defense plants in California, bank failures in New Hampshire, corporate mergers, and "downsizing." The unemployment rate hit 7.6 percent in August 1992.[15]

Owing to his success against Saddam Hussein in the First Gulf War, Bush had briefly enjoyed job approval ratings that approximated 90 percent. More prominent Democrats than Bill Clinton looked at the polls and opted not to run for their party's nomination in 1992.[16] However, with Saddam routed from Kuwait, victory celebrations concluded, and the economy again preoccupying most Americans, Bush's job approval rating fell back to the prewar level of 51 percent. It eventually bottomed out at 33 percent (with 57 percent disapproving) near the end of the fall campaign. Other polls showed that only one out of four Americans took a favorable view of his economic stewardship.[17] Looking back at this race, political scientist Walter Dean Burnham wrote that issues of the domestic economy had dominated to a degree not seen since 1936.[18]

No economic issue vexed Bush more than breaking his 1988 campaign promise never to let Congress raise taxes. "Read my lips: No new taxes" soared to the top of the list of violated vows when Bush entered into a 1990 budget agreement with the majority Democrats. Eventually efficacious, the package included tax increases as well as spending cuts, all deemed necessary to deal with a burgeoning deficit.[19] To conservative Republicans already uneasy about the administration's unwillingness to stand up for their causes, the 1990 budget deal smacked of betrayal.[20] Pundit Pat Buchanan exploited this bitterness in his failed primary challenge to Bush.

If Bush had his troubles, so did William Jefferson Clinton. Although he was touted by outsiders as a progressive son of the New South, Clinton's reputation in his home state was as much libertine as liberal. Allegations of lechery, lying, and draft dodging had dogged his career in Arkansas politics, and they hardly abated when he ran for president. The tabloid revelations of a former mistress, as well as news that Clinton had evaded the draft by lying about his intent to sign up for the Reserve Officers' Training Corps (ROTC) hurt him in the New Hampshire primary. Early polls in 1992 showed that he had higher negatives and lower positives than Bush, and focus groups furnished additional evidence that Clinton suffered from a "debilitating" image.[21]

In the first part of 1992, Ross Perot looked more like a winner than a spoiler, an image helped by early polls and his professed willingness to spend upwards of $100 million on the campaign.[22] Polls showed that he threatened Clinton as well as Bush prior to the Democratic convention (see Table 3.1). In May, Gallup showed Perot running even with Bush and ten points ahead of Clinton. In June, he led Bush by eight points and Clinton by fourteen. Then, owing to developments that will be discussed later, Perot fell behind Bush.[23]

Table 3.1. 1992 Campaign before Labor Day

Polls	Two-Way Trial Heat (%)		Three-Way Trial Heat (%)			Perot Impact (%)		Favorable Opinion (%)		
	Clinton	Bush	Clinton	Bush	Perot	Clinton	Bush	Clinton	Bush	Perot
April 1	34	54	25	44	24	-9	-10	—	—	—
April 12	41	48	27	42	20	-14	-6	34	48	—
April 22	34	50	26	41	25	-8	-9	42	55	41
May 10	40	45	29	35	30	-11	-10	51	50	48
May 20	39	50	25	35	35	-14	-15	42	48	50
June 8	40	46	25	31	39	-15	-15	—	—	—
June 14	37	45	24	32	34	-13	-11	41	44	52
June 30	41	44	27	33	32	-14	-11	45	44	48
July 8	40	48	28	35	30	-12	-13	41	49	45
July 18	56	34	—	—	—	—	—	—	—	—
August 2	57	32	—	—	—	—	—	—	—	—
August 12	56	37	—	—	—	—	—	57	43	—
August 17	58	35	—	—	—	—	—	—	—	—
August 22	52	42	—	—	—	—	—	57	50	—

Notes: Poll dates represent the final day of each polling period. Not every trial heat poll asked for a positive or negative opinion; Gallup did not include Perot in its April 12 questions asking for opinions of the candidates. The July 8 favorable rating of Perot was obtained by special request from Maura A. Strausberg, data librarian at the Gallup Organization. Perot withdrew before completion of the July 18 poll.

— = not asked

Source: The Gallup Poll: Public Opinion 1992 (Wilmington, DE: Scholarly Resources, 1993).

Perot frightened both parties enough for Bush and Clinton operatives to discuss a joint effort to discredit him. The Clinton camp backed off, however, leaving Republicans the task, in Bush's words, of taking on "the little bastard."[24] A few highly publicized attacks soon followed. One from Vice President Dan Quayle branded Perot a "temperamental tycoon" who had little regard for the Constitution. "Those sound bites left some teeth marks," Quayle later recalled.[25] When the *Washington Post* ran a story of a Perot investigation into Bush's business dealings, Press Secretary Marlin Fitzwater spoke of Perot's "delusions and paranoia."[26] Behind the scenes, Republicans peddled questions about Perot's stability to leading news organizations. Meanwhile, Perot developed a poisonous relationship with the press, fell out with big-name consultants hired to organize his campaign, referred to African Americans as "you people," and took issue with the gay-rights agenda. Fed up and frustrated by the drumbeat of criticism, he dropped out of the race on July 16.

Perot's withdrawal came as a shock to almost every observer of the 1992 campaign. It occurred during the Democratic convention and only hours before Clinton's acceptance speech. The timing of his withdrawal, along with his statement that the revitalization of the Democratic Party had obviated the need for his candidacy, suggests that Perot acted in no small part to help Clinton defeat Bush.[27] In any case, Clinton received a huge bounce in the Gallup Poll, which Bush never overcame.

When Perot began signaling that he might return to the race, the Clinton camp made a major effort to keep him on the bench even as desperate Bush advisers welcomed the prospect.[28] Regardless of his intense desire to see Bush defeated, Perot may have been more concerned at that juncture to rebut characterizations of him as a "quitter" and the "Yellow Ross of Texas."[29] In any case, by September 22, it had become obvious that he wanted to rejoin the fray and make a major issue of deficit reduction.[30] Perot's return coincided with a drop in Clinton support as well as upward movement for Bush (see Figure 3.3).[31] Exit polls on election day indicated that Perot cost Clinton about as many votes as Bush. Some postelection studies concluded that he had helped Clinton by hurting Bush, although at least one found that Clinton would have won a clear majority of the popular vote had Perot remained on the sidelines.[32]

The 1996 Race

Of the three somewhat competitive races in our study, 1996 most resembled a runaway. On Labor Day, few doubted that Clinton would win another term. Gallup showed him slipping below 50 percent only twice during the fall campaign (see Figure 3.4), whereas Bob Dole's support exceeded 39 percent only once (possibly because this poll marked Gallup's shift to polling likely voters instead of registered voters). Overall, the Democratic lead averaged 16.8 percent, seemingly the makings

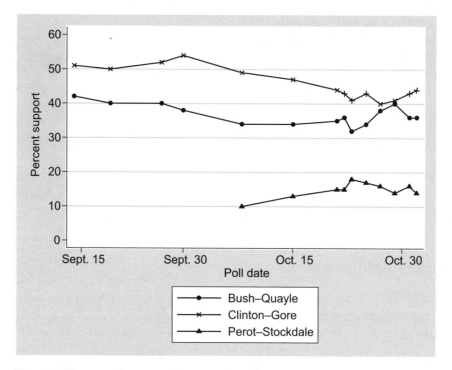

Figure 3.3 The somewhat competitive campaign of 1992
Source: The Gallup Poll: Public Opinion 1992 (Wilmington, DE: Scholarly Resources, 1993).

of a runaway race.[33] Clinton made history as the first Democrat since Franklin D. Roosevelt to win a second consecutive term. He also entered the history books as the first president to win a second term with less than a majority of the popular vote (49.2 percent) since Woodrow Wilson in 1916. At 40.7 percent, Dole fared better than Bush had in 1992 but not as well as Dukakis in 1988. Still, more than half of the 1992 Perot voters who turned out in 1996 voted for Dole. (Only a third stuck with Perot.) Perot finished with 8.4 percent of the popular vote, a decline of more than 10 percent from 1992.[34] Clinton won handily in the Electoral College, with 359 votes to Dole's 159.[35]

Like Bush in 1988, Clinton had to stage a near-miraculous recovery to take the lead in 1996. This was because the first half of Clinton's initial term proved disastrous, as demonstrated by the 1994 midterm elections. His resurrection started in 1995 and was confirmed by the 1996 outcome. Several analysts have referred to these rather different periods as Clinton's first and second presidencies.[36]

Clinton enjoyed initially high job approval ratings upon taking office in 1993, as well as early success in moving his programs through Congress. Soon, however,

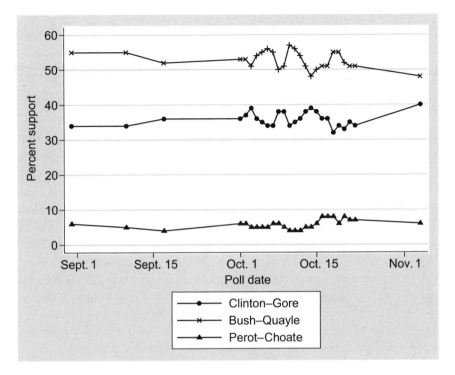

Figure 3.4 The somewhat competitive campaign of 1996
Note: Perot did not name Choate as his running mate until September 10. Survey
questions about the Perot ticket prior to that date mentioned only Perot.
Source: The Gallup Poll: Public Opinion 1996 (Wilmington, DE: Scholarly Resources, 1997).

charges of ineptitude and scandal overshadowed these early accomplishments.
Questions about Bill and Hillary Clinton's role in the Whitewater scandal led to
a long-running investigation by special prosecutors and to the First Lady's appearance before a federal grand jury. President Clinton's bid to admit gays into
the military met with fierce resistance in Congress and the Pentagon. Ultimately,
the resulting "don't ask, don't tell" compromise fell far short of what Clinton had
promised during the 1992 campaign. His stimulus package failed in Congress,
and the effort jointly undertaken with his wife to transform health care also went
down to a crushing defeat. While all of this was going on, congressional Democrats reeled under the impact of several scandals, including overdrawn accounts
at the House "bank."[37] Ways and Means Committee chairman Dan Rostenkowski
eventually ended up in federal prison for abuse of funds. These and other incidents reinforced Republican efforts to portray the Democratic majority as arrogant, corrupt, and unresponsive.

Perot played to the national mood, at one point urging voters to help Republicans win control of the House. Republicans, in turn, inserted some of Perot's ideas into their Contract with America.[38] Sensing the coming storm, Democratic pollster Stanley Greenberg urged his party's incumbents to run away from the president. Many followed his advice.[39] Republicans made the most of Clinton's unpopularity in television spots that "morphed" him with Democratic candidates for Congress.

On election day in 1994, the GOP recaptured the House, picking up fifty-two seats (including the one represented by Speaker Tom Foley), and it reclaimed the Senate, with a net gain of eight seats. The number of Republican governors shot up from nineteen to thirty, as did bicameral legislatures wholly controlled by the GOP (from eight to nineteen). Republicans seized control of one of the two chambers in thirteen other state legislatures. For the first time since 1920, every governor, senator, and House member running on the Republican ticket won reelection, and for the first time since 1913, nary a Democrat turned up in the new crop of senators.[40] Exit polls indicated that disdain for Clinton had much to do with this rout, a belief shared by prominent Democrats who urged the president not to run for a second term.[41] Although at least one poll showed that most Democrats favored a challenge to Clinton's renomination, no challenger of consequence stepped forward.[42]

"Presidency Two" began as Clinton dug himself out of the rubble of 1994. Pursuing a strategy of triangulation, he eschewed much of his party's policy agenda in Congress while attacking the excesses of the new Republican majority. The shift in net job approval graphed in Figure 3.5 indicates that this triangulation strategy began to pay off in the early spring of 1995. Some of this movement occurred after Clinton delivered a moving speech in Oklahoma City just after the terrorist bombing there. Two months later, he stunned liberal Democrats by proposing to balance the budget within ten years. He regained his party's confidence by vetoing the Republican budget bill, thereby setting the stage for a struggle that brought about two government shutdowns, one in November and another in December, which carried over to January. Polls indicated that Clinton had gotten the better of congressional Republicans in the battle for public opinion. He upset fellow Democrats again by proclaiming an end to the "era of big government" in his State of the Union speech. For the sake of a sound bite, White House aide George Stephanopoulos later mused, Clinton had repudiated every Democratic president from Franklin Roosevelt to Lyndon Johnson. "But," Stephanopoulos added, "it was solid-gold politics, testing at 80 percent in the polls."[43]

Clinton launched his reelection campaign more than a year before Dole became the Republican nominee. Ads extolling Clinton's record on domestic issues began airing in selected states as early as July 1995. Starting in October and continuing up to the 1996 Democratic convention, the DNC unleashed an advertising blitz caricaturing Dole as a menace to senior citizens, students, and the environment.[44]

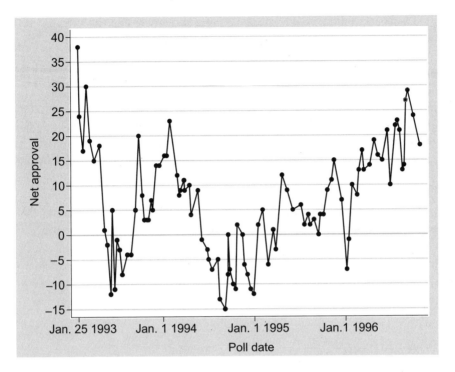

Figure 3.5 Clinton's net job approval ratings, 1993–1996
Note: Net job approval was calculated by subtracting disapproval from approval.
Source: The Gallup Poll: Public Opinion (Wilmington, DE: Scholarly Resources, 1993, 1994, 1995, and 1996).

Much of the money to pay for these ads came from questionable fund-raising at White House coffees and Buddhist temples. Clinton and Gore played leading roles in this scandal, a fact that became apparent as the campaign ended.[45]

Even before the end of the Republican primary season, Senate Majority Leader Robert Dole had fallen well behind Clinton in the polls. His inability to gain ground, as well as his limitations as a campaigner, cast a pall over congressional Republicans, who became increasingly fearful of associating with him. Congressional Republicans reportedly wrote off Dole by passing a welfare reform bill that Clinton would sign. The law helped House and Senate Republicans even though it deprived Dole of a key campaign issue. Clinton seized the opportunity and signed it over the passionate objections of liberal Democrats. In yet another manifestation of its "losing to win" strategy, the GOP aired a "blank check" ad that conceded the presidential contest to Clinton, even as it asked voters if they also wanted the Democrats to take over Congress.[46]

Desperate to shake up the race, Dole called on Perot to endorse him and drop out of the running. Perot promptly dismissed Dole's appeal as "weird."[47]

Except for the attacks he unleashed against Clinton, Perot reiterated the themes of his 1992 campaign. But much had changed in the interim, with economic recovery, a related shrinkage of the "angry electorate," and corresponding increases in the job approval ratings of both the president and Congress. Perot, in short, played to a much smaller crowd, having lost a substantial chunk of his middle-class support.[48] In 1992, he had spent $60 million, mostly out of his own pocket; in 1996, he accepted a federal grant with all of its spending limits. Moreover, he spent relatively little until quite late in the race.[49] In 1992, Perot had performed impressively in all three presidential debates, thereby overcoming some of the negative response to his July departure, but in 1996, the Commission on Presidential Debates ruled against his participation on grounds that he had no realistic chance of getting elected.[50] Perot faced another daunting problem in that his polling negatives greatly exceeded his positives. In the final Gallup Poll asking for evaluations of the candidates, 57 percent of the respondents gave him a negative rating, compared with a favorable assessment of 27 percent.[51]

ATTACKERS AND TARGETS

We turn now to the attack propensities of each campaign in the 1988, 1992, and 1996 races, beginning with exchanges between major-party tickets. Once again, we call attention to the Skaperdas-Grofman prediction that trailers will attack leaders more frequently than vice versa, and as before, we compare the attack propensities of each side.

Looking first at overall scores, Table 3.2 shows that the trailing ticket exhibited substantially greater negativity than the leading ticket. Contrary to the popular impression that the Dukakis camp failed to counter Republican attacks, we found that it gave more than it got. Fully 65 percent of all Democratic statements in 1988 leveled attacks against the Republicans, whereas Republican negativity came to 58 percent. The Democrats also showed up as more negative than their Republican adversaries in seven of the nine weeks. Further, Democratic negativity surpassed 70 percent in weeks four, five, and eight. Only in week eight was the Republican propensity as high. In 1992, the Bush camp blasted the Clinton-Gore ticket in 64 percent of its campaign statements, and it outattacked the Democrats in all but one of the eight weeks observed. In comparison, the 1996 exchange appeared relatively mild: 55 percent negativity for the underdog Republicans and 45 percent for the favored Democrats, with Republicans registering higher attack scores than Democrats in seven of nine weeks of fall campaigning.

Perot seriously distracted both of the major parties in 1992, but he was largely ignored in 1996. Of all the reasons that induced him to run for president in 1992, few (if any) matched his intense loathing of Bush.[52] Evidently, this ill will originated in the 1980s, when Perot dealt with Vice President Bush's office on the question of Americans missing in action because of the Vietnam War. Moved by rumors of prisoner sightings in remote parts of Indochina, Perot came to believe not only that a substantial number of U.S. personnel had been abandoned to the Communists but also that the Reagan administration was unwilling to secure their return. As Reagan's point man in these discussions, Bush failed to persuade Perot that no such rumor had been confirmed. Bush's subordinate, Richard Armitage, incurred Perot's wrath by making the same argument. Convinced that Bush, Armitage, and perhaps others in the administration either were covering up or were incompetent, Perot went all out to discredit now president Bush's nomination of Armitage to be secretary of the army. Perot also excoriated Bush for going back on his "no new taxes" vow, for a family link to the savings and loan scandal, and for "coddling" Saddam Hussein before the First Gulf War.[53]

Much less has been written about Perot's reasons for running in 1996. Taking him at his word, it seems he believed strongly that only a new party founded on a mix of populism and sound business principles could bring needed reform to national councils.[54] Largely funded out of his pocket, the Reform Party was to be Ross Perot's gift to the nation. Of course, it also served as his vehicle for another presidential bid.

In sum, we had ample reason to assume that in 1992 Perot attacked Bush and the GOP much more than Clinton and the Democrats. At least at the point he rejoined the race, Perot took on the role of spoiler, bent upon preventing Bush's reelection. Ironically, the Bush camp welcomed his return, whereas the Clinton camp tried to keep him on the bench. This is not to deny that Perot had other reasons for rejoining the race, as we reveal later. However complex his motives, a spoiler's intent becomes manifest in his choice of targets. In 1996, we discerned no rationale behind Perot's attacks other than holding Clinton in greater contempt than Dole.

Table 3.3 provides a weekly breakdown of Perot's attacks on the major parties, as well as their attacks against him. As before, we focus on the totality of each campaign's attacks. Consistent with the interpretation offered earlier, Perot went after the Republicans twice as frequently as contra the Democrats in 1992. Except when he spared both parties, his weekly negativity against the Republicans consistently exceeded his propensity to bash the Democrats. In 1996, he criticized the favored Democrats more frequently than the trailing Republicans, a pattern more consistent with the general Skaperdas-Grofman model of three-candidate competitions. Overall, the Republicans exhibited slightly more negativity toward Perot in 1992 than the Democrats did. Both parties all but ignored him in 1996.

Table 3.2. Negativity of Democrats versus Republicans in Somewhat Competitive Races

Campaign Week	1988 Democratic Propensity to Attack Republicans	1988 Republican Propensity to Attack Democrats	1992 Democratic Propensity to Attack Republicans	1992 Republican Propensity to Attack Democrats	1996 Democratic Propensity to Attack Republicans	1996 Republican Propensity to Attack Democrats
1	.551	.520	.450	.456	.412	.467
2	.500	.551	.426	.600	.700	.434
3	.635	.545	.714	.706	.622	.448
4	.756	.675	.607	.692	.303	.580
5	.729	.529	.329	.512	.424	.526
6	.596	.516	.630	.650	.300	.574
7	.595	.583	.463	.674	.429	.746
8	.708	.747	.593	.663	.560	.571
9	.694	.529	—	—	.375	.541
Overall	.650	.578	.563	.637	.455	.549
N statements	691	758	608	787	354	566

Notes: Scores are for the fall campaign, beginning on Labor Day and ending on election day. The 1992 fall campaign lasted eight weeks instead of nine weeks as in 1988 and 1996. Date ranges for 1988 campaign weeks are: September 5–11 (week one), September 12–18 (week two), September 19–25 (three), September 26–October 2 (four), October 3–9 (five), October 10–16 (six), October 17–23 (seven), October 24–30 (eight), and October 31–November 8 (nine). For 1992 campaign weeks, the dates are: September 7–13 (week one), September 14–20 (two), September 21–27 (three), September 28–October 4 (four), October 5–11 (five), October 12–18 (six), October 19–25 (seven), October 26–November 3 (eight). For 1996: September 2–8 (week one), September 9–15 (two), September 16–22 (three), September 23–29 (four), September 30–October 6 (five), October 7–13 (six), October 14–20 (seven), October 21–27 (eight), and October 28–November 5 (nine).

— = no cases

Table 3.3. Attack Propensities of Perot and Major Parties, 1992 and 1996

Campaign Week	1992 Perot against Democrats	1992 Perot against Republicans	1992 Democrats against Perot	1992 Republicans against Perot	1996 Perot against Democrats	1996 Perot against Republicans	1996 Democrats against Perot	1996 Republicans against Perot
1	.000	.500	.000	.018	.333	.333	.000	.000
2	.000	.000	.000	.000	.167	.222	.000	.000
3	.250	.625	.000	.000	.625	.375	.000	.000
4	.091	.182	.067	.066	.200	.600	.000	.000
5	.091	.227	.012	.012	.167	.167	.000	.000
6	.185	.296	.014	.019	.500	.400	.000	.019
7	.128	.277	.063	.062	.375	.375	.000	.000
8	.250	.500	.065	.114	.333	.333	.020	.014
9	—	—	—	—	.777	.111	.014	.009
Overall	.173	.354	.036	.051	.418	.319	.006	.005
N statements	243	243	608	787	91	91	354	566

— = no cases

We now take up specific sources and targets of attacks. According to Table 3.4, all of the presidential candidates except Clinton in 1996 personally accounted for a large portion of their campaigns' attacks, around 40 percent. Presidential nominees figured even more prominently as targets of attacks. In 1988, for instance, 93 percent of the GOP's total of 438 attacks fell on Dukakis, as did 97 percent of Bush attacks and 94 percent of those made by Quayle. Republican attackers also concentrated more on presidential nominees than their Democratic counterparts did in the 1992 and 1996 campaigns. Lloyd Bentsen made more attacks than any other vice-presidential nominee, and Jack Kemp made remarkably few.

Table 3.5 shows that nearly every Democratic and Republican attack singled out Perot, an entirely logical finding in view of the paucity of other targets. As expected, the GOP flayed him more frequently than the Democrats did in 1992. Not surprisingly, the number of Bush attacks on Perot exceeded the Clinton figure by more than three to one. Perot made nearly all of his side's attacks in 1992, lacerating Bush in more than twice the number of attacks he directed at Clinton, even though the targeting score for Clinton was slightly higher. Similarly, Perot directed more attacks against Clinton than at Dole in 1996, even though his targeting score of Dole was higher.

Neither of Perot's running mates appears to have played an important part in his assault on the major party tickets. In 1992, Perot ran with James Stockdale, a retired admiral and Vietnam War hero; in 1996, he chose Pat Choate, a published author and policy analyst unknown outside academic and government circles. Although their contributions may have been underreported, it appears that little was expected of either man. Stockdale lent his name to the ticket on the understanding that someone better suited to the rough-and-tumble of presidential campaigning eventually would replace him.[55] "Campaign?" Stockdale reportedly exclaimed to a reporter. "What do you mean by campaign? I don't see why I have to make a fool of myself."[56] His most memorable statement came at the opening of the vice-presidential debate with Quayle and Gore: "Who am I? Why am I here?"[57] A vocal critic of international trade agreements, Choate provided a degree of policy expertise that Perot lacked.

CAMPAIGN TOPICS

Convergence characterized the discourse of these somewhat competitive contests much more than issue avoidance (see Table 3.6). In 1988, Democrats and Republicans emphasized eight of the same topics in the ten most mentioned, albeit with varying degrees of priority. Democrats talked more about leadership, the campaign, the economy, and foreign policy than Republicans, whereas Republicans

Table 3.4. Democratic and Republican Targeting in Somewhat Competitive Races

	1988 Democratic Targeting of Republicans	1988 Republican Targeting of Democrats	1992 Democratic Targeting of Republicans	1992 Republican Targeting of Democrats	1996 Democratic Targeting of Republicans	1996 Republican Targeting of Democrats
All party attacks						
Presidential nominee	371	406	305	470	101	259
Other targets	78	32	35	31	60	52
N attacks	449	438	342	501	161	311
Nominee targeted	.826	.927	.898	.938	.627	.833
Solo attacks of presidential nominee	Dukakis	Bush	Clinton	Bush	Clinton	Dole
Presidential nominee	178	180	130	207	17	163
Other targets	12	5	11	10	33	27
N attacks	190	185	141	217	50	190
Nominee targeted	.937	.973	.922	.954	.340	.858
Solo attacks of vice-presidential nominee	Bentsen	Quayle	Gore	Quayle	Gore	Kemp
Presidential nominee	20	30	24	31	12	6
Other targets	25	2	5	5	1	2
N attacks	45	32	29	36	13	8
Nominee targeted	.445	.938	.828	.861	.923	.750

Note: Some attacks on presidential candidates also targeted others of the same party.

Table 3.5. Major-Party and Third-Party Targeting in 1992 and 1996

	1992 Democratic Targeting of Perot	1992 Republican Targeting of Perot	1996 Democratic Targeting of Perot	1996 Republican Targeting of Perot	1992 Perot Party Targeting of Democrats	1992 Perot Party Targeting of Republicans	1996 Perot Party Targeting of Democrats	1996 Perot Party Targeting of Republicans
All party attacks								
Presidential nominee	22	37	2	3	30	54	24	19
Other targets	0	3	0	0	12	32	14	7
N attacks	22	40	2	3	42	86	38	26
Nominee targeted	1.00	.925	1.00	1.00	.714	.628	.632	.731
Solo attacks of presidential nominee	Clinton	Bush	Clinton	Dole	Perot	Perot	Perot	Perot
Presidential nominee	4	15	1	1	21	48	21	14
Other targets	0	0	0	0	7	25	10	5
N attacks	4	15	1	1	28	73	31	19
Nominee targeted	1.00	1.00	1.00	1.00	.750	.658	.677	.737
Solo attacks of vice-presidential nominee	Gore	Quayle	Gore	Kemp	Stockdale	Stockdale	Choate	Choate
Presidential nominee	1	0	1	0	1	0	1	1
Other targets	0	0	0	0	4	3	0	0
N attacks	1	0	1	0	5	3	1	1
Nominee targeted	1.00	0	1.00	0	.200	0	1.00	1.00

Notes: No candidate of consequence ran on a third-party ticket in 1988; some attacks on presidential candidates also targeted others in same party.

pushed military and defense issues, crime, ideology, and patriotism more than Democrats. All of these topics, however, figured among those most emphasized by each side. Republicans made a big issue of the environment, a subject not showcased by Democrats. Similarly, Democrats tried to pin Bush down on Iran-Contra and the savings and loan scandals, issues that Republicans played down. Likewise, Democrats emphasized social policies and health care, not among the subjects most important to Republican campaigners. Although saddled with a recession, the Republican side nonetheless said more about the economy than any other topic in 1992. Quite likely, the GOP could not avoid this fight because of the undeniable fact of recession. Consistent with Clinton's vow to focus laserlike on these concerns, the domestic economy also topped the Democratic list. Leadership ranked second in importance for both parties, and campaign matters also got a lot of play. Defense lagged behind these topics and others, placing sixth in Democratic emphasis and fifth for Republicans. In 1996, Democrats and Republicans attached considerable importance to seven of the same topics: the economy, campaign matters, myriad scandals associated with Clinton's presidency, social policy and health care, leadership, crime, and liberalism versus conservatism. Democrats pitched school uniforms and other education issues, tapping a subject area that was not among those most emphasized by Republicans. Defense ranked eighth on the Republican agenda but did not make the Democratic top ten.

For the most part, Perot addressed the same concerns as his opponents. The economy topped his 1992 agenda, and he also focused heavily on campaign matters, leadership issues, and defense. Like the Democrats, he declaimed on scandal, and, like Republicans, he made much of patriotism. In 1996, he said more about the scandals swirling around Clinton than any other topic, and he also complained about his exclusion from the presidential debates. Still, he addressed some of the same concerns as Democrats and Republicans: the economy, leadership, campaign matters, and ideology.

Convergence also dominated in the attacks exchanged between Democrats and Republicans. Nearly every topic listed in Table 3.6 shows up in Table 3.7. In making these attacks, both of the major parties again addressed the same topics, albeit with varying degrees of emphasis. In 1988, for example, Democrats highlighted leadership, the economy, foreign policy, and campaign negativity more than their Republican adversaries did, and Republicans put substantially more emphasis on crime, liberal-conservative differences, military and defense issues, patriotism, and Boston's polluted harbor. Even so, the parties joined battle on nine of the top ten topics in 1988, a pattern essentially repeated in 1992 and 1996.

Table 3.8 shows that neither party allowed Perot's attacks to go unanswered in 1992. More than half of Perot's relatively few criticisms of Clinton had to do with leadership and economic issues, but he saved some ammunition to take potshots

Table 3.6. Topics Most Emphasized in Somewhat Competitive Races

1988 Democrats	1988 Republicans	1992 Democrats	1992 Republicans	1992 Perot	1996 Democrats	1996 Republicans	1996 Perot
Leadership (94)	Military/defense (89)	Domestic economy (138)	Domestic economy (169)	Domestic economy (51)	Domestic economy (56)	Domestic economy (80)	Corruption, abuse of power (20)
Campaign (83)	Crime (86)	Leadership (74)	Leadership (100)	Campaign (47)	Campaign (46)	Campaign (79)	Debates (16)
Domestic economy (68)	Campaign (77)	Campaign (65)	Patriotism/war record (88)	Leadership (29)	Social/health programs (40)	Leadership (67)	Domestic economy (13)
Crime (52)	Domestic economy (74)	Debates (35)	Campaign (83)	Personal (14)	Corruption, abuse of power (27)	Corruption, abuse of power (59)	Leadership (10)
Foreign policy (38)	Ideology/party (71)	Foreign policy (31)	Military/defense (40)	Military/defense (10)	Crime (22)	Crime (51)	Campaign (9)
Military/defense (36)	Leadership (67)	Military/defense (28)	Personal (38)	Ideology/party (9)	Education (22)	Social/health programs (32)	Wasted vote (3)
Corruption, abuse of power (33)	Patriotism/war record (44)	Social/health programs (27)	Energy/environment (35)	Wasted vote (8)	Leadership (17)	Ideology/party (28)	Campaign finance (3)
Social/health programs (30)	Foreign policy (36)	Corruption, abuse of power (27)	Foreign policy (33)	Patriotism/war record (7)	Energy/environment (17)	Military/defense (24)	Foreign policy (3)
Patriotism/war record (28)	Energy/environment (34)	Patriotism/war record (25)	Debates (21)	Corruption, abuse of power (7)	Ideology/party (16)	Women's rights (17)	Patriotism/war record (2)
Ideology/party (27)	Debates (30)	Energy/environment (21)	Social/health programs (18)	Debates (6)	Women's rights (8); foreign policy (8)	Personal (16)	Ideology/party (2)

Notes: The top-ten topics of the Democrats accounted for 71 percent of all Democratic statements in 1988, 77 percent in 1992, and 73 percent in 1996; corresponding percentages for the Republicans were 70 in 1988, 81 in 1992, and 80 in 1996. Perot-Stockdale's top ten accounted for 73 percent of their total; corresponding figure for Perot-Choate in 1996 was 89 percent.

Table 3.7. Leading Attack Topics of Democrats and Republicans in Somewhat Competitive Races

1988 Democrats Targeting Republicans	1988 Republicans Targeting Democrats	1992 Democrats Targeting Republicans	1992 Republicans Targeting Democrats	1996 Democrats Targeting Republicans	1996 Republicans Targeting Democrats
Leadership (83)	Crime (71)	Domestic economy (93)	Domestic economy (118)	Domestic economy (27)	Corruption, abuse of power (56)
Domestic economy (53)	Ideology/party (63)	Leadership (57)	Leadership (89)	Corruption, abuse of power (22)	Domestic economy (41)
Crime (36)	Military/defense (52)	Corruption, abuse of power (26)	Patriotism/war record (83)	Social/health programs (21)	Leadership (40)
Corruption, abuse of power (31)	Domestic economy (51)	Dirty campaign (18)	Energy/environment (26)	Education (14)	Crime (35)
Foreign policy (25)	Patriotism/war record (33)	Debates (16)	Military/defense (25)	Crime (12)	Social/health programs (25)
Dirty campaign (24)	Leadership (32)	Military/defense (16)	Foreign policy (24)	Ideology/party (11)	Ideology/party (21)
Patriotism/war record (22)	Energy/environment (26)	Foreign policy (16)	Personal slurs (19)	Leadership (10)	Military/defense (17)
Energy/environment (20)	Foreign policy (21)	Social/health programs (14)	Women's rights (16)	Dirty campaign (10)	Dirty campaign (10)
Military/defense (19)	Dirty campaign (14)	Patriotism/war record (13)	Social/health programs (10)	Energy/environment (9)	Foreign policy (10)
Ideology/party (17), personal slurs (17)	Personal slurs (8), religion (8)	Energy/environment (11)	Ideology/party (10)	Women's rights (3), personal slurs (3)	Personal slurs (9)

Note: The Democrats' top-ten statements accounted for 77 percent of all their campaign statements in 1988, 82 percent in 1992, and 88 percent in 1996; corresponding percentages for the Republicans were 86 in 1988, 84 in 1992, and 85 in 1996.

at the Arkansas economy and Clinton's experience. Except for wasted-vote arguments, the Democrats played defense, occasionally responding to a Perot attack with one of their own on the same topic. Perot, of course, vented his wrath at the GOP with particular emphasis on allegations that he had been driven from the race in July by a Republican dirty-tricks operation. And as is hinted in Table 3.8, Republicans responded by questioning Perot's sanity. Four years later, Perot lacerated Clinton more often than his Republican opponent, yet he seldom got the satisfaction of a reply from either rival.

ATTACK METHODS

Recall that attacks employ one or more of the following methods: fear arousal (accusations that things will get worse or have gotten worse under the opposition), ridicule, labeling (or guilt by association), apposition or contrast, and accusations of lying or inconsistency. Table 3.9 reveals that fear arousal figured more prominently than any other tactic in four of the six campaigns the two parties waged against each other. Its most disproportionate use occurred in the Democratic campaign of 1996, followed closely by the Republican campaign of the same year. Clinton clearly made greater use of this tactic than any other candidate, working it into 72 percent of his solo attacks on Republican targets. Dole and Dukakis also relied heavily on this method of attack.

The other methods of attack varied in relative frequency from campaign to campaign, no doubt in response to candidate style. Labeling topped the list of attack methods only once—when it was the tactic of choice for the 1988 Republicans, who tirelessly used the "L word" against Dukakis. Probably no Republican matched President Reagan's record of calling Dukakis a liberal nineteen times in only two speeches, delivered on the same day.[58] Similarly, accusations of lying ranked first only once, when the Democrats invoked it in nearly 42 percent of all their 1992 attacks on Republicans, as in Clinton's denunciation of Bush: "I mean, this guy's been out there for two months making up charges about me, deliberately falsifying my plan. . . . And if you're totally shameless and somebody tells you you're not telling the truth, and you keep on doing it anyway, which is what Bush does, it's hard for the American people to know what to make of it."[59] Apposition generally ranked as the third or fourth most used method, with ridicule in last place. We found no relationship between a ticket's resort to a particular method of attack and its standing in the polls.

Table 3.10 indicates that Perot tailored his attack methods to the target. In 1992, he resorted to fear arousal most frequently when attacking Bush, and he used ridicule when taking aim at the Arkansas governor.[60] He also exhibited a greater

Table 3.8. Attacks Exchanged between Perot and Major Parties

1992 Perot Attacks on Democrats	1992 Democratic Attacks on Perot	1992 Perot Attacks on Republicans	1992 Republican Attacks on Perot	1996 Perot Attacks on Democrats	1996 Perot Attacks on Republicans
Leadership (13)	Leadership (5)	Dirty campaign (28)	Personal slurs (15)	Corruption (15)	Debates (7)
Domestic economy (10)	Domestic economy (5)	Domestic economy (14)	Dirty campaign (9)	Domestic economy (5)	Domestic economy (6)
Personal slurs (4)	Wasted vote (2)	Leadership (11)	Domestic economy (3)	Debates (5)	Leadership (5)
Ideology/party (4)	Personal slurs (1)	Military/defense (7)	Military/defense (3)	Leadership (3)	Corruption (4)
Backward Arkansas (3)	Campaign finance (1)	Scandals (5)	Wasted vote (2)	Patriotism (2)	Foreign policy (1)
Wasted vote (2)	Backward Arkansas (1)	Personal slurs (4)	Leadership (2)	Dirty campaign (1)	Ideology/party (1)
Energy/environment (2)	Social/health (1)	Ideology/party (3)	Campaign finance (2)	Ideology/party (1)	Wasted vote (1)
Patriotism (1)		Wasted vote (2)		Military/defense (1)	Dirty campaign (1)

Note: Democrats attacked Perot only twice in 1996 on corruption issues; Republicans made only three attacks, two of which raised the wasted-vote issue, the other the domestic economy.

Table 3.9. Democratic and Republican Attack Methods in Somewhat Competitive Races

	Presidential Candidate (solo)	Vice-Presidential Candidate (solo)	All Attackers
1988 Democrats targeting Republicans			
Fear arousal	.453	.422	.394
Ridicule	.137	.267	.183
Labeling	.242	.356	.274
Apposition	.242	.289	.205
Dishonesty	.247	.222	.261
1988 Republicans targeting Democrats			
Fear arousal	.270	.344	.253
Ridicule	.092	.313	.110
Labeling	.449	.375	.420
Apposition	.303	.094	.208
Dishonesty	.135	.125	.142
1992 Democrats targeting Republicans			
Fear arousal	.312	.379	.330
Ridicule	.050	.138	.091
Labeling	.248	.310	.208
Apposition	.291	.138	.225
Dishonesty	.383	.379	.415
1992 Republicans targeting Democrats			
Fear arousal	.350	.333	.323
Ridicule	.147	.111	.118
Labeling	.295	.111	.238
Apposition	.194	.222	.190
Dishonesty	.300	.472	.295
1996 Democrats targeting Republicans			
Fear arousal	.720	.385	.484
Ridicule	.040	.077	.062
Labeling	.180	.385	.373
Apposition	.480	.308	.267
Dishonesty	.060	.154	.149
1996 Republicans targeting Democrats			
Fear arousal	.463	.375	.415
Ridicule	.132	.125	.100
Labeling	.421	.375	.415
Apposition	.316	.250	.248
Dishonesty	.326	.375	.305

Note: Entries are percentages of attacks that employed a particular method. For example, in 1988, Dukakis used fear arousal in 45.3 percent of his attacks on Republicans.

propensity to label Clinton rather than Bush. Of course, he accused both rivals of dissembling. By way of a response, Clinton limited himself to claims that Perot had misrepresented his views or his record, but Democratic surrogates resorted most to fear arousal and apposition. Republicans went in for labeling when letting fly at Perot, branding him "paranoid," "loony," "strange," and a "conspiracy nut" in well over half of their attacks. They also challenged his veracity in more than one of every five ripostes. In 1996, Perot used the same tactics against both rivals, relying most on fear arousal and labeling and least on apposition and ridicule.

ECHOES FROM THE CAMPAIGN TRAIL

The 1988 Democratic Attacks on Republican Leadership

For purposes of our study, the concept of leadership extends beyond the candidate's record in public office to substance, vision, and responsiveness to public opinion (when not specific to a particular policy). The Democrats made much of Bush's supposed lack of vision and dearth of policy specifics in 1988. According to Governor Mario Cuomo of New York, the choice between Dukakis and Bush turned on the "size" of each candidate's vision, a contest that Dukakis was certain to win.[61] Dukakis adviser John Sasso hit on the same theme: "Who is George Bush? Where does he stand? What does he believe? We already know the answer: He's willing to say practically anything."[62] Democrat John Sharp of the Texas Railroad Commission accused Bush of waging a "mushroom campaign"—one that kept voters "in the dark" while "throwing manure on them."[63]

Dukakis tirelessly painted Bush as lacking both in vision and in policy substance. In Ohio, he charged that Bush "sees no challenges. He offers no solutions. And he would lead America nowhere as president of the United States."[64] "Mr. Bush offers complacency, I offer change," he proclaimed in Chicago. "He offers slogans, we offer solutions to the problems that American families face every day and every week and every month."[65] During an interview with the *Times,* Dukakis summarized Bush's perspective as follows: "Don't rock the boat, don't change anything, everything's okay, don't change horses in the middle of the stream. That's not what this country is all about, that's not what made us a great nation."[66] "How can we trust his values when he says nothing and does nothing?" Dukakis said of Bush at rally after rally. "How can we make him the man in the Oval Office, when for the past eight years, he's been the man who wasn't there?"[67] By the end of October, Dukakis and other Democrats spoke repeatedly of the "cocoon" in which Bush sought refuge from the tough questions.[68] Entering the final week, Dukakis inveighed against "an adversary that doesn't understand the fundamental challenges that face American people, average citizens across this country."[69]

Table 3.10. Attack Methods Used in Perot Attacks on Major Parties and Vice Versa

	Presidential Candidate (solo)	All Attackers
1992 Perot targeting of Democrats		
Fear arousal	.107	.167
Ridicule	.321	.238
Labeling	.143	.238
Apposition	.107	.095
Dishonesty	.179	.143
1992 Democratic targeting of Perot		
Fear arousal	.000	.364
Ridicule	.000	.000
Labeling	.000	.182
Apposition	.000	.273
Dishonesty	.250	.182
1992 Perot targeting of Republicans		
Fear arousal	.233	.233
Ridicule	.055	.070
Labeling	.068	.105
Apposition	.096	.105
Dishonesty	.137	.116
1992 Republican targeting of Perot		
Fear arousal	.000	.050
Ridicule	.000	.050
Labeling	.600	.550
Apposition	.000	.025
Dishonesty	.267	.225
1996 Perot targeting of Democrats		
Fear arousal	.548	.447
Ridicule	.062	.079
Labeling	.387	.421
Apposition	.290	.263
Dishonesty	.355	.368
1996 Perot targeting of Republicans		
Fear arousal	.368	.308
Ridicule	.105	.115
Labeling	.316	.385
Apposition	.158	.154
Dishonesty	.263	.346

Note: No column for vice-presidential nominees or for 1996 Democrats and Republicans targeting Perot owing to small N's.

The record of Democratic attacks on leadership indicates that Dukakis, Bentsen, and others viewed Quayle as a particularly inviting target on leadership and substance issues. Until Bush put him on the ticket, few Americans knew much, if anything, about Indiana's junior senator.[70] This changed after the news media began probing into Quayle's background. Reporters pounced on a claim that family connections had landed Quayle in the National Guard, thereby sparing him a tour of duty in Vietnam. Similarly, the press pursued rumors that Quayle had partied his way through four years at DePauw University, had landed a seat in law school despite poor grades, and had cheated on his wife.[71] Visibly rattled by such allegations, Quayle added to his image problem by displaying a penchant for malapropisms, grammatical errors, and misstatements of fact. In the event, he became the butt of countless jokes on late-night TV and a prime target for the Democrats.

Indeed, Quayle's problems gave the Democrats additional reason to pound away on leadership issues. Democrats took encouragement from a *New York Times*/CBS poll that revealed that nearly a third of likely voters thought Quayle unqualified to serve as vice president.[72] Dukakis conjured up scenarios of what might happen if Quayle had to take over: "Think about it: The Cuban Missile Crisis with Dan Quayle in charge? The nuclear alert during the 1973 war in the Middle East with Dan Quayle in charge? A future crisis, war and peace at stake, with Dan Quayle in charge?"[73]

Before their October 5 debate, Lloyd Bentsen had said little about Quayle, other than that he might not be up to the job of vice president and that the Republican Right had forced him on Bush.[74] During the debate, however, Bentsen delivered one of the most memorable putdowns in the history of presidential campaigns. The moment came just after Quayle had likened his experience in Congress to that of John F. Kennedy before the 1960 election. "Senator, I served with Jack Kennedy," Bentsen exclaimed. "I knew Jack Kennedy. Jack Kennedy was a friend of mine. Senator, you're no Jack Kennedy."[75] The look on Quayle's face and his lack of an effective retort left no doubt that Bentsen's verbal punch had staggered him.

Democrats wasted no time in exploiting Quayle's weakness. Campaigning with Bentsen in Texas one day after the debate, Dukakis said that Quayle had been "programmed beyond belief." "After listening to Dan Quayle for ninety minutes last night," Bentsen quipped, "I can understand why he kept talking about job training."[76] Evidently unaware of JFK's family history, Jesse Jackson maintained that Kennedy and Quayle had nothing in common: "What Kennedy earned from the bottom up, Quayle had bequeathed and bestowed on him from the top down."[77] A Dukakis spot homed in on Quayle's facial expression just after Bentsen delivered the Kennedy line, and as this image of distress faded to black, "President Quayle?" appeared on screen.[78]

Democratic attackers took up the cry that Bush had disqualified himself for the presidency by putting Quayle on the ticket.[79] Dukakis, for one, asked repeatedly if America's future should be entrusted to the man who picked Dan Quayle.[80] Bentsen took a similar line: "Now Republicans have to ask questions about Dan Quayle's qualifications and George Bush's judgment in picking him." He also accused Bush of trying to run away from Quayle: "By his own words, he said that the American people should judge him by his choice. . . . Dan Quayle is the latest entry in the diary of George Bush's decision-making, and the American people don't like it." Quayle, he continued, was someone "that the image makers and poll takers thought could be packaged and sold to the American people."[81]

Quayle's real and imagined failings had plagued Bush since their first appearance together at the New Orleans convention, and they were greatly enhanced by the vice-presidential debate. Pressed by reporters to comment on Quayle's performance shortly afterward, Bush insisted that his running mate "did well in that debate." Bush also denounced as "ridiculous" and "ludicrous" rumors that he no longer supported Quayle.[82] Still, among Republicans, only President Reagan appeared eager to acknowledge Quayle's candidacy.[83] At the first debate with Dukakis, Bush accused the press of using "rumor and innuendo" to smear Quayle. Dukakis countered with what had become a staple of his stump speeches: "I doubt very much that Dan Quayle was the best qualified person Mr. Bush could have chosen. I think for most people the notion 'President Quayle' is a very, very troubling notion tonight."[84] A similar exchange occurred during the second debate. When Bush insisted that he had made "a good selection," Dukakis responded: "Mr. Bush picked Dan Quayle, and before he did he said: 'Watch my choice for vice president. It will tell all.' It sure did."[85] Quayle, Dukakis avowed on November 6, was not a crisis manager but "a crisis who has to be managed."[86]

The 1988 Republican Attacks on Dukakis's Crime Policies

As previously noted, the issue of weekend passes for imprisoned murderers figured critically in Republican attacks on Dukakis prior to the Democratic convention. This early effort included a fund-raising letter about Willie Horton signed by Bush and sent out in August.[87] One of the first Republican television spots of the fall campaign asked viewers to identify the candidate who had a record of giving weekend passes to convicted killers and opposing the death penalty for slayers of police officers. The ad left viewers in no doubt about the correct answers.[88] Asked in a *Reader's Digest* interview to elaborate on his disagreement with Dukakis on crime, Bush replied that the difference on furloughing murderers was fundamental. Moreover, he said, Dukakis should be held accountable not so much for the individual result ("when a person like Willie Horton goes and kills, rapes and terrorizes") but for endorsing such a misguided program. Bush went on to parry a Dukakis claim that federal prisons also let inmates out on furloughs: "But it was not the federal government or any other state government that did what he at one point strongly supported—and so I'm not going to let him get away with that."[89]

By early October, Bush had worked the movie cop Dirty Harry into his attacks on Dukakis: "Clint Eastwood's answer to violent crime is: 'Go ahead, make my day.' My opponent's answer is slightly different. His motto is: 'Go ahead, have a nice weekend.'"[90] Holding forth in Kansas City on October 7, Bush criticized Dukakis for not admitting "that his furlough program was a tragic mistake."[91] Hours later, he labeled Dukakis "the furlough king."[92] In Washington, D.C., with the national president of the Fraternal Order of Police looking on, Bush struck again: "America's police officers work to put criminals behind bars and they do not want to have their work undermined by weak judges and governors whose revolving-door prison policies give dangerous felons a weekend pass to our citizens' backyards and living rooms."[93] Capitalizing on his endorsement by the Boston police union (a patent repudiation of Dukakis), Bush advocated "a philosophy that honors the rights of victims and not just the rights of those criminals."[94] By October, he had framed Dukakis as one of the "liberal thinkers" whose misguided advocacy of light sentencing and early release had harmed the interests of society. After all, he added, "the victims of crime are given no furlough from their pain and suffering. Suffice it to say that I think there is something very wrong when there is so much sympathy for criminals that there is none left over for victims."[95]

The Republican offensive on crime extended beyond Willie Horton to paint Dukakis and liberal Democrats generally as wrongheaded on drug lords, cop killers, and the death penalty. Campaigning in California, Bush likened Dukakis to Rose Bird, a state judge recently forced off the bench by a recall election: "If you loved Rose Bird, you'll love my opponent. They both hate and oppose the death penalty, no matter how brutal the crime that's been committed."[96] He stuck to this message during the first presidential debate: "When a narcotics-wrapped-up guy goes in and murders a police officer, I think they ought to pay with their life."[97] Commenting on the slaying of two police officers in Detroit, Michigan, Bush highlighted his "tremendous differences" with Dukakis "in this whole field of crime," a subject he embellished in Akron, Ohio: "Yes, I do believe that, when a police officer is gunned down in some drug-related killing, that that killer should pay with his life. My opponent is totally against it."[98]

Other Republicans joined the crime offensive, including President Reagan, who ridiculed weekend passes for the likes of Willie Horton as "the most liberal prison program since Billy the Kid sprung the Lincoln County jail." Reagan also decried liberal opposition to the death penalty in general.[99] Senator Alfonse D'Amato made an issue of Dukakis's refusal to meet with Horton's victims, noting that the Massachusetts governor was far more willing to hear the complaints of incarcerated felons.[100] State Republican parties hurled even tougher charges via mailings and leaflets. One Illinois flyer stated that "all the murderers and rapists and drug pushers and child molesters in Massachusetts vote for Michael Dukakis." State party officials rejected criticism from the Dukakis camp. "Of course, he says it's garbage," an Illinois Republican official said of Dukakis, "because he refuses to face the facts. The facts are that he basically sympathizes with the criminals, sides with the criminals, bends over backward to protect their rights instead of their victims."[101] A Maryland handout juxtaposed pictures of Horton and Dukakis with the following text: "Is this your pro-family team for 1988? You, your spouse, your children, your parents, and your friends can have the opportunity to receive a visit from someone like Willie Horton if Mike Dukakis becomes president."[102]

Although slow to get off the mark, Dukakis fought back, vowing that Bush would not "get away with this furlough business." He denounced the attacks on his crime record as "pathetic," "totally cynical," and hypocritical.[103] In Michigan, he urged voters not to be taken in by Republican ads.[104] Seeking to show that he knew something about crime victims, he spoke of the hit-and-run death of his brother and a violent assault on his elderly father. Meanwhile, the Democrats aired a television spot charging that "thousands of drug kingpins" had been furloughed from federal prison while Bush led the administration's war on drugs. "One of his furloughed heroin dealers," the ad asserted, had raped and murdered "a pregnant mother of two."[105] Stumping in the South, Dukakis decried the way that Republicans had linked him to Horton: "I think to use human tragedy for political purposes is one of the most cynical and hypocritical things I've seen in public life."[106] Eventually, Democrats decried Republican exploitation of Horton's criminality as racist, a charge that Bush and Quayle termed "ridiculous," "absurd," and "desperate."[107]

The 1992 Exchange on the Economy

Both parties focused more of their 1992 attacks on economic issues than on any other topic, even though that exchange hardly helped the president. Frequently, Bush had to acknowledge just how hard the times were. Right before Labor Day, he conceded that growth over the previous five quarters had been "anemic," and during a swing through New Jersey, he said the economy was "lousy."[108] Other Republicans acknowledged that the economy was a drag on Bush's reelection hopes. "It's still clearly uphill," said Representative Vin Weber, a Republican from Minnesota. "We still have a heavy burden of proof in a change-oriented environment."[109] Bush sounded a plaintive note in late October: "Now I know the only way he [Clinton] can win is to make everybody believe the economy is worse than it is. But this country's not coming apart at the seams, for heaven's sake. We're the United States of America."[110]

Bush repeatedly tried to steer the argument away from a retrospective judgment of his economic leadership toward concerns about what Clinton would do if elected. This meant portraying Clinton as a southern-fried Michael Dukakis: "He has more than doubled Arkansas state spending since 1983, and he has paid for it by raising the taxes that hurt the poor working families the most."[111] The opening salvo of the Republican air war blasted Clinton's record as governor: "To pay for his increased spending in Arkansas, Bill Clinton raised state taxes. And not just on the rich. He increased the sales tax by 33 percent. Imposed a mobile home tax. Created a cable TV tax. Supported a tax on groceries. And now, if elected president, Bill Clinton has promised to increase government spending—$200 billion. Guess where he'll get the money."[112]

Sensing correctly that voters harbored doubts about Clinton's character, the Bush team injected trustworthiness into its economic arguments: "You can't trust Clinton economics," one Republican TV spot proclaimed. "It's wrong for you. It's wrong for America."[113] Similarly, a Texas radio ad declared: "Fewer jobs for Texans. You can't trust Bill Clinton. He's all wrong for America."[114] Quayle pounced during the vice-presidential debate when Gore prevaricated on taxes: "You're pulling a Clinton. You know what a Clinton is? He says one thing one day and another thing the next."[115]

Unfortunately for Bush, all this talk about taxes served to remind voters of his "read my lips" vow from the 1988 campaign—his promise not to raise taxes. Two years later, however, he agreed to a tax hike as part of a deficit-reduction package brokered with congressional Democrats. Many Republicans in the House and Senate opposed the legislation, as did conservative opinion leaders throughout the nation. Primary opponent Pat Buchanan made a major issue of the broken tax vow in New Hampshire, where he repeatedly referred to Bush as "King George." The president later apologized and tried to put the issue behind him at the 1992 convention. The question before the American people, he stated, was, "Who do you trust in this election: The candidate who's raised taxes one time and regrets it? Or the other candidate, who raised taxes and fees 128 times and enjoyed it every time?"[116] But as Quayle acknowledged shortly after Labor Day, anger over the broken promise still lingered: "He [Bush] looks back on that and he says not only does he regret it, but it was a mistake." And, in a remarkable show of contrition, Quayle added: "We raised taxes on the American people and we put this country right into a recession. We are struggling to get out of it."[117] Two days later, Bush sought to reassure critics: "I went along with one Democratic tax increase, and I'm not going to do it again. Ever. Ever."[118]

Throughout the fall, Bush continually caricatured Clinton as a big-government man, a planner in the bureaucratic mode, a liberal tax-and-spender. Speaking at a Labor Day rally in Wisconsin, he accused Clinton of using scare tactics "so that he can slip into office with that failed tax-and-spend policy of the past."[119] After two days, he spied an opportunity to equate Clinton with the $2.8 billion tax increases of New Jersey's governor, Jim Florio: "I don't have to tell New Jersey about that old saxophone song sounding the familiar tax-and-spend theme. You know what a liberal governor and a liberal legislature can do to wreck an economy."[120] Attacking Clinton's "investment" program in Detroit, he proclaimed: "Our nation has never been seduced by the mirage that my opponent offers of a government that accumulates capital by taxing it and borrowing it from the people, and then redistributing it according to some industrial policy."[121] Stumping across Georgia in mid-September, he dismissed Clinton's "investment" scheme as "big-time government spending, directed by Washington planners who want to reorder social and economic priorities."[122]

Bush pounded away on taxes and big government for the rest of the campaign. In Ohio, for example, he ridiculed Democratic arguments that only "those people who drive Jaguars and eat that quiche and drink that champagne" would pay for Clinton's programs. "We've heard that song before," he continued. "Jimmy Carter sang it, Walter Mondale sang it, Michael Dukakis sang it, and they're going after the rich, but the middle class always gets up singing the blues. Big government gets the gold and you get the shaft."[123] He made similar appeals to Perot followers: "Mine is the only agenda that includes cutting the growth of mandatory government spending, cutting the size of government, and reducing the federal deficit. . . . Governor Clinton offers more of the old big taxes, big government—no serious plan to control the deficit."[124] During the third presidential debate, Bush implored "Mr. and Mrs. America" not to be taken in by Clinton: "When you hear him say we're going to tax only the rich, watch your wallet because his figures don't add up, and he's going to sock it right to the middle-class taxpayer and lower, if he's going to pay for all the spending programs he proposes."[125] By that time, Bush had come up with the phrase *trample down,* as in "tramples down business with those deadly new mandates and regulations, tramples down individual initiative with higher taxes, and tramples down the dreams of people."[126] At the end, he mixed derision with rarely reported good news about the economy, such as a 2.7 percent increase in growth for the previous quarter. Clinton and Gore, he charged, kept talking about "change": "That's all you will have left in your pockets if Governor Clinton becomes president of the United States!"[127]

With Stanley Greenberg's polls indicating Bush's vulnerability on the economy, the Clinton-Gore ticket made extensive use of "trickle-down economics," a staple of Democratic presidential campaigns since 1896.[128] Clinton fittingly spoke of trickle down in Harry Truman's hometown of Independence, Missouri, and he played the same card in New England, Detroit, and Los Angeles, as well as during the presidential debates.[129] "We've had trickle down for twelve years," he said in a typical speech, "I want you to give Al Gore and Bill Clinton a chance to invest, to educate, to cooperate, and to compete."[130]

Clinton and Gore naturally framed this contest as a retrospective judgment on Bush's economic record. In New Mexico, Clinton accused Bush of hiding "from a record that has given this country its worst economic performance in fifty years, the first decline of $1,600 a year in the average family income, 2 million more people in poverty since he's been president."[131] Gore served up more of the same in Georgia: "Unemployment under Bush and Quayle is up. New housing starts are down. Poverty is up. Personal income is down. Bankruptcies are up. Consumer confidence is down. Everything that should be down is up; everything that should be up is down. They've got it upside down. We want to turn it right-side up."[132] In Ohio, Gore called the Bush record on the economy the worst since the Great Depression, and during the first presidential debate, Clinton blamed Bush for the loss of 200,000 jobs in California.[133] By the end of October, Gore had found inspiration in a popular film: "If George Bush went to Hollywood and made a movie, they'd have to call it 'Honey, I Shrunk the Economy,' and, if he made a sequel, they'd have to call it 'Honey, I Blew Up the Deficit.'"[134]

Democratic attack ads posed the retrospective question, "Can we afford four more years of this?" First aired on September 20, one spot ticked off the grim statistics of a protracted recession—a three-year high in unemployment reached in 1990, a six-year high in lost jobs reached in March 1992, and the highest unemployment in eight years posted in July 1992.[135] Another spot reminded voters that Bush had promised an increase of 30 million jobs in eight years: "He's 29 million short."[136] Still another quoted a Bush promise that Americans would be better off economically at the end of his first term. "Well, it's four years later," the ad concluded. "How are you doing?"[137] A Michigan radio ad took aim at autoworkers: "According to the Department of Labor, the American auto industry has lost 89,000 jobs under George Bush, nearly 30,000 auto jobs right here in Michigan."[138]

Clinton parried Bush's attacks on taxation by reminding voters of his "read my lips" promise. When Marlin Fitzwater sought to qualify a new Bush promise never to raise taxes, Gore retorted, "Well it sounds to me as if Marlin Fitzwater has learned to be a lip reader. We are now greatly in debt to Mr. Fitzwater for interpreting the president's commitments. Many Americans might have otherwise been fooled into believing . . . that the president actually meant what he said."[139] In Michigan, Clinton charged that Bush had "betrayed" those who had voted for him in 1988 by breaking his tax pledge.[140] Reacting to Bush's warnings of higher taxes on the middle class, Clinton exclaimed: "He has no credibility on taxes and he can't even count. Everything he says is wrong. He raised taxes on everybody. It's just bull."[141] First aired on October 2, a Democratic attack ad continually juxta-posed "Read my lips: No new taxes" with claims that Bush had signed the biggest tax increase in American history, increased taxes on the middle class, doubled the beer tax, and increased the tax on gasoline by 56 percent. The spot concluded with a charge that Bush wanted to give millionaires a tax break of $180,000.[142]

Clinton also exulted in Bush's predicament when Democratic majorities pushed through Congress a tax relief bill that also contained rate increases. He stated, "There's no question that if he signs it, it's inconsistent with his position, which is that he is not going to raise any taxes, even though we all know he's raised a slew of them."[143]

The 1992 Exchanges between Perot and the Major Parties

Ostensibly, Perot rejoined the fray to showcase his ideas for ending the deficit, but after making some headway on this front, he initiated a nasty exchange with the GOP over alleged dirty tricks, and that reflected badly on him. This episode also dis-tracted the Republicans and likely benefited Clinton. At the October 1 press confer-ence called to announce his return, Perot faced reporters who clearly saw him as out to spoil Bush's chances of reelection. "Isn't your strategy to disrupt George Bush's vote in a number of key states, including this one, Texas?" one reporter asked. Perot's heated reply hardly laid the spoiler charge to rest: "Absolutely not. That's press myth number 615. . . . He has called me every name in the book. All I have ever said, fine man, fine family. The only thing I've ever criticized is his mistakes in office. That's it. We're talking about performance here and not personality. See? I'm everything from a 'monster' to 'crazy,' though, coming from them, right?"[144]

For the next several weeks, Perot concentrated on deficit reduction. Bravura performances in the debates restored his standing with many voters, as did his infomercials on television. Just before the third debate, however, Perot's daughter Susan—evidently with his permission—claimed that the real reason for her fa-ther's withdrawal from the race in July had been to stop a Republican smear cam-paign against another daughter, Carolyn. "We were told that they were planning to destroy her wedding by spreading the story that she was a lesbian," Susan told a reporter. "It was just terrible. It wasn't true, but they were going to do it anyway and put the story out in the news media to embarrass my dad."[145] When Susan's interview failed to arouse much of a media reaction, Perot tried to plant the story with the *Boston Herald* on October 23. Dissatisfied by that paper's response, he wrangled an invitation to appear on the CBS television show *60 Minutes*, where he finally succeeded in igniting a media firestorm. The real reason for getting out in July, Perot declared, was to foil a Republican plot to ruin Carolyn's wedding and destroy her reputation. But his departure had not stopped the Republicans from trying to bug his phones and otherwise get inside his Dallas headquarters. Three "sources" supposedly associated with the GOP had warned him of the conspiracy. "I couldn't believe that anyone representing the President of the United States would stoop to these lows," he exclaimed. "This is Watergate II."[146] When pressed for proof, however, Perot revealed that he had no solid evidence to back up any of these charges and, further, that he had never met his principal source, one Scott Barnes.[147] After the *60 Minutes* interview, Perot spoke to rallies in New Jersey and Pennsylvania, where he repeated his allegations.[148]

The uproar that followed these claims dominated coverage of the presidential campaign for the next several days. Six of eleven campaign stories in the next day's *Times* reported and mulled over Perot's accusations, as well as the Republican and Democratic reactions. Soon, however, the Perot camp realized that this coverage was hurting Perot more than Bush. Accordingly, Perot aides implored the press to drop the matter. "We're trying to stop talking about it," spokesman Orson Swindle said. "If you'll cooperate, we'll quit talking about it."[149] But the plot thickened when news surfaced that, just before dropping out in July, Perot had enlisted the Federal Bureau of Investigation (FBI) in an effort to implicate the chairman of Bush's Texas campaign as a conspirator in the alleged plot to drive him out of the race.[150] Now, in October, he still could not let go of the dirty-tricks charge, even as he pooh-poohed its significance. "Until the Republican dirty-tricks guys started after it in June," Perot stated in Denver, no one had questioned his integrity. The present imbroglio, he insisted, amounted only to "silly putty," having "nothing to do with anything that concerns the American people, and I just look at it and marvel."[151]

The airing of Perot's charges on *60 Minutes* provoked immediate outrage from the Bush camp. "Nonsense," Marlin Fitzwater exclaimed. "I don't want to attack Perot, but I don't know where he's getting it from. I mean, fantastic stories about his daughter and disrupting her wedding and the CIA, it's all loony."[152] Fitzwater had more to say the following day: "It's so crazy that he seems to have latched onto this theory like other people latch onto UFO theories, and he seems to believe it. I think the news media needs to take a look at this because they're the only ones left who can investigate it and prevent us from electing a paranoid person who has delusions. This man simply cannot see the truth."[153] Bush campaign manager James A. Baker revealed that he and other Republicans, including First Lady Barbara Bush, had contacted Perot to deny the truth of these claims just before Perot rejoined the race. "When someone makes this kind of charge," Baker observed, "they ought to provide some little scintilla of evidence."[154] Bush took a hand on October 27, telling the *Times* that Perot's charges were "strange, strange."[155] Marilyn Quayle, wife of the vice president, added her voice to this attack by repeatedly labeling Perot as "bizarre" and a "conspiracy nut."[156]

Democrats welcomed this distraction from relentless Bush attacks on Clinton's character. "So now we've got this bizarre situation where Bush and Perot have accused each other of investigating each other's children," Clinton chortled. "Let me tell you something, I want to investigate your children—their problems, their promise, and their future."[157] But he soon took a different tack by hinting that Perot's charges were plausible because Bush would say and do anything to stay in power.[158]

All told, Perot took it easy on Clinton in 1992, lessening the sting in part by also targeting Bush or the Republicans when knocking Clinton and the Democrats. Perot justified his October reentry in this way: "I thought both political parties would address the problems that face the nation. We gave them a chance. They didn't do it."[159] Perot tipped his hand later by delivering a public rebuke to his aide Orson Swindle for having suggested that Perot voters should prefer Bush to Clinton as their second choice.[160] He did take a slap at Clinton during the final debate, making light of the responsibilities of governing such a small, atypical, and "irrelevant" state as Arkansas.[161] In the final days, Perot avowed that neither of his rivals had enough sense to run a small business, and he urged voters not to vote for either of them.[162]

The 1996 Exchanges over Corruption Issues

Both Perot and the Republicans made a major issue of Clinton's fund-raising irregularities and other scandals during the fall of 1996. Clinton called on surrogates to answer the Republican charges while ignoring Perot. By that point, Clinton had overcome almost all of his early setbacks except for persistent questions about his character and involvement in assorted scandals. Whitewater, a real estate fiasco in Arkansas in which the president and the First Lady had played a part during his time as governor, led to the appointment of a special prosecutor, grand jury testimony by Hillary Clinton, criminal indictments, and the jailing of some close Clinton associates. Other dustups also attracted media attention, such as the dismissal of the White House travel staff for reasons of political patronage, the White House response to the suicide of a despondent adviser, and revelations that the White House had acquired FBI files on 900 Republicans in government service.[163] Typically, as in their response to Travelgate, Clinton aides chose to dismiss such charges as election-year partisanship rather than to dispute their veracity: "There's nothing here that will change anybody's mind one way or the other."[164]

Despite his reputation as a hatchet man, Dole signaled in 1996 that he wanted to forego personal attacks on President Clinton.[165] And to the chagrin of

Republicans, he passed up opportunities to make an issue of White House scandals during the first debate with Clinton. Under intense pressure to wage a more aggressive campaign, Dole promised to take a tougher line in the next debate. Still, when a reporter asked him to comment on Clinton's ethics and morality, he replied, "It's a very close question."[166]

Dole's reticence reflected disagreements among his advisers about the costs of going negative. Some felt that hammering Clinton would revive unpleasant memories of Dole's earlier campaigns. Moreover, his running mate, former congressman Jack Kemp, had given assurances on national television that Dole would not stoop to making personal attacks.[167] Yet Dole could hardly ignore reports that Clinton had dangled the prospect of presidential pardons to his partners in the Whitewater affair. The strategic shift became apparent on October 9, when Dole alluded to Whitewater and Filegate during a speech in Wheaton, Illinois.[168] The following day, he served notice that corruption would be an issue of his campaign: "I'm running for president. I think the FBI files are fair game. I think the pardon is fair game."[169]

Others joined this offensive. Clearly stung by Republican denunciations of him as a "powder puff," Kemp uncorked a rare attack on the president: "Four years later [after Clinton promised the "most ethical administration in history"], the words that seem to characterize the ethics of this administration are words like Travelgate, Filegate, independent counsels, and possible presidential pardons."[170] House Speaker Newt Gingrich decried irregularities in Democratic fund-raising. Money had flowed into Democratic coffers from all over Asia, he charged, and a scandal was brewing that surely would dwarf Watergate.[171]

Meanwhile, Dole crisscrossed the nation and hammered away on ethics, pardons, Filegate, and fund-raising. "He talks about an ethical administration," Dole exclaimed in Kansas City, Missouri. "He does not have an ethical administration. . . . It's time the President of the United States made it very clear: no pardons, no pardons to anybody he did business with who may be in jail. . . . There were people who went to jail in the Nixon administration for looking at two FBI files. They've got 900 files."[172] Dole kept up the pressure in California, denouncing foreign contributions, naming disgraced Clinton administrators, and charging that Democratic corruption had diminished the presidency.[173] Immediately after the second debate with Clinton, he pounced on news of Gore's fund-raising prowess at a Buddhist temple in Los Angeles: "You have to take a vow of poverty to be in that temple. Well, several [monks] gave $5,000. Next thing you know, they're going to be having fundraisers at homeless shelters. They've got such a laundering machine going, they've got their own Laundromat."[174] Conservative talk-show host Rush Limbaugh provided Dole with another venue to reiterate these charges, as did a rally in Albuquerque, New Mexico: "Here's a president who often talks

about a bridge to the future. More often it seems it's a bridge to wealthy political donors. It goes through a laundromat first, and takes a left at the Democratic
National Committee, and then rolls all the way down to the Oval Office."[175] "Our
elections are not for sale to some foreign influence or some foreign interest," he
affirmed in Colorado; he reiterated the point in a nationwide radio address.[176] In
New Hampshire, Dole spoke of parallels to Watergate and proposed new restrictions on campaign contributions, some of which provoked immediate opposition
from Gingrich and other Republicans.[177]

With less than two weeks remaining before election day, some Dole advisers
urged him to change the subject because the corruption charges had not helped
his poll ratings.[178] Dole persisted all the same, as did Speaker Gingrich, who described Clinton's philosophy as "break the law, bruise the law, cover it up, and then
frankly lie about the cover-up." Gingrich likened the Clinton administration to an
octopus embracing Indonesian bankers, Buddhist temples, vanished Koreans, and
Cuban drug smugglers.[179] At the same time, Dole pantomimed the White House
pitch: "You want to spend the night in the Lincoln Bedroom for say, $100,000?
We'll get it for you. Whatever you want, we'll do it. You want to visit Indonesia?
We'll arrange a trip. You want to go to India to see some of Gandhi's relatives, who
gave $300,000 and owe $10,000 in back taxes? We'll work it out for you."[180]

Dole kept up the assault to the end. Referring to foreign money, he exclaimed:
"It's coming from Indonesia! It's coming from India! All over the world, money's
coming into America, right into the president's coffers."[181] "Where's the outrage?"
became his mantra. The White House became "the animal house," where Clin-
tonites swilled beer while poring through FBI files on Republicans: "Let's look
through Bob Dole's file today, yeah, and see what he's got going. Set 'em up boys,
have another beer."[182] When Clinton proposed reforming the Federal Elections
Campaign Act (FECA) at this eleventh hour, Dole reacted scornfully: "Apparently
all the money . . . has been counted. Now he can go ahead and make the speech."[183]
Meanwhile, RNC chairman Haley Barbour likened Clinton's credibility on campaign finance reform to O. J. Simpson's pledge to find the murderer of his wife.[184]

In 1992, Perot had helped the Democrats by attacking Bush, but in 1996, he
lashed out at Clinton and the Democrats with a ferocity seldom matched by the
Dole-Kemp ticket. In San Francisco, for example, Perot spoke of the likelihood
that Clinton would buy the silence of his confederates in the Whitewater scandal
with the promise of presidential pardons.[185] By mid-October, he was arguing that
the moral and ethical lapses of the Clinton gang would lead to more criminal
prosecutions. His contempt for Clinton and company increased as the campaign
neared its end: "I never thought I would live to see a major drug dealer give 20,000
bucks in Florida and then be invited to a big Democratic reception by the Vice
President of the United States, Al Gore. . . . Now, then, right after his trip to the

White House, they caught him with 5,828 pounds of cocaine. Don't you think we should set a higher standard? I hope you do."[186]

On October 28, Perot called on Clinton to do the responsible thing and resign. How, he asked, could anyone who loved his country and his family "even consider voting" for a president confronted by such moral, ethical, and criminal problems?[187] On the eve of the presidential vote, he likened Bill and Hillary Clinton to Bonnie and Clyde, the celebrated bank robbers of the 1930s, and for good measure, he called Clinton corrupt to the core.[188]

Consistent with Clinton's maxim of replying immediately to every Republican attack, his team usually had a ready response to Dole's allegations. Typically, the response took aim at the attacker's credibility rather than addressing the substance of the charge. When Dole took up the Filegate issue, for instance, George Stephanopoulos reminded the press of Dole's reputation as a negative campaigner: "When you're faced with a campaign that doesn't have a current theme, you revert to type: hatchet man."[189] When Gingrich accused the Clinton White House of illegal fund-raising, campaign spokesman Joe Lockhart suggested that Gingrich should "look pretty deep inside before he starts throwing stones about ethical problems."[190] Similarly, Lockhart characterized Dole's fund-raising effort as "a full-service Laundromat."[191] Responding to Republican allegations of illicit contributions from foreigners, Lockhart claimed that Dole, too, had accepted foreign lucre: "It's the height of hypocrisy for them to rail at taking contributions from foreign nationals when they are doing the same thing."[192] White House chief of staff Leon Panetta asserted that the GOP had collected roughly $24 million from subsidiaries of foreign corporations.[193] When Dole issued his call for finance reform, Lockhart likened the Republican nominee to Jack Kevorkian "giving a lecture on the sanctity of life." Similarly, White House press secretary Michael McCurry dismissed Dole's proposal as the political version of a "deathbed conversion."[194] Aired on October 22, a Democratic spot made Clinton out as a champion of campaign finance reform while charging that Dole had raked in $2.4 billion from "foreign oil, foreign tobacco, foreign drug companies."[195] Another spot released about the same time—and quickly disavowed by the expert source cited—named Dole as the senator "most responsible for blocking any serious campaign reform."[196] Defending Clinton's eleventh-hour call for campaign finance reform, Stephanopoulos dismissed the notion that Dole was a "tribune of campaign finance reform" as "ludicrous."[197]

SUMMARY AND CONCLUSIONS

Despite the obvious difference between Clinton's big lead in 1996 and the more problematic leads of eventual winners in 1988 and 1992, the races analyzed in this chapter had enough in common for us to characterize them as somewhat competitive. Bush won a higher percentage of the popular vote in 1988 than Clinton did in 1992 or 1996; Bush also got a bigger share of the electoral vote in 1988. Like Bush's lead in 1988, Clinton's lead in 1992 began with a big convention bounce. Similarly, both Bush in 1988 and Clinton in 1992 came close to losing that advantage. Clinton looked like a sure winner on Labor Day 1996—but only after clawing his way back from the setbacks of "Presidency One."

The Skaperdas-Grofman model suggests that the trailing candidate will always wage a more negative campaign than the leading candidate. This expectation held true of the major parties in all three races examined in this chapter. Even though Dukakis absorbed devastating blows from Bush in the spring and summer, his side outattacked the Republicans in the fall. Likewise, Republican underdogs in 1992 and 1996 waged more negative campaigns than the favored Democrats. Consistent with his big lead in the polls, Clinton did far less attacking in the second campaign.

Perot made a much bigger splash in 1992 than in 1996: he overtook Clinton early in the polls and briefly snatched the lead from Bush before falling back. His bizarre exit while the Democratic convention was meeting undeniably helped catapult Clinton past Bush in the polls. Then, after Clinton had built up a strong lead, Perot returned to the fray, evidently for personal reasons. Back in the running, Perot reverted to the role of spoiling Bush's chances for reelection, even though his presence hurt Clinton. The odd charges that Perot made regarding skullduggery against his family not only reflected poorly on Bush but also raised questions about Perot's sanity. These twists and turns bore no resemblance to either part assigned third-ranked candidates in the Skaperdas-Grofman model.

In 1996, Perot looked more like what Skaperdas and Grofman had in mind for third-ranked candidates in their general model. He attacked front-runner Clinton more frequently than runner-up Dole. Also consistent with the model, the Democrats and Republicans largely ignored him. The Skaperdas-Grofman formulations fall short, however, in that they make no allowance for the egoism and animosity so obvious in Perot's case.

Interesting similarities showed up in the targeting of campaign attacks in these somewhat competitive races. Except for Clinton in 1996, presidential candidates figured prominently as attackers. And every candidate figured principally as a target of attacks.

As for methods of making attacks, in the 1988 race, the Republicans' continual labeling of Dukakis as a liberal gibes with general accounts of this heavily ideological contest. Across all eight campaigns (three Democratic, three Republican, and two by Perot), however, we uncovered no systematic relationship between standing in the race and choice of attack methods. Rather than tailor attack methods to the strategic situation, candidates evidently resort to familiar, if not always successful, tactics. That is, a candidate long given to labeling opponents most likely will label opponents in the next campaign.

Once again, we were struck by the degree of topical convergence. If ever a concern worked in favor of one party and against the other, the domestic economy did so in 1992. Yet the Republicans engaged the Democrats, even though their efforts can only be described as desperate. In 1996, the Democrats not only hit back on corruption but also made Dole out as part of the problem rather than the solution. Only in 1988 did the two parties vary much on the topics they emphasized, but even then, the Democrats answered Republicans on crime and Willie Horton. Likewise, although Bush rued his choice of a running mate, the Republicans denied Democratic charges that Dan Quayle was unfit to be vice president; they also disputed that Bush had shown poor judgment in choosing Quayle. In 1996 as well as in 1992, Perot addressed many of the same topics as his major-party opponents.

4. The Comeback
Races of 1968 and 1976

Unlike a "somewhat competitive" race, the runner-up in a "comeback" contest gains ground against the favored candidate until the outcome becomes too close to call. What once looked like a runaway ends as a cliff-hanger.

Shortly before Labor Day in 1968, Democrat Hubert Humphrey lagged sixteen percentage points behind Republican Richard Nixon. The same poll showed George C. Wallace, the American Independent Party (AIP) candidate, in third place with 18 percent.[1] "It's as if we've been pushed off the rim of the Grand Canyon," Humphrey lamented, "and now we have to claw our way up the sides."[2] Six weeks later, Wallace nipped at Humphrey's heels.[3] However, Humphrey's stock began rising in October as Wallace's dropped. Nixon remained flat at around 43 percent. In the last of Gallup's preelection polls, Humphrey trailed Nixon by only two points (see Figure 4.1). Harris showed him in front of Nixon by three.

On election day, early returns favored Nixon, but he soon fell behind Humphrey as the national tally proceeded. Pennsylvania and Texas unexpectedly fell to Humphrey as Nixon carried New Jersey by a smaller than anticipated margin. Eventually, the outcome hinged on what happened in California, Missouri, Ohio, and Illinois.[4] Although Nixon won all four states, he led Humphrey by little more than half a million in the popular vote nationwide, 43.4 to 42.7 percent. The electoral vote broke down more impressively for Nixon at 301 to Humphrey's 191.[5] Wallace made history by garnering 13.5 percent of the popular vote and corralling 46 electoral votes.

No third-party or independent candidate of consequence figured in the 1976 comeback race. Before Labor Day, Jimmy Carter led President Gerald Ford by an astonishing 33 percent in the Gallup Poll. By election day, however, Ford's support had surged and Carter's had plunged to the point that the race was too close to call (see Figure 4.2).[6] As in 1968, the early favorite squeaked by in the popular vote (Carter with 50 percent, Ford with 48 percent). In the electoral vote, Carter defeated Ford by 297 to 240.

THE 1968 STRATEGIC ENVIRONMENT

Three powerful issues unsettled the American electorate in 1968, as described by Philip Converse, Warren Miller, Jerome Rusk, and Arthur Wolfe:

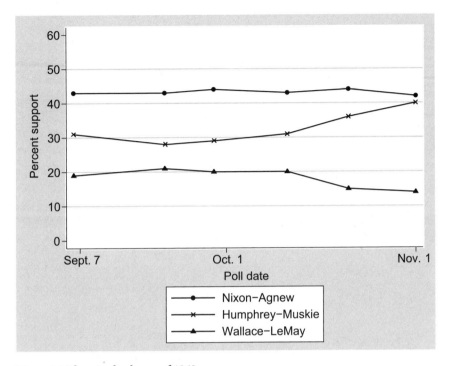

Figure 4.1 The comeback race of 1968
Source: George H. Gallup, *The Gallup Poll: Public Opinion 1935–1971, vol. 3* (New York: Random House, 1972); "Humphrey Trims Gallup Poll Gap," *NYT*, October 27, 1968, A68.

From Vietnam and the racial crisis a corollary discontent crystallized that might be treated as a third towering issue of the 1968 campaign, or as nothing more than a restatement of the other two issues. This was the cry for "law and order" and against "crime in the streets." While Goldwater had talked in these terms somewhat in 1964, events had conspired to raise their salience very considerably for the public by 1968. For some, these slogans may have had no connotations involving either the black race or Vietnam, signifying instead a concern over rising crime rates and the alleged "coddling" of criminal offenders by the courts. More commonly by 1968, however, the connection was very close: there were rallying cries for more severe police suppression of black rioting in the urban ghettoes, and of public political dissent of the type represented by the Vietnam peace demonstrations at Chicago during the Democratic convention.[7]

Similarly, when Gallup inquired about the "most important problems" facing the nation in 1968, Vietnam always received the most mentions, at 53 percent in

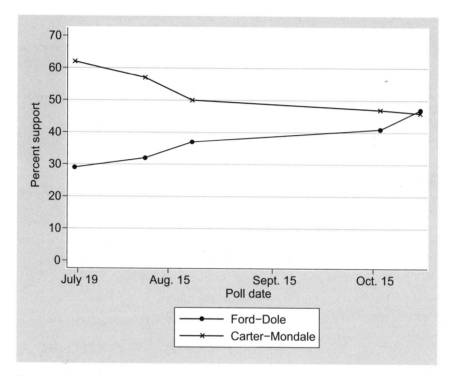

Figure 4.2 The comeback race of 1976
Source: George H. Gallup, The Gallup Poll: Public Opinion 1972–1977 (Wilmington, DE: Scholarly Resources, 1978).

January, 41 percent in May, 52 percent in June, and 51 percent in August. Unfortunately, because Gallup loaded up its "crime" category with references to "riots" and "looting," it may have depressed choices of "unrest" and "race," which were listed separately. In any case, the racially tinctured category of crime ranked second in May, June, and August.[8]

Few who remember the sixties have forgotten the urban riots from 1963 to 1968. Owing chiefly to the assassination of Martin Luther King in April, the year 1968 was marked by the most riots, the most days of rioting, and the most arrests of any year in that troubled decade (see Table 4.1). As could be expected, the slayings, arson, and looting of so many "long hot summers" had heightened fears of social collapse. Symptomatic of such feelings, one 1968 poll found that 47 percent of the public favored the idea of allowing police to shoot looters on sight.[9] Liberal Democrats in 1964 had denounced race riots as "Goldwater rallies." Now, the riots underscored the problems of a conflicted Great Society, and they aided the Wallace and Nixon candidacies as well.

Table 4.1. Urban Riots, 1963–1968

	1963	1964	1965	1966	1967	1968	Total
Cities	8	16	20	44	71	106	265
Riots	12	16	23	53	82	155	341
Riot days	16	42	31	92	236	286	703
Arrests	780	2,000	10,245	2,216	16,741	21,697	53,409
Injuries	88	580	1,206	467	3,348	2,770	8,459
Deaths	1	9	43	9	85	75	221

Source: Bryan T. Downes, "A Critical Reexamination of the Social and Political Characteristics of Riot Cities," *Social Science Quarterly* 51 (September 1970): 349–360.

Humphrey, Johnson, and the War

In his autobiography, Humphrey looked back on "the chaos of 1968" and concluded that "one place" (Vietnam) and "one person" (Lyndon Johnson) had determined his fate.[10] Clark Clifford, Johnson's secretary of defense and a friend to both men, described Humphrey as a liberal trapped between his natural constituency and the man to whom he owed his job.[11] Johnson and Humphrey had known each other since their early days in the Senate, and of course, Johnson had put Humphrey on the ticket in 1964.[12] Still, Johnson never fully respected or trusted Humphrey.[13]

Having failed to win the Democratic nomination in 1960, Humphrey entertained no thought of a 1968 bid until March 31, when Johnson announced his decision not to seek another term. At that point, however, the deadlines for candidate filings had expired in all but two of the primary states, and in any case, Humphrey lacked the organization, money, and inclination to take on Senators Eugene McCarthy and Robert F. Kennedy in the primaries.[14] Rather, he counted on party regulars and labor supporters to corral most of the convention delegates in nonprimary states, as well as in primary states such as Pennsylvania, where party rules did not link the allocation of delegates to the candidate-preference vote.[15]

By late May, Humphrey had lined up more delegates than McCarthy or Kennedy.[16] Kennedy's assassination on June 5 cleared the way for the Democratic convention in Chicago to nominate Humphrey. It also emboldened Johnson to take a tougher stand on Vietnam. Indeed, Johnson even contemplated getting himself renominated.[17] Marvin Watson, Johnson's chief of staff and a Texas delegate, asked Mayor Richard Daley to launch such a trial balloon, even though the real objective may have been to scare Humphrey into supporting Johnson's position on the war.[18] Specifically, Johnson wanted Humphrey to embrace the administration's plank against an antiwar substitute when the convention took up the party platform. John Connally, another Texas ally, warned Lawrence O'Brien, a top Humphrey adviser, that any sign of weakness on Humphrey's part might stampede the southern delegations into renominating LBJ.[19]

By that point, Humphrey had holed up in a Chicago hotel room with O'Brien and others to draft a compromise plank.[20] He frequently called Secretary of State Dean Rusk and National Security Adviser Walt Rostow to discuss proposed revisions, knowing that they had a direct line to Johnson. Eventually, Rusk and Rostow approved Humphrey's new language, leading him to assume that they also spoke for Johnson. Johnson, however, dispatched Watson to tell Humphrey that none of his changes was acceptable. When Humphrey called him directly to protest, Johnson delivered a withering rebuke: "Well, this plan just undercuts our whole policy, and, by God, the Democratic Party ought not be doing that to me and you ought not to be doing it; you've been a part of this policy."[21] His hand forced and fearful that Johnson might block his nomination, Humphrey declared for the administration plank, which carried after several hours of rancorous debate. In a sign of things to come, delegates on the losing side donned black armbands and sang the civil rights anthem "We Shall Overcome."[22]

In yet another blow to Humphrey, the networks frequently cut away from convention speeches to show clashes between the Chicago police and demonstrators. In one melee, police bloodied some of Eugene McCarthy's young volunteers. The cameras refocused on the convention, however, when Senator Abraham Ribicoff of Connecticut used the podium to accuse the Chicago police of behaving like Hitler's Gestapo, and they also captured Mayor Daley shouting obscenities while Ribicof spoke. Like tear gas, rancor lingered in the hall when Humphrey and his running mate, Senator Edmund Muskie of Maine, delivered their acceptance speeches.[23]

Even the timing of the Chicago convention worked against Humphrey. Scheduled to coincide with Johnson's August 27 birthday, it allowed Humphrey almost no respite before Labor Day, which fell on September 1 that year.

Humphrey had to cope with other setbacks as well. He soon learned that no funds would be forthcoming from a bankrupt Democratic National Committee and also that the President's Club refused to turn over the $600,000 it had raised to reelect Johnson. A word from Johnson might have unlocked this war chest, but it never came.[24] In yet another turn of the screw, Johnson barred political appointees in his administration from taking time off to help Humphrey.[25] George Ball accordingly resigned as U.S. ambassador to the United Nations before signing up with the Humphrey campaign. "For Humphrey, and for many of us in the White House who were close to him," one Johnson official recalled, "it was a bitter time."[26]

Unable to pay for TV ads and poorly organized, Humphrey hit the campaign trail, hoping to get his message out via the "free media." He soon ran afoul of Johnson by predicting the early return of some American troops from Vietnam, perhaps by year's end. Very soon after Humphrey spoke these words at the University of Pennsylvania, Secretary of State Rusk denied that any such plan was in the works. Irked by the repudiation, Humphrey repeated his claim and pointed to a newspaper headline that declared: "Marine Regiment Heads Home from Vietnam." Upon reading the story, he had to admit that it pertained to the rotation of troops rather than a reduction of the force in Vietnam. He had to eat more crow after telling reporters that he would have happily run on the rejected antiwar plank. The reaction of his press entourage soon forced a retraction.[27]

Speaking to a convention of the American Legion in New Orleans, Johnson poured salt on Humphrey's self-inflicted wounds. "We yearn for the day when our men can come home," Johnson said. "But *no man* can predict when that day will come because we are there to bring an honorable—to bring a stable—peace to Southeast Asia, and no less will justify the sacrifices that our men have died for."[28] "Not an act of friendship," Humphrey grumbled.[29] "At a time when Vice President Humphrey appeared to be trying to soften the psychological impact of the war in the presidential campaign," the *Times* noted, "Mr. Johnson took a decidedly hard line in his New Orleans speech."[30]

Several days later, Johnson met with Humphrey in the White House. Reportedly, the president told the vice president not to play commander-in-chief until elected to the office. Humphrey conceded Johnson's point but stated clearly that the policy would change if he won the election. Humphrey returned to the hustings with a new theme, which he tested in South Dakota: "I'm going to seek peace in every way possible, but only the president can do it now. Come January, it's a new ball game." The audience cheered and applauded this declaration. Humphrey repeated the line in Louisville, Kentucky, and got a standing ovation.[31]

At that juncture, such positive reinforcement must have seemed sweet indeed to one of the most reviled and harassed candidates in the history of modern presidential campaigns. Humphrey barely could be heard over the chants, curses, and jeers of antiwar protestors in Boston. In Portland, Oregon, hundreds of Reed College students walked out in the middle of his speech. "Oh, for God's sake," he shouted at a determined heckler in Seattle. "Shut up and let the decent people listen!" Shortly afterward, Humphrey tearfully told George Ball that he wanted to run as the candidate of peace rather than the candidate of war.[32]

Ball and others set to work on a speech that would set Humphrey apart, not only from Johnson on the war but also from Nixon and Wallace. Wealthy backers put up the money to pay for a September 30 broadcast from Salt Lake City. In the final version, Humphrey declared that he was prepared to take "an acceptable risk for peace" as president by unilaterally halting U.S. bombing of North Vietnam. "In weighing that risk, and before taking action," his text read, "I would place key importance on evidence—direct or indirect, by word or deed—of Communist willingness to restore the demilitarized zone between South and North Vietnam."[33]

When Humphrey informed Johnson of the speech, LBJ replied, "I gather you're not asking my advice." Johnson also brushed aside Humphrey's assurances that the speech would not depart significantly from administration policy. After more of the same, Johnson cut the conversation short: "Well, you're going to give the speech anyway. Thanks for calling, Hubert."[34]

Consistent with Johnson's expectations, Humphrey aides played the speech up as his declaration of independence. Humphrey's podium no longer bore the vice-presidential seal, and he angered Johnson further by relaxing his already loose terms for a bombing halt.[35]

Years later, Johnson looked back on the Salt Lake City speech as the event that decided Humphrey's defeat. According to Johnson, the government of South Vietnam interpreted the vice president's language as an official change of administration policy rather than as the act of a desperate candidate. Saigon officials lost faith in the administration's commitment, and this lack of trust explained their refusal to participate in the peace talks that Johnson announced only days before the presidential election. LBJ concluded that Humphrey would have won had he kept faith with administration policy.[36]

The desideratum in Johnson's account was his refusal to acknowledge just how Humphrey was able to close the gap enough to come within striking distance of defeating Nixon. It seems unlikely that Humphrey could have caught up with Nixon had he not publicly broken with administration policy. Whatever the impact of the Salt Lake City speech on the South Vietnamese government, it marked the start of Humphrey's comeback in the polls. Moreover, organized disruptions of his campaign events ended soon after the speech.[37]

Still, Humphrey owed his comeback to more than just the Salt Lake City speech. He gained ground not because of a falloff in Nixon support, which remained remarkably stable at about 43 percent, but because of the decline in Wallace support. Two developments that undermined Wallace likely boosted Humphrey in the polls.

The first development occurred only four days after the Salt Lake City speech, when Wallace called a press conference to show off his choice of a running mate, retired air force general Curtis LeMay. Acclaimed in World War II for masterminding the air raids that devastated Tokyo and other Japanese cities, LeMay figured importantly in the creation of an air force deterrent to the Soviets. His fierce anticommunism and willingness to fight a nuclear war against the Russians came out during the Cuban missile crisis. To liberals, LeMay became the real-life equivalent of the mad general in the film *Dr. Strangelove*, a black comedy about nuclear annihilation.

Hardly unaware of LeMay's reputation, Wallace probably picked him to symbolize a tough approach to national defense. Still, Wallace wanted LeMay to duck questions about possible uses of nuclear weapons. Briefed by Wallace aides before the press conference, LeMay nonetheless took the bait as soon as it was dangled. As a discomfited Wallace looked on, LeMay spoke about using whatever weapons were necessary to assure national survival. He also maintained that the effects of nuclear fallout were more benign than commonly understood.[38] Ignoring Wallace's effort to minimize the impact of LeMay's language, reporters rushed to file their stories. An avalanche of bad press fell on the Wallace-LeMay campaign.[39]

Wallace also lost support in Michigan and other industrial states of the North because of a massive effort by organized labor to paint him as no friend of the worker.[40] Although labor's drive had gone on for some time, it likely enhanced the negative impact of LeMay's press conference on white, working-class Democrats in must-win states for Humphrey.

In any case, antiwar Democrats began declaring for Humphrey, although McCarthy held back until the eleventh hour.[41] Even Johnson stumped on Humphrey's behalf, and he likely made the difference in Texas.[42] Johnson also pulled an "October surprise" meant to help Humphrey by misleadingly declaring that a new round of peace talks would soon start in Paris. To increase the chances of peace, Johnson also ordered a halt in the bombing of North Vietnam. "I've been hoping for months that it would happen," an ebullient Humphrey exclaimed.[43]

Nixon, Johnson, and the War

Like Humphrey, Nixon had known Johnson since their time together in Congress. Nixon attracted more notice in the House, but Johnson cut a much bigger swath in the Senate.[44] Nixon made an enemy of Johnson in 1950 by defeating his good friend and likely mistress in the race for California's open Senate seat.[45] And as Eisenhower's vice president, Nixon clashed with Johnson over the 1957 civil rights bill.[46] LBJ blasted Nixon when he ran with Kennedy in 1960. Six years later, Nixon repeatedly criticized Johnson's conduct of the Vietnam War as he crossed the nation on behalf of Republican congressional candidates. He also took aim at LBJ's "credibility gap."[47] Johnson unintentionally aided Nixon's presidential aspirations by blaming Democratic losses on the efforts of Nixon, the "chronic campaigner."[48]

Still, in 1968, Nixon saw an opportunity to exploit Johnson's disdain for Humphrey's fecklessness on the war. As Clark Clifford later wrote, Nixon proved far more adept than Humphrey in "the insider game of dealing with Lyndon Johnson."[49] The opening gambit likely occurred when Nixon, then a candidate for the Republican nomination, attended a national security briefing at the White House. Meeting privately with Johnson after the formal session, Nixon expressed support for the president's policy of continuing to bomb North Vietnam until Hanoi accepted his conditions for a pause.[50] The next move occurred when Nixon stopped off at the LBJ ranch right after the Republican convention for friendly banter and a good meal.[51] Nixon also got Johnson's attention when he showed up in Chicago only days after the Democratic convention. Although critical of Humphrey, he pointedly refused to criticize Johnson's war policy.

Nixon stepped up the courtship on September 8 by dispatching evangelist Billy Graham with a personal message for Johnson. While LBJ listened appreciatively, Graham read aloud from Nixon's statement. It praised Johnson as "the hardest working and most dedicated president in 140 years," promised to give Johnson full credit when the Vietnam conflict ended, and pledged to acknowledge Johnson's greatness for posterity. Although "administration mistakes" would be mentioned during the campaign, no personal attacks on Johnson would be allowed. Johnson reportedly enjoyed the letter so much that he asked for a second reading. Graham returned with Johnson's reply: "I intend to loyally support Mr. Humphrey, but if Mr. Nixon becomes the president-elect, I will do all in my power to cooperate with him."[52]

It appears that neither man deceived nor trusted the other, even though both went to considerable lengths to honor their nonaggression pact.[53] Nixon tipped his hand when speechwriter William Safire questioned his instructions to go easy on LBJ: "Look," Nixon said while holding up his right thumb and forefinger, "I don't want to give LBJ this much—not this much reason to help Humphrey toward the end."[54] Johnson's press secretary, George Christian, hinted at Johnson's position when telling reporters that he would respond to Nixon criticism of the administration only when "thoroughly aroused."[55]

Still, Nixon never dismissed the possibility that Johnson might make some "eleventh-hour masterstroke" on the war to help Humphrey. Accordingly, the Nixon team sought insider information from Henry Kissinger, on loan to Johnson from Nelson Rockefeller to help out in the Paris negotiations with the North Vietnamese. Via Kissinger and perhaps others, Nixon regularly received updates about happenings in Paris. One such report alerted him to the possibility that Johnson might stop the bombing of North Vietnam before election day—even if Hanoi refused to budge on his conditions.[56]

On October 16, Johnson called Nixon (as well as Humphrey and Wallace) to say that he was about to stop the bombing if Hanoi properly reciprocated.[57] Nixon endorsed the Johnson proposal on condition that it would not increase the risk to U.S. forces or reduce the chances of obtaining peace with honor.[58] Hours later, Nixon used up some of his speaking time at the twenty-third annual dinner of the Alfred E. Smith Memorial Foundation to praise Johnson's commitment to peace.[59] However, Hanoi rejected Johnson's conditions, and the bombing continued.

Another source in the Johnson administration, recruited by Bryce Harlow and later described by Nixon as "impeccable," reported that Johnson was desperate to end the bombing before election day.[60] When Kissinger could not confirm this claim, Nixon asked Senator Everett Dirksen to raise the issue with Johnson on his behalf. Johnson led Dirksen to believe that there would be no bombing halt unless

Hanoi met his conditions. Dirksen passed this assurance on to Nixon, adding that he took Johnson at his word.[61] Meanwhile, the "impeccable source" informed Nixon that a deal to end the bombing already had been struck.

His fear of an October surprise seemingly confirmed, Nixon moved to lessen its impact on the election.[62] On October 26, he issued a statement that Safire described as "a shot across Johnson's bow—a message couched in pious, I-just-can't-believe-it terms, that he had better not pull any fast ones on the weekend before the election."[63] Over the preceding thirty-six hours, Nixon revealed, "I have been advised of a flurry of meetings in the White House and elsewhere on Vietnam. I am told that top officials in the administration have been driving very hard for an agreement on a bombing halt, accompanied by a cease-fire, in the immediate future. I have since learned that these reports are true." And in a transparent effort to say the very opposite of what he really meant, Nixon expressed doubt that Johnson personally would take part in such a "cynical, last-minute attempt" to help Humphrey.[64]

Johnson quickly hit back in a New York City speech. Charging that Nixon had lodged "ugly and unfair charges" unhelpful to the cause of peace, the president heaped scorn on Nixon's history of losing elections. Neil Sheehan of the *Times* wrote that Johnson had "abandoned the restraint he had shown earlier toward Mr. Nixon."[65]

Hours later, Hanoi agreed to take part in a new round of talks if the United States not only halted the bombing but also accepted the Viet Cong as a participant in the talks as Saigon's equal. Johnson immediately recalled the U.S. commander in South Vietnam to Washington to discuss Hanoi's terms.

In Saigon, however, President Nguyen Van Thieu wanted neither a bombing halt nor talks that accorded equal status to the Viet Cong. Opposition to Johnson's plan also ran high in the national assembly.

The White House had good reason to suspect that a Nixon agent had stiffened Thieu's opposition to Johnson's proposal. The emissary in question was Anna Chan Chennault, the Chinese widow of World War II general Claire Chennault. Madame Chennault had become a staunch Republican as well as an American citizen, and her position as a columnist for a Chinese-language newspaper provided the perfect cover for frequent visits to Saigon. When in town, she frequently met with high officials in the South Vietnamese government, including Thieu. Likewise, when in Washington, she regularly communicated with Bui Diem, South Vietnam's ambassador. Johnson's inner circle knew all about these contacts because of intercepts of Diem's diplomatic cables, taps on Chennault's phones, and surveillance of Chennault herself. Because of the telephone taps, Johnson knew that Chennault often spoke with John Mitchell, Nixon's campaign manager. Adding up what they had, Clifford and other White House aides concluded that Nixon was subverting Johnson's peace initiative through a chain of communications that began with Mitchell and ended with Thieu, with Chennault acting as the go-between. In short, they believed that Nixon was urging Thieu to hold off for a better deal after the election.[66]

Clark Clifford, an insider in Democratic administrations since Truman and one of those privy to the information on Chennault's activities, later wrote of the "extraordinary dilemma" facing the White House:

> On the one hand, we had positive evidence that the Little Flower [Chennault] and other people speaking for the Republican candidate were encouraging President Thieu to delay the negotiations for political reasons. On the other, the information had been derived from extremely sensitive intelligence-gathering operations of the FBI, the CIA, and the National Security Agency; these included surveillance of the Ambassador of our ally, and an American citizen with strong political ties to the Republicans.[67]

After much discussion, Johnson decided against accusing Nixon of subverting the peace process.[68]

But he did make his move to help Humphrey. On October 31, Johnson announced an end to the bombing and the beginning of new talks in Paris. Nixon, Humphrey, and Wallace learned of this speech only two hours before its delivery. Nixon recalled that Johnson "had just dropped a pretty good bomb in the middle of my campaign." Nonetheless, Nixon pledged that neither he nor his running mate, Spiro Agnew, would say anything "that might destroy the chance to have peace."[69]

Still, as the White House knew only too well, Saigon had not assented to Johnson's plan. The fact that LBJ announced the bombing halt and new talks anyway lent credibility to Nixon's fear of an October surprise. Indeed, a call that Johnson made to Humphrey aide James Rowe corroborated this interpretation. "Tell Hubert we've got a problem," Johnson informed Rowe just four days before the election. "I'm not going to work out this Vietnam peace negotiation early enough to help him."[70] The next day, Saigon formally refused to take part in the new talks. Nixon seized the moment to declare that the prospect of peace was "not as bright as we would have hoped a few days ago."[71] He then planted a story with the wire services that Johnson had rushed to declare a bombing halt in order to help Humphrey. The United Press reported this charge, naming Nixon aide Robert Finch as the source.[72]

Enraged, Johnson told Dirksen that he had known all along about the Chennault channel and Nixon's part in it. Dirksen, in turn, warned Nixon that Johnson might publicly accuse him of subverting the peace effort. Nixon quickly reached Johnson at home in Texas and, by his own account, lied when denying that Finch had spoken for him. According to some, Nixon also insisted that Madame Chennault had not acted on his behalf.[73]

At long last, Johnson passed the Chennault file to Humphrey. After much discussion with top advisers, Humphrey decided against going public. Reportedly, Johnson had expected him to expose Nixon, but Humphrey dared not reveal how he had come by such information. He also doubted that evidence against Nixon was conclusive.[74] By one account, Humphrey threatened to expose both Madame Chennault and Ambassador Diem unless Saigon immediately embraced the Paris talks.[75] If actually made, Humphrey's threats had no discernible effect.

THE 1968 ATTACK SCORES AND TARGETS

We now take up the question of whether the Skaperdas-Grofman models made sense of the negativity exhibited by each side in this complex race. According to these models, Nixon should have attacked Humphrey less frequently than Humphrey assailed Nixon. To act in accordance with Skaperdas and Grofman's definition of a spoiler, Wallace should have ignored both rivals and waged an entirely positive campaign. Similarly, Nixon and Humphrey should have paid no attention to Wallace. And, consistent with the three-candidate model, both Humphrey and Wallace should have directed their attacks at Nixon rather than at each other. In fact, Wallace attacked both of his rivals in a remarkably evenhanded fashion.

Our findings jibe with much that has been written about Wallace's 1968 bid for the White House. Several accounts agree that Wallace ran not to win the presidency for himself or to spoil a rival's chances but to prevent both rivals from carrying enough states to garner a majority of electoral votes. To pull off this feat, he needed to carry the South and an industrial state or two in the North. If that stratagem worked, he meant to trade the electoral votes pledged to him for major concessions from Nixon or Humphrey. Whoever conceded the most would pick up enough electors from Wallace to become president. The transaction would happen after the popular vote on November 5 and before the presidential electors balloted in mid-December. To this end, Wallace exacted a sworn pledge from each of his electors to vote according to his instructions.[76] He made no secret of what he wanted from the next president: ending the enforcement of certain civil rights laws, nominating states' rights advocates to the federal courts, making a good-faith effort to return basic powers to the states, and terminating foreign aid to countries unfriendly to the United States.[77]

Wallace posed far too great a threat for either rival to ignore him. Unlikely to win in any southern state except Lyndon Johnson's Texas, Humphrey had to compensate by carrying big industrial states in the North, where white ethnics and union members traditionally voted Democratic. Wallace, however, appeared to be winning the hearts and minds of such voters in Michigan and other must-win states.

At the same time, Wallace's strength in the South ran afoul of Nixon's southern strategy. Expecting a close race, Nixon deduced that disgruntled Democrats would supply most of Wallace's vote. However, when Republican polls omitted Wallace from the vote-choice question, Nixon beat Humphrey more than two to one among Wallace supporters, especially in the South. Nixon accordingly set out to suppress the Wallace vote as much as possible by playing the wasted-vote card. Especially in Florida, North Carolina, Tennessee, Kentucky, and Virginia, the major Republican argument against Wallace became "don't waste your vote."[78]

Table 4.2 points up several findings contrary to the spirit, if not the letter, of the Skaperdas-Grofman models. Despite Humphrey's underdog standing, the Republicans outattacked the Democrats in seven of the nine weeks of fall electioneering, and over the entire fall campaign, Republican negativity surpassed Democratic negativity by 44 to 42 percent. Moreover, Republican negativity was at its highest level when Humphrey's poll standings were at their lowest—in weeks two and four *before* the Salt Lake City speech.[79] Far from ignoring Wallace, both of the major parties dedicated a significant proportion of their campaign statements to bashing Wallace and LeMay. Such attacks peaked in weeks five and six, no doubt inspired by LeMay's discourse on nuclear weapons, and they fell off as Wallace sank in the polls.

One cannot take the full measure of negative campaigning in 1968 without combining the attack propensities that each side exhibited against both of its rivals. By adding attacks on Wallace-LeMay to those scored against the Republicans, we found that Democratic negativity rose to 57 percent. Similarly, the Republicans' propensity to attack climbed to 54 percent when attacks on Wallace-LeMay were included, and Wallace-LeMay negativity against both parties totaled 41 percent (see Table 4.3). The combined measure of Democratic negativity exceeded 60 percent in four of the nine weeks; Republican negativity reached or surpassed 60 percent only twice. The weekly scores for Wallace-LeMay ranged from a low of 23 percent to a high of 72 percent.

Turning to targets of negative campaigning, we found that Democrats went after Nixon more frequently than Republicans took aim at Humphrey (see Table 4.4). Nixon showed up as a target in 89 percent of all Democratic attacks directed against Republicans, in 94 percent of Humphrey's attacks on the GOP, and in twenty-five of twenty-six such attacks by Muskie. Conversely, Humphrey figured as a target in 69 percent of all Republican attacks on Democrats, in 66 percent of Nixon's attacks, and in two-thirds of those unleashed by Agnew. Wallace and LeMay bore the brunt of nearly all the attacks aimed at their ticket, a finding wholly consistent with the fact that the AIP amounted to little more than a front for Wallace's ambitions.[80] Wallace personally targeted Nixon more than Humphrey.

Table 4.2. Attack Propensities, 1968

Week	Democratic Attacks on Republicans	Democratic Attacks on Wallace	Republican Attacks on Democrats	Republican Attacks on Wallace	Wallace Attacks on Democrats	Wallace Attacks on Republicans
1	.196	.043	.378	.075	.364	.227
2	.494	.148	.507	.027	333	.389
3	.470	.200	.400	.017	.250	.250
4	.453	.116	.500	.096	.176	.058
5	.294	.255	.378	.222	.095	.143
6	.411	.242	.415	.245	.125	.167
7	.351	.170	.487	.066	.269	.115
8	.333	.125	.404	.064	.273	.212
9	.576	.056	.489	.064	.143	.200
Overall	.417	.153	.440	.096	.215	.193

Notes: Total statement N's are 844 for Democrats, 647 for Republicans, and 228 for Wallace-AIP. Negativity scores for each party reflect percentage of its campaign statements that contained attacks on the other party. Week 1 began on Sept. 2 and ended Sept. 8; week 2, Sept. 9–15; week 3, Sept. 16–22; week 4, Sept. 23–29; week 5, Sept. 30–Oct. 6; week 6, Oct. 17–13; week 7, Oct. 14–20; week 8, Oct. 21–27; week 9, Oct. 28–Nov. 5.

Table 4.3. Total Negativity of 1968 Campaigns

Week	Democratic	Republican	AIP
1	.239	.453	.591
2	.642	.534	.722
3	.670	.417	.500
4	.569	.596	.234
5	.549	.600	.238
6	.653	.660	.292
7	.521	.553	.384
8	.458	.468	.485
9	.632	.553	.343
Overall	.570	.536	.408

Note: Democratic total negativity = attacks on Republicans + attacks on Wallace-LeMay; Republican total negativity = attacks on Democrats + attacks on Wallace-LeMay; Wallace-LeMay total negativity = attacks on Democrats + attacks on Republicans.

LEADING TOPICS IN 1968

Table 4.5 shows that convergence clearly trumped avoidance in topics most emphasized by each side. All three tickets stressed military and defense issues more than any other. They also allocated considerable time to race and crime concerns. Indeed, had we coded race and crime issues under a single heading, that topic would have risen to the top of the Democratic and AIP agendas. Each side also played up leadership and ideological themes. Republicans put major emphasis on

Table 4.4. Targeting of 1968 Attacks

	Democratic Targeting of Republicans	Republican Targeting of Democrats	Democratic Targeting of Wallace Party	Republican Targeting of Wallace Party	Wallace Party Targeting of Democrats	Wallace Party Targeting of Republicans
All party attacks						
Presidential nominee	312	196	120	57	18	26
Other targets	40	89	9	5	31	18
N attacks	352	285	129	62	49	44
Nominee targeted	.886	.688	.930	.919	.367	.591
Solo attacks of presidential nominee	Humphrey	Nixon	Humphrey	Nixon	Wallace	Wallace
Presidential nominee	163	90	50	16	12	20
Other targets	10	46	3	1	21	14
N attacks	173	136	53	17	33	34
Nominee targeted	.942	.662	.943	.941	.364	.588
Solo attacks of vice-presidential nominee	Muskie	Agnew	Muskie	Agnew	LeMay	LeMay
Presidential nominee	42	43	26	10	2	4
Other targets	1	21	0	3	3	0
N attacks	43	64	26	13	5	4
Nominee targeted	.977	.672	1.00	.769	.400	1.00

Note: Some attacks on presidential candidates also targeted others of the same party.

eight of the ten topics also given top priority by Democratic campaigners. Wallace and LeMay emphasized six of the ten topics most emphasized by the Democrats and Republicans. Table 4.5 also highlights the topics emphasized only by one side. Democrats understandably dwelled on labor issues, as well as Nixon's unwillingness to debate Humphrey;[81] Wallace played on regional pride and called for putting states' rights conservatives on the federal courts.

Most of these topics reappeared as prime subjects of attack statements (see Table 4.6). Race particularly mattered in that riotous year, and Democrats sometimes tarred Nixon and Wallace with the same brush. Humphrey accused Nixon of "openly competing" with Wallace for the racist vote.[82] Likewise, Lawrence O'Brien charged that Nixon exploited fear, hatred, and bigotry no less than Wallace.[83] On other occasions, such attacks fell only on Wallace.[84] Democrats also made much of Wallace's treatment of unions while he was governor of Alabama.

Republicans placed most emphasis on national defense, crime, and leadership qualities when going after the Democrats. Agnew also ignited a contretemps over patriotism by calling Humphrey "soft" on communism.[85] Consistent with Nixon's memoir, Republicans used the wasted-vote argument against Wallace more than any other line of attack. Especially in Florida, North Carolina, and Michigan, Nixon urged Wallace supporters not to perpetuate four more years of misguided policies by throwing away their votes "on a third-party fling."[86] Agnew took a similar line: "The candidacy of George Wallace is Hubert Humphrey's last best hope of squeaking through this election to become a minority president."[87] Wallace countered the wasted-vote argument by accusing both parties of not facing up to real problems.[88] Most of his attacks pertaining to the war and other defense issues fell on the Democrats. On crime, leadership, race, and composition of the federal judiciary, however, he attacked both parties.

Table 4.5. Leading Topics of 1968

Democrats	Republicans	AIP
Military/defense (164)	Military/defense (133)	Military/defense (44)
Leadership (107)	Leadership (78)	Crime (35)
Campaign (96)	Crime (74)	Race (22)
Race (89)	Campaign (45)	Campaign (24)
Crime (73)	Patriotism (41)	Ideology/party (24)
Ideology/party (59)	Race (34)	Leadership (13)
Domestic economy (43)	Domestic economy (34)	Patriotism (12)
Social/health programs (33)	Social/health programs (31)	Regional bias (9)
Debates (26)	Foreign policy (24)	Federal judiciary (7)
Labor (21)	Ideology/party (21)	Foreign policy (7)

Note: The ten topics most emphasized by Democrats accounted for 84 percent of all Democratic statements; the corresponding figures for the Republicans and AIP were 80 and 86 percent, respectively.

Table 4.6. Leading Attack Topics of 1968

Democrats Targeting Republicans	Republicans Targeting Democrats	Democrats Targeting AIP	Republicans Targeting AIP	AIP Targeting Democrats	AIP Targeting Republicans
Leadership (62)	Military/defense (67)	Race (24)	Wasted vote (16)	Military/defense (8)	Ideology/party (6)
Military/defense (52)	Crime (38)	Crime (23)	Leadership (14)	Crime (7)	Crime (5)
Race (40)	Leadership (37)	Dirty campaign (15)	Military/defense (10)	Leadership (6)	Regional bias (5)
Crime (28)	Domestic economy (28)	Labor (14)	Race (7)	Ideology/party (5)	Leadership (5)
Domestic economy (26)	Social/health programs (20)	Military/defense (12)	Ideology/party (5)	Race (3)	Race (4)
Ideology/party (21)	Patriotism (19)	Ideology/party (11)	Crime (3)	Regional bias (2)	Military/defense (4)
Debates (19)	Residual domestic (12)	Leadership (10)	Patriotism (2)	Federal judiciary (1)	Federal judiciary (1)
Social/health programs (17)	Debates (8)	Domestic economy (6)	Personal (2)	Farm policy (1)	Farm policy (1)
Education (12)	Ideology/party (8)	Wasted vote (3)	Residual domestic (1)	Residual domestic (1)	Residual domestic (1)
Personal (11)	Foreign policy (8)	Personal (3)	Dirty campaign (1)	Personal (1)	Personal (1)

Note: Top-ten Democratic topics accounted for 82 percent of all Democratic attacks against Republican targets, as well as 94 percent of all Democratic attacks against the AIP; Republican topics accounted for 86 percent of all Republican attacks on the Democrats and 98 percent of attacks on the AIP. The AIP topics listed above accounted for 77 percent of all attacks against the Democrats and 75 percent against the Republicans.

THE 1968 ATTACK METHODS

Fear arousal and labeling showed up as the methods most frequently employed by each side in 1968 (see Table 4.7). Nearly two-thirds of Nixon's attacks against the Democrats projected a dim future if Humphrey won, and he resorted to labeling in a similar portion of his attacks on Wallace-LeMay. Agnew was especially prone to label the opposition, using his branding iron in 73 percent of his attacks on the Democrats and in 85 percent of attacks on Wallace-LeMay. The major parties invoked apposition when assailing each other but not when going after Wallace and LeMay. Wallace used the charge of lying more against Republicans than against Democrats.

Little more than a trace of humor showed up in the attacks exchanged between campaigns in 1968. Among the nominees for vice president, only Agnew made much use of ridicule (and then mostly against the Democrats). However, one Nixon ally, Senator Strom Thurmond of South Carolina, took obvious delight in playing up Humphrey's penchant for verbosity. In Lake Charles, Louisiana, and doubtless other venues, he regaled audiences with the following analogy: "I live down near the Savannah River in South Carolina, and there used to be a steamboat that ran up and down that river. It had such a small boiler that, when they blew the whistle, the paddle wheel would stop. And when the paddle wheel turned, the whistle couldn't blow. You know Hubert Humphrey. When he talks, he stops thinking, and when he's thinking, he can't talk. But he talks just about all the time."[89]

ECHOES FROM THE 1968 CAMPAIGN TRAIL

Democrats Attacking Republicans on Vietnam and Other Defense Issues

Of the fifty-two defense-related attacks launched by Democrats against Republicans, a mere twenty pertained to Vietnam. More than half of these occurred in the last two weeks of the campaign. Neither finding is surprising in view of the Soviet invasion of Czechoslovakia on September 1, as well as Humphrey's difficulty in taking a stand on Vietnam.

It follows that most of the case on national defense that Democrats made against Republicans focused on two issues not directly linked to the conflict in Southeast Asia. The first pertained to Nixon's reputation as an unyielding anti-Communist. Humphrey initiated this line of attack only days after the Chicago convention by arguing that Nixon could not achieve détente with the Soviets.[90] The second issue pertained to an arms-control treaty with the Soviets that had bogged down in the Senate. Johnson and Humphrey sought a Senate vote before the election, whereas Nixon urged delay because of the Kremlin's crackdown on

Table 4.7. Attack Methods, 1968

	Presidential Candidate (solo)	Vice-Presidential Candidate (solo)	All Attackers
Democrats targeting Republicans			
Fear arousal	.405	.256	.366
Ridicule	.064	.047	.054
Labeling	.549	.372	.514
Apposition	.318	.326	.270
Dishonesty	.231	.302	.216
Republicans targeting Democrats			
Fear arousal	.662	.531	.544
Ridicule	.066	.125	.070
Labeling	.419	.734	.540
Apposition	.397	.313	.337
Dishonesty	.176	.156	.218
Democrats targeting AIP			
Fear arousal	.509	.615	.597
Ridicule	.038	.000	.016
Labeling	.585	.538	.612
Apposition	.189	.308	.186
Dishonesty	.094	.000	.078
Republicans targeting AIP			
Fear arousal	.353	.462	.500
Ridicule	.000	.077	.016
Labeling	.647	.846	.645
Apposition	.118	.077	.065
Dishonesty	.000	.000	.000
AIP targeting Democrats			
Fear arousal	.515	.600	.408
Ridicule	.000	.000	.000
Labeling	.455	.600	.469
Apposition	.061	.400	.122
Dishonesty	.152	.000	.143
AIP targeting Republicans			
Fear arousal	.500	.250	.455
Ridicule	.059	.000	.045
Labeling	.441	1.00	.477
Apposition	.088	.250	.091
Dishonesty	.265	.000	.250

Czechoslovakia. Johnson took aim at Nixon and Senate Republicans: "So I warn those who postpone and procrastinate or delay this treaty. They will live to regret the day when they threw overboard everything that America has worked so long and so hard to try to achieve."[91] Humphrey latched on to this issue hoping to improve his standing with the doves.[92] Both issues surfaced in his attacks on Nixon throughout the campaign. On October 27, for example, he accused Nixon of not knowing "how to come to grips with the problem of arms control and the Cold War."[93]

For reasons already related, Humphrey struggled to find his footing on Vietnam before the Salt Lake City speech.[94] By mid-September, he and Muskie had hit upon a share-the-blame argument that made Nixon out as no less responsible for the quagmire in Vietnam than Johnson. Provoked by Nixon's condemnation of the administration's "past mistakes" in Vietnam, Muskie maintained that the most basic of mistakes had been made by the "Eisenhower-Nixon administration" in 1954. The Republicans, Muskie charged, had prevented South Vietnam from holding free elections.[95] Similarly, Humphrey devoted a part of his Salt Lake City speech to Nixon's 1954 advice as vice president to President Eisenhower on the possibility of sending U.S. troops to help the French in Indochina: "He advocated American armed intervention in Vietnam in aid of French colonialism. It was necessary for President Eisenhower to repudiate his proposal. Since then, he has taken a line on Vietnam policy, which I believe could lead to greater escalation of the war."[96]

Humphrey came up with another line of attack by way of response to the demonstrators and hecklers who tormented him at most campaign events: "I am a more likely peacemaker than Nixon."[97] George Ball sounded this note on September 26, telling reporters that the war would end shortly after Humphrey's election. "I have no idea of what Nixon would do," he added.[98] The next day, Ball predicted that Nixon would escalate the war if elected.[99]

Republican talk of a "secret plan" to end the war gave Humphrey another opening to blast Nixon. "If he has such a plan," Humphrey said in his Salt Lake City speech, "he has an obligation to so inform President Johnson and the American people. A few days ago the Republican vice-presidential nominee said there is not now and never has been a Nixon-Agnew plan for peace in Vietnam. It was, he said, a ploy to 'maintain suspense.' And then he said: 'Isn't that the way campaigns are run?' I think we need some answers about this from Mr. Nixon."[100]

Humphrey also insinuated that Nixon shared LeMay's delusions about nuclear war: "Mr. Nixon's statements on the same subject give grave cause for doubt among the American people."[101] (In fact, Nixon had condemned LeMay's remarks as dangerous and irresponsible.)

The frequency of Vietnam-related attacks on Republicans rose dramatically in the final two weeks of the race. When Nixon released his statement of October 26 that so provoked Johnson, Humphrey accused him of undercutting Johnson's position on the bombing halt and of spreading "an unfounded rumor" about attempts to help the Democratic ticket.[102] Humphrey also saw through the Finch gambit: "This seems to be a rather carefully constructed Nixon tactic," he opined, "which gives Mr. Nixon the chance to always knock down the rumor in case that it proves to be totally unfounded, which is the case in this instance once again."[103] Humphrey also pioneered the tactic of "rapid response." While appearing live on ABC, he learned Nixon on NBC had just claimed that Communist supplies were flowing down the Ho Chi Minh Trail unimpeded by American bombers. Humphrey immediately exclaimed:

> Now Mr. Nixon. I think you know very well that the president's order to stop the bombing of the North did not include the Ho Chi Minh Trail. The entire Ho Chi Minh Trail is subject to intensive American airpower as it has been in the past and is even more so now. To frighten the American people at this time, when delicate negotiations are underway, I think is a rather irresponsible act. What you and I should be doing is asking the government of South Vietnam to attend that peace conference in Paris.[104]

During his final day of campaigning, Humphrey removed any lingering doubt that he would abandon Saigon if necessary to end the U.S. presence in Vietnam. The Paris negotiations, he insisted, had to proceed without the South Vietnamese:

> The foreign policy of the United States and the fate of young Americans in Vietnam should and will be determined by the United States and not by any foreign government. That policy and those young Americans should not be placed at the mercy of domestic political considerations in another country.[105]

Republicans Attacking Democrats on Vietnam and Other Defense Issues

Of the sixty-seven defense-related attacks that the Republicans unleashed against the Democrats, forty-two, or 62 percent, pertained to Vietnam. (Other issues included the Democratic response to Soviet intervention in Czechoslovakia, the nuclear nonproliferation treaty, arms control in general, North Korea's seizure of the USS *Pueblo*, aid to Israel to offset Soviet backing of Arab nations, Cuba, and a naval buildup.) Republicans outattacked the Democrats on Vietnam, and the frequency of these attacks surged after the Salt Lake City speech. Only in week eight did Democratic attacks on defense exceed those of the Republicans.

More or less true to his word, Nixon avoided singling out LBJ when attacking Democrats on the war. Even before the first round of peace talks began in May 1968, he scrapped a major speech on Vietnam and vowed to say nothing specific for the rest of the campaign about how best to end the conflict.[106] But he did not rule out criticizing the administration's "past mistakes." By one account, Nixon turned the multiple facets of public opinion on the war to his advantage by "proposing politically appealing courses of action to particular portions of the electorate."[107] He spoke of ending the war, conducting negotiations, and withdrawing American forces while at the same time advocating continual pressure on the enemy and remaining true to South Vietnam. Only a new administration not linked to the mistakes of the past, he tirelessly maintained, could bring a successful end to the conflict.[108]

Nixon's careful handling of Johnson left him ample latitude to attack Humphrey, especially when Humphrey deviated from administration policy. Thus, when Humphrey called on Nixon to join him in a bipartisan pledge not to jeopardize the Paris negotiations, Nixon accused him of not keeping faith with Johnson's envoys. Robert Ellsworth, Nixon's national political director, leveled this charge, accusing Humphrey of undermining the American negotiating team in Paris. Ellsworth also recalled Humphrey's reluctance to embrace the administration plank at the Democratic convention.[109]

Humphrey's early blunders over troop withdrawals and the platform inspired a fusillade of Republican attacks. Agnew led off, characterizing the Democratic contender as "pretty malleable" when trying to appease antiwar Democrats willing to end U.S. participation in the war "at any cost."[110] Agnew soon had more to say, accusing Humphrey of creating "false hopes for American mothers" in his desperation to placate the doves.[111] Nixon surrogates pointed up Humphrey's advocacy of unilateral troop withdrawals and bombing pauses.[112] Representative Melvin Laird of Wisconsin lambasted "a flailing Humphrey" for misrepresenting troop rotations as withdrawals.[113] And Humphrey gave Republicans yet another opening when he talked about reducing the number of U.S. combat troops in Vietnam before the end of 1969, regardless of what resulted from the Paris talks. Nixon quickly contrasted his view with his opponent's: "I don't want to pull the rug out from under our negotiators in Paris." He also suggested that Humphrey had signaled to the enemy "that they don't really have to negotiate now."[114]

The Salt Lake City speech set off a Republican offensive, starting with a Nixon press conference the following morning. Nixon called on Humphrey to clarify his stand in view of divergent reports about whether he had broken with Johnson. Humphrey could not call for a bombing halt and claim to support American negotiators at the same time. Characterizing a bombing halt as the "trump card" in a highly complex game, Nixon said that Humphrey had tipped his hand too soon.[115] Agnew accused Humphrey of being disloyal to Johnson and of aiding the enemy.[116] Led by Dirksen, Republican solons assailed Humphrey for two hours on the Senate floor.[117] Nixon struck again on October 23. "In this terribly important function of keeping the peace," he intoned, "you must remember that when there is miscalculation, when a potential enemy is not sure of what you stand for—that's when the danger of war escalates." He continued this line of attack into the next week, at one point chiding Humphrey for "ceaselessly chattering" about peace as if it could be easily obtained.[118]

On October 27, the GOP aired a soundless attack ad on television that juxtaposed images of a grinning and laughing Humphrey with scenes of carnage in Vietnam, urban rioting at home, and malnourished children. The Nixon camp pulled the ad after two days of adverse public reaction.[119]

Although Nixon held back when Johnson announced the bombing halt on October 31, key Republicans in Congress immediately questioned the president's motives. Senator Bourke B. Hickenlooper of Iowa, the ranking Republican on the Foreign Relations Committee, spoke of playing games with American lives. Senator John Tower of Texas wrongly called the bombing halt "unconditional." House Minority Leader Gerald Ford suggested that Johnson had acted to help Humphrey.[120]

With election day only forty-eight hours away, the *Times* took note of "thinly veiled" suggestions that the bombing halt "had been motivated by a desire to influence the election." These insinuations, correspondent Warren Weaver wrote, had "moved a step closer to open charges" as Nixon campaigned across Texas. Weaver alluded to Finch's statement and repeated a Nixon claim that such a bombing halt would cast doubt on Johnson's credibility as well as jeopardize the military and diplomatic situations in Vietnam.[121]

To the very end, Nixon held true to the strategy of appealing to almost every segment of opinion on the war. In a final address to the voters, he credited Johnson with the "best of intentions" and pledged to help nudge Saigon to the table before Johnson left office. Yet he also spoke of how the "tired men" around Johnson had failed to arrange viable talks. Their failure, he said, had dashed "tremendously high" hopes for peace. The time had come to elect a new team, unite the country, and secure an honorable peace.[122]

Democrats Attacking Wallace-LeMay on Defense

Before the Salt Lake City speech, voters had difficulty in separating the vice president's stand on Vietnam from that of Johnson, Nixon, and Wallace. Moreover, before LeMay's ill-considered remarks of October 3, Humphrey lacked an opening to blast Wallace on national security grounds. The choice of LeMay, however, exposed Wallace to such attacks. Representative Henry Reuss denounced LeMay as a "Neanderthal" who, if elected, would "make the atom bombs fly soon after the election."[123] "Between them," Humphrey intoned, "General LeMay says he would bomb North Vietnam back to the Stone Age and probably start World War III in the process; and George Wallace says he would drive over demonstrators in his car and probably unleash violence and bloodshed at home."[124] Humphrey referred to Wallace and LeMay in subsequent speeches as the "Bombsy Twins."[125] Muskie also chimed in: "Then there's Wallace, whose running mate would not hesitate to use the nuclear bombs. He's said so."[126]

Republicans Attacking Wallace-LeMay on Defense

Republican campaigners also aroused fears about what LeMay might attempt as vice president. Nixon, for one, warned of a catastrophic war, and Agnew spoke of the "single careless incident" that could turn "this nation and the world into a cinder."[127] Agnew also decried LeMay's "casual, offhand way" of talking about nuclear weapons.[128] Loath to criticize Humphrey and uneasy about Agnew, liberal Republicans such as Jacob Javits and George Romney helped Nixon by assailing Wallace and LeMay.[129]

Wallace and LeMay Attacking Both Parties on Defense

Physical as well as rhetorical violence characterized the typical Wallace rally in 1968. A bantamweight boxer in his youth, Wallace took delight in throwing verbal uppercuts at antiwar protestors, liberal academics, federal bureaucrats, rioters, looters, and still others at odds with his vision of America. He also took undisguised pleasure in putting down hecklers. Such incidents generally aroused his supporters. "You better have your say now, I can tell you that," Wallace typically retorted when interrupted by protestors. "After November 5, you anarchists are through in this country." Long-haired youths, including one young man who gave him the finger, felt his lash: "Hey there, sweetie. Oh, excuse me, I thought you were a girl!"[130]

No observer of Wallace's campaign style accused him of accentuating the positive. Yet he scored relatively low on our attack propensity measure because so many of his attacks targeted individuals and groups, such as rioters and antiwar protestors, who were not supportive of either party.

When Wallace did condemn a party's defense policy, he usually targeted the Democrats. On October 18, for example, he recited America's history of fighting wars declared by Democrats. As for the administration's performance on Vietnam, he exclaimed: "We've spent $122 billion of our money, we're about broke, we've got less friends than we've ever had, and we've got Communists running wild in the United States."[131]

LeMay took on the responsibility of attacking both of the opposing tickets on the war. Shortly before undertaking a "fact-finding" mission to South Vietnam, he promised to expose the "no-win" policy that had protracted the conflict and prevented an American victory. Neither Nixon nor Humphrey, he avowed, understood that *victory* was still a word in the English language.[132] Back in the United States, LeMay complained of wasted lives and contended that American pilots had not been permitted to bomb "the right targets."[133] Picking up on rumors of an imminent bombing pause, he spoke of political tricks to keep Wallace out of the White House. The big nightmare of the Communists, he continued, was a vote that rejected Nixon and Humphrey's no-win policy and elected Wallace.[134] Responding to subsequent talk of an October surprise, LeMay warned against giving the enemy time to rebuild his forces and launch future offensives.[135]

THE YEAR 1968 IN SUMMARY

Only one prediction of the Skaperdas-Grofman model held up in our analysis of the 1968 campaign—Humphrey attacked Nixon more frequently than vice versa. Overall, however, Humphrey's side waged the less negative campaign. Numerous developments help account for this discrepancy, the most fundamental of which was the splintering of his party. Hawks spurned him because he wobbled on the war, and doves reviled him as Johnson's tool. Many of the latter returned to the fold after Salt Lake City, but McCarthy and a few other doves in high places held back until the bitter end. Lack of funds early in the contest handicapped Humphrey's ability to hire staff and run TV ads against Nixon. Meanwhile, Wallace cast a pall over prominent southern Democrats none too keen on sharing a platform with Humphrey. And labor invested heavily in attacking Wallace, thereby using up resources that might have been expended against Nixon.

Wallace's behavior bore little resemblance to that of third-ranked candidates in the Skaperdas-Grofman model. Hardly the disinterested spoiler, he attacked Humphrey and the Democrats about as often as he blasted Nixon and the GOP. Further, Wallace adhered to a rational strategy quite different from what the model stipulates for the lowest-ranked candidate in a three-way contest. He attacked both parties evenly in hopes of denying each an electoral-vote majority.

Similarly, we found scant support for the issue-ownership thesis in this comeback contest. For the most part, the tickets engaged one another on the same topics, and this was particularly true of the two major parties. Convergence, not avoidance, dominated the campaign discourse of 1968.

THE STRATEGIC ENVIRONMENT OF 1976

To comprehend the context in which the 1976 campaign played out, one must look back to the circumstances that landed Gerald Ford in the Oval Office. Watergate cast a shadow over his bid to become an elected president. Although unharmed in two assassination attempts, he never recovered from the political wounds incurred by pardoning Nixon. South Vietnam's collapse occurred on Ford's watch, thus bringing America's war in Indochina to an inglorious end. Although expert in the complexities of economic policy and federal budgets,[136] Ford had to contend with an unholy combination of high inflation and high unemployment. These problems and strong opposition from Democratic majorities broke his lance when tilting with Congress. Meanwhile, doubts among Republicans about Ford's conservatism and competence emboldened Ronald Reagan to mount a primary challenge in 1976 that jeopardized Ford's nomination right up to the convention. While Ford grappled with Reagan, Democratic primary voters passed over better-known aspirants such as Senator Henry "Scoop" Jackson of Washington State to settle on Jimmy Carter, a former governor of Georgia and born-again Baptist who was unfamiliar to most of his fellow citizens.

Repercussions of Watergate

Although news of Watergate had not prevented Nixon from winning by a landslide in 1972, this burgeoning scandal eventually drove him from office. Before his departure on August 9, 1974, federal prosecutors negotiated a plea bargain with Vice President Agnew, who resigned in October 1973. Federal authorities had put together a strong case against Agnew on bribery charges, but they let him off with a small fine and no jail time. The principal reason for leniency was to get rid of a corrupt vice president before the House impeached Nixon.[137] Agnew's departure triggered the Twenty-fifth Amendment, which empowered Nixon to appoint a new vice president subject to the approval of both houses of Congress. Although Nixon preferred former Treasury secretary John Connally, he settled on Representative Gerald Ford of Michigan because the latter stood a better chance of winning speedy confirmation.[138] First elected to the House in 1948, Ford had also served on the Warren Commission in 1963 and 1964 before becoming the House Republican leader in 1965. As expected, the nomination sailed through both houses, allowing Ford to take the oath of office on December 6, 1973.[139]

At first, Ford stood up for Nixon against labor and other pro-Democratic groups. But he went too far in January 1974, asserting that Nixon had known nothing about the misdeeds committed on his behalf. Sobered by the public's angry reaction to his remarks, Ford recruited new speechwriters and moderated his tone. Events in July forced Nixon to produce the incriminating tape recordings that sealed his fate. When word of what Nixon had said on the "smoking gun" tape reached him, Ford abandoned the president. Similarly, Nixon's staunchest defenders on the House Judiciary Committee no longer stood in the way of

impeachment proceedings. After hearing from a delegation of Republican senators that he would be convicted in an impeachment trial, Nixon announced that
he would resign the presidency on August 9. After being sworn in as the nation's
thirty-eighth president, Ford hailed the end of a long, national nightmare.[140]

But the nightmare did not end. Rather, it took on new form when Ford uncon-
ditionally pardoned Nixon. Earlier, as Nixon had sunk into a deep melancholy, the
aides who had followed him into exile pleaded for a presidential pardon. Secretary
of State Henry Kissinger and other Nixon holdovers in the Ford administration
added their voices to this call. Alerted to these appeals, the Washington press corps
fastened on the likelihood and legality of a pardon before the issuing of any criminal indictment. To Ford's dismay, questions about a possible pardon dominated
his first press conference as president, leading him to conclude that the best way to
move the country beyond the episode was to pardon Nixon.[141]

At least two presidential advisers argued against this idea. Speechwriter Robert Hartmann warned of a media firestorm should the pardon be issued, and he
correctly predicted that it would take a heavy toll on Ford's public support. Jack
Marsh, Ford's liaison with Congress, urged the president to consult congressional leaders before proceeding further. When Ford rebuffed this suggestion, Marsh
presciently warned that Ford's conversation with Nixon's chief of staff, General Al
Haig, would become an issue. Shortly before Nixon resigned, the pardon issue had
come up when Ford met with Haig to plan for a likely transition. Ford insisted to
Marsh that the discussion had been entirely proper. He also expressed an intense
desire to go ahead with the pardon as soon as possible so that the country could
move beyond Watergate. Unwilling to pry a clear confession of wrongdoing out of
Nixon, Ford issued the pardon on September 8, 1974.[142]

In the overwhelmingly negative reaction that followed Ford's announcement,
irate callers tied up the White House switchboard and angry denunciations filled
the presidential mail. Editorial writers at the *Times* and other leading publications railed against the pardon, and Ford's press secretary abruptly resigned in
protest.[143] Gallup captured the popular reaction when it next asked the presidential approval question. Previously, Ford had received 71 percent job approval, but
the first postpardon poll put him at 50 percent. The same poll showed that disapproval had shot up by twenty-five points.[144]

As Marsh had predicted, Democrats in Congress began insinuating that the
pardon had been Ford's ticket to the Oval Office. Bella Abzug of New York and
fourteen other Democrats in the House introduced two resolutions calling for an
investigation of Ford's motives. William Hungate of Missouri, a prominent figure
in the House Judiciary Committee's hearings on Watergate and a subcommittee
chairman, asked Ford to provide written answers to the questions raised in these
resolutions. Fearing that the Democrats would distort a written response, Ford

surprised the committee by appearing in person. At one particularly testy moment, Representative Elizabeth Holtzman indicated that she doubted Ford's assurance that no corrupt bargain had been struck. Visibly angered, Ford shot back: "There was no deal, period, under no circumstances."[145]

The controversy did not end with Ford's testimony. The pardon proved damaging to the Republican Party in the 1974 midterm elections, hurt Ford in the Republican primaries of 1976, and plagued him again in the fall campaign (see Table 4.8). Watergate and its offshoots also contributed to a loss of public trust in government. The percentage of Americans who claimed to trust the government to do the right thing "always" or "most of the time" had already fallen by twenty-three points between 1964 and 1970. It dropped another seventeen points between 1972 and 1974.[146]

Even before Nixon's landslide victory in 1972, Jimmy Carter had begun building a 1976 candidacy on the theme of restoring trust in government. Three years later and still unknown to the great majority of his fellow citizens,[147] Carter published a slender autobiography that called for presidential leadership based on morality, trust, competence, and adherence to principle.[148] His concluding chapter took aim at the pardon: "Recently we have discovered that our trust has been betrayed. . . . It is obvious that the best way for our leaders to restore their credibility is to be credible, and in order for us to be trusted we must be trustworthy!"[149]

In innumerable encounters with activists and voters during the nominating struggle, Carter called for government "as good and honest and decent and truthful and fair and competent and idealistic and compassionate and as filled with love as are the American people."[150] He also promised never to lie to the American people. Michael Schudson recounted an early contradiction of that promise: "A few days before his nomination, Carter said he would not use Watergate as an issue, but his whole stance of ethical purity made political sense only with a Watergate backdrop." Peter Rodino, chairman of the House Judiciary Committee and a key figure in moving Nixon's impeachment, put Carter's name in nomination. Carter's running mate, Walter Mondale, roused the convention with the line "We have just lived through the worst political scandal in our history and are now led by a president who pardoned the person who did it."[151]

Watergate and Ford's pardon of Nixon persisted as issues for the fall campaign. In September, Carter pounced on news reports that FBI director Clarence Kelley had received unauthorized gifts and assistance on personal matters from bureau employees. For the most part, these accusations melted away under scrutiny—but not before Carter had made a case for Watergate II.[152] He similarly summoned the spirits of Watergate when decrying "the lush green fairways of privilege" that Ford had enjoyed on golf outings financed by corporate interests.[153]

Other allegations against Ford's probity as a congressman also provided

Table 4.8. Public Reaction to Nixon Pardon

"Do you think Ford did the right thing or the wrong thing in granting Nixon a pardon?"	Right Thing (%)	Wrong Thing (%)	No Opinion (%)	Right Thing-Wrong Thing
Total sample	35	55	10	−20
Republicans	57	33	10	+24
Democrats	25	67	8	−42
Southern Democrats	34	53	13	−19
Independents	37	52	11	−15
College educated	42	50	8	−8
High school	33	58	9	−25
Grade school	28	55	17	−27
Easterners	35	58	7	−23
Midwesterners	37	54	9	−17
Southerners	36	52	12	−16
Westerners	30	58	12	−28
Aged 18-24	35	57	8	−22
Aged 25-29	28	67	5	−39
Aged 30-49	38	51	11	−13
Aged 50 and older	34	55	11	−21
Manual labor	31	61	8	−30
Clerical/sales	38	51	11	−13
Professional/business	41	50	9	−9

Source: *The Gallup Poll: Public Opinion 1972–1977*, vol. 2 (Wilmington, DE: Scholarly Resources, 1978), 799–801; question asked June 11–14, 1976.

material for the Carter-Mondale camp. One of these turned on the charge that Ford had improperly accepted money from the Marine Engineers Beneficial Association (MEBA). Ford maintained that these campaign contributions had been legal and fully disclosed. The matter went to the new Watergate special prosecutor, Charles F. C. Ruff, who finally cleared Ford of all wrongdoing in October. Mondale repeated rumors that Ford, as House Republican leader, had tried to squelch the House Banking Committee's investigation of Watergate and that he had pressured the Senate to conduct its Watergate hearings behind closed doors.[154] More claims of improper campaign contributions swirled around Senator Robert Dole, Ford's running mate.[155]

Economic Doldrums

For all the attention lavished on the legacies of Watergate, the combined effects of high inflation (driven in large part by the high cost of oil) and high unemployment figured even more importantly in the 1976 campaign. The economy topped Gallup's list of the nation's most pressing problems in this election year, and that issue probably tipped the balance in Carter's favor.[156]

The summer of 1974 produced grim tidings. Already a problem under Nixon, inflation reached double digits for the first time since the 1940s. The wholesale price index jumped by 3.7 percent in July, the second-biggest hike for a single month since 1946. By August, unemployment had risen to 5.5 percent. Third-quarter figures for the gross national product (GNP) showed a dip of 2.3 percent.[157]

Promptly upon taking office, Ford proclaimed inflation to be "public enemy number one." Preparing the ground for tax increases and austerity measures, he convened a September 23 "summit" to underscore the need for swift action against inflation. Speaking to a joint session of Congress on October 8, 1974, the new president proposed a 5 percent surcharge on corporate earnings and family incomes of more than $15,000. He also advocated $4.4 billion in spending cuts to force federal expenditures below $300 billion. And in an ill-fated public relations gesture, he called on the public to take steps to "Whip Inflation Now" (WIN).[158]

With midterm elections looming, few members of Congress wanted to raise taxes or scale back popular programs. They also had good reason to doubt Ford's diagnosis. Unemployment was rising (it would top out at 7.2 percent at year's end and reach 8.9 percent in May 1975), fourth-quarter figures showed a 7.5 percent drop in GNP, and the October index of leading indicators registered the biggest monthly decline in twenty-three years. Fixated on inflation, Ford disputed that the economy was technically in recession. Influenced by the Nixon pardon as well as a bad economy, the 1974 midterm elections ended in a Republican rout, in which Democrats picked up forty-nine seats in the House and four in the Senate.[159]

After this rebuff, Ford struggled to find an alternative to cutting taxes and increasing the deficit. Accordingly, he used the State of the Union address to propose $16 billion in tax rebates. In return, he asked for a cap on domestic spending and a moratorium on new programs except those pertaining to energy. Congress instead passed a tax cut of nearly $23 billion, along with much bigger spending bills than Ford had requested. A veto war followed until Ford agreed to accept $17 billion more in expenditures than he had asked for.[160] He returned to the fray in October 1975, offering permanent tax cuts that were far greater than any the Democrats had in mind in return for an expenditure cap. Congress provoked another veto by passing its tax cut without a spending cap. Even though Ford prevailed in the override vote, he capitulated when Congress passed a similar bill just before the Christmas holidays.[161]

More thrusting and parrying took place during the election year, with Ford wielding his veto pen as well as the power to defer spending as allowed by the 1974 Budget and Impoundment Control Act. With an eye to the 1976 presidential campaign, Democrats devised a so-called misery index (inflation combined with unemployment) that would serve Carter well. Ford worsened his plight by failing to articulate his case in a coherent manner, a failing acknowledged by his advisers.[162]

Still, he enjoyed some success in resisting passage of the Humphrey-Hawkins "full employment" bill, whereby the federal government would become the employer of last resort for all who were unable to find work.[163]

The picture brightened in early 1976, when inflation declined to 4.8 percent and unemployment fell to 7.3 percent. By late summer, however, the jobless rate rose again, reaching 8 percent in November. Stock market averages also dropped as wholesale prices shot up. Ford had passed up an opportunity to ask for a stimulus package in 1975, gambling that another downturn would not happen before the election.[164]

Electoral and Campaign Strategies

Both sides saw the 1976 race in remarkably similar ways. The Carter team thought their man could not lose, whereas Ford's people thought only a miracle could make their candidate the winner. Republican and Democratic strategists agreed that New York, New Jersey, Pennsylvania, Ohio, Illinois, Michigan, and California held the keys to electoral victory. They further agreed that Ford had to carry at least five of the biggest states to win.[165]

Uncertain only about the size of Carter's victory, Hamilton Jordan mistakenly advised his candidate that Ford possessed neither a popular base nor an electoral strategy.[166] Riding extraordinarily high in the polls, Carter waited almost until Labor Day to discuss campaign themes with his advisers. At a rather casual gathering, he asked, "What are our themes going to be?" With Mondale present, the group settled on: "Leadership: Carter has it, Ford doesn't. Competence: Carter has it, Ford doesn't. The economy: The Republicans have messed it up; inflation is soaring, and so is unemployment."[167]

Dick Cheney and other Ford advisers pulled no punches when apprising their candidate of the strategic situation. "If the past is prologue," they declared in one memorandum, "you will lose on November 2nd—because to win you must do what has never been done: close a gap of about 20 points in 73 days from the base of a minority party while spending approximately the same amount of money as your opponent."[168]

Still, they held out the slim possibility of winning if the president ran the right kind of campaign. Ford had to convince voters that he deserved a term of his own while Republicans worked to destroy Carter's image. Television ads and Republican surrogates would depict Carter as untested and inexperienced, more liberal on social issues than he pretended, vague and inconsistent on numerous issues, and no less ruthless and manipulative than Nixon. Aside from Republican stalwarts (greatly outnumbered by Democratic loyalists), Ford had to win over upwardly mobile Catholics and other swing voters in the Northeast and Midwest.[169]

Having become a figure of fun for his verbal and physical pratfalls, Ford was told to stay in Washington and make a show of managing the nation's affairs. Counseled by one adviser that he was "no [expletive deleted] good," Ford agreed to this "Rose Garden strategy."[170] He later wrote:

> Frantic trips across the country in search of votes could well cause a continuing slide in the polls. Carter would be the candidate constantly on the road. The press . . . would cover his appearances; yet, to be fair, they'd report on what I had done that day no matter what it was, and the contrast would be clear. I was in the White House doing my job, and he was flying from place to place making extravagant promises.[171]

This strategy soon irked Carter, who complained that

> President Ford can walk out in the Rose Garden and make a minute-and-a-half statement and that's his only confrontation with the American people on the evening news. I make a hundred different statements a day.[172]

Table 4.9 shows a striking contrast in how Ford and Carter allocated their time early in the campaign. The Rose Garden strategy soon fizzled, however, once the press began playing up old allegations of improper fund-raising by Ford and Dole.

Costly Campaign Blunders

As Ford's strategists suspected, their man was not the only 1976 candidate prone to stumble on the campaign trail. Carter had exhibited similar failings during the primaries, and now the Republicans counted on him to make more mistakes. Carter obliged in September when explaining his Baptist conceptions of sin and redemption to *Playboy* magazine, a curious choice for an interview in view of its erotic photos. Frustrated by the interviewer's inability to take his meaning, Carter restated his ideas in graphic terms:

> Christ said, "I tell you that anyone who looks on a woman with lust has in his heart already committed adultery." I've looked on a lot of women with lust. I've committed adultery in my heart many times. This is something that God recognizes I will do—and I have done it—and God forgives me for it. But that doesn't mean that I condemn someone who not only looks on a woman with lust but leaves his wife and shacks up with somebody out of wedlock.

For good measure, he avowed that Lyndon Johnson had lied and cheated no less than Nixon.[173]

Playboy leaked these passages to a network news program just three days before Carter's first debate with Ford. Public reaction ranged from outrage to puzzlement. "Bad, bad, bad," said a spokesperson for the Georgia Democratic Party

Table 4.9. Rose Garden versus Stump

September 6 (Labor Day)	Ford works at his desk in the Oval Office; tells ABC News that a victory in November will strengthen his hand with Congress	Carter speaks in Warm Springs, Georgia; greets fans at the Darlington, South Carolina, stock car races; and appears in Norfolk, Virginia
September 7	Ford signs disaster-relief and child-care bills in the Rose Garden, talks about serving the people well, and reads a statement decrying Vietnam's "callous and cruel" release of names of U.S. war dead previously listed as missing in action	Carter campaigns in New York, Connecticut, and Pennsylvania
September 8	Ford appears on White House lawn to denounce Carter attacks on FBI director Kelley, noting that Mrs. Kelley is terminally ill	Carter campaigns in Pittsburgh and Washington, Pennsylvania, as well as Columbus and Cleveland, Ohio
September 9	Ford reads a statement to reporters about the death of Mao Tse-tung, signs an interstate sewage bill for New Hampshire and Vermont, receives the ambassador of Guinea, and speaks at a Washington hotel	Carter campaigns in Carbondale, Springfield, Peoria, Chicago, and Milwaukee

Sources: Martin Schram, *Running for President: The Carter Campaign* (New York: Stein and Day, 1977), 287; Jules Witcover, *Marathon: The Pursuit of the Presidency 1972–1976* (New York: Viking, 1977), 546.

when asked about the likely impact.[174] Carter's daily tracking polls registered an alarming slump in support, with a drop of roughly twelve points over the next several days before it recovered.[175] Gallup reported that the episode lowered his favorability rating by a net eleven points (16 percent viewed him less favorably than before, compared with 5 percent who took a more positive view). Carter suffered most among persons aged fifty or older, professionals and businesspeople, residents of the Midwest, and those with college degrees.[176] In Texas immediately after the debate, he repeatedly apologized for calling LBJ a liar. "This frankness," he conceded, "might very well not be a good safe thing to do in a campaign."[177] A California crowd laughed when a local official ended his introduction of Carter by extending a "lusty welcome, really, for the next president."[178]

Republicans made hay out of this episode, at one point taking out a newspaper ad that showed the cover of the *Playboy* issue containing Carter's interview. It depicted "a voluptuous young woman with an unbuttoned shirt." When Carter complained, Ford suggested that presidents should not grant interviews to magazines "featuring photographs of unclad women."[179]

Ford's most costly blunder occurred during the second debate, held on October 6. The event focused wholly on foreign policy, the one policy area where Ford was perceived as better qualified than Carter. Responding to a question from journalist Max Frankel about U.S. policy toward Eastern Europe, Ford proclaimed: "There is no Soviet domination of Eastern Europe and there never will be under a Ford administration." Taken aback, Frankel asked if the Russians were not "using Eastern Europe as their own sphere of influence and occupying most of the countries there." Yet Ford did not seize this opportunity to make a critical distinction between the de facto domination of Eastern Europe by the Soviets and the U.S. view that such domination was illegitimate:

> I don't believe, Mr. Frankel, that the Yugoslavians consider themselves dominated by the Soviet Union. I don't believe that the Rumanians consider themselves dominated by the Soviet Union. I don't believe that the Poles consider themselves dominated by the Soviet Union. Each of these countries is independent, autonomous. It has its own territorial integrity. And the United States does not concede that those countries are under the domination of the Soviet Union. As a matter of fact, I visited Poland, Yugoslavia, and Rumania to make certain that the people of those countries understood that the president of the United States and the people of the United States are dedicated to their independence, their autonomy, and their freedom.[180]

Carter capitalized on Ford's confused, if adamant, declarations:

> I would like to see Mr. Ford convince the Polish-Americans and the Czech-Americans and the Hungarian-Americans in this country that those countries don't live under the domination and supervision of the Soviet Union behind the Iron Curtain.[181]

Cheney and other Ford advisers sensed immediately that their man had blundered badly and urged him to issue a correction. Ford, however, refused to confess error until a week of bad publicity changed his mind.[182] Carter put that interval to good use, ridiculing Ford's intellect and questioning his knowledge. In Kansas City, for example, he described the president's newest position as follows: "Well, maybe Eastern Europe is free after all—or is not free after all."[183] A comparison of Gallup Poll findings indicates that this episode cost Ford dearly. The last pre-debate poll showed him well ahead of Carter (50 to 21 percent) on the question of who would best handle relations with the Soviet Union. But the twenty-nine-point lead fell to five points in the first postdebate poll. Before the debate, Ford had enjoyed a fifteen-point advantage on national defense. The next poll showed him three points behind.[184]

ATTACK SCORES AND TARGETS IN 1976

Let us return to the familiar prediction that the trailing ticket in a two-party race will wage a much more negative campaign than its favored rival. This did not happen in 1976. Rather, the overall attack score of Democrats exceeded that of the Republicans, 50 to 44 percent. Democratic negativity also topped that of the Republicans in six of the eight weeks of campaigning (see Table 4.10).

Consistent with their strategy of making Carter the issue of the campaign, Republicans targeted him 89 percent of the time. Ford blasted Carter in 92 percent of his attacks, a higher targeting score than Dole's. Conversely, Ford figured in nearly 85 percent of all Democratic attacks and in 92 percent of Carter's. Three-quarters of Mondale's attacks fell on Ford as well (see Table 4.11).

LEADING TOPICS OF 1976

Turning to the topics most emphasized in the 1976 campaign, Table 4.12 shows that both sides placed a premium on seven of the same concerns. Moreover, the Democrats and Republicans exhibited a remarkable consensus on which topics deserved the most attention: the economy, leadership, campaign issues, and the complex of military and defense issues. They also engaged on ideology, debates, and race. Not surprisingly, the Carter-Mondale side pressed hard on scandals and corruption whereas Republicans put much more stock in foreign policy. Democrats stressed poverty and women's issues; Republicans focused more on farm policy.

Table 4.12 also shows that both sides put major emphasis on six of the same attack topics. Remarkably little difference showed up in the order of importance that each side accorded to the top four categories: the economy, leadership, defense, and foreign policy. They also converged on ideology and farm policy. Republicans exploited Carter's *Playboy* interview, and Democrats made a major issue of the Nixon pardon, post-Watergate flaps, and Ford's personal finances.[185]

ATTACK METHODS IN 1976

As for the methods of making attacks, both sides relied most on fear arousal and labeling (which includes guilt by association). Charges of lying and the drawing of unflattering contrasts (apposition) showed up more frequently than ridicule. As might have been expected, Dole exhibited a greater propensity to joke at an opponent's expense than did the other principals in this contest (see Table 4.13).

Table 4.10. Negativity of Major Parties in 1976

Campaign Week	Democratic Attacks on Republicans	Republican Attacks on Democrats
1	.434	.392
2	.450	.326
3	.367	.412
4	.644	.571
5	.661	.379
6	.682	.567
7	.431	.359
8	.451	.505
Overall	.505	.440
N statements	473	470

Note: Week 1 began September 6 and ended September 12; week 2, September 13–19; week 3, September 20–26; week 4, September 27–October 3; week 5, October 4–10; week 6, October 11–17; week 7, October 18–24; and week 8, October 25–November 2.

Table 4.11. Targeting of 1976 Attacks

	Democratic Targeting of Republicans	Republican Targeting of Democrats
All party attacks		
Presidential nominee	202	185
Other targets	37	22
N attacks	239	207
Nominee targeted	.845	.894
Solo attacks of presidential nominee	Carter	Ford
Presidential nominee	125	78
Other targets	11	7
N attacks	136	85
Nominee targeted	.919	.918
Solo attacks of vice-presidential nominee	Mondale	Dole
Presidential nominee	33	43
Other targets	11	9
N attacks	44	52
Nominee targeted	.750	.827

Note: Some attacks on presidential candidates also targeted others of the same party.

ECHOES FROM THE 1976 CAMPAIGN TRAIL

Leadership figured as the foremost attack topic for Republicans and ranked second in the Democratic arsenal. Polls taken at the time revealed that both of the presidential candidates left much to be desired by way of leadership. One such

Table 4.12. Topics Most Mentioned and Most Utilized in 1976 Attacks

Leading Democratic Topics	Leading Republican Topics	Leading Democratic Attack Topics	Leading Republican Attack Topics
Domestic economy (95)	Domestic economy (81)	Domestic economy (61)	Leadership (50)
Leadership (72)	Leadership (58)	Leadership (53)	Domestic economy (49)
Campaign (49)	Campaign (58)	Military/defense (25)	Military/defense (30)
Military/defense (41)	Military/defense (55)	Foreign policy (25)	Foreign policy (14)
Ideology/party (21)	Foreign policy (30)	Social/health programs (16)	Ideology/party (12)
Corruption/abuse of power (19)	Ideology/party (24)	Corruption, abuse of power (15)	Patriotism (6)
Debates (18)	Campaign finances (24)	Ideology/party (7)	Race (6)
Race (17)	Debates (21)	Women's rights (4)	Personal morality (5)
Social/health programs (13)	Race (17)	Farm policy (4)	Farm policy (5)
Women's rights (11)	Women's rights (12), farm policy (12)	Personal finances (4)	Religion (4)

Notes: The top-ten Democratic topics accounted for 75 percent of all Democratic campaign statements; the corresponding figure for the Republicans was 88 percent. The ten topics most utilized to assail the Republicans accounted for 89 percent of total Democratic attacks; the corresponding figure for Republicans was 87 percent.

sampling revealed that only 22 percent of the public credited Ford with exceptional ability, that a mere 30 percent found him imaginative and innovative, that just over one-third thought he had a clear plan for the future, that only 36 percent felt he had been a "strong" leader, and that a meager 40 percent thought that he was sincere. The same poll uncovered serious misgivings about Carter's leadership: barely 28 percent credited him with consistency on the issues, a mere 34 percent claimed to know what he stood for, only 38 percent thought he said what he really meant, 40 percent perceived exceptional ability, and another 40 percent divined a clear plan for the future. Carter enjoyed a huge advantage over Ford on the question of siding with the average citizen, yet he trailed notably on experience, consistency, and credibility.[186] William Loeb, New Hampshire's dyspeptic newspaper publisher, summarized these doubts after the election in a headline that shouted, "Shifty Beats Stupid."[187]

Table 4.13. Attack Methods, 1976

	Presidential Candidate (solo)	Vice-Presidential Candidate (solo)	All Attackers
Democrats targeting Republicans			
Fear arousal	.478	.568	.469
Ridicule	.066	.023	.059
Labeling	.515	.364	.469
Apposition	.206	.068	.184
Dishonesty	.154	.114	.188
Republicans targeting Democrats			
Fear arousal	.494	.404	.425
Ridicule	.059	.154	.077
Labeling	.318	.462	.411
Apposition	.400	.231	.300
Dishonesty	.365	.288	.275

Note: Entries are percentages of attacks employing a particular method.

Democratic Attacks on Republican Leadership

Throughout the fall campaign, Carter painted Ford as a failed leader, starting with a Labor Day speech at Warm Springs, Georgia. Standing in front of the cottage where FDR had spent his final hours, Carter called for a "new generation of leadership" and likened Ford to Herbert Hoover. "This year, as in 1932," the Democratic nominee added, "our nation is divided, our people are out of work and our national leaders do not lead. Our nation is drifting without vision and without purpose." Hours later in Norfolk, Virginia, he denounced "quiet, dormant, timid leadership" in the Oval Office.[188] In late September, the Democratic standard-bearer offered a more sarcastic appraisal: "Ford is a good automobile. It's not doing too well in the White House. Stuck in the mud, flat tires, gears locked in reverse. If it ever does move again, which I doubt, I'm sure we're going to back into the future."[189] During the October 6 debate, he asserted that Ford had failed overseas as well as at home.[190] He stressed leadership in his third debate with Ford on October 23. Americans wanted an end to weak leadership: "We've been drifting too long. We've been dormant too long. We've been discouraged too long."[191] Carter reiterated this argument during his final days of campaigning.[192]

Carter worked the Rose Garden strategy into his leadership offensive. In Florida, evidently without sensing the contradiction, he accused Ford of evading presidential responsibilities by "hiding in the White House."[193] In the wake of the *Playboy* incident, he contrasted his willingness to answer tough questions with Ford's avoidance of real press conferences.[194]

The Eastern Europe flap enhanced Carter's efforts to paint Ford as inaccessible and ignorant of how Eastern European immigrants felt about Soviet domination.[195] The following day, he told an Indianapolis audience that there was "just about as much openness in the Ford administration as there is freedom in Eastern Europe."[196]

Having long linked Ford to Nixon, Carter came up with a new angle by claiming that Nixon had been the stronger leader. During the first debate, for instance, he said that Nixon had been "a strong leader, at least."[197] Six days later, he proclaimed Ford worse than Nixon: "In 1972, we got two [presidents] for the price of one. I'm afraid the second one, as far as people's lives are concerned, is even worse than the first one."[198] He took a similar line when responding to attacks on his own lack of experience: "I think Gerald Ford is on shaky grounds when he starts talking about experience. If we had wanted experience, we would have kept Richard Nixon."[199] Nixon also surfaced in criticisms of the Rose Garden strategy: "Gerald Ford has hidden himself from the public even more than Richard Nixon at the depths of Watergate."[200] Similarly, he worked Nixon into a list of mistakes that Republican presidents had made by secluding themselves in the White House and not listening to the people.[201] In mid-October, Carter promised to correct the leadership failures of Nixon and Ford.[202]

Carter also seized on the indiscretions of Earl Butz, the secretary of agriculture and a close friend of Ford's. Already controversial, Butz had told a racist joke overheard by John Dean of Watergate fame, now a correspondent for *Rolling Stone*. Carter made a point of Ford's reluctance to part with Butz: "The way this whole embarrassing and disgusting episode was handled by President Ford shows a continuation of the lack of leadership."[203]

Dole's poor showing during his vice-presidential debate with Mondale gave Carter yet another angle from which to attack Ford's leadership. "The one major decision that President Ford and I have had to make since our nominations," he informed a Pittsburgh rally on October 28, "was to choose our vice-presidential running mates. I searched the nation over and I had one thought in mind—to choose the one person who I thought would make the greatest president. I chose Walter Mondale and I think all of you know I made the right choice." Ford, he suggested, could not make the same case for Dole.[204]

Other Democrats seconded Carter's leadership attacks. Mondale lambasted "the appointed president of the United States" for "hiding behind his desk in Washington."[205] Weeks later, he described the Ford White House "as a bunker to hide from the American people."[206] Rosalynn Carter compared her husband favorably with politicians penned up in Washington.[207] Ford's long record of public service, she pointed out, did not prevent "the mess the government is in."[208] Governor Hugh Carey of New York challenged Ford to "come out of the Rose Garden and meet the people."[209] On another occasion, Carey recalled serving in some of the same Congresses as Ford, saying that Ford had never supported a constructive program during that period. He also blamed the continuing decline of trust in government on Ford's presidency.[210] Representative Louis Stokes of Ohio roused a Cleveland crowd by making fun of Ford's blunder on Eastern Europe.[211]

Republican Attacks on Carter's Leadership

As previously noted, the Rose Garden strategy delegated most negative campaigning to Dole and other stand-ins for Ford. Dole liked to joke that he had been dispatched to the briar patch while Ford got to stay in the Rose Garden. At first, Dole exhibited a similarly light touch when going after the Democrats, calling them "Mondale, Tuesdale, and all those folks." "Now we've had the New Deal and the Fair Deal and the Fast Deal," he exclaimed at one rally, "and we're about to have the Ordeal if Carter's elected."[212]

Dole made an issue of Carter's inconsistency on certain issues throughout the campaign. In the early stages, he tied this theme to negotiations over the number of presidential debates: "I don't blame him for wanting three debates. He needs one to explain each position."[213] He used this staple of the campaign trail during his debate with Mondale, asserting that Carter took "three positions on everything. That's why they're having three television debates. I wish Mr. Mondale would tell us Mr. Carter's views."[214] Campaigning in Marietta, Ohio, he worked the three-positions-on-every-issue line into a broader assault on Carter's character: "He wants to be president so bad, he'll tell any group anything anytime to get their votes."[215] After noting the enthusiasm of young people for McCarthy in 1968 and McGovern in 1972, he said, "I don't see those young people around Governor Carter because they don't know where he stands on the issues."[216]

Most of what Dole made of Carter's *Playboy* interview fastened on the characterization of the late Lyndon Johnson as a liar and cheater of Nixonian proportions. "It just strikes me as rather strange," Dole said on the stump, "that he [Carter] can go around to the widow and say, 'I didn't really mean it.'"[217] He turned up the heat in North Carolina: "Don't you kind of wonder at those people who make snap judgments, then rush to the phone to apologize?"[218]

Branded as a hatchet man by Democrats, Dole eventually carried the Ford banner to forty-four states. He finished up in Nebraska, Iowa, Missouri, and Kansas, charging that Carter and Mondale were "desperate men devoid of issues."[219]

Bowing to the Reagan wing of his party, Ford had abandoned Nelson W. Rockefeller—the nation's second unelected vice president—to pick Dole as his running mate.[220] Under the circumstances, the aging prince of the Eastern Liberal Establishment could have sat out the campaign. Instead, he stumped energetically for

Ford across New York. As an attacker, Rockefeller wielded a needle rather than a cleaver. Carter had not tried to mislead people, he deadpanned, he just had trouble making up his mind. Similarly, "Rocky" proclaimed *Playboy* an "unusual forum" for Christ's message. When hecklers orchestrated a show of middle fingers in Binghamton, New York, Rockefeller replied in kind, later describing the gesture as "a spontaneous response to a sustained salute from a small group."[221]

Ford received almost no help from Ronald Reagan, but other prominent Republicans rallied to his cause. Senator Barry Goldwater panned Carter's performance in the first debate.[222] John Connally contrasted Ford's steady leadership with Carter's unpredictability. "In President Ford we have a leader," he said at a Houston rally. "We know how he will act. We know how he will react. His opponent we do not know; we really don't know what he would do, or how he would act, or how he would react."[223]

Other notables backing Ford included Democrats who were uncomfortable with Carter. On October 6, Ford appeared in San Francisco to herald the formation of Citizens for Ford, a committee composed of "non-Republicans" such as Edith Green (former Democratic congresswoman from Oregon) and George J. Feldman (former U.S. ambassador to Luxembourg). Green, who had seconded the nominations of Adlai Stevenson and John F. Kennedy, praised Ford as honest, decent, and capable if not "flamboyant," and she attacked Carter: "I do not know Carter, do not know what he stands for and, believe me, I've tried to find out." Sporting a "Fordocrat" button, Feldman nodded in agreement.[224]

Of course, Ford also took a hand in these matters, early on calling Carter's bludgeoning of FBI director Kelley "callous," "indecisive," and "contradictory."[225] He countered charges that he was hiding in the White House with slaps at Carter's inconsistency: "A few weeks ago he was complaining that I was campaigning too much and not spending enough time in government business. Now that I'm spending virtually 100 percent of my time on being president, he is being critical of the fact that I'm not out politicking."[226]

Ford made an issue of trust when he departed the Rose Garden to speak at the University of Michigan. "Trust is not having to guess what a candidate means," he declaimed. "Trust is leveling with the people before an election about what you're going to do after the election. Trust is not being all things to all people, but being the same thing to all people. Trust is not cleverly shading words, so that each separate audience can hear what it wants to hear, but saying plainly and simply what you mean, and meaning what you say."[227]

Ford hammered Carter on leadership issues during their first debate, saying at one point that "the president can't be all things to all people."[228] Responding to Carter's opening statement, he said, "I don't think Mr. Carter has been any more specific on this case than he has been on many other instances."[229] He continued this line of attack after the second debate, charging that his opponent had not answered questions and had contradicted himself on various policy matters: "I still don't know where Mr. Carter stands on most issues."[230] Immediately after the second debate, he expanded the assault on Carter's lack of specificity to include accusations of lying, distortion, and exaggeration. Ford claimed that fourteen "distortions, misrepresentations, inaccuracies, or untruths" had issued from Carter in ninety minutes of debate time, more than one misstatement every six minutes. "That's too darn many for a president of the United States," he concluded.[231]

Once liberated from the Rose Garden, Ford pushed the inconsistency theme. In New York, he spoke of searching the nation in vain for that candidate who promised never to lie to the people: "He seems to have disappeared."[232] On October 15, joining in the laughter after telling an Iowa State University crowd that it was great to be at Ohio State, Ford maintained that Carter was a "quick-change artist" who sounded like Cesar Chavez in California, Mayor Daley in Chicago, Ralph Nader in New York, and George Meany in Washington. "Then he comes to the farm belt and he becomes a little old peanut farmer," he declared.[233] Ford served up more of the same while stumping in Springfield, Illinois, claiming that Carter came on like Bella Abzug in New York and the little old peanut farmer in Illinois. "He wiggles, he wanders, he wiggles and he waffles, and he shouldn't be president of the United States." Echoing Dole, Ford added that Carter would "say anything anywhere to be president of the United States."[234]

When Carter sent Ford a telegram demanding an end to misrepresentation of his positions, the Ford camp issued a reply "rich in sarcasm and pointed irony," noting that Carter had changed positions so frequently that it was difficult to figure out "who you are and what you really represent." "It is, of course, your right to change your position on any or all of these issues, but what you have done instead is to claim that you never took the positions in the first place."[235]

By this time, both sides had come under criticism for lowering the quality of campaign discourse. An Ohio Republican said that neither candidate had given the electorate "anything to vote for" and compared the level of campaign exchanges to that of "a student-council race."[236] Ford acknowledged a need to improve the dialogue but added, "I think it is graphic and accurate to say that Mr. Carter does waver, wander, wiggle, and waffle."[237]

Robert Maynard, an editorial writer for the *Washington Post*, raised the issue with both candidates during their final debate on October 22. Maynard started with Carter:

> Governor, by all indications, the voters are so turned off by this election campaign so far that only half intend to vote. One major reason for this apathetic electorate appears to be the low level at which this campaign has been conducted.

It has digressed frequently from important issues into allegations of blunder and brainwashing and fixations on lust and *Playboy*. What responsibility do you accept for the low level of this campaign for the nation's highest office?[238]

Carter responded with a lengthy recitation of campaign themes, attributing the falloff in voting since 1960 in part to "the deep discouragement of the American people about the performance of public officials," citing inflation and unemployment statistics, mentioning Watergate and related issues, and linking these scandals to public unease about government officials. Eventually, he acknowledged having made mistakes in twenty-two months of campaigning for his party's nomination as well as the presidency. The "*Playboy* thing," he added, "has been of very great concern to me. I don't know how to deal with it exactly." After more such ruminations, Carter pledged not to run television and newspaper ads containing a "personal attack on President Ford's character."[239]

Ford conceded to Maynard that voters had just cause for their unhappiness and acknowledged that Watergate—"a very, very bad period of time in American political history"—had contributed significantly to the problem. Still, he pointed up the bicentennial celebrations as evidence of positive feelings about the country. Moreover, he claimed to have encountered plenty of optimism and a willingness to vote on the campaign trail. He continued,

> Now, like any hard-working person seeking public office, in the campaign inevitably sometimes, you will use rather graphic language, and I'm guilty of that just like I think most others in the political arena. But I do make a pledge that in the next ten days when we're asking the American people to make one of the most important decisions in their lifetime—because I think this election is one of the most vital in the history of America—that we do together what we can to stimulate voter participation.[240]

Only moments after this exchange of vows, Carter provoked Ford by accusing him of "callous indifference" to families struggling to make ends meet. Ford hit back at the first opportunity, charging Carter with inconsistency and distortion.[241]

When polls showed the race dead even in the final days, Ford waged a television blitz centered on his chats with Joe Garagiola, the popular sports announcer. For the most part, Garagiola lobbed softballs for Ford to hit out of the park. In one such exchange, Garagiola asked, "How many leaders have you dealt with, Mr. President?" "One hundred twenty-four leaders of countries around the world, Joe," was the reply. Occasionally, however, Ford took aim at Carter: "He doesn't have the kind of experience I think is essential."[242]

CONCLUSION

Noteworthy differences marked the circumstances under which the 1968 and 1976 campaigns played out. The war that figured so critically in 1968 came to its inglorious finale before the 1976 contest. Similarly, the "long hot summer" years of race rioting had ended before Ford replaced Nixon, although violence over busing flared up in Boston. Crippled in 1972 by the bullets of a would-be assassin, Wallace lost his second try for a Democratic nomination in 1976 to a little-known former governor from Georgia.

Almost every aspect of the 1976 strategic environment worked against Ford— a wretched economy, Watergate and related scandals, an accidental presidency, the disastrous pardon, the 1974 midterm elections, Democratic control of both houses of Congress, a bitter fight for the Republican nomination, and Ford's limited abilities both as presidential candidate and chief executive. Like Humphrey in 1968, he paid a high price for his association with an unpopular president, and he, too, struggled to overcome the bitter disappointment of party loyalists. Still, like Humphrey, he came within a whisker of winning.

The Skaperdas-Grofman model was even less applicable to the attack politics of 1976 than to those of 1968. Nonetheless, the model's postulate that an attacker loses as well as gains by going negative sheds light on Carter's drop in the polls that corresponded with Ford's remarkable comeback. Carter appears to have suffered a great deal for waging so righteous, shrill, and humorless a campaign against the likable, and bumbling Ford, and what should have been a romp in a year when almost every issue favored the Democrats turned into a cliff-hanger. Convergence dominated campaign discourse in 1976 despite the economy and a hunger for change that greatly advantaged the Democrats.

5. The Dead Heat Race of 1960

Kennedy speechwriter Richard N. Goodwin described the 1960 race as a virtual tie "from beginning to end," regardless of what the polls showed.[1] Between Labor Day and election day, the lead shifted from Nixon to Kennedy, whose margin in the Gallup Poll never exceeded 4 percent (see Figure 5.1).

Assuming that Vice President Richard Nixon would receive the Republican nomination, Gallup began matching him against potential Democratic rivals as early as 1958. Nixon not only beat Adlai Stevenson in all but one of these trial heats, he also trounced Senate Majority Leader Lyndon Johnson and Senator Stuart Symington of Missouri.[2] However, Senator John F. Kennedy looked more formidable. Gallup showed him trailing Nixon in four polls, tying in one, and winning in four.[3] Nixon expected to face Kennedy in the fall and rightly anticipated that the race would be tough and close.[4]

No event looms larger in the popular accounts of the 1960 race than the first Kennedy-Nixon debate. Radio listeners thought that Nixon had performed well, but most television viewers thought that he looked wan and irresolute compared with a robust and confident Kennedy.[5] Postdebate commentary helped boost Kennedy a point or two in the polls. Although Nixon performed and looked much stronger in all three of the later debates, none of those impacted the contest as much as the first.

Nixon may have pulled his punches in the first debate as part of a more general stratagem to appear more presidential than Kennedy. In part, he needed to shed the character-assassin persona of the 1950s, an image that Herbert Block had long projected in editorial cartoons for the *Washington Post*. ("Herblock" repeatedly drew Nixon as a ruthless and mendacious practitioner of gutter politics.) Owing to hot studio lights and inadequate makeup, Nixon's appearance in the first debate reinforced his five o'clock shadow, a staple of the Herblock caricature.

But most of the problems with Nixon's haggard visage in the first debate had to do with his freak accident in mid-August. While Kennedy and his running mate, Lyndon Johnson, were bogged down in a special session of Congress, Nixon seized the opportunity to make a sweep of the South.[6] During that sweep, he banged his knee against a car door in North Carolina, and the serious infection that quickly developed landed him in Walter Reed Hospital. Nixon had planned to spend these bedridden days conferring with advisers, refining issue stands, meeting with volunteers, and getting a head start on a foolish promise to stump in all fifty states.[7]

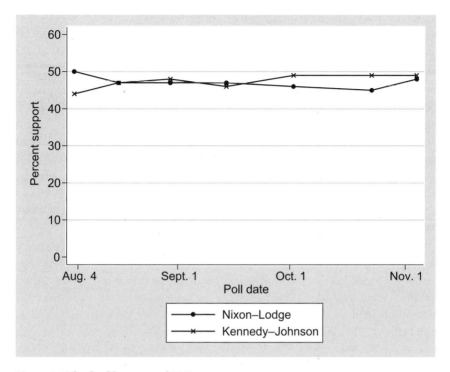

Figure 5.1 The dead heat race of 1960
Note: Dates are shown according to the final day of the polling sequence.
Source: George H. Gallup, *The Gallup Poll: Public Opinion 1935–1971, vol. 3* (New York: Random House, 1972).

But almost none of this preliminary work had been done when, still feverish, he tried to make up for lost time by scheduling appearances in twenty-five states.[8] Nixon accordingly showed up for the first debate physically spent and ten pounds underweight.[9] His regular shirt collar was now a full size too large, his gray suit blended into the gray studio backdrop, and he had reinjured his knee upon arriving at the studio.

Ironically, despite a lifetime of serious illnesses and hospital stays, Kennedy looked much fitter on that occasion than the normally healthy Nixon. Indeed, due to an extraordinary regimen of steroids and other medications, JFK's imposing physique unsettled Nixon, who remembered his opponent, from their congressional time together, as a puny specimen.[10] Before a television audience of 70 million, a cool, confident, and tanned Kennedy played offense to Nixon's defense.

On the campaign trail, however, Kennedy made no less a superhuman effort than his opponent. His eighteen-hour days typically included eight to ten speeches on top of press interviews, meetings with local politicians, and strategy sessions.[11] Although pundits panned Nixon's decision to campaign in every state, Kennedy appeared in forty-five.[12] Unlike Nixon, he appeared to pick up steam as this war of attrition ground on. In contrast with his humorless opponent, Kennedy cloaked his travail in self-deprecating humor. On one such occasion, he urged the earliest possible passage of a bill to provide health care for the elderly because "we are all aging very fast these days."[13]

In the final days of the campaign, Nixon, down but hardly out, trotted out the popular Eisenhower, who landed some telling blows on Kennedy. Nixon also executed a long-standing plan to saturate the airwaves with campaign ads. His blitz caught the Democrats flat-footed and helped close the gap between the two contenders. And what began as a "confident adventure" for Kennedy ended in a fog of "fatigue and doubt."[14]

The candidates ended their campaigns on opposite coasts. Nixon uncharacteristically frittered away election day before repairing to his command post at the Ambassador Hotel in Los Angeles. Kennedy spoke at Fannuel Hall in Boston before retiring to Hyannis Port for a long night with family and aides. Early returns prefigured a Kennedy sweep of the Northeast, and Connecticut, New York, and Pennsylvania (twice carried by Eisenhower) quickly fell into line. Only rock-ribbed Maine, Vermont, and New Hampshire remained in the Republican column. As Kennedy's margin increased, CBS and NBC projected that he would win a clear majority of the popular vote.[15]

In his worst-case analysis, Nixon had allowed for all of these reverses. However, he expected the change of fortune to begin in Texas.[16] A victory in the Lone Star State also would humiliate Lyndon Johnson, Kennedy's running mate and an old Nixon enemy. Kennedy had chosen Johnson largely to nail down Texas, but the antipathy that conservative Democrats felt toward LBJ boosted Nixon's chances.[17] Further, Eisenhower had carried the state in 1952 and 1956. The tipping point in Texas likely occurred only four days before the election, when a mob of right-wingers accosted Lyndon and Lady Bird Johnson in Dallas. Pictures of the ugly spectacle on TV and in the newspapers sparked a good deal of public indignation, which Johnson skillfully stoked. Texas hung in the balance for most of election day before slipping into Kennedy's column.

At that point, Nixon knew that he had to carry nearly all of the states yet to be called. Wins in Florida, Tennessee, Virginia, and Kentucky (all Eisenhower states in 1956) provided encouragement, as did confirmation of Republican victories in Indiana, Iowa, Kansas, Oklahoma, Nebraska, North Dakota, and South Dakota. Nixon also won Ohio (a bitter disappointment for Kennedy) and stood a good chance of claiming Michigan's electoral votes until the final tally put the Wolverine State in Kennedy's column. Most of the Mountain West states voted for Nixon, as did Oregon, Washington, and newly admitted Alaska. Kennedy carried New Mexico, Nevada, and newly admitted Hawaii (the latter by just 115 votes out of 733,349 cast).[18]

Shortly after midnight, Nixon spoke to a gathering of supporters at the Ambassador as his wife, Patricia, choked back tears. "The present trend," he said, favored Kennedy. As diehards shouted, "No, no, don't concede," Nixon asked for national unity. "I want Senator Kennedy to know, and I want all of you to know, that certainly if this trend continues, and if he does become our next president, he will have my wholehearted support."[19] In Hyannis Port, some of Kennedy's inner circle excoriated Nixon for not giving up. "Why should he?" Kennedy asked. "I wouldn't under these circumstances."[20]

The circumstances to which Kennedy referred were shaping up to produce one of the closest outcomes in the history of American presidential elections. His popular-vote margin had slipped below 900,000, and there was every reason to expect further attrition. Yet Kennedy needed just four more electoral votes to win, and only California, Illinois, Michigan, and Minnesota were still in play. For his part, Nixon never doubted that he would prevail in California, but he questioned his chances of carrying all of the others.[21]

With some state outcomes still up in the air the following morning, Nixon took a hard look at the numbers. Assuming a victory in California, he had carried twenty-six states to Kennedy's twenty-three. Kennedy, however, appeared to control 303 electoral votes, or 34 more than needed for election. The popular vote in Alabama and Mississippi had set aside 14 electoral votes for Senator Harry F. Byrd, a Dixiecrat from Virginia. To win, Nixon somehow had to deprive Kennedy of 49 electoral votes unofficially credited to him. Reports of massive voter fraud in Cook County, Illinois, as well as in a number of Texas counties seemingly provided grounds for legal challenges, if Nixon were so inclined. He also held out hope that the final tally in Minnesota would eliminate Kennedy's wafer-thin margin.

In a 1978 account of his thinking on the morning after the 1960 election, Nixon wrote that Senator Everett Dirksen had telephoned him to vent his anger over massive voter fraud in Chicago. Nixon claimed that Dirksen had implored him to file an immediate legal challenge to the Cook County vote. If he did not do so, Dirksen warned, "voting records would be destroyed or otherwise disappear."[22] Nixon shared Dirksen's view that Mayor Daley had stolen Illinois for Kennedy, but he doubted that he would prevail in a court case. Reports of similar wrongdoing in Texas led Nixon to consider a legal challenge there, but he dropped that idea when he learned that Texas law made no provision for a recount. Had he raised the challenge in Illinois, Nixon wrote, the matter might have dragged on for half a year, thereby draining the legitimacy of Kennedy's presidency.[23] Moreover, U.S. foreign policy and the national interest would have suffered. For good measure, he added: "And what if I demanded a recount and it turned out that despite the vote fraud Kennedy had still won? Charges of 'sore loser' would follow me through history and remove any possibility of a further political career."[24]

More so in 1978 than in his 1962 memoir, Nixon bitterly recalled the disinformation and dirty tricks that the Democrats had used against him in 1960. He had harsh words for Robert Kennedy's use of the Catholic issue. Alluding to Dick Tuck, a foe who had hounded him for decades, Nixon sourly commented on the dirty tricks that had "captivated many politicians and overcame the critical faculties of many reporters."[25] From that point on, Nixon stated, "I had the wisdom and wariness of someone who had been burned by the power of the Kennedys and their money and by the license they were given by the media. I vowed that I would never again enter an election at a disadvantage by being vulnerable to them—or anyone—on the level of political tactics."[26]

THE STRATEGIC ENVIRONMENT OF 1960

The Eisenhower Factor

Of the many shadows that individuals cast on the 1960 campaign, Eisenhower's loomed as potentially the largest. The last president born in the nineteenth century and the most successful military man in American politics since Ulysses S. Grant, Ike was the first Republican to occupy the Oval Office in twenty-four years. Reelection in 1956 made him the first president covered by the Twenty-second Amendment's ban on third terms. Although ailing and aged by the burdens of office, he enjoyed an average job approval rating of 62.7 percent in his last two years in office. Never between January 1959 and October 1960 did his approval number fall below 57 percent.[27]

One can only speculate on whether a more engaged Eisenhower could have changed the 1960 outcome in critical states such as Illinois and Missouri. In any case, he contributed too little and too late to help Nixon's campaign. Ike's ambivalent relationship with Nixon dated back to 1952, and as one White House insider recalled of the 1960 race, a "peculiar distance" existed between the White House and the man "striving so actively to defend it and so ardently to inherit it."[28]

That relationship had soured shortly after Eisenhower accepted Nixon as a running mate in 1952. Nixon had risen high in some party circles for unmasking Alger Hiss, he hailed from a state rich in delegates at the Republican convention, and he had helped deliver that delegation to Ike in Chicago. Eisenhower evidently had decided on Nixon even before the convention, and the party leaders with whom he discussed the choice expressed wholehearted agreement.[29] Soon, however, Ike developed a case of buyer's remorse, when his running mate came under fire for allegedly accepting improper donations from supporters. Pressured by old friends and leading newspapers to dump Nixon, Ike shifted from a statement of initial support to a demand that Nixon prove himself to be "cleaner than a hound's tooth." Although this ordeal reduced Nixon to tears on occasion, it also aroused his fighting spirit. The affair famously climaxed with the Checkers speech, in which Nixon not only denied the charge, detailed his personal finances, and called attention to Democratic practices but also outflanked the general by asking viewers and listeners to decide his fate in calls and telegrams to the Republican National Committee. The tidal wave of support that flooded the RNC quickly forced Ike off the fence (or off the pot, as Nixon indelicately put it). Although Ike publicly embraced Nixon as "my boy," the episode indelibly stained their association.[30]

Three years later, the heart attack that cast a shadow over Ike's reelection bid also inspired another effort to get rid of Nixon. Eisenhower answered the question of his candidacy at a February 1956 news conference, but he also set off a frenzy of press speculation by refusing to discuss Nixon's role in the campaign. Unquestionably, this "lack of a clear-cut and enthusiastic endorsement cut Nixon deeply."[31] Eisenhower further aroused Nixon's suspicions by signaling that he should forfeit the vice presidency for a cabinet seat. Accounts differ on what motivated him to make this offer. Some say that he wanted to help Nixon build a more impressive record of executive leadership in time for the 1960 race, but others conclude that he wanted to replace Nixon with someone more likely to win in 1960. In any case, Nixon stayed on the ticket by rebuffing the gambit and thereby forcing Ike's hand.[32]

More tensions arose on the eve of the 1960 convention, when Nixon entered into the so-called treaty of Fifth Avenue with Governor Nelson Rockefeller of New York, an on-again, off-again rival for the nomination. Rockefeller had angered Eisenhower by questioning his defense budget and by warning state governors of a decline in U.S. power. To head off a convention challenge, Nixon negotiated changes in the platform to Rockefeller's liking. Although these changes infuriated Eisenhower, Nixon ultimately orchestrated compromises that not only placated the president but also satisfied Rockefeller. Thanks to Nixon's skillful maneuvering, the Chicago convention showcased unity rather than fratricide.[33] Interestingly, however, Eisenhower never mentioned Nixon by name in his speech to the delegates.[34]

Not long afterward, Ike dealt a serious blow to Nixon's argument that, as vice president, he had acquired executive experience wholly lacking in Kennedy. Nixon had frequently spoken of the meetings that he had attended and often chaired in the White House, and on at least one occasion, he implied that he had also influenced some of Eisenhower's decisions. *Time* correspondent Charles Mohr pressed the president hard to cite one decision that Nixon had influenced. "If you give me a week," Ike snapped, "I might think of one. I don't remember." Sensing the injury just done, Eisenhower apologized to Nixon, but as both men realized, the Democrats had been given a stick to beat Nixon with for the rest of the campaign.[35]

In yet another awkward exchange, Eisenhower and Nixon discussed the president's role in the fall campaign. Accounts differ on whether Nixon wanted more or less from Eisenhower than he got, but in any case, they agreed that Ike would remain above the fray until the last two weeks. Then, the president would blast the Democrats in key states.

Kennedy's attacks, however, so angered Eisenhower that he wanted to do more for the ticket than the agreement called for. Both men realized that Nixon needed Ike's help when they sat down on October 31 to discuss the remainder of the campaign. When the president said that he wanted to go all out in the final days, Nixon urged him to make even fewer stops than previously planned. Visibly hurt by what he took to be Nixon's rejection, Eisenhower reluctantly agreed to follow orders. Twelve years later, Nixon related that he restricted Ike's schedule because Mamie Eisenhower had begged him not to overtax her husband's weak heart. Nixon also promised to keep Mamie's request secret.[36] In any case, Ike used his limited time to pummel Kennedy on the campaign trail. More use of Eisenhower in that role, Nixon later wrote, might have won the day in Illinois and Missouri.[37]

Cold War Developments

Although the 1960 campaign took place in what technically passed for peacetime, it occurred in a context dominated by the continual threat of war (see the appendix to this chapter). In that difficult time of Sputnik and the purported missile gap, American schoolchildren learned to "duck and cover," authorities designated public buildings as bomb shelters, and homebuilders hawked family bunkers. Tensions dropped when Nikita Khrushchev toured the United States at Eisenhower's invitation, but they surged anew after the Soviets downed an American U-2 spy plane, captured the pilot, and demanded a formal apology from the United States. The collapse of a four-power summit on Berlin soon followed, leading Adlai Stevenson to predict that "this year's campaign will be waged under the darkest shadows that ever hovered over the world—the mushroom clouds of a nuclear war that no one wants."[38] The Russians downed another American plane before the end of Eisenhower's second term, a time also punctuated by Nixon's narrow escape from a violent mob in South America, Japan's cancellation of President Eisenhower's state visit, the emergence of a Soviet ally only 90 miles off the Florida Keys, and Khrushchev's bellicose antics at the United Nations. It is small wonder, then, that worries about national security and related difficulties in foreign policy dwarfed domestic concerns when Gallup asked Americans to name the most important problem of 1960.[39]

Concerns about a missile gap favoring the Soviets arose after the *Sputnik* launch of 1957. Although administration officials downplayed this feat of Russian rocketry, Congress did not. In and out of committee hearings, members expressed fears about the number and superiority of Soviet intercontinental ballistic missiles (ICBMs) that could be launched against the United States. With one eye on the 1960 nomination, Senator Symington took a leading role in challenging a tight defense budget. By 1962, he warned, the Soviets would deploy more than three times as many ICBMs as the United States. The former air force secretary declared that the times required "a missile man for a missile age," and he offered himself for the job.[40]

Senator Kennedy took up the cry in August 1958, warning that "the missile striking power of the Soviet Union" would increase as the "retaliatory power" of the United States declined. Failing a major shift in policy, Kennedy insisted, "the deterrent ratio during 1960–64 will in all likelihood be weighted very heavily against us."[41] "I would not say that the Russians possess an overall superiority," he told Wisconsin Democrats in November 1959. "But we have fallen behind the Soviet Union in the development and production of ballistic missiles. . . . They have surpassed us in the thrust of rocket engines, jet engines, and new types of fuel." He went on to note, "They have more long-range, modernized submarines than we do . . . and they may well be pulling ahead of us in the numbers of long-range jet bombers with a nuclear bomb capacity. Their continental air defense is thought to be superior—their installations better dispersed, better concealed, and better protected."[42]

At times, the prospect of a war against the People's Republic of China (PRC) appeared more likely than one with the Soviet Union. In August 1958, Communist batteries on the mainland began bombarding Nationalist troops entrenched on the nearby islands of Quemoy and Matsu.[43] Fearing that the PRC would try to seize these outposts, Eisenhower and Secretary of State John Foster Dulles vowed to defend Quemoy and Matsu.[44] No Democrat took greater exception to this policy than Senator Kennedy: "Here is a real example of how control of events—even the critical issues of war and peace—can pass from our own hands. For there is a real possibility that the tail in this case will wag the dog—that . . . we will be dragged into a war—possibly an atomic war, probably a world war—at a time and place *not* of our choosing, in an argument over two islands *not* essential to our security" (emphasis original).[45]

In December 1959, Kennedy told a *New York Times* correspondent that the 1960 campaign would turn on defense issues, especially the Republican failure to sustain American superiority. When formally declaring his candidacy on January 2, 1960, he promised dynamic leadership in a "time of maximum peril," and he spoke of reversing the recent decline in America's standing among nations.[46]

Unfortunately for Kennedy, the U-2 crisis that began in May 1960 raised new doubts about his youth and executive inexperience. About the same time, a Gallup Poll showed Nixon far ahead on national security issues. Virtually all of the Republicans polled—as well as most independents and many Democrats—preferred Nixon to Kennedy as the man to negotiate with Russia. Nixon enjoyed a similar advantage on who would be more likely to keep the United States out of another world war.[47]

Kennedy gave his critics in the Democratic Party an opening by suggesting that Eisenhower could have salvaged the Paris summit by expressing regret for the U-2 incident. Although diplomats distinguished between regret and apology, Republicans in Congress and most of Kennedy's rivals for the nomination did not. Senator Hugh Scott labeled him a "turnquote," and Majority Leader Johnson bellowed that he, for one, would never apologize to Khrushchev. Eleanor Roosevelt and Harry Truman called on Kennedy to step aside for a more mature and seasoned leader. "New problems and new opportunities," Kennedy responded, called for new leadership.[48]

In short, both Kennedy and Nixon had good reason to make national security a major issue in the fall of 1960. As one analyst correctly noted, "Kennedy's concern with military preparedness reflected his decision to make America's position in the world a central campaign issue."[49] Similarly, the Cold War had catapulted Nixon onto the national stage, and his representation of the United States abroad as vice president (especially in the celebrated "kitchen debate" with Khrushchev) chiefly accounted for his advantage over Kennedy. Evidence of this showed up in polls that asked which party would be more likely to avoid another world war. In August 1960, the GOP led by thirteen percentage points.[50]

Nixon sought to capitalize on such sentiment by selecting America's "foremost spokesman" on the Cold War as his running mate—Henry Cabot Lodge. Polls at the time indicated that he had made a popular choice; for instance, Gallup found that Lodge got slightly more "highly favorable" mentions than Nixon or Kennedy and twice as many as Johnson.[51] Nixon wanted to focus chiefly on national security and foreign policy issues, not only to showcase his and Lodge's credentials but also to offset the Democratic advantage on domestic issues.[52] It is no wonder, then, that Lodge devoted his acceptance speech at the Republican convention entirely to the struggle against communism.[53]

Recessions and Democratic Majorities

Two of the three recessions during Eisenhower's presidency took place during his second term. The most severe of these began in 1957 and persisted into the next year, contributing to massive Republican losses in the 1958 midterm elections. The vote for Republican candidates in House elections was the lowest since 1936, and forty-nine Republican incumbents lost their seats. RNC analysts found that the level of unemployment in congressional districts correlated strongly with the defeat of Republican incumbents. The GOP also lost thirteen seats in the Senate, reducing the Republicans' number in the next Congress to thirty-four, the party's smallest representation since 1940. Beyond that, 7 Republican governors and 686 Republican legislators lost their seats as well.[54]

According to Nixon, the 1958 setback seriously hurt his chances two years later. Kennedy won a big reelection victory in Massachusetts, whereas Republican losses had reduced Nixon's "stock" to "an all-time low." (Nixon had stumped for many of the Republican losers.) Moreover, so many defeats undermined the Republican capacity to help out in the presidential campaign. Yet another ill effect of the 1958 elections, from Nixon's perspective, was the solidification of the Democrats' advantage among party identifiers. "To win in 1960," he wrote, "the Republican candidate would have to get practically all of the Republican votes, more than half of the independents—and, in addition, the votes of between five and six million Democrats."[55]

Although correct in recounting the Democratic advantage in numbers, Nixon failed to mention that Eisenhower had overcome similar odds in 1952. Then, self-identified Democrats had outnumbered Republicans by 51 to 29 percent, with another 19 percent calling themselves independents. In the 1960 poll cited by Nixon, the breakdown was 47 percent Democrats, 30 percent Republicans, and 23 percent independents.[56]

Signs of the second recession to influence the Kennedy-Nixon contest first showed up in March 1960. It was at that point that Arthur E. Burns, a former chairman of the President's Council of Economic Advisors (CEA) and a Nixon supporter, predicted substantial job losses by October unless the administration moved quickly to increase defense spending and seek lower interest rates. Nixon raised the alarm at the next cabinet meeting but to no avail.[57] The recession became evident "at the very time that Kennedy was calling for greater economic growth and job development."[58]

Religion

The 1928 defeat of Alfred E. Smith, governor of New York and the first Catholic nominee of a major party for president, clouded Kennedy's candidacy thirty-two years later. Although Catholicism figured critically in Smith's loss, other factors also worked against him. Small-town, rural, and "dry" voters took offense at his accent, his Tammany background, and his "wet" position on Prohibition. Moreover, since 1916, the Democrats had not carried one state in New England, the Middle Atlantic region, the Midwest, or the West. Secure only in the South and a few urban outposts, Democratic tickets headed by James E. Cox in 1920 and John W. Davis in 1924 had been buried in Republican landslides.[59]

In some respects, Smith clearly surpassed Cox and Davis. Not only did he win a substantially larger share of the popular vote than either of his predecessors, he also mobilized Catholics and immigrants, whose ballots led to the capture of cities not carried by the Democrats since the 1890s.[60] Likewise, Massachusetts and Rhode Island fell into the Democratic column for the first time since 1912. But it was also the case that large numbers of southern Democrats either defected to Hoover, blanked their presidential ballot, or stayed home. Accordingly, Florida, North Carolina, Tennessee, Texas, and Virginia voted Republican by huge margins, and Alabama and Georgia remained in the Democratic fold by smaller than normal margins. In the South, then, Smith compared poorly not only with Cox, who had swept every one of the former Confederate states except Tennessee, but also with Davis, who had carried all eleven states. Only in Louisiana and Arkansas did Smith do better than Davis.[61] Most Democratic leaders concluded that the nomination of another Catholic for president would wreak similar havoc with the party's southern base.[62]

Kennedy had to reckon with this presumption in 1956, when he made a serious effort to win nomination as Adlai Stevenson's running mate. The Kennedy camp adduced statistics suggesting that JFK would help Stevenson carry big states with lots of Catholic voters that had been lost to Eisenhower in 1952. Stevenson, however, left the choice to the convention, which settled on Estes Kefauver instead of Kennedy. Even so, Kennedy came across on national television as youthful, bright, articulate, and attractive—as well as a worthy prospect for 1960. That Stevenson garnered only a dismal share of the Catholic vote added to talk of nominating Kennedy the next time.[63]

The Kennedy camp could also point to major demographic and attitudinal changes in American society since Al Smith's era. Census figures showed that the Catholic population had more than doubled since the 1920s and that a large part of that population had joined the middle class. Americans also had grown accustomed to Catholics serving in Congress and as governors.[64] Further, Gallup Polls in 1958 and 1959 showed that about two-thirds of the public might vote for a well-qualified Catholic for president if he was nominated by their party. Of course, the same polls indicated that one in four rejected the idea of a Catholic president no matter what his qualifications or party.[65]

Kennedy also distanced himself from "those aspects of Catholicism most likely to generate suspicion of, and opposition to, his candidacy among non-Catholics."[66] Rather than repeat Smith's mistake of defending church doctrine, he quoted his own record and views, focused on legislative rather than theological issues, and spoke only for himself.[67] "Whatever one's religion in private life may be," he told a *Look* magazine reviewer in 1959, "for the office-holder nothing takes precedence over his oath to uphold the Constitution and all its parts."[68] When Catholics complained that he had conceded too much, Kennedy replied that "a Catholic can serve as President of the United States and fulfill his oath of office with complete fidelity and with no reservations."[69]

Knowing that he needed primary victories to win over party chieftains, Kennedy was only too happy to whip Hubert Humphrey in the Wisconsin primary and finish him off in West Virginia. Although much of the press framed Wisconsin as a win for a Catholic in a heavily Catholic state, Kennedy's victory in Protestant West Virginia established him as the leading contender for the nomination.

The "religious issue" also posed a problem for Nixon, who went to great lengths to restrain his supporters.[70] "There should be no discussion of the religious issue in any literature prepared by any volunteer group or party organization supporting the vice president," he declared, "and no literature of this kind from any source should be made available at campaign headquarters or otherwise distributed."[71]

Norman Vincent Peale—a minister, popular author, and longtime supporter of Nixon's—soon tested his candidate's resolve by signing, along with other clergy, a manifesto that opposed Kennedy's election solely on religious grounds. Virtually all of the fury that followed fastened on the befuddled Peale. Nixon refused to repudiate his old friend, but he did come to Kennedy's defense. He also called for an end to the discussion of religion as a campaign issue.[72]

A day later, Kennedy informed a gathering of mostly Protestant ministers in Houston that he was not "the Catholic candidate for president." Rather, he insisted, "I am the Democratic Party's candidate for president, who happens also to be a Catholic. I do not speak for my church on public matters—and the church does not speak for me." He went on to oppose federal funding of religious instruction, White House consultation with ecclesiastical authorities, sending an ambassador to the Vatican, and imposing any religious belief on the public. He also recalled that nobody had challenged his religious views when he joined the navy in World War II. Watching the proceedings on television, House Speaker Sam Rayburn whooped that Kennedy was "eating" his antagonists "blood raw."[73] "The Houston confrontation," Theodore Sorensen recalled, "helped divide the citizens legitimately concerned about Kennedy's views from the fanatics who had condemned him from birth."[74]

Still, as Sorensen also noted, the furor over Kennedy's faith did not subside: "Well over three hundred different anti-Catholic tracts, distributed to more than twenty million homes, and countless mailings, chain letters, radio broadcasts, television attacks and even anonymous telephone calls inflamed and assaulted the voters' senses, at a cost to someone of at least several hundred thousands of dollars."[75]

Although Kennedy absolved Nixon of any part in this hate mongering, other Democrats offered a contrary view. On national television, Robert Kennedy accused the Republicans of distributing hate literature.[76] Lyndon Johnson blasted Nixon for "letting his minions underneath the table spread their hate."[77] Former president Truman railed against Missouri Republicans for "sending out all the dirty pamphlets they can find on the religious issue."[78] DNC chairman Scoop Jackson charged that "religious prejudice" animated Nixon's campaign in the Show-Me State.[79] Representative Charles Diggs of Detroit accused "the propaganda masters of the Republican Party" of keeping up "a continuous, well-financed attack" on Kennedy's religion.[80] Harlem's Adam Clayton Powell ranted that "all bigots will vote for Nixon and all right-thinking Christians and Jews will vote for Kennedy rather than be found in the ranks of the Klan-minded."[81] Adorned with a cover contrasting the Statue of Liberty with a robed Klansman, a United Automobile Workers (UAW) pamphlet asked voters to choose between "liberty and bigotry."[82]

Still other Democrats made an issue of Nixon's Quaker faith. Adlai Stevenson expressed doubt that a Quaker should be commander-in-chief, and North Carolina's governor, Luther Hodges, reminded voters of the last time a Quaker faced a Catholic for president: Hoover versus Smith in 1928. "We elected a Quaker and lived to regret it," Hodges cautioned. "And if you vote for a Quaker this time, you will live to regret it horribly."[83]

Of course, not all Republicans heeded their candidate's injunction against discussing religion. Clare Boothe Luce, formerly a member of Congress as well as U.S. ambassador to Italy, maintained that religion should be a factor in the campaign.[84] RNC chairman Thruston B. Morton accused Truman and Jackson of lying about Republican involvement in attacks on Kennedy's religion.[85] Representative William E. Miller, himself a Catholic, accused the Democrats of playing on the fears of Catholic voters.[86] His remarks reappeared in a New York Republican pamphlet, "BIGOTRY IN REVERSE or How the Kennedy Supporters Are Using His Religion for Political Purposes."[87] Ramsey Pollard, president of the Southern Baptist Association and an outspoken supporter of Nixon, called on the Vatican to "lift its bloody hand from the throats of those that want to worship in the church of their choice."[88]

Republicans pressed Nixon to denounce Democratic exploitation of the religious issue. "If this type of smear continues," Nixon press secretary Herb Klein told reporters, his candidate would "have no choice but to discuss the tactics of our opponents."[89] Nixon, however, held back and thereby won postelection acclaim from Cardinal Richard Cushing and the Fair Campaign Practices Commission. Years later, however, he vented his anger at Robert Kennedy and other "key associates" of JFK for making the religious issue into a "heads I win, tails you lose proposition."[90]

On the one hand, the religious issue evidently hurt Kennedy more in the popular vote than it helped. Surveys after the election revealed that the religious issue had mobilized Catholics to vote overwhelmingly for Kennedy but also that it had mobilized a near-critical mass of nominal Democrats and devout Protestants to vote against him in the South and Midwest. Because of this "new stream" of anti-Catholic Democrats, the popular vote was much closer than it would otherwise have been.[91] On the other hand, the Catholic vote figured critically in Kennedy's victory in the Electoral College.[92]

Civil Rights and the Black Vote

Prior to the Great Depression, most blacks favored the party of Abraham Lincoln and Thaddeus Stevens rather than the party of Woodrow Wilson and Theodore Bilbo. True, Franklin D. Roosevelt and Harry Truman, along with liberal northerners in state parties and the Congress, made the Democratic Party more appealing to African Americans, but the party was also home to Richard B. Russell, James Eastland of Mississippi, and other southern grandees in the Senate who consistently fended off civil rights legislation. Dixiecrats similarly controlled key committees in Sam Rayburn's House of Representatives.[93] A protégé of Russell's, Lyndon Johnson became the most powerful majority leader in Senate history with solid southern backing. Bills and resolutions to enact an antilynching law, establish a Fair Employment Practices Commission (FEPC), or abolish the poll tax died in committee or foundered against Senate filibusters.[94] Support for such measures came from northeastern liberals in both parties who competed for black votes at election time; conservative Republicans of the Midwest and Great Plains made common cause with southern Democrats to defeat this legislation.[95] The New Deal, however, offered blacks a package of economic programs unmatched by the party of Herbert Hoover and Alf Landon. By 1952, Samuel Lubell observed, the Democrats had proven far more effective than the Republicans in addressing "the climbing aspirations of the black masses."[96] Yet Eisenhower's 40 percent share of the black vote in 1956 suggested that the right Republican could nonetheless appeal to African Americans.[97]

In the buildup to the 1960 campaign, Nixon appeared considerably stronger on civil rights issues than Kennedy. During his first term in the House, he had taken out membership in the National Association for the Advancement of Colored People (NAACP) and had voted to abolish the poll tax. As vice president, he had spoken in favor of school desegregation; dined with the president of Howard University; entertained African dignitaries; defended the use of the army to implement the court-ordered school desegregation in Little Rock, Arkansas; headed a commission that promoted employment and promotion of blacks; and advocated a much stronger civil rights bill in 1957 than the one enacted. Black leaders, including Martin Luther King Jr., applauded Nixon's "courage" and urged him to court the northern black vote in 1960.[98]

Nixon also joined Rockefeller in imposing a stronger civil rights plank on his party than conservatives such as Barry Goldwater at the 1960 convention could stomach. The Nixon-Rockefeller version pledged to enforce all civil rights laws, support court-ordered school desegregation, take steps to end racial discrimination in housing, and promote equal opportunity in employment.[99] By matching the Democrats on racial equality, Nixon signaled his intent to compete for the votes of northern blacks.

Although Kennedy, too, had backed a strong civil rights plank, blacks had cause to question his sincerity. No doubt mindful of Al Smith's dismal showing in Dixie, Kennedy made a point of wooing southern segregationists for his vice-presidential bid in 1956. Moreover, the NAACP had rebuked him in 1957 for having helped Johnson weaken the civil rights bill. Likewise, Kennedy had criticized Eisenhower's enforcement of court-ordered desegregation of Little Rock's Central High School in a speech to Mississippi Democrats.[100]

As Kennedy's choice for vice president, Lyndon Johnson's record held even less appeal to African Americans. With his eye on the 1948 Senate race in Texas, Johnson, a congressman at the time, had gone on record as an opponent of the antilynching bill and a fair employment commission.[101] He used his maiden speech as a senator to extol the filibuster as a means of protecting the South against such measures.[102] By 1956, however, he had developed an appetite for the presidency and, in pursuit of that goal, had begun to remake his image. Accordingly, Russell and the other Senate Dixiecrats gave him a pass on signing their "Southern Manifesto" condemning the Supreme Court ruling in *Brown v. Board of Education*.[103] In 1957, Majority Leader Johnson figured critically in enacting the first civil rights bill in eighty years—but not until it was rendered tolerable to Russell and most of the other southern senators.[104] Three years later, Johnson weakened another civil rights act "to the point of meaninglessness."[105]

In a bid for black support just before the Democratic convention, Kennedy had promised the NAACP that he would chart a bold course on civil rights. (In the fall, however, he declined to meet publicly with Martin Luther King in Atlanta for fear of offending white Democrats.)[106] Johnson also gave assurances that he would support the party's civil rights plank.

All too soon, Everett Dirksen put this resolve to the test. Johnson and Rayburn had scheduled a special session of Congress in August as part of a postconvention ploy to put Republicans on record as opposing popular housing and education measures showcased by the Democrats. But Senator Dirksen seized this opportunity to introduce legislation that called for prompt implementation of every commitment to civil rights in the Democratic platform. He reveled in the consternation that his measure sowed among the Democrats and was delighted when Johnson and Kennedy took the lead in voting it down.[107]

The Kennedy camp prepared strikingly different instructions on how surrogates in different parts of the country should go after Nixon on race. Northerners were told to paint him as prejudiced against blacks, whereas southerners were to play up his NAACP membership and his socializing with blacks. Democratic operatives in the South also distributed flyers with photos of Nixon and prominent persons of African descent.[108]

As the campaign got under way, however, Nixon reached a fork in the road regarding civil rights. His ardor for a tough civil rights message cooled upon encountering unexpectedly large and enthusiastic crowds of whites in the South, and he soon began speaking of his belief in states' rights.[109] Oblivious to this shift, Lodge made headlines by suggesting that his running mate would appoint a Negro to his cabinet. Nixon promptly countered that neither race nor creed nor color would figure in his cabinet nominations. Immediately after meeting with Nixon on the matter, Lodge opined to reporters that "it would be a wonderful thing to have a Negro in the cabinet—and I'm still for it."[110] While black supporters of Nixon scratched their heads, Kennedy seized the moment to accuse Nixon of taking contrary stands on race issues.

The most telling moment of the campaign happened near the end, after Atlanta police had jailed Martin Luther King Jr. for taking part in a sit-in. The affair turned ominous when a local judge ordered that King be transferred to a state prison, where his life would have been at risk. Acting on impulse and much to the consternation of his younger brother, Kennedy called King's wife to express his concern. Robert Kennedy followed up by negotiating King's release. After assessing the situation, Nixon opted to say nothing. Word of Kennedy's intervention circulated quickly among African Americans, and King endorsed Kennedy as soon as the jail door closed behind him. On the Sunday before election day, the Kennedy camp distributed 2 million leaflets that contrasted their man's compassion with Nixon's "no comment" to black churchgoers.[111] Until the jailing of his son, the elder Martin Luther King had supported Nixon because of Kennedy's religion. Now, he vowed to dump a "suitcase full of votes" in Kennedy's lap.[112]

ATTACK PROPENSITIES AND TARGETING

Recall that the Skaperdas-Grofman model casts the decision to go negative as a rational assessment of likely benefits versus potential costs, and because the leader in the race has less to gain and more to lose by going on the attack, the leader always runs a more positive race than the trailer. But this did not happen in 1960. Although the Democrats never held a convincing lead, they outattacked the Republicans in every week of the fall campaign (see Table 5.1). Democratic negativity exceeded 60 percent in eight of these weeks and surpassed 70 percent in six. Kennedy's propensity to attack exceeded 60 percent in every one of these weeks, and it topped 80 percent in three of them. Weekly negativity on the Republican side peaked at 61 percent, and Nixon scored 70 percent or higher only twice.

Although Kennedy's attack strategy appears to have been influenced by the closeness of the race, a mix of idiosyncrasies and strategic calculations doubtless contributed to the ferocity of the Democratic campaign and, likewise, to the Republican show of restraint. According to Theodore H. White, who knew both candidates well, Kennedy believed in going all out from the outset, whereas Nixon subscribed to the notion of not peaking too soon—that is, of maximizing the vote by building steadily to a climax.[113] Sorensen described the Nixon strategy as one of "careful pacing of campaign efforts, going all out the last two weeks to reach his peak on Election Eve."[114] Stephen Ambrose agreed that Nixon subscribed to the "theory" of peaking but concluded that he deviated from the plan as circumstances necessitated.[115]

Although the *negativity scores* of candidates reported earlier indicate that Kennedy waged a go-for-broke campaign, they provide no comparable support for the proposition that Nixon's negativity increased steadily as the race progressed. But the sheer *number of attacks* that Nixon made each week does lend support to the idea of a peaking strategy (see Table 5.2). His attacks increased gradually in number until topping out at forty-five in the final week. Kennedy's attacks followed no apparent pattern, other than that they almost always exceeded the number of Nixon attacks.

Of course, *peaking* refers to all campaign statements, negative or otherwise. Allowing for Nixon's stint in the hospital—which overlapped with the first week of fall campaigning—both his surge in week two (to make up for lost time) and his falloff in week three (because of fatigue and lingering illness) make sense. From the third week on, however, the frequency of his campaign utterances increased gradually until topping out in week nine. This pattern suggests that Nixon did follow a peaking strategy, even though it also supports Sorensen's conclusion that Nixon peaked too late because his pace was "too slow."[116] As for Kennedy, the figures on total campaign statements suggest that he, too, stepped up the tempo in the final four weeks.

Interesting differences also surfaced in regard to the targeting of attacks (see Table 5.3). Although the Democrats waged the decidedly more negative campaign, the Republicans speared Kennedy more frequently than Democrats skewered Nixon. Again, the disparity can be traced to competing strategies. Kennedy chose to frame the contest as a choice between parties; Nixon, by contrast, endeavored to

Table 5.1. 1960 Attack Propensities

Week	Democratic Attacks on Republicans	Kennedy Attacks on Republicans	Republican Attacks on Democrats	Nixon Attacks on Democrats
1	.770	.766	.464	.000
2	.640	.703	.398	.298
3	.638	.733	.610	.700
4	.547	.826	.354	.625
5	.723	.822	.580	.703
6	.783	.745	.488	.580
7	.805	.823	.504	.586
8	.702	.720	.519	.567
9	.711	.687	.583	.652
Overall	.713	.755	.511	.578
N statements	998	416	1,069	386

Notes: Weekly starting and ending dates are: week one, September 4–11; two, September 12–18; three, September 19–25; four, September 26–October 2; five, October 3–9; six, October 10–16; seven, October 17–23; eight, October 24–30; and nine, October 31–November 8. Week one overlapped with Nixon's hospital stay; the first debate took place at the beginning of week four, the second during week five, the third in week six, and the fourth in week seven.

Table 5.2. Weekly Candidate Statements, 1960

Week	Kennedy Attacks	Total Kennedy Statements	Nixon Attacks	Total Nixon Statements
1	36	47	0	3
2	26	37	14	47
3	22	30	21	30
4	19	23	20	32
5	37	45	26	37
6	41	55	29	50
7	51	62	34	58
8	36	50	34	60
9	46	67	45	69
Total	314	416	223	386

cast the struggle as a means to elect the better man. To reunite a party twice splintered by Eisenhower's appeal, Kennedy continually reminded Democrats of their heritage. In Duluth, Minnesota, for example, he avowed that "parties do make a difference. . . . The Republican Party would never choose me, and the Democratic Party would never choose Mr. Nixon. If parties don't mean something, we ought to get rid of them."[117] As the nominee of the minority party, Nixon repeatedly urged voters to set party labels aside and vote for the better man.[118] "It isn't enough," he said in Windsor Locks, Connecticut, "simply to say 'well this is my party label and

I am going to vote that way. . . . You've got to look beneath the label . . . vote for what is best for America."[119]

LEADING TOPICS

Both sides focused on the same topics to a remarkable degree, even to the point of attaching the same importance to military and defense issues, the domestic economy, foreign policy, ideology and party tradition, and farm policy (see Table 5.4). Similarly, religion showed up in third place for Democrats, fourth for Republicans. Democrats talked more about campaign matters, and Republicans said more about race. Social and health programs showed up as a priority only for Democrats, just as Republicans made much more of patriotism.

The same table shows that even greater convergence surfaced in the topics most emphasized in attacks. Both sides utilized national security issues and the domestic economy as their foremost subjects when attacking the other. Democratic efforts to associate Nixon with independent attacks on Kennedy's religion provoked an even greater number of Republican counterattacks. For a detailed example of just how

Table 5.3. Targeting of 1960 Attacks

	Democratic Targeting of Republicans	Republican Targeting of Democrats
Targets of all party attacks		
Presidential nominee	536	439
Other targets	176	107
N attacks	712	546
Nominee targeted	.753	.804
Solo attacks by presidential nominee	Kennedy	Nixon
Presidential nominee	201	195
Other targets	113	28
N attacks	314	223
Nominee targeted	.640	.874
Solo attacks by vice-presidential nominee	Johnson	Lodge
Presidential nominee	44	23
Other targets	37	1
N attacks	81	24
Nominee targeted	.543	.958

Note: Some attacks on presidential candidates targeted others of the same party.

Table 5.4. Topics Most Mentioned and Most Utilized in 1960 Attacks

Leading Democratic Topics	Leading Republican Topics	Leading Democratic Attack Topics	Leading Republican Attack Topics
Military/defense (147)	Military/defense (227)	Military/defense (105)	Military/defense (110)
Domestic economy (104)	Domestic economy (102)	Domestic economy (90)	Domestic economy (73)
Religion (86)	Leadership (98)	Foreign policy (65)	Religion (66)
Campaign (74)	Religion (94)	Social/health programs (52)	Leadership (41)
Foreign policy (71)	Foreign policy (79)	Leadership (50)	Foreign policy (36)
Leadership (68)	Race (69)	Ideology/party (47)	Ideology/party (31)
Social/health programs (63)	Campaign (68)	Farm policy (43)	Farm policy (30)
Ideology/party (59)	Ideology/party (47)	Religion (42)	Race (30)
Farm policy (50)	Farm policy (46)	Race (35)	Patriotism (29)
Race (41)	Patriotism (46)	Patriotism (30)	Social/health programs (27)

Notes: The ten topics most emphasized by the Democrats accounted for 76 percent of all Democratic statements; the corresponding figure for the Republicans was 82 percent. The ten attack topics most utilized by the Democrats accounted for 78 percent of total Democratic attacks; likewise, the attack topics most employed by the Republicans accounted for 86 percent of all Republican attacks.

much the two sides converged on an important issue belonging to the military and defense category, see the "Echoes" section later in this chapter.

ATTACK METHODS

Idiosyncratic factors appear to have determined the choice of attack methods on both sides (see Table 5.5). Both Kennedy and Nixon relied most on fear arousal; apposition figured next in importance for Kennedy, whereas Nixon made extensive use of labeling. Johnson resorted chiefly to labeling his targets; Lodge usually worked charges of lying into his remarkably few attacks on the Democrats. Humor generally showed up as the least utilized method in 1960, although Democrats made occasional and likely effective use of it. Aside from the stiletto that Kennedy wielded so skillfully at the Al Smith memorial dinner, one of the most notable quips issued from Stevenson, who parodied the title of Rev. Peale's best seller when assailing Nixon's stand on Quemoy and Matsu: "I suppose you could

Table 5.5. Attack Methods, 1960

	Presidential Candidate (solo)	Vice-Presidential Candidate (solo)	All Attackers
Democrats targeting Republicans			
Fear arousal	.478	.346	.427
Ridicule	.105	.259	.118
Labeling	.220	.444	.374
Apposition	.331	.160	.260
Dishonesty	.315	.247	.302
Republicans targeting Democrats			
Fear arousal	.520	.292	.399
Ridicule	.054	.125	.048
Labeling	.413	.208	.469
Apposition	.269	.208	.231
Dishonesty	.300	.542	.337

Note: Entries are percentages of attacks utilizing each method.

call that the power of positive brinking."[120] Truman took particular pleasure in conjuring up a fantasy theme park named "Nixonland," where everything "would be as clean as a hound's tooth."[121]

ECHOES FROM THE CAMPAIGN TRAIL: QUEMOY AND MATSU

Many issues fell under the military and defense heading in 1960, including the failed summit of 1959, the New Look and massive-retaliation doctrines with their implications for defense spending and missile production, the space race, the Congo, Communist threats to allied occupation of West Berlin, Fidel Castro's takeover in Cuba, the potential for war over Quemoy and Matsu, and America's prestige in the world.[122]

Kennedy typically attacked Republican leadership on two or more of these problems, for instance, coupling Castro's takeover of Cuba with developments in the Congo. Other Democrats took up the cry, including Stevenson, Truman, party chairman Jackson, and J. William Fulbright, chairman of the Senate Foreign Relations Committee.[123] Nixon likewise received help from surrogates when making the Republican case. His lineup included RNC chairman Morton, Thomas E. Dewey, Senator Jacob Javits, Governor Rockefeller, and a "truth squad" consisting of House and Senate members.[124] Aside from Secretary of Defense Thomas Gates and President Eisenhower, however, little assistance was forthcoming from the administration.

No exchange of attacks on military and defense matters better illustrates the ferocity exhibited by both sides on the issue of whether to defend the islands of Quemoy and Matsu against invasion by the Chinese Communists. Seldom in the annals of American presidential contests have the campaigns shown a greater willingness to converge on the same issue.

Although Quemoy-Matsu had simmered on the back burner since Labor Day,[125] it boiled over during the second presidential debate on October 7. When asked about the defense of these outposts, Kennedy argued that neither could be defended and that both should be abandoned. Their evacuation, he maintained, not only would reduce the risk of a major war with mainland China but also would clarify America's obligations to the Nationalist government of Chiang Kai-shek. Nixon promptly accused Kennedy of engaging in the same kind of "woolly thinking" that had encouraged North Korea's aggression against South Korea in 1950. More than "two tiny pieces of real estate," Nixon declared, Quemoy and Matsu stood for nothing less than the principle of not giving ground to the Communists.[126]

After the debate, Kennedy charged that Nixon's doctrine of defending "every rock and island around the world" risked dragging the United States into an "unnecessary or futile war."[127] An entire speech on Quemoy-Matsu followed, in which Kennedy warned that the United States might find itself fighting "the wrong war at the wrong place and the wrong time." Nixon, he said, had made "a commitment where we have no commitment now."[128]

Hitting back in Albuquerque, Nixon countered that Kennedy's policy would bring war, surrender, or both.[129] The correct course, he stated, was to yield "not one inch of free territory" to communism.[130] In Long Beach, California, just before the third debate on October 13, he parried Kennedy's characterization of him as "trigger happy" by reminding voters of wars launched by Democratic presidents.[131]

Quemoy and Matsu dominated the third and most acrimonious of the debates. When asked a convoluted question about how he, as president, would respond to an effort to take Quemoy and Matsu, Nixon gave a convoluted reply that avoided a possible use of nuclear weapons. At the same time, he professed a willingness to fight for the islands *if attacks on them were a prelude to an attack on Formosa itself.* Whether his response was calculated or not, Nixon on this occasion had tempered his original vow not to give up an inch of free soil to communism. In the next breath, he cast Kennedy's position in the worst possible light: "To do what Senator Kennedy has suggested . . . that we will surrender these islands or force our Chinese Nationalist allies to surrender them in advance, is not something that would lead to peace. It is something that would lead, in my opinion, to war."[132]

Evidently, Kennedy missed the opening that Nixon had just given him, for he reverted to the familiar claim that his opponent was willing to risk war for the sake of tiny islands that the United States had no obligation or good reason to defend. This exchange led to a heated argument over the precise obligations that the United States had to Chiang Kai-shek according to a 1955 pact. Kennedy maintained that the treaty only committed the United States to defend Taiwan (roughly 130 miles from the mainland) as well as the nearby Pescadores. In Kennedy's account, Quemoy and Matsu (no more than several miles off China's coast) did not fall under U.S. protection. Moreover, Kennedy continued, both President Eisenhower and Secretary of State Dulles were at odds with Nixon's unequivocal commitment to defend Quemoy and Matsu. Nixon accused Kennedy of gross distortion on every point, as well as misrepresentation of a Senate vote that had gone heavily against Kennedy's interpretation of the treaty.

This slugfest continued despite the panelists' attempts to change the subject. Nixon seized on every question, regardless of its topic, to associate Kennedy with the word *surrender*. Showing his anger, Kennedy came up with a quote that Quemoy and Matsu were not worth the bones of a single American solider. He reiterated his understanding of "the disagreement between Mr. Nixon and myself. He's extending the administration's commitment." Nixon got the last word, responding to a question about America's prestige in the world to avow that it would suffer if the next president "surrendered" free territory to the Communists.[133]

The debate hardly put an end to the wrangling over Quemoy and Matsu. "If Mr. Nixon wants to engage the United States in military action four miles from the mainland of China," Kennedy vowed on October 15, "I will talk about it from now on." In New Castle, Pennsylvania, he declared: "I do not want any young man in this community involved in a military action on islands not worth the bones of a single American solider."[134]

At that point, Eisenhower intervened via his press secretary, James Hagerty, who issued a statement declaring that the president and vice president were wholly in agreement about the defense of Quemoy and Matsu. "In effect," the *Times* reported, "President Eisenhower associated himself with Mr. Nixon's position. This restated the policy of defending the offshore islands if necessary to the defense of Nationalist China on Taiwan."[135]

Kennedy seized the moment to declare victory, arguing that Nixon had retreated from his previous posturing. "The position outlined in the White House statement," Kennedy insisted, "has been my position throughout and is my position now."[136] In Springfield, Illinois, Nixon likewise played up the Hagerty statement, but he also accused Kennedy of wanting to "surrender" Quemoy and Matsu. Such a "naïve, dangerously irresponsible, frighteningly foolish" policy, Nixon thundered, would only encourage aggression.[137] Sensing that the issue was becoming a liability, Kennedy tried to change the subject, saying on *Meet the Press* that it was time to stop talking about Quemoy and Matsu. Nixon immediately issued a statement declaring that the dispute would not end until Kennedy had conceded that "surrendering the islands" was unwise and unacceptable.[138]

The exchange continued when both men turned up in Florida to address a meeting of the American Legion. Warming up for the event, Kennedy played to the home crowd: "I wish I could take Mr. Nixon's attention for just five minutes from the coast of China, and move him just ninety miles off the coast of Florida." In his convention speech, Kennedy promised to honor all "present commitments" to freedom around the world, including the Formosa Strait. "Anyone who says the reverse," he added, "is guilty of a malicious distortion."[139] Nixon warned the Legionnaires against a policy of surrender: "Whenever you deal with a dictator, you must never abandon people or territory at the point of a gun because, if you do, it never satisfies him. It only whets his appetite and leads to war and not to peace."[140]

Quemoy and Matsu also figured in the final debate of October 21. Nixon devoted considerable time to the fate of these islands in his opening remarks, contrasting Eisenhower's record of "keeping the peace without surrender" with Kennedy's stand. Kennedy picked up the gauntlet:

> Mr. Nixon earlier indicated that he would defend Quemoy and Matsu even if the attack on these islands, two miles off the coast of China, were not part of a general attack on Formosa and the Pescadores. I indicated that I would defend those islands if the attack were directed against Pescadores and Formosa, which is part of the Eisenhower policy.

Now, he concluded, the controversy had been mooted because Nixon had come around to the Eisenhower position—that is, to Kennedy's view.[141] Nixon flatly rejected this interpretation:

> Senator Kennedy persists in what I think is a fundamental error. He says he supports the president's position. He says he voted for the resolution. Well just let me point this out: He voted for the resolution in 1955 which gave the president the power to use the forces of the United States to defend Formosa and the offshore islands. But he also voted for an amendment—which was lost, fortunately—an amendment which would have drawn a line and left out those islands and denied the right to the president to defend those islands if he thought that it was an attack on Formosa. He repeated the error in 1959, in the speech that he made. He repeated it again in a television debate that we had. . . . Senator Kennedy has to be consistent here. . . . Either he's for the president and against that position, or we simply have a disagreement here that must continue to be debated. Now, if the Senator . . . will say "I now will . . . retract my previous views; I think I was wrong in 1955; I think I was wrong in 1959; and I think I was wrong in our television debate" . . . then this will be right out of the campaign because there will be no issue between us.[142]

Kennedy stood his ground:

> Well, the resolution commits the president . . . to defend Formosa, the Pescadores, and if it was his military judgment [Quemoy and Matsu]. . . . And, therefore, the president's judgment has been that we should defend these islands if . . . the attack on these islands should be a part of an overall attack on Formosa. . . . That's the only position we can take. That's not the position you [looking at Nixon] took, however. The first position you took . . . was that we should draw the line and commit ourselves, as a matter of principle, to defend these islands. Not as part of the defense of Formosa and the Pescadores. . . . And I challenge you tonight to deny that the administration has sent at least several missions to persuade Chiang Kai-shek's withdrawal from these islands.

At this point, time for give-and-take expired, and the candidates delivered their concluding statements, neither of which mentioned Quemoy and Matsu.

CONCLUSION

In the dead heat race of 1960, neither side behaved in accordance with the Skaperdas and Grofman model. Rather, it appears that the instinct of candidates held far greater importance for candidate attack strategies than their standing in the race. Although Kennedy led by a tiny margin most of the time, he and his surrogates exhibited the sort of negativity that one would expect of hopeless trailers. Nixon may have held back from attacking to keep faith with his peaking theory. In any case, the strategies of both candidates reflected electoral considerations wholly lacking in the Skaperdas-Grofman model. Because Nixon needed to win over so many Democrats and independents, his side attacked Kennedy while sparing Kennedy's party. And because Kennedy needed to win back the Eisenhower Democrats, his side barraged Eisenhower and the GOP as well as Nixon. The knee injury that hospitalized Nixon artificially depressed his negativity score in the first week of the fall campaign.

Seldom has a presidential contest so clearly contradicted the notions of issue ownership and avoidance. Indeed, the agreement of Kennedy and Nixon to engage in four debates meant that both men would speak to the same topics. Further, both wanted to fight over national defense and security issues, and so they did.

6. The Dead Heat Race of 1980

Among the possible endings to the 1980 contest, Jimmy Carter's loss of all but four states to Ronald Reagan was surely the least anticipated. The lead in this dead heat changed twice between Labor Day and election day (see Figure 6.1), one-third of all likely voters had not settled on a candidate prior to the final week of campaigning, and roughly one of every ten voters made up his or her mind on election day.[1]

Campaign events take on exaggerated importance in close races, and there is no better case in point than the one and only debate between President Carter and former California governor Reagan, which took place in Cleveland one week before the election.[2] Polls completed a few hours later indicated the beginning of a groundswell for Reagan.[3] Carter had blundered by quoting his daughter Amy on the proliferation of nuclear weapons, and Reagan's "there you go again" retort reminded viewers of Carter's much criticized penchant for personal attacks. Reagan also made maximum use of his closing argument to frame the election as a referendum on Carter's performance:[4]

> Next Tuesday all of you will go to the polls, will stand there in the polling place and make a decision. I think when you make that decision, it might be well if you would ask yourself, are you better off than you were four years ago? Is it easier for you to go and buy things in the stores than it was four years ago? Is America as respected throughout the world as it was? Do you feel that our security is as safe, that we're as strong as we were four years ago? And if you answer all of those questions yes, why then I think your choice is very obvious as to whom you will vote for. If you don't agree—if you don't think that this course that we've been on for the last four years is what you would like to see us follow for the next four— then I could suggest another choice that you have.[5]

Carter suffered another blow only forty-eight hours before the polls opened regarding the fate of fifty-two Americans held hostage in Iran since November 4, 1979. After learning that the Iranian parliament had set out its terms for freeing the hostages, Carter canceled his campaign appearances to study Tehran's terms. He also scheduled a national television address. Close study of the Iranian message, however, revealed that key points had not been resolved, and Carter was obliged to admit that he could not say when the hostages would come home.[6]

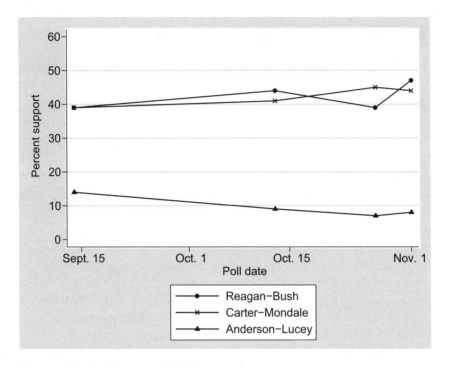

Figure 6.1 The dead heat race of 1980
Source: The Gallup Poll: Public Opinion 1980 (Wilmington, DE: Scholarly Resources, 1981).

Although the tracking polls of both sides showed a Reagan gain after the Cleveland debate, they differed greatly on what was going on in the final days. Pat Caddell's polls for Carter led the president to think he had a chance, but Richard Wirthlin's indicated that Reagan was on track to win by a landslide.[7] Wirthlin had gotten it right, as Caddell realized when looking at the results of his final poll. While returning from campaign appearances in Oregon and Washington, Carter learned from Caddell that his base was collapsing.[8] After a dolorous finale in Plains, Georgia, Carter returned to the White House to prepare his concession speech. Speaker Tip O'Neill called to urge him not to concede before the polls had closed on the West Coast. O'Neill feared for the reelection of vulnerable Democrats in the Pacific time zone, and he reportedly wrung a promise from the president to hold off until the polls had closed. However, early network projections of a Republican sweep changed Carter's mind. After telephoning congratulations to a surprised Reagan, he formally conceded the election before all of the polls in the West had closed.[9]

Unlike 1960, the dead heat contest of 1980 ended with a "negative landslide," in which Reagan carried all but six of the fifty states, for a total of 489 electoral votes;

he also trounced Carter in the popular vote, 50.7 to 41 percent. Running on a National Unity ticket, Representative John Anderson of Illinois garnered 6.6 percent in the popular vote. Though respectable for a third-party candidate, Anderson's share was substantially less than his support in earlier polls.[10]

A critical factor in Carter's defeat was the loss of support among voters who had backed him in 1976. Exit polls revealed a massive falloff even among groups that gave him a majority of their votes in both elections: a 19 percent drop among Jews (from 64 percent in 1976 to 45 percent in 1980) as well as a decline of 13 percent among self-declared liberals, 12 percent among voters belonging to union families, 11 percent among professed Democrats and among Hispanics, and 10 percent among unemployed voters. Other groups that had voted for him in 1976 flocked to Reagan in 1980, including moderates, Catholics, blue-collar workers, suburbanites, and small-town inhabitants.[11]

Carter also suffered because millions of voters who had voted for him in 1976 refrained from casting a presidential ballot in 1980. According to a *Los Angeles Times* poll, 28 percent of the 1976 Carter voters blanked their presidential ballot or stayed home this time around, taking a greater toll than that caused by the defection of former Carter voters to Reagan and Anderson. All told, only 37 percent of the voters who backed Carter in 1976 did so again in 1980. Conversely, two-thirds of the 1976 Ford voters pulled the lever for Reagan. Carter also lost badly among so-called late switchers, or voters who had supported him in preelection polls but voted two-to-one for Reagan on election day.[12] Anderson took away almost as many votes from Reagan nationwide as he wrested from Carter, but a state-by-state analysis revealed that he had seriously hurt the president in must-win states such as Massachusetts and New York while doing no comparable harm to Reagan.[13]

Explanations for Reagan's unexpected landslide vary to this day. Most agree with Paul Abramson, John Aldrich, and David Rohde that the outcome constituted more of a repudiation of Carter than an ideological or policy mandate for Reagan.[14] Although approval of Carter's performance declined drastically (see Figure 6.2), a sizable portion of Reagan voters were uneasy about their choice. Exit polls revealed that "time for a change" was the most-cited reason for choosing him.[15] Some analysts opined that Reagan had benefited from a rightward shift in public opinion indicative of realignment; others attributed his victory to dealignment.[16]

In any event, returns from House, Senate, gubernatorial, and state legislative elections indicated that the Carter factor extended well beyond presidential voting. Republicans gained twelve seats in the Senate, unseating nine Democratic incumbents in the process and recapturing the chamber for the first time since 1954. Among the Democratic losers were such liberals as Birch Bayh of Indiana, Frank Church of Idaho, John Culver of Iowa, George McGovern of South Dakota, Warren Magnuson of Washington (Appropriations chairman and Senate president

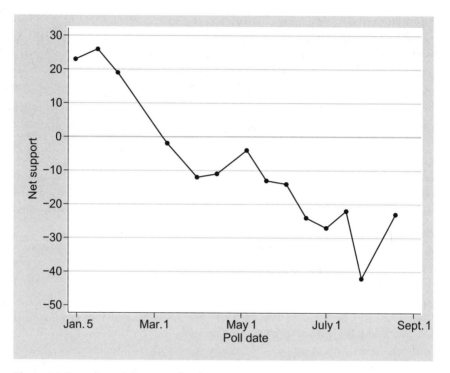

Figure 6.2 Carter's net job approval ratings, 1980
Source: The Gallup Poll: Public Opinion 1980 (Wilmington, DE: Scholarly Resources, 1981).

pro tempore), and Gaylord Nelson of Wisconsin. Likewise, the GOP picked up thirty-three seats in the House, including twenty-seven wrested from incumbents such as Majority Whip John Brademas; Ways and Means chairman Al Ullman; and James Corman, chairman of the Democratic Congressional Campaign Committee. Although the Democrats held on to the House, Speaker O'Neill readily allowed that the outcome had been disastrous for his party. Republicans also came out on top in seven of thirteen gubernatorial elections, unseating three Democratic incumbents (including Bill Clinton of Arkansas), even as they won all of their contested races. The breakdown among governors shifted from thirty-two Democrats and eighteen Republicans to twenty-six Democrats and twenty-four Republicans. With 5,000 legislative races on the ballot in forty-three states, the Republicans picked up 200 seats and won control over both chambers in four additional legislatures.[17]

Carter's problems undoubtedly helped Republicans nationalize contests that usually were dominated by state or local concerns. To symbolize Republican unity, Reagan had appeared at the Capitol with hundreds of congressional candidates to formalize the Capitol Compact, a precursor of the 1994 Contract with America.[18] The GOP also recruited "high-quality" challengers (candidates previously elected to public office) to go after Democratic incumbents, and along with supportive political action committees (PACs), the party invested heavily in good challengers and open-seat candidates. Democratic campaign committees and PACs funneled most of their money to incumbents.[19] Seniority also figured as a factor in these contests because of the anti-incumbent mood of voters in many districts.[20] Accordingly, the pull of Reagan's coattails remained a matter of debate, although few experts dispute that he proved to be a "significant asset" for his party in selected House and Senate races.[21]

THE STRATEGIC CONTEXT OF 1980

Carter's Style and Relations with Congress

Most accounts agree that Carter's personal style, which he projected onto the bigger-than-life stage of the presidency, undermined his leadership of congressional Democrats. "We came to Washington as outsiders," Carter later wrote, "and never appreciably changed this status. Nowhere within the press, Congress, or the ranks of the Washington power structure were there any long-established friends and acquaintances who would naturally come to our defense in a public debate on a controversial issue."[22] His southern identity, born-again Christianity, and relative inexperience in government enhanced his prideful outsiderism.[23] Before becoming president, Carter had served seven years as head of a county school board, two terms in the Georgia senate, one term as governor, and a brief time as chairman of the National Democratic Campaign Committee. "Nothing in Mr. Carter's prior experience as a politician," Nelson Polsby has written, "certainly nothing in his experience of the nomination process, led him to the view that he had to come to terms with the rest of the Democratic Party."[24]

As governor of Georgia, Carter had made no secret of his disdain for legislative politics, an opinion he reiterated during the 1976 campaign. Decrying the incapacity of congressional leadership to get things done, he promised to overcome this "inherent" flaw in the system when he became president.[25] When Speaker O'Neill urged the president-elect to respect and work closely with Congress, Carter replied that he would take the same approach he had used with the Georgia legislature.[26] One House Democrat quipped that the new president had "hit the ground shunning."[27] Nearly a year into his presidency, Carter complained about the time that Congress took to enact major bills, and not surprisingly, his presidential memoir teems with condemnations of stubborn committee chairmen and "ravenous" special interests.[28]

This is not to deny that Carter enjoyed apparent success in getting his programs enacted. Congress enacted sixteen of the twenty "significant domestic laws" on which he took a stand, and he endorsed the four others. However, nearly all of the important measures passed only after he made major concessions, and this was especially true of the energy package. His victory on water projects can only be described as Pyrrhic, and the tax bill enacted in 1978 contained so little of what he wanted that a veto appeared almost as likely as a signature.[29]

Congressional Democrats might have followed Carter's lead more willingly if a significant number had ridden his coattails in 1976, but more than nine of every ten Democrats elected or returned to a House or Senate seat won a bigger share of the two-party vote than Carter did in their districts and states.[30] Further, owing to recent reforms, members of his own party in the House possessed both the means and the opportunity to defy him if so motivated.[31]

The Economy

In 1977, Carter entered the Oval Office bent on stimulating the economy with tax cuts and rebates, as well as a federal jobs program. Remarkably little of this package survived the opposition of congressional Democrats.

Economic indicators at the time gave the Carter team reason to believe that a modest stimulus effort would not fuel higher inflation, but one indicator that escaped notice was the annual growth in productivity.[32] From 1963 to 1973, it had inched up by a mere 2 percent, compared with almost 9 percent for Japan and nearly 5 percent for France and Germany. The rate rose by less than half a percentage point in 1979, compared with about 3 percent in Japan, Germany, and France.[33] Of all the shocks to the economy on Carter's watch, this one supposedly had the greatest impact.[34] Worker efficiency could not compensate for wage increases, and when employers passed labor costs on to consumers, the resulting jump in prices stifled increases in real wages.

Several explanations of why productivity had fallen so low got top billing by conservatives: high inflation, high marginal tax rates, and high costs of compliance with government regulation. By one estimate, the cost of business compliance with regulations including those designed to promote worker safety and clean up the environment exceeded $100 billion.[35]

The "Great Inflation" that raged during the Nixon, Ford, and Carter administrations also wreaked havoc with the Keynesian paradigm. That is, the trade-off between inflation and unemployment no longer occurred, and more government spending did not lower unemployment. One economist summarized the economy in 1979 as follows: "We were at the end of two decades in which government spending, government taxes, government deficits, government regulation, and government expansion of the money supply had all increased rapidly. And at the end of those two decades the inflation rate was high, real economic growth was slow and our 'normal' unemployment rate—the rate we experienced in good times—was higher than ever."[36]

Carter had played up the so-called misery index in 1976, pointing out that both unemployment and inflation had reached unprecedented highs on Ford's watch. In 1980, however, the index reached 20.76 (see Table 6.1). Ford gleefully reminded voters of that fact when stumping on Reagan's behalf in 1980.

Inflation on the order of 13 percent led to "bracket creep," that is, it moved taxpayers into higher tax brackets. By one account, the number paying "high" marginal rates quadrupled between 1966 and 1980, and the average rate jumped from 25 to 37 percent. Middle-income Americans felt uneasy about being taxed at rates once reserved for the rich, especially when taxes claimed nearly half of each new dollar earned.[37] Likewise, because inflation also boosted property values, local property taxes shot up. Tax revolts broke out in California and other states, where initiatives to cap the rates easily carried.[38] This movement complemented one of Reagan's principal messages, even though he focused on the federal code, and it brought middle-income taxpayers together with "right-wing populists" such as Howard Jarvis.[39]

Determined to pass an austerity budget for fiscal 1980, Carter proposed major cuts in entitlements in his January 1979 message to Congress. But congressional Democrats recoiled at his plan to take away $400 million from school lunches, $600 million from Social Security, and $2.1 billion from social services. He further raised Democratic hackles by calling for a 3 percent increase in defense spending. "I'm not going to allow people to go to bed hungry for an austerity program," Speaker O'Neill growled.[40] Senator Edward Kennedy roused the Democrats' midterm convention with a fierce denunciation of Carter's plan: "The party that tore itself apart over Vietnam in the 1960s cannot afford to tear itself apart over budget cuts in basic social programs."[41] NAACP director Benjamin Hooks warned of black opposition to Carter's renomination. Meanwhile, the wholesale price index for the first three months of 1979 indicated an increase of 14.1 percent.[42]

Monetary policy before 1979 may have done more harm than good with respect to inflation. Although the Federal Reserve Board had criticized congressional spending and growing deficits, it had done little to offset the effects of such policies and thereby allowed a rapid, if erratic, expansion of the money supply.[43] Outgoing Fed chairman Arthur Burns had exhibited little enthusiasm for Carter's stimulus package in 1977, but he took only modest steps to dampen its effect.[44] Under William Miller, the Fed did increase key rates in 1978—by 3.5 points in federal funds rate (raising it almost to 10 percent), moving the discount rate up from 7.25 percent in August to 9.5 percent in November, and escalating the prime rate from 8 percent in March to 11.5 percent in December. Even so, acceleration of the

Table 6.1. The "Misery Index," 1960–2004

Years	Unemployment	Inflation	Misery Index
1960	5.54	1.46	7.00
1964	5.16	1.28	6.44
1968	3.56	4.27	7.83
1972	5.60	3.27	8.87
Ford years			
1974	5.64	11.03	16.67
1975	8.48	9.20	17.68
1976	7.70	5.75	13.45
Carter years			
1977	7.05	6.50	13.55
1978	6.07	7.62	13.69
1979	5.85	11.22	17.07
1980	7.18	13.58	20.76
Reagan years			
1981	7.62	10.35	17.97
1982	9.71	6.16	15.87
1983	9.60	3.22	12.82
1984	7.51	4.30	11.81
1985	7.19	3.55	10.74
1986	7.00	1.91	8.91
1987	6.18	3.66	9.84
1988	5.49	4.08	9.57
Subsequent years			
1992	7.49	3.03	10.52
1996	5.41	2.93	8.34
2000	3.97	3.38	7.35
2004	5.53	2.68	8.21

Note: For inflation rates, 1982 base = 100.

Sources: http://www.miseryindex.com.us; http://inflationdata.com.

money supply persisted. "If one looked at these increases in the money supply instead of the interest rate," one student of the Carter economy concluded, "one would conclude that money was not tight but easy."[45] In 1979, Paul Volcker succeeded Miller as Fed chair and began his ultimately successful, albeit painful, effort to tame inflation. However, by the time his policy began to work, Reagan had replaced Carter in the Oval Office.

Energy, Crisis of Confidence Speech, and Cabinet Purge

Although no issue mattered more to Carter than formulating a comprehensive energy policy, few issues hurt him more politically. In the course of pushing his program, Daniel Yergin wrote, "Carter received a firsthand education in how special interests operate in the American system, including liberals, conservatives, consumer groups, automobile companies, pro- and anti-nuclear activists, coal producers, utility companies and environmentalists—all with conflicting agendas."[46] To Carter and his energy secretary, James Schlesinger, America's growing dependence on foreign oil (up from 35 percent at the time of the 1973 oil embargo to nearly 50 percent in 1977) constituted a serious threat to national security, one that necessitated serious efforts to reduce consumption.[47] Carter delivered five speeches on energy during his presidency, four to the nation at large and another to a joint session of Congress.[48]

The first of these addresses occurred on February 2, 1977, when Carter alerted the public to the limited sources of oil and gas, advocated development of coal and alternative sources, decried the waste of energy at home, asserted the need for a new energy department, demanded an honest accounting of profits from oil and gas suppliers, and urged citizens to conserve by lowering their thermostats. His appearance on camera in a cardigan sweater underscored the latter point. He followed up with town hall meetings across the nation. Still, as he later acknowledged, neither his party in Congress nor the public answered the call.

Carter tried again on April 18, 1977, this time referring to the eventual energy crisis as "the moral equivalent of war," a phrase openly scorned by pundits of various persuasions. Schlesinger later characterized the response as more akin to Chinese water torture than to William James's moral equivalent of war.[49] Two days later, Carter submitted a package of five bills to Congress, none of which passed before adjournment in December.[50]

Under pressure from European leaders at the 1978 economic summit in Bonn, Carter had committed the United States to a policy of gradually decontrolling artificially low prices on domestically produced oil, with the intent of allowing them to rise to the world level. Although Carter deemed this pledge necessary to exact concessions from the Europeans, he also wanted to reduce energy consumption at home, as well as force domestic manufacturers to produce more fuel-efficient vehicles. Accordingly, on April 5, 1979, he vowed to exercise his executive authority if necessary to decontrol the price of domestic oil. To make this policy acceptable to Congress, he called for a 50 percent windfall-profits tax on oil company income attributable to decontrol or to future price increases by the Organization of Petroleum Exporting Countries (OPEC).[51] (OPEC had doubled the price of imported crude oil in February.) He also sought authorization to impose emergency rationing of gasoline, a proposal quickly voted down in the House.[52]

Meanwhile, the high cost of energy figured in inflated prices for agricultural goods, which shot up by 15 percent between the fourth quarter of 1978 and April 1979. Charles Schultze, chairman of Carter's Council of Economic Advisers, predicted that prices would jump another 10 percent by the fourth quarter of 1979.[53]

Unfortunately for Carter, decontrol coincided with shortages of gasoline supplies, which led to long lines at filling stations across the country. Even before
decontrol went into effect, lines at some California stations numbered 500 cars.
In the New York metropolitan area, 90 percent of all gas stations closed down
over the Fourth of July weekend, as did 80 percent of all filling stations in Pennsylvania.[54] A wildcat strike among independent truckers exacerbated the plight of
motorists, whose outrage attracted considerable coverage on the nightly news.[55]

In yet another instance of unfortunate timing, the July shortages made news
while Carter was holding forth at an economic summit in Tokyo. At the urging of
Vice President Mondale and others, he returned promptly to Washington to address the problem rather than take a few days of vacationing in Hawaii.

July 3 found the president back at Camp David and at work on yet another energy speech. His focus changed, however, after reading a memorandum from Pat
Caddell, which argued that "the American people had become completely inured
to warnings about future energy shortages," in part because they saw both government and the oil companies as "incompetent or dishonest—or both." Carter
agreed with this analysis and also concurred in Caddell's judgment that "the problem transcended the single issue of energy, and applied to the basic relationship
between the people and their government and other major institutions." In short,
"Americans were rapidly losing faith in themselves and in their country." Carter
accordingly embraced Caddell's recommendation that he move beyond energy in
the next speech to address the national mood.[56]

Having settled on this course, Carter canceled the energy speech and likewise
backed out of a commitment to speak at the National Governors' Conference.
Word of these developments aroused the news media, and the plot thickened
when Carter and wife, Rosalynn, holed up at Camp David, where they planned to
seek advice from people they trusted on what to do next. Carter recalled feeling
"a remarkable sense of relief and renewed confidence" after taking these steps.[57]
His behavior, however, hardly inspired confidence in government circles or in
the news media, where many speculated about the president's state of mind. The
White House responded with a statement that Carter was "all right."[58]

Meanwhile, Carter summoned Vice President Mondale, Caddell, Communications Director Gerald Rafshoon, Domestic Policy Aide Stuart Eizenstat, and
Press Secretary Jody Powell to a July 5 meeting at Camp David. In what soon became a heated confrontation, Mondale took on almost everyone else, including
the president. Caddell began the session by distributing poll data to support his
view that a self-indulgent public lacked confidence in government. Carter agreed
with Caddell, at one point exclaiming that "we're irrelevant and people don't listen to us." More programs, he added, would not ameliorate the country's "sense of
despair." Rather than give another energy speech that no one would heed, Carter

wanted to talk about deeper and more spiritual concerns. Visibly upset by such talk, Mondale countered that the problem was a lousy economy, not spiritual malaise. Carter replied that the time had come for a show of "drama and mystery" rather than just another energy speech. "You can't castigate the American people," Mondale shot back, "or they will turn you off once and for all."[59]

Taken aback, Carter abruptly ended the meeting and asked Mondale to take a stroll with him around Camp David. As they walked, he tried to persuade Mondale that a speech of the sort proposed by Caddell was the "right thing to do."[60] Mondale disagreed. "Everything in me told me that this was wrong, " he said later. "I thought it would destroy Carter and me with him."[61]

Until that moment, Carter evidently had not sensed the depth of Mondale's unhappiness as vice president. Although friendly with Jordan and with director of the Office of Management and Budget (OMB) Bert Lance (forced out in 1977 due to allegations of scandal), Mondale had made no secret of the ill will he felt toward Caddell, Rafshoon, and Attorney General Griffin Bell. Nor did he hide his dismay over how Carter aides in the White House treated congressional Democrats. Further, Mondale now viewed the association with Carter as detrimental to his own chance of becoming president. Indeed, he gave serious thought to resigning his office before the 1980 convention, as well as to refusing to seek reelection as Carter's running mate. In June, after much soul-searching, he had decided to stay the course. Although the July 5 meeting at Camp David shook that resolve, Mondale hoped to refocus the next Carter speech (scheduled for July 15) on energy policy.[62]

In the interim, Carter summoned roughly 150 people to Camp David for "leisurely conversations" about the state of the union, the effectiveness of his administration, and energy. Members of Congress, Washington insiders, governors, labor leaders, educators, prominent journalists, economists, energy experts, religious leaders, and experienced political advisers trooped to the mountaintop.

One such group (consisting of senior political adviser Charles Kirbo, Jesse Jackson, former defense secretary Clark Clifford, and six others) met with Carter late one afternoon, talked through supper, and reconvened for a wrap-up session in the presidential cabin. Reposed on the floor, Carter took notes as his guests literally looked down on him as they spoke. In this, as in previous sessions of this sort, Carter heard a lot of criticism of the cabinet, the White House staff, and himself. "It was not pleasant for me to hear this," he revealed in his memoir, "but I felt their analysis was sound." Indeed, he looked back on the Camp David experience as "the most thought-provoking and satisfying" of his presidency.[63]

As Mondale feared, Carter devoted more than half of the new speech to Caddell's malaise thesis. He spoke of national problems that went "much deeper" than long lines at gas stations, energy shortages, and even inflation or recession. He related some of the criticisms aired at Camp David, and he warned that a crisis of confidence might "destroy the social and political fabric of America." The choice was clear: indulgence and self-destruction versus sacrifice and eventual energy independence. "Energy," Carter declared, "will be the immediate test of our ability to unite this nation." In a bow to Mondale, he proposed relying less on foreign oil, imposing import quotas, developing alternative fuels, pushing utility companies to switch from oil to other fuels, establishing an energy mobilization board, and promoting conservation in the workplace and at home.[64]

To Mondale's immense relief, the speech was favorably received in most quarters. But public opinion quickly changed when Carter decided to follow the advice of Camp David participants and purge his administration. Thirty-four high officials, including senior White House staff and cabinet members, were instructed to sign undated letters of resignation. The ax fell on the secretaries of energy, transportation, and treasury, as well as the attorney general. One of Mondale's staunchest allies—Health, Education, and Welfare Secretary Joseph Califano—also lost his post.[65] Carter's poll standings reflected a general discontent, as in a report by the Harris Poll that disapproval of his performance as president had risen to 75 percent.[66]

Foreign Policy and the Iranian Hostage Crisis

As in domestic policy, Carter experienced some hard-won successes and endured some stinging defeats. Successes included the Camp David Accords, which ended the state of war between Israel and Egypt. Less acclaimed was the severing of ties with the Nationalist Chinese government on Taiwan in order to establish full relations with the PRC. Congress responded to this executive action by passing a veto-proof bill that assured Taiwan of future American arms sales. Carter reluctantly signed this measure, which also contained a warning that the United States would not countenance military or economic action against Taiwan.[67] With the backing of former president Ford and other Republicans, Carter pushed the Panama Canal Treaty through the Senate, and without Republican votes in the House, legislation to implement the treaty would not have passed.[68]

Carter's earliest setback on foreign and military policy arose from his attempt to pull all U.S. ground troops out of South Korea. Several motivations appear to have shaped this campaign promise: a desire to avoid another Korean war, a hope of reducing military expenditures, and a wish to punish South Korea's abuses of human rights. At the same time, he appeared oblivious to the greater risk of North Korean aggression, Pyongyang's far worse record of human rights abuses, and the improbability of forcing so basic a policy change entirely on his own. After encountering fierce opposition from Congress, the Pentagon, and the governments of South Korea and Japan, Carter abandoned the effort in 1979.[69]

Another reverse occurred just after the signing of the SALT II Treaty in 1979, when the Soviets invaded Afghanistan. Sensing that he had to protest this aggression yet desirous of ratifying the treaty, Carter pushed for a UN resolution condemning the Soviets. He also ordered an embargo on grain sales to the USSR and canceled American participation in the Moscow Olympic Games. The embargo backfired, allowing Argentina and Canada to increase their exports and giving Reagan an issue to push in the Farm Belt.[70] Meanwhile, the Senate refused to approve SALT II, a disappointment that Carter later called "the most profound" of his presidency.[71]

No debacle hurt Carter more than the Iranian hostage crisis that started on November 4, 1979, and dragged on for 444 days. Most accounts of the 1980 campaign agree that his failure to free the hostages by election day exhausted the electorate's tolerance for weak and ineffectual leadership.[72]

From the American standpoint, the origins of the hostage crisis probably went back no further than November 15, 1977, when the president and First Lady hosted Shah Mohammad Reza Pahlavi of Iran and his wife in an outdoor ceremony at the White House. A nearby protest of Iranian students provoked the police to use tear gas, which drove the presidential party inside. After this inauspicious beginning, Carter and the shah took up the touchy subject of human rights abuses in Iran. For the most part, Carter listened while the shah justified his measures as essential to combating domestic Communists backed by the Kremlin.[73]

Carter's apparent reticence to make an issue of human rights on this occasion may have encouraged the shah to order a crackdown upon returning home. In any case, a new policy of repression had begun when President and Mrs. Carter visited Tehran in January 1978. It was during this state visit that Carter famously toasted the shah and proclaimed Iran "an island of stability in a turbulent corner of the world." The Ayatollah Ruholla Mussaui Khomeini, a bitter enemy of the shah's who was exiled to Saddam Hussein's Iraq at the time, denounced Carter as a hypocrite on human rights.[74]

The irony in Carter's toast became apparent in little more than a month, when riots erupted in more than fifty Iranian cities; security forces killed and wounded hundreds. The violence reached a boiling point when roughly a million protestors marched in Tehran chanting "Death to the Pahlavis," "America out of Iran," and "Khomeini is our leader." The shah moved quickly to impose martial law and to demand Khomeini's ejection from Iraq. Khomeini soon turned up in Paris, where he enjoyed much greater freedom to agitate as well as increased access to Western media.[75]

On November 2, National Security Adviser Zbigniew Brzezinski called the shah to pledge Carter's support in resolving the crisis. America's ambassador to Iran reaffirmed this commitment to the shah, and in Washington, Secretary of

State Cyrus Vance read a similar statement to reporters. By that time, however, Pahlavi had grown loath to unleash the "iron fist." Rather, he talked of taking his family on a long "vacation" and appointed a famously diffident general to head up a new government.[76]

Encouraged by the shah's show of weakness, the rapidly growing opposition cried out for his death and Khomeini's return from exile.[77] Rolling strikes shut down the oil sector and soon crippled the economy. Rebellious customs officers opened the floodgates to smuggled weapons. Immobilized by the lack of fuel, the military limited its patrols. Carter cabled the shah on December 28, urging him either to establish a stronger military government or to abdicate in favor of his son. Instead, the shah ended martial law, deposed his military government, and appointed the liberal Shapour Bakhtiar as prime minister. By that time, large numbers of soldiers had begun to desert, and many of those who remained at their posts refused orders to fire on protestors.[78]

Within days, Carter dispatched General Robert E. Huyser to Tehran for the purpose of rallying the Iranian military to defend the Bakhtiar government. Huyser was also to help engineer a military coup if necessary to block a Khomeini takeover, but he soon learned that Ambassador William Sullivan was trying to reach an accommodation with Khomeini. Their differences mirrored a larger conflict between Secretary of Defense Harold Brown and National Security Adviser Zbigniew Brzezinski, on the one hand, and Secretary of State Cyrus Vance, on the other.[79] Matters grew even more complicated on January 16, 1979, when the shah, his family, and a few aides left the country.

Unwilling to arrest Khomeini upon his February 1 arrival in Tehran, Iran's military leaders soon lost control of the situation. General Huyser left the country on February 3, and Prime Minister Bakhtiar followed suit a few days later. Even as it struggled to evacuate Americans from Iran, the Carter administration decided to keep the embassy in Tehran open. The White House found encouragement in Khomeini's appointment of Medhi Bazargan as prime minister. Khomeini hardliners, however, viewed the relatively pro-American Bazargan with suspicion. Still, when Iranian Marxists overran the U.S. embassy two weeks after Khomeini's return, Khomeini loyalists quickly evicted them and returned the compound to American officials. Similarly, the seizure of Americans monitoring Soviet communications in more remote parts of the country quickly ended with their release.

Once inclined to grant the shah asylum in the United States, Carter now sought to fob him off on other governments. Meanwhile, the shah departed Morocco for the Bahamas and eventually Mexico, where doctors discovered that he was suffering from lymphoma as well as other ailments. Unable to obtain adequate care in Mexico, the shah requested a visa to receive treatment at Columbia University's hospital. David Rockefeller and Henry Kissinger aggressively lobbied the White House on the shah's behalf, and after intense discussions with Mondale, Vance, and others, Carter reluctantly agreed to admit the shah on a temporary visa. "What are you guys going to recommend that we do," Carter presciently queried his advisers, "when they take our embassy and hold our people hostage?"[80] The ailing monarch, his immediate family, and a few aides arrived in New York on October 23. Hoping to temper Iranian reaction to his decision, Carter sent word to Tehran that the shah would stay no longer than his treatment required.[81]

Carter's fear of a hostage crisis became reality on November 4, when 150 militants overran the embassy and seized 66 Americans. Unable to free them, Prime Minister Bazargan and his cabinet resigned. In a crude gesture meant to impress the West, Khomeini released all of the black and female hostages. Fifty-two remained in bondage.[82]

An ordeal that steadily eroded Carter's chances of reelection had begun. From November 5, 1979, to the failed attempt to rescue the hostages on April 24, 1980, the administration launched numerous diplomatic initiatives without result.[83] All the while, Secretary Vance counseled patience and restraint, insisting that Khomeini eventually would reach a point at which he would trade the hostages for concessions acceptable to the United States. "As painful as it would be," Vance wrote later, "our national interests and the need to protect the lives of our fellow Americans dictated that we continue to exercise restraint."[84] Still, as Vance admitted, dealing with the Iranians was like talking into the wind.[85] American diplomacy failed to get European allies to go along with imposing sanctions against Iran, and the effort foundered even before the Soviet Union got a chance to veto it in the UN Security Council. Meanwhile, Hamilton Jordan began communicating with lawyers supposedly employed by the Iranian government in hopes of establishing a back channel to Tehran.

Frustrated by the lack of movement on the diplomatic front, Carter froze all Iranian funds held by Chase Manhattan Bank, ended American purchases of Iranian oil, and eventually expelled Iran's diplomats.[86] Committed to bringing every hostage back alive and averse to spilling Iranian blood, Carter ruled out punitive strikes unless Khomeini put the hostages on trial or ordered their execution.[87] He also rejected proposals to blockade Iranian ports, interrupt oil shipments, and bomb oil facilities for fear of an Islamic backlash.

Eventually, the failure of diplomacy and the mounting frustration of the public led Carter to sanction a high-risk commando raid to free the hostages. This mission came to grief well short of Tehran, when unforeseen weather problems, mechanical failures, inadequate intelligence, and a shortage of helicopters impelled the ground commander to abort. Tragically, one helicopter collided with a refueling plane as the force prepared to depart its first staging area in Iran, thereby igniting a fireball that incinerated eight people. The raiders fled this ghastly scene, leaving behind the charred remains of men and machines, as well as sensitive documents, for the Iranians to display on television. Carter acknowledged the failure as his own in a nationally televised speech delivered the following day.[88]

Despite a short-lived rally effect in the polls, the hostage imbroglio lowered public esteem for the president. Even before the failed rescue attempt, approval of his handling of the problem had dropped from 71 percent in December 1979 to 40 percent in March 1980. Following the debacle in the desert, disapproval topped approval, 48 to 42 percent.[89]

Diplomatic efforts petered out for a time after the failed rescue mission, but a combination of events eventually led to the hostages' release. Although the shah's demise appeared to have no discernible effect on the Iranian leadership, it mooted demands for his extradition. Saddam Hussein's invasion of Iran in September 1980 may have moved Khomeini toward a settlement with the United States, although Tehran at first excoriated Hussein as the Great Satan's agent. This aggression not only unified Iran but also underscored its need for military supplies and equipment that the shah had purchased from the United States but never received. Khomeini may also have hoped to recover some of the shah's money held by American banks. Still other developments probably contributed to a change of mind, including the magnitude of Reagan's victory over Carter in November. To the degree that Khomeini took Carter's repeated denunciations of Reagan as a dangerous warmonger seriously, he must have worried about what thunderbolts this newly elected Mars might hurl at Iran upon taking office. Further, thanks to Vance's diplomacy, Iran had become an outlaw state at the United Nations. Algeria stepped into the diplomatic breach at that critical moment to offer its services as an intermediary. Although an agreement to spring the hostages was concluded hours before Carter left office, Tehran deliberately postponed their release until Reagan had taken the oath of office.

John Anderson's Independent Candidacy

Congressman John B. Anderson (R-IL) began thinking about a run for the presidency in 1978, when he faced a stiff primary challenge from the right wing of his party. First elected to the House in 1960, he had moved considerably to the left by 1978.[90] Rather than seek another term in 1980, he launched a long-shot bid for the Republican presidential nomination. Strong debate performances and a penchant for plainspeaking made him the favorite of the national news media, but good press neither filled his coffers nor propelled him to victory in any primary or caucus state. He departed the race after losing must-win primaries in Illinois, Connecticut, and Wisconsin. Twenty-seven days after the Wisconsin loss, he declared himself a "national unity" candidate for the fall presidential campaign. Two weeks after the Democratic convention, Anderson persuaded a Democrat, former Wisconsin governor Patrick Lucey, to join the ticket.[91]

At the point of Anderson's April announcement, it was clear not only that Carter and Reagan would face off in the fall campaign but also that millions of voters held both men in low esteem. Anderson used his declaration of candidacy at the National Press Club to offer himself as a realistic alternative. Eight Gallup Polls in the spring and summer of 1980 uncovered a range of support from 18 to 24 percent.[92] Invariably, however, Anderson trailed well behind Carter and Reagan when the public named the candidate best able to handle various problems. Moreover, his base looked even softer than that of either opponent.[93]

Anderson did not help his chances by spending far more to get his name on the ballot of every state than necessary and by traveling abroad as a commentator for NBC News while the Democratic primary battle raged. Upon returning, he held a widely publicized meeting with Ted Kennedy, which became all the more newsworthy when Anderson hinted that he might drop out if Kennedy defeated Carter. This ill-considered remark made no sense in view of Carter's solid lead in the Democratic delegate count. Further, it rankled most Anderson supporters, who did not regard Kennedy as an acceptable alternative, and it freshened doubts about Anderson's seriousness.[94] Whatever the import of these mistakes, support for the Anderson-Lucey ticket dropped from 15 percent in mid-September to 8 percent at the end of October.[95]

ATTACK PROPENSITIES AND TARGETS

Neither side in the Democratic-Republican exchange consistently outattacked the other (see Table 6.2). Rather, Democrats waged the more negative campaign in four of nine weeks, Republicans were more negative in four other weeks, and the two sides waxed equally negative in the final week. Overall, the Republicans conducted a slightly more negative campaign against the Democrats than vice versa.

Contrary to either of the three-candidate scenarios proposed by Skaperdas and Grofman, the National Unity ticket attacked the Democrats more than the Republicans (especially in weeks two through four). Overall, Anderson and Lucey attacked the Democrats in 35 percent of their statements, compared with 22 percent negativity against Republican targets.

A plausible explanation of this pattern can be found in the rather different ways that Reagan and Carter responded to Anderson's candidacy. Probably because of the threat that Anderson posed to Carter, Reagan took the view that he should be allowed to take part in the presidential debates. When word circulated in early September that the League of Women Voters (the debate sponsor) wanted

Table 6.2. Attack Propensities, 1980

Week	Democratic Attacks on Republicans	Democratic Attacks on Anderson	Combined Democratic Negativity	Republican Attacks on Democrats	Republican Attacks on Anderson	Combined Republican Negativity	Anderson Attacks on Democrats	Anderson Attacks on Republicans	Combined Anderson Negativity
1	.355	.016	.371	.522	.000	.522	.300	.250	.550
2	.461	.115	.576	.632	.000	.632	.536	.214	.750
3	.507	.029	.536	.613	.000	.613	.500	.017	.517
4	.643	.036	.679	.552	.017	.569	.375	.188	.563
5	.639	.049	.688	.491	.000	.491	.263	.210	.473
6	.521	.033	.554	.617	.000	.617	.348	.217	.565
7	.596	.021	.617	.451	.000	.451	.286	.214	.500
8	.600	.000	.600	.580	.000	.580	.272	.227	.499
9	.500	.018	.518	.500	.000	.500	.342	.233	.575
Overall	.533	.031	.564	.545	.001	.546	.353	.219	.572
N Statements	715	715	715	664	664	664	283	283	283

Note: Week one: September 1–7, week two: September 8–14, week three: September 15–21, week four: September 22–28, week five: September 29–October 4, week six: October 5–11, week seven: October 12–18, week eight: October 19–25, and week nine: October 26–November 4.

to include Anderson in the first of several projected debates, Reagan expressed approval, labeled him a "viable" candidate, and took a poke at Carter: "I can't for the life of me understand why Mr. Carter is so afraid of him."[96] Reagan also helped Anderson gain valuable exposure by debating him on September 21; however, as perhaps Reagan foresaw, he benefited more from the exchange than Anderson did.[97]

The Carter camp plainly viewed Anderson as a threat. Tim Smith, chief counsel to Carter-Mondale, maintained that Anderson took away six or seven votes from Carter for every one he lured away from Reagan. "While Anderson is leading in no state," Smith argued, "he makes Reagan the leader in states where Carter would have been ahead. Anderson has no serious chance to be elected but he has become a significant factor in the election."[98] To lessen the threat, the Democrats tried to keep Anderson off the ballot in their must-win states, they reportedly pressured banks not to lend him money, and they played dirty tricks against his volunteers.[99] Carter's son Chip warned college audiences that "giving a vote for John Anderson is the very same thing as giving a vote to Ronald Reagan."[100] In Massachusetts (where Anderson had made deep inroads into the president's base) Carter likened his nemesis to George Wallace in 1968.[101] Responding to the League of Women Voters, he refused to take part in any debate that included Anderson: "I see Anderson as primarily a creature of the press. He's never won a primary even in his own home state. He's never won a caucus contest in any state. . . . He ran as a Republican and he still is a Republican. . . . He doesn't have a party. He and his wife handpicked his vice presidential nominee."[102]

At first, Anderson rejected the charge that he was out to spoil Carter's reelection. "Talk about being a spoiler," he exclaimed to reporters. "What's to spoil?"[103] But the characterization of him as a creature of the media struck a nerve, as did another Carter charge that he was the second Republican in the race.[104] Anderson's resentment flared in October, when he exclaimed that Carter—"an incompetent moderate"—was worse than Reagan—"a competent extremist."[105]

Table 6.2 also compares combined negativity scores in this three-way contest. Attacks against Anderson increased Democratic negativity by three points. The combination of Anderson-Lucey attacks on both Republican and Democratic targets resulted in an overall negativity score of 57 percent, the highest of the three tickets.

As for targeting patterns, Reagan came under fire in nearly every Democratic assault on the Republicans, whereas the Republicans worked Carter into 88 percent of their attacks against Democrats (see Table 6.3). Carter and Reagan let fly at each other in virtually all of their solo attacks. Only one Republican attack on Anderson surfaced in *Times* accounts, compared with twenty-two attacks against him by the Democrats. Nearly all of the National Unity attacks targeted opposing presidential nominees.

Table 6.3. Targeting of 1980 Attacks

	Democratic Targeting of Republicans	Republican Targeting of Democrats	Democratic Targeting of Anderson	Republican Targeting of Anderson	National Unity Targeting of Democrats	National Unity Targeting of Republicans
All attackers						
Presidential nominee	364	318	21	1	93	58
Other targets	18	44	1	0	7	4
Total attacks	382	362	22	1	100	62
Nominee targeted	.953	.878	.954	1.00	.930	.935
Solo attacks by presidential nominee	Carter	Reagan	Carter	Reagan	Anderson	Anderson
Presidential nominee	194	167	6	1	75	52
Other targets	2	10	0	0	5	2
Total attacks	196	177	6	1	80	54
Nominee targeted	.990	.943	1.00	1.00	.937	.963
Solo attacks by vice-presidential nominee	Mondale	Bush	Mondale	Bush	Lucey	Lucey
Presidential nominee	43	43	0	0	3	1
Other targets	0	5	0	0	2	0
Total attacks	43	48	0	0	5	1
Nominee targeted	1.00	.937	0	0	.600	1.00

Note: Some attacks on presidential nominees targeted others of the same party.

LEADING TOPICS

A remarkable degree of convergence showed up in the topics emphasized by each side (see Table 6.4). Republicans and Democrats showcased the same top-ten topics, nine of which were addressed by Anderson-Lucey. Not surprisingly, the Republicans and Anderson stressed the economy much more frequently than the beleaguered Democrats, a strategy that made perfect sense in light of polls that consistently ranked inflation as the nation's most serious problem. (When responses citing unemployment as the leading problem were added, the combined figure for the high cost of living and job loss exceeded 70 percent.)[106] Given the salience of such concerns, the Democrats had to address them.

Substantial convergence also surfaced in the attacks exchanged between Democrats and Republicans (see Table 6.5). Both sides stressed eight of the same topics, albeit with different degrees of emphasis. The Carter camp painted Reagan as dangerous on military and defense issues, repeatedly cast him as an enemy of Social Security, questioned his capacity for leadership, claimed that he was in league with racial bigots, insisted that he was antilabor, blasted his views on energy, ridiculed his "killer trees" concept of environmental policy, likened him to Goldwater, and warned of the havoc he would wreak in the realm of foreign policy. The Reagan camp blamed the current economic woes wholly on Carter, accused the White House of cutting defense spending as well as of revealing plans for a top-secret stealth bomber, repeatedly denigrated Carter's leadership ability, denounced his foreign policy, turned Carter's charges of racism against him, played up his penchant for personal attacks, inveighed against his policies on energy and the environment, disputed Democratic charges that Reagan wanted to do away with

Table 6.4. Leading Topics of 1980

Democrats	Republicans	National Unity
Military/defense (132)	Domestic economy (136)	Domestic economy (47)
Campaign (79)	Military/defense (99)	Military/defense (42)
Leadership (61)	Campaign (69)	Leadership (39)
Social/health programs (60)	Foreign policy (51)	Campaign (31)
Domestic economy (58)	Leadership (40)	Debates (17)
Race (55)	Debates (39)	Energy/environment (14)
Energy/environment (33)	Race (38)	Foreign policy (12)
Debates (32)	Iranian hostage crisis (35)	Ideology/party tradition (10)
Iranian hostage crisis (30)	Energy/environment (26)	Race (9)
Foreign policy (29)	Social/health programs (24)	Iranian hostage crisis (8)

Notes: The ten topics most emphasized by the Democrats accounted for 80 percent of all Democratic campaign statements; the corresponding figure for the Republicans was 84 percent. The topics most emphasized by Anderson and Lucey accounted for 81 percent of the National Unity total.

Social Security, and eventually got around to questioning Carter's handling of the hostage crisis. On the one hand, Carter wanted to frame the contest around fears of what Reagan would do if elected; on the other, Reagan endeavored to focus voter attention on the economic havoc supposedly wrought by Carter's policies.

A Gallup Poll completed in mid-September must have reinforced Reagan's decision to stress economic woes when barraging Carter. In a series of questions asking which candidate would handle various problems better as president, Reagan enjoyed substantial leads over Carter on inflation (44 to 29 percent) and unemployment (41 to 32 percent). He also edged Carter on resolving the Iranian hostage crisis (39 to 33 percent) and, more tellingly, on who was better on energy policy (40 to 34 percent). Conversely, the figures on keeping the country out of war doubtless reinforced Carter's decision to make the most of military and defense issues when attacking Reagan (Carter led on the war question, 50 to 25 percent). On the same questions, support for Anderson ranged from 8 percent on the Iranian crisis to 14 percent on unemployment and energy.[107]

As for attacks exchanged between Anderson-Lucey and the Democrats, we observed convergence only on leadership and race. On leadership, Anderson replied to Democratic disparagement of his potential with accusations that the president lacked a "clear and compelling" vision of the future. He also branded Carter's stewardship as "incompetent" and "incoherent." "He wants power, yes," Anderson told a gathering of the Liberal Party in New York, "but he seems to have no idea of how to use it."[108] Most of the firefight over race took place near the end of the campaign, when the Democrats aired radio ads in Chicago and Detroit charging that Anderson had voted against the civil and voting rights acts of 1964 and 1965. "This is an undisguised lie," Anderson thundered, "a reprehensible attack to scare black voters away from the Anderson-Lucey ticket. It takes the idea of dirty politics to a new low."[109] Otherwise, the Democrats and Anderson-Lucey shouted past one another—with Democrats making no reply to Anderson attacks on the economy, military and defense issues, Carter's refusal to debate, foreign policy, charges of dirty campaigning, the Iranian hostage issue, and abortion. The lack of response was all the more interesting because the Republicans' resort to the same topics provoked a vigorous response from the Carter camp. Against Anderson, however, Democrats played the wasted-vote card more than any other.

No convergence took place between Anderson and the Republicans for the simple reason that Reagan and his supporters refused to exchange attacks. Even when debating Anderson, Reagan pulled his punches.

Table 6.5. Leading Attack Topics of 1980

Democrats Attacking Republicans	Democrats Attacking Anderson-Lucey	Republicans Attacking Democrats	National Unity Attacks on Democrats	National Unity Attacks on Republicans
Military/defense (98)	Wasted vote (7)	Domestic economy (94)	Domestic economy (20)	Leadership (13)
Social/health (51)	Leadership (6)	Military/defense (70)	Military/defense (18)	Domestic economy (12)
Leadership (39)	Race (3)	Leadership (30)	Leadership (18)	Military/defense (12)
Race (35)	Labor (2)	Foreign policy (28)	Debates (9)	Ideology/party (5)
Domestic economy (26)	Ideology/party (1)	Race (28)	Foreign policy (7)	Personal slurs (5)
Labor issues (20)	Social/health (1)	Dirty campaign (20)	Dirty campaign (4)	Social/health (3)
Energy/environment (14)	—	Debates (16)	Race (4)	Energy/environment (3)
Ideology/party (13)	—	Iranian hostage crisis (15)	Iranian hostage crisis (4)	Race (2)
Foreign policy (11)	—	Energy/environment (11)	Personal slurs (3)	Women, abortion (2)
Dirty campaign (10)		Social/health (10)	Women, abortion (2)	Education (1)

Notes: The top topics used in Democratic attacks on Republicans accounted for 83 percent of all such attacks; the corresponding figure for the Republicans against Democrats was 89 percent. The six topics used by Democrats to assail Anderson accounted for 91 percent of all Democratic attacks on the National Unity ticket. The ten attack topics listed for National Unity against the Democrats accounted for 89 percent of such attacks; the corresponding figure for National Unity attacks on the Republicans was 93 percent.

— = no cases

ATTACK METHODS

As for attack methods, all three tickets relied most on fear arousal, labeling, and charges of dishonesty, making less use of apposition and ridicule (see Table 6.6). Carter sought to stir up fears about Reagan in nearly half of his solo attacks on Republican targets, and Reagan and Bush returned the favor when assailing Democrats. Labeling surfaced as Anderson's preferred method of attack. Accusations of lying figured most frequently in Republican attacks on Democrats.

Of the six presidential and vice-presidential attackers, Mondale made the greatest use of humor. In Arkansas, for example, he ridiculed Reagan's call for the restoration of diplomatic relations with Taiwan, a suggestion he cited as one of several instances in which "the Gipper" wanted to turn back the clock. Continuing in this vein, he deadpanned that Reagan had just come up with a new plan "to win the war in Vietnam" and also that Reagan had picked up the "hot potato that William Jennings Bryan dropped in 1925" by questioning the theory of evolution.[110] In Iowa, Mondale made light of Reagan's environmental record while he was governor of California, chortling that the Republican's plane could not land in Burbank because of the smog.[111]

Anderson had some fun at his opponents' expense in the final days of the campaign. Playing off Carter's reference to his daughter, Amy, during the Cleveland debate, Anderson explained that his own nine-year-old, Susan, was unable to appear with him because she was at home studying up on nuclear nonproliferation. Following a performance of "Dixieland Blues," he thanked a New Jersey combo for playing Carter's song. Fairness, he added, also required a "golden oldie" for Reagan.[112]

ECHOES FROM THE CAMPAIGN TRAIL

On Labor Day, the *Times* ran a front-page assessment of each candidate's situation at the start of the fall campaign, authored by Adam Clymer. Carter was about to speak to 20,000 or more of the party faithful in Tuscumbia, Alabama, where he hoped not only to shore up his southern base but also to showcase ideas for economic recovery that had been promulgated the previous week. His managers conceded that inflation, unemployment, and the dim prospects of freeing the hostages before election day had created serious problems for Carter. Even when his standing rose in the polls, Clymer noted, "approval of his handling of his job remains low. The Carter camp talks of his 'vision of the future,' but concedes a failure to convey it as a strong positive force for his reelection." Still, Carter's team took comfort in the "uncertain state" of Reagan's campaign. After handily winning

Table 6.6. Attack Methods, 1980

	Presidential Candidate (solo)	Vice-Presidential Candidate (solo)	All Attackers
Democrats attacking Republicans			
Fear arousal	.495	.256	.446
Ridicule	.041	.233	.071
Labeling	.362	.256	.402
Apposition	.199	.233	.223
Dishonesty	.173	.279	.226
Democrats attacking Anderson			
Fear arousal	.167	—	.227
Ridicule	—	—	—
Labeling	.500	—	.636
Apposition	—	—	—
Dishonesty	—	—	.045
Republicans attacking Democrats			
Fear arousal	.480	.500	.459
Ridicule	.068	.042	.050
Labeling	.424	.438	.467
Apposition	.198	.250	.182
Dishonesty	.362	.250	.334
Anderson-Lucey attacking Democrats			
Fear arousal	.413	.800	.460
Ridicule	.075	—	.070
Labeling	.438	.200	.450
Apposition	.125	—	.120
Dishonesty	.263	.200	.250
Anderson-Lucey attacking Republicans			
Fear arousal	.315	—	.290
Ridicule	.111	—	.129
Labeling	.463	—	.500
Apposition	.241	—	.242
Dishonesty	.204	—	.210

Note: Entries are percentages of attacks employing a particular method.

— = no cases

the Republican nomination, Reagan had "appeared to many to be headed for a landslide victory." But gaffes over evolution, Taiwan, and the Vietnam conflict had revived impressions of him as "a conservative extremist." The Republican candidate was to speak at an ethnic festival in Jersey City, New Jersey, where he hoped to negate this perception among blue-collar whites of the Northeast. According to Clymer, Reagan's slump in the polls had given rise to a show of confidence in the Carter camp "that would have seemed remarkable a month ago." That mood stopped well short of euphoria, however, because of the threat that Anderson, running at 17 percent in the latest Roper Poll, seemingly posed to Carter. "The belief that Mr. Anderson will take votes from the president," Clymer claimed, "is so firmly ingrained in the Carter camp that it is weighing whether to take the blame for blocking all debates if that is the cost of keeping Mr. Anderson out." Anderson was scheduled to spend part of Labor Day in Calumet City, Illinois, where he, too, hoped to build support among blue-collar voters. Over all of this activity hovered the volatility of voter preferences. Clymer quoted Democratic pollster Peter Hart's contentions that most of the vote would be cast against rather than for a particular candidate and that "as many as 50 percent" would change their minds between Labor and election day."[113]

Republican Attacks on the Carter Economy

Reagan sought to frame the contest as a retrospective judgment on "the things that had gone wrong in America during the previous four years, especially regarding the economy."[114] Of the 318 attack statements for topics most emphasized by Republicans, 29 percent focused on the economy. Reagan took the lead in making the economic case against Carter, although his running mate, former president Ford, and other Republicans added their voices to the assault.[115] At times, Reagan linked his economic attacks to Carter's unwillingness to take part in a debate that included Anderson, charging that the president could not defend so wretched an economy. Reagan similarly melded economic woes with criticism of the administration's tepid stands on Israel and the plight of Soviet Jews. Israel could expect even less support, he warned, "if the United States of America continues its descent into economic impotence and despair."[116] Carter's push for more fuel-efficient cars gave Reagan an opening in Michigan to link this policy to high unemployment in the domestic auto industry.[117]

Even before Labor Day, Reagan had described the economy as being in a state of "depression," a characterization that understandably set off cries of gross distortion and woeful ignorance. On Labor Day, he dismissed such "semantic quibbles," claiming that the voters knew what he meant: "They're out of work, and they know who put them out of work. Let Mr. Carter go to their homes, look their children in the eye and argue with them that it is 'only' a recession that put dad or mom out of work."[118] For the rest of the campaign, he pushed the depression theme. Stumping in the Midwest, for example, he asserted that unemployment had soared to 19.5 percent in Kokomo, Indiana, and to a stunning 25 percent in Flint, Michigan. "These are the figures of the Great Depression of the 1930s," he told a cheering crowd in Kokomo. "That's not the recession he [Carter] speaks of, that's depression."[119]

In Chicago on the following day, Reagan fired off a fusillade of charges, contending that the policies of the Carter administration had "damaged our economy much more than virtually anyone could have foreseen." Noting the "unconscionably high" interest rates and inflation, the loss of 2 million jobs "this year alone," and an increasing tax burden, he characterized the president's "economic failures" as "an assault on the hopes and dreams of millions of American families." More accusations followed: "Every visit to the supermarket reminds us of what Mr. Carter's policies have done. We pay the price of Carter's inflation every time we buy food or clothing or other essentials. We are dealing with an unprecedented crisis that takes away not only wages and savings, but hopes and dreams."[120]

An Associated Press interview furnished Reagan yet another opportunity to frame the contest as a referendum on the Carter economy:

> Here's a man with almost four years' record as chief executive of this nation, and the simple question is, on the basis of the record, do we want four more years of this? . . . I think it is fair game to say when his policies have taken us from 4.8 percent inflation to as high as 18 percent inflation. . . . I can understand his not wanting to run on the record. . . . He has to retreat from it or hide from it. . . . I'm going to keep talking about his record.[121]

Still on message at a "save our steel" rally in Ohio, the Republican nominee spoke of "massive unemployment, the highest interest rates since the Civil War, and prices which have turned simple shopping trips into an oppressive burden."[122]

With only ten days left in the campaign, Reagan, who was trailing at that point, unleashed a half-hour assault against Carter's economic policies on ABC television. Those policies, he charged, had failed

> on a scale so vast in dimensions, so broad with effects so devastating, that it is virtually without parallel in American history.

Reagan invoked the misery index:

> As a candidate four years ago, Mr. Carter adopted what he called the "misery index." Now he added the rate of inflation to the rate of unemployment, and for 1976 it totaled 12.5 percent . . . and he suggested no president had a right to seek reelection with an index of 12.5 percent. Well, today, by his own standard, he does not deserve reelection. The misery index is two-thirds higher than it was four years ago.

Reagan also offered up an example of inflation's pernicious effects:

> Each American family has its own story about what the Carter economy has done. The other day I came across a story that sums up what the American people have been through. And the story is all the more poignant because it

concerns a child's disappointment . . . a Fort Wayne fifth-grader named Andrea Baden who wanted to buy a pair of roller skates. So, in the great American tradition, she saved her allowance until she had the money to buy them. Andrea put it this way: "When I went back to the store, the price had gone up. So I saved more money, but when I got back again, the price had gone up again. It's just not fair." Well that's right, Andrea. What Mr. Carter has done to this country's economy just isn't fair. It just isn't right. But Andrea has learned something as a fifth-grader that Mr. Carter seems to have forgotten or not to have learned at all: inflation hurts people.[123]

Reagan also pitched his "humane" proposal to cut taxes with the "crushing tax burden" imposed by Carter, and for good measure, he declared that the administration had "jimmied" the latest inflation figures.[124]

For the most part, the debate between Carter and Reagan on October 28 mirrored the efforts of each side to frame the contest to its own advantage. According to the *Times* account,

> Mr. Carter returned again and again to the theme that nuclear policy was "the most important crucial difference in this election campaign," and said that his opponent had an "extremely dangerous and belligerent" attitude on that matter. Mr. Reagan said that the president had allowed the country's economic position to deteriorate and suggested that voters ask themselves: "Are you better off than you were four years ago?"[125]

Despite the difference in emphasis, both men had no choice on this occasion but to engage on the same issues, such as Reagan's tax-cut proposal and the principal causes of high inflation.[126]

In what remained of the race after the debate, Reagan continued to pound away on the economy, at one point charging that Carter cared little for the "economic suffering of millions of Americans."[127] In Lodi, New Jersey, where the Democratic mayor endorsed him, Reagan aroused fears about what might happen in a second Carter term: "If the present rate of food price inflation continues for the next four years, a pound of ground beef that now costs $2 would cost $4.92, chicken that costs 80 cents a pound would cost $1.97, a dozen eggs that now cost $1.10 would cost $2.71, and a gallon of milk that now costs $1.75 would cost $4.31."[128] At a rally in Peoria, Illinois, on the eve of the election, Reagan spoke of "worsening economic problems" and warned that another term for Carter would mean only "more rhetoric and more misery."[129]

Television attack ads by the Reagan camp supplemented the economic message. A *Times* account described Reagan's negative spots as "fairly predictable." One ad presented "a chart with computer-like graphics showing that food prices

have increased 35 percent since Mr. Carter took office, automobile prices 31 percent, clothes 20 percent." Another linked Carter's refusal to debate with a record
of 18 percent inflation, 8.5 million out of work, declining housing starts, and rising
interest rates.[130]

In a subsequent piece, the same reporter pointed up major differences between Democratic and Republican attack strategies: "Essentially, while the Carter
advertisements . . . seek to make Mr. Reagan the issue of the campaign, the Reagan
media drive is focusing almost totally on Mr. Carter's economic record." One such
ad showed a gray plaster slab labeled "the Carter promise: an inflation rate of 4
percent." Cracks appeared in the slab as the voice-over ticked off price increases
during Carter's term. Reagan spoke for himself in yet another spot: "Everywhere
I travel in America I hear this phrase over and over again. Everything is going up.
Where is it going to end? Record inflation has robbed the purchasing power of
your dollar. And, for three and a half years the administration has been unable to
control it."[131] After asking, "Can we afford four more years of broken promises?"
another ad cited increases in inflation, job loss numbers, and the federal deficit.[132]

Ostensibly independent of the Republican campaign, the Fund for a Conservative Majority promised to spend upwards of $1.5 million for its air war against
Carter in New York, Pennsylvania, Florida, and Connecticut. One of its ads reminded viewers that Carter had promised to do something about unemployment
in 1976 and, indeed, *had* done something: "Two million more people became unemployed this year."[133] Another of these offerings reminded viewers of Carter's 1976
promise to curb inflation: "When the president who said we could depend on him
to lower the cost of living took office in 1977, the annual inflation rate was under 5
percent. And things did change. One year later it was almost 7 percent. By '79 it was
9 percent. By this year it was over 13 percent. America did depend on you, Mr. President. Now we're going to make some changes, and you can depend on that."[134]

Democratic Attacks on Reagan's Economic Plan

On October 24, the Labor Department's Bureau of Statistics reported that consumer prices in the previous month had risen by a whole percentage point and
that it had jumped by 12.7 percent over the last twelve months. The timing of
this news could not have been worse for the White House, which was reduced to
claiming that the numbers confirmed not only Carter's restraint on spending but
also his opposition to Reagan's "massive election-year tax cut."[135]

Carter had played the tax card much earlier in the contest, as on September 9,
when he used the dedication of a New Jersey steel mill to warn against the "devastating blow to the American economy" that three consecutive years of Reagan
tax cuts would surely inflict. According to Carter, the economic situation called for

a "carefully targeted, nonpolitical approach to taxation and to economic revitalization" rather like the package of tax breaks and grants from various governments that had enabled this mill to open. Carter also held forth at a news conference, where he denounced "tremendous tax cuts for the rich" that would bring even higher inflation to average Americans. Even some Republicans, he added, would reject "so bad" an idea. At the same time, the White House released an analysis showing that the Reagan tax cuts would deprive the government of $280 billion in revenues. Other administration officials told reporters that Reagan's tax depreciation proposal would worsen inflation and thereby reduce incentives for investment.[136]

The White House launched another offensive on October 11, when Press Secretary Jody Powell and Domestic Affairs Adviser Stuart Eizenstat railed against the "economic mishmash" of Reaganomics. Specifically, they decried Reagan proposals to abolish the estate tax, lift the limit on earnings for senior citizens on Social Security, and grant tuition tax credits for parents of children in private schools. Taking other Reagan proposals into account, such as a reduction in the windfall-profit tax on oil and the income tax cuts, Powell and Eizenstat warned that the total package would add perhaps $40 billion to the deficit, none of which would be offset by new or existing revenues.[137] Carter followed up the next day with a fifteen-minute radio speech in which he urged voters to reject the dreams of "earlier times, simple problems, and painless solutions." He also argued that his administration's efforts to meet the energy challenge and modernize American industry would "propel us past our current economic obstacles and build the new foundations for economic greatness."[138]

The president kept up the attack two days later in a speech that the *Times* interpreted as an effort to make "the economy a primary issue for the final phase of the campaign." One of the most important issues facing the voters, Carter argued, was: "Do we want policies that encourage growth—without driving up inflation—through needed investments in new plant[s] and new equipment, or do we want to place our emphasis on immediate consumption through a quick, regressive, across-the-board tax cut?" After listing the revenues that would be lost to Reagan's tax cut, he warned that the cut would increase the deficit for fiscal 1983 by $130 billion—unless current programs were eliminated as well. Of course, Carter acidly noted, his opponent had not specified which programs would be cut. "I call upon him to do so," he added. "For it's clear that the only way he could balance the budget under his program is to eliminate almost all of the federal government, except for defense and entitlement programs."[139] In New York to attend the Alfred E. Smith dinner two days later, Carter warned Nassau County taxpayers to expect even higher property taxes if Reagan won the election.[140]

The aforementioned inflation report of October 24 came out only four days before the Cleveland debate. Carter learned of the latest inflation figures while stumping in Michigan and New Jersey. Taken aback, he gamely joked about Republican claims that he had "jimmied" previous data. "If I could control the figures on the Consumer Price Index," Carter told a hundred residents of Grand Rapids, Michigan, "it would have been better today than it came out." He appeared steadier in Gloucester City, New Jersey, where he alluded to the new inflation numbers as further proof of the folly of Reagan's tax cuts. To make such reductions, he claimed, would be "just like pouring gasoline on a fire." For good measure, Carter reminded his audience that Reagan's running mate had earlier labeled Reagan's tax proposals as "voodoo economics." But as Carter's own words on this grim occasion made clear, the hex was on him. Accordingly, he offered the lame defense that the overall inflation rate of the previous three months was "only" 7 percent and that the September jump had resulted, in part, from the higher cost of food production, as well as a grain shortage. Inflation, he maintained, would have risen even higher had he not imposed budgetary and fiscal restraints.[141] Carter said relatively little about economic issues in the last week of the campaign, partially because of his preoccupation with the Iranian hostage problem.[142]

The *Times* record indicates that Vice President Mondale devoted most of his attacks on Reagan and the GOP to topics other than the economy. On occasion, however, he reiterated the White House line about a grim economic future under President Reagan. On October 16, for example, he issued the following admonition in Toledo, Ohio: "Mr. Reagan's economic program is simple—cut taxes by $1 trillion by 1987. If you cut taxes by $1 trillion, and balance the budget, increase defense, and maintain basic entitlement programs—all of which Mr. Reagan says he will do—the only way his plan will work is if you eliminate the housing and development and mass transit and other programs that cities count on."[143]

Similarly, the economic woes relentlessly emphasized by the Republicans evidently elicited little, if any, response in Democratic ads assailing Reagan. By way of exception, one spot alluded to unemployment by accusing Reagan of not respecting recipients of unemployment insurance.[144] Taxes and spending figured in one of several Democratic ads attacking Reagan's record as governor of California: "He increased state spending by 120 percent. He brought three tax increases to the state. He added 34,000 employees to the state payroll. The Reagan campaign is reluctant to acknowledge the accuracy of these facts today. But can we trust the nation's future to a man who refuses to remember his own past?"[145]

Anderson Attacks on the Economic Policies of Carter and Reagan

When going negative on the economy, Anderson and Lucey frequently used the occasion to attack Reagan as well as Carter. Even so, Carter figured as a target more frequently than Reagan. When aiming at the president, Anderson called attention to current woes and called for a retrospective judgment on Carter's performance. In Park Forest, Illinois, for instance, Anderson charged: "He planned a recession, and by golly, it worked." That sound bite made the evening news on two networks. The case against Reagan had to be prospective, and accordingly, Anderson took issue with Republican proposals to slash taxes, increase defense spending, and balance the budget. After accusing Reagan of offering "slick and simplistic" explanations, he concluded: "I don't think any one-liner is going to supply the answer to the question: Mr. Reagan, how are you going to do it?"[146] Similarly, Anderson maintained on September 12 that Carter's economic policy lay in ruins, that the Carter and Reagan budgets had been constructed with mirrors, and that "neither of these approaches makes any sense." After labeling Carter's record "abysmal," he disparaged Reagan's approach as both "confused" and equally prone to failure.[147]

During his September 21 debate with Reagan, Anderson seized on a question about inflation to remind viewers of "the poor rate of performance of the American economy over the last four years." Governor Reagan, he granted, was not responsible for what had happened, nor was he. Moreover, "the man who should be here tonight to respond to those charges chose not to attend." He then denounced tax cuts proposed by Reagan and Carter as irresponsible at a time when a deficit loomed in excess of $60 billion. Responding to another question on tax cuts and inflation, he echoed a Reagan attack ad by noting that "we haven't gotten the 4 percent inflation that we were supposed to get at the end of Mr. Carter's first term. Instead we had, I think, in the second quarter, a Consumer Price Index registering around 12 percent. And nobody knows, with the latest increase in the Wholesale Price Index—that's about 18 percent on an annualized basis—what it's going to be." At that juncture, he turned on Reagan, insisting that "my programs are far less inflationary" while ridiculing the difference in what the average taxpayer would receive from the Carter and Reagan tax cuts. Echoing or anticipating a Carter attack ad, Anderson maintained that government spending in California had doubled when Reagan was governor. He closed his performance by asking: "Do you really think that our economy is healthy? Do you really think that 8 million Americans being out of work and the 50 percent unemployment among youth are acceptable?"[148]

In San Diego on October 4, Anderson unleashed a blistering attack on Carter during a speech to the National Savings and Loan League: "Housing starts earlier this year hit a near-record postwar low. The Carter housing recession has cost hundreds of thousands of jobs and billions in lost tax revenues. We simply cannot afford as a nation Carter's anti-housing policies. . . . The president let the inflation fight rest on tight money and high interest rates. We will suffer from this miscalculation long after he leaves the White House." Anderson did not spare Reagan on that occasion: "My program rejects the president's Tinker-Toy economics and the self-evident untruth of Reagan's new math. Each is too weak to defeat the double-digit inflation and interest rates. It's hard to take Tweedle Ron and Tweedle Jimmy very seriously."[149]

Ten days later, Anderson told the Chicago Association of Commerce and Industry that each candidate had a duty to lay out the costs of his economic program and explain how he would pay for it. Neither of his opponents, he continued, had offered "a full and fair cost accounting of his party's platform." According to his calculations, a Reagan administration would run up deficits over the next four years ranging from $60 billion to $91 billion per annum. Another Carter term, he predicted, would incur a $106 billion deficit in fiscal 1982 before declining to $38 billion in fiscal 1984. Anderson allowed that Carter could end up with a surplus of $13 billion in fiscal 1985. For his own part, he promised to defer any reduction in personal income taxes until fiscal 1983, at which time he hoped to balance the budget.[150]

Anderson attacked both rivals immediately after the Cleveland debate, but he directed most of his ire at Carter. Picking up on Reagan's "are you better off" question, he snorted: "Can anyone say after four years of the Carter administration that this country is more prosperous, that we are more respected, that we are more secure than when he took office?" Labeling inflation "the cruelest tax of all," he contended that the administration had come up with "seven different economic plans" in less than four years, all of them failures. He also faulted Carter for imitating Reagan's call for tax cuts at a time of high deficits.[151]

Over the course of the fall campaign, Anderson heaped scorn on the economic proposals of both rivals. Yet it became increasingly clear that he wanted Carter to lose. Perhaps in an unguarded moment, he told reporters that it would not greatly trouble him to take enough votes away from Carter to elect Reagan: "I don't want on my conscience reelecting a president who has given us 8 million unemployed in this country, who has given us a core inflation rate of almost 10 percent."[152]

CONCLUSION

In 1980, the lead changed hands more than once, and neither nominee of a major party enjoyed a long or convincing lead over the other. Still, the contest ended in a negative landslide for Reagan that national polling organizations failed to detect.

The Skaperdas-Grofman model shed relatively little light on the 1980 contest. Contrary to the model, the Democrats blasted Anderson instead of concentrating all of their fire on the Republicans. The model takes no account of the kind of threat that Anderson posed to Carter in his must-win states. Moreover, Anderson developed into a spoiler bent on defeating Carter. The Republicans refrained from attacking Anderson for a reason not stipulated in the model: he posed a much graver threat to Carter than to their own candidate.

The CBS/*New York Times* National Election Day Survey revealed that one-third of the voters designated "inflation and the economy" as an important determinant of their choice: 61 percent for Reagan, 28 percent for Carter, and 9 percent for Anderson. Nearly a quarter of those casting ballots claimed that "jobs and unemployment" had influenced their voting. Carter led Reagan in the preferences of this group, 48 to 42 percent, and another 7 percent voted for Anderson. In a direct test of the relative importance of inflation and unemployment, the poll asked respondents whether they agreed or disagreed with the claim that "unemployment is a more important problem today than inflation." Among the 39 percent agreeing, 40 percent voted for Reagan and 51 percent supported Carter. Among the 45 percent disagreeing, 60 percent cast a Reagan vote and only 30 percent backed Carter. Just 10 percent of all voters cited "reducing federal income taxes" as a major factor in making up their minds, and unsurprisingly, Reagan ran away with their votes, receiving 64 percent to Carter's 29 percent. Responding to the statement that "cutting taxes is more important than balancing the budget," 30 percent of all voters agreed; 53 percent disagreed. Among those agreeing, Reagan beat Carter by 50 to 42 percent; among those disagreeing, Reagan led 53 to 37 percent.[153]

In sum, inflation helped Reagan's cause more than unemployment, but his unrelenting attacks on the latter demolished the notion that the Democrats "owned" the unemployment issue. Reagan enjoyed considerable success in transforming traditional Democratic claims of lowering unemployment into an issue of jobs lost because of Carter's flawed leadership. Even though Reagan's tax cuts scored decisively with only a minority of the voters, he ran ahead of Carter even among voters who preferred balancing the budget to lowering federal taxes. Although the Democrats emphasized the economy less frequently than their opponents, it figured as one of their top-ten topics. Like it or not, Carter had to defend his economic policies against Reagan's onslaught.

7. The Dead Heat
Races of 2000 and 2004

Few contests for the presidency have exhibited greater similarities than the back-to-back dead heats discussed in this chapter. In 2000, Vice President Al Gore roared out of the Democratic convention with a lead that erased the summer gains of Texas governor George W. Bush. "Everyone expected a bounce," said a disconcerted Fred Upton, a Republican congressman from Michigan, "but not nearly as much as this."[1] In Gallup Polls, Bush displaced Gore in early October and clung to a narrow lead for most of what remained of the race. The final poll showed Bush ahead by only two points (see Figure 7.1).[2] Annenberg's rolling cross-sectional surveys showed a slightly different pattern. The first of three phases began with the convention bounce that moved Gore ahead of Bush. Governor Bush recaptured the lead on September 27 and held on to it for twenty-three days. A "dead heat" stage began on October 21 and lasted through election day.[3] Monitoring statewide polls to track shifts in likely shares of the electoral vote, Daron Shaw found that Bush never reached 270 until the very end, whereas Gore moved above that threshold in mid-September only to fall below it in mid-October.[4]

In the contest four years later, after winning six of eight early primaries as well as the precinct caucuses in Iowa, Senator John Kerry of Massachusetts moved twelve points in front of President Bush in Gallup's poll of February 16–17, 2004. Kerry led by eight points shortly after wrapping up his party's nomination on March 2. Bush overtook Kerry a few weeks later, but for the rest of the run-up to the Democratic convention in July, the president usually trailed. Even so, Kerry's support never topped 50 percent, and depending on the poll, the Democratic convention gave him little or no bounce. The Gallup Poll showed him losing a percentage point among registered voters and two points among likely voters. This had not happened to any presidential nominee of a major party since George McGovern in 1972.[5] Bush moved four points in front and retained a slender lead going into the Republican convention that began on August 30. Although Bush's bounce amounted to a mere two points in the Gallup Poll, it boosted his lead over Kerry to seven percent.[6] Postconvention polls commissioned by *Time* and *Newsweek* showed Bush ahead by a staggering eleven points.[7] The race tightened after the first presidential debate in October, which briefly put Kerry back in front. The lead switched back to Bush, only to vanish in Gallup's final poll, which showed

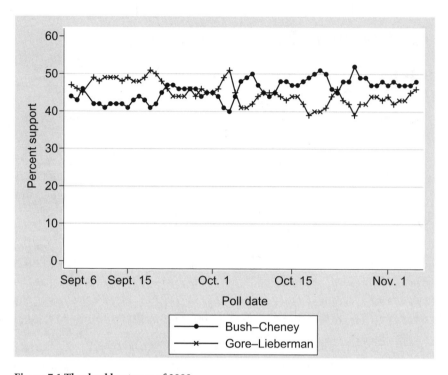

Figure 7.1 The dead heat race of 2000
Note: The entries are three-day rolling averages.
Source: www.gallup.com.

Bush tied with Kerry at 49 percent each.[8] Figure 7.2 tracks these fluctuating poll standings from late July to the end of October.[9]

SIMILAR STRATEGIES AND VOTING PATTERNS

The similarities between the 2000 and 2004 races extended well beyond the fact that they were close and hard fought. In both contests, the Democrats and Republicans lavished their advertising dollars and candidate appearances on the same battleground states. Regardless of the electoral votes at stake, residents of safe states in both election years saw few, if any, campaign ads and even less of the presidential and vice-presidential candidates. The candidates turned up in fewer than half of the nation's media markets in 2000. Four years later, they returned time and again to the same battleground states, "sometimes even appearing literally within earshot of each other, in the same city on the same day."[10]

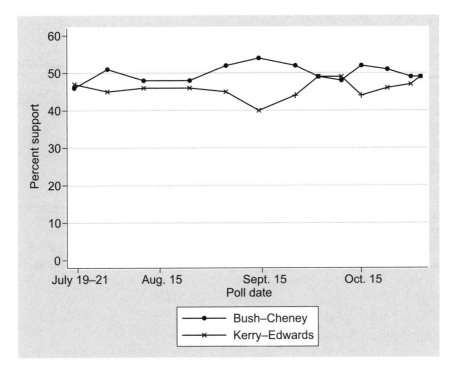

Figure 7.2 The dead heat race of 2004
Source: www.gallup.com.

Both times, Bush succeeded in transforming predominantly Democratic states into battlegrounds.[11] In 2000, he counted on the Republican governors of Michigan, Pennsylvania, and Wisconsin to tip the scales in his favor, and when that did not happen, he had another go at those states in 2004. Bush lost Wisconsin to Gore by a mere 0.2 percent (out of 2,598,607 votes cast) and to Kerry by 0.4 percent (with just under 3 million cast).[12] Bush's efforts in Michigan and Pennsylvania also fell short both times.[13] Likewise, he forced Gore and Kerry to fight for Minnesota, which no Republican presidential candidate had carried since 1972.[14]

Like Gore, Kerry set out to win Ohio and Florida. Ohio had gone for Clinton in 1992 and 1996, and although Gore eventually gave up on the Buckeye State, he garnered more than 46 percent of its vote. Kerry finished with nearly 49 percent. The actual winner of Florida's 2000 vote will never be known for certain, but no one doubted Bush's win in 2004 (with 52 percent to Kerry's 47 percent).[15]

Both sides also lavished time and money on Colorado, Nevada, New Hampshire, New Mexico, and Iowa. Colorado went for Bush in 2004 but by roughly half the 2000 margin. He carried Nevada again by a small margin, lost New Hampshire by a whisker after eking out a slim victory there in 2000, took New Mexico in 2004 by 0.8 percent after losing it in 2000 by 0.1 percent, and squeaked by in Iowa after losing it by a fraction of a point in 2000.[16]

Bush won lopsided victories in the Mountain West, the Great Plains, and the South, besting both Gore and Kerry by more than thirty percentage points in Utah, Wyoming, Alaska, and Idaho; by more than twenty points in Kansas, Montana, Nebraska, North Dakota, Oklahoma, South Dakota, and Texas; and by more than ten in Alabama, Georgia, Indiana, Kentucky, Mississippi, North Carolina, and South Carolina. Conversely, both Gore and Kerry won landslide victories in California, Hawaii, New York, New Jersey, Connecticut, Massachusetts, Rhode Island, Vermont, Maryland, and Illinois.[17]

All told, in 2004, Bush lost only one of thirty states that he had carried in 2000 (New Hampshire), while depriving Kerry of two (Iowa and New Mexico) that had voted for Gore. Conversely, Kerry beat Bush in eighteen of the twenty states that had voted for Gore. According to Alan Abramowitz, Bush improved on his 2000 vote almost everywhere, gaining an average 2.6 percent in the states that he had carried earlier and 2.8 percent in those lost to Gore.[18] Gerald Pomper has described the correlation of state voting for Bush in 2000 to that of 2004 as the highest ever for successive presidential elections.[19]

Analysis of exit polls and other voter surveys uncovered additional similarities. According to the Voter News Service (VNS) exit poll, 86 percent of self-identified Democrats cast ballots for Gore in 2000, and 91 percent of Republicans who went to the polls voted for Bush.[20] Four years later, exit polls showed that 89 percent of Democrats voted for Kerry, and 93 percent of Republicans supported Bush.[21] Similarly, Gallup found that the 2004 election set a new record of party-line voting, with 93 percent of all Democrats marking their ballots for Kerry and 95 percent of all Republicans voting for Bush.[22] This extraordinary show of partisan unity moved John Kenneth White to comment on the paucity of "George W. Bush Democrats," on the one hand, and "John Kerry Republicans," on the other.[23] Gary Jacobson found that polarization and partisan mobilization efforts in 2004 resulted in the highest level of party-line voting in the fifty-two-year history of the American National Election Studies (ANES), eclipsing the previous record set in 2000.[24] Further, the percentage of voters identifying with a major party reached a historic high in 2000, only to be surpassed by the 2004 figure.[25]

Ideology, as Figure 7.3 shows, slightly modified the influence of party loyalty on the vote in both contests while profoundly affecting the vote choice of independents. Thus, Republican and Democratic configurations showed up as mirror images, with nearly every conservative Republican voting for Bush both times and almost every liberal Democrat backing Gore and Kerry. Conservative independents voted overwhelmingly for Bush; liberal independents backed Gore and

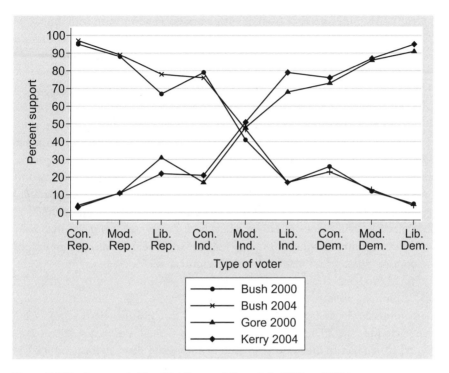

Figure 7.3 Ideology, party identification, and the vote in 2000 and 2004

Kerry by similarly lopsided margins. Only among moderate independents did the vote divide evenly between Bush and his Democratic opponents.

Religion figured importantly as a predictor of presidential vote choice in both elections, although it likely was a weightier factor in 2004. Bush garnered 56 percent of all votes cast by Protestants of varying descriptions in 2000, compared with 59 percent in 2004. He won 63 percent of votes cast by white Protestants in 2000 and likely increased his share of that vote four years later.[26] Exit polls indicated that he won a majority of the white Catholics both times and that he garnered more than half of all Catholic votes in 2004. The latter outcome was all the more remarkable because John Kerry was only the third Catholic to win the presidential nomination of a major party.[27]

Analysts of both elections also noted that the degree of religious commitment modified the relationship between religion and vote choice. Overall, 63 percent of voters who attended religious services more than once a week voted for Bush in 2000, compared with less than a third of those who seldom, if ever, set foot in a house of worship. In 2004, he garnered 70 percent of the vote of the most religious Protestants, as well as 56 percent among Catholics who regularly attended Mass.[28]

Although Bush won 80 percent of voters in 2000 who identified with the "white religious Right," the turnout of such voters fell 4 million short of what Karl Rove had anticipated.[29] Leaving nothing to chance in 2004, Republican operatives tirelessly worked the churches, interest groups, and media organizations that bring conservatives of religious faith together.[30] This effort paid off on election day, when 78 percent of the 22 million evangelicals who turned out voted for Bush.[31]

Additional similarities showed up in the demographics of the vote. Both times, Bush won solid majorities among men, whites, persons with some college education, those with undergraduate degrees, most groupings of married people, gun owners, and persons earning $50,000 or more. In 2004, however, his vote improved markedly among women, Hispanics, the elderly, and the least educated.[32] Still, as in 2000, most of the women, blacks, Hispanics (except Cuban Americans), unmarried individuals, childless couples, persons with the least schooling, those with the most formal education, voters earning $30,000 or less, and members of union households who turned out voted Democratic.[33]

IMPORTANT DIFFERENCES

For all of the similarities just described, the 2004 and 2000 contests differed in noteworthy respects, starting with campaign agendas. Both sides addressed the great majority of their 2000 campaign statements to domestic issues, even though terrorist bombings of U.S. embassies in Africa, retaliatory missile strikes against Al Qaeda targets in Afghanistan and the Sudan, continual U.S. bombing of Iraqi antiaircraft sites, American air raids on Serbian targets, and the loss of seventeen sailors in the bombing of the USS *Cole* belied perceptions of a nation at peace. In 2004, the United States waged war in Iraq and Afghanistan, and war issues dominated the campaign agendas of both parties.

By all accounts, the 2000 contest ended with one of the narrowest vote differences in American history.[34] Bush trailed Gore in the popular vote by more than half a million ballots, and he also garnered only one more vote than needed for a majority in the Electoral College.[35] Worse, the protracted fight over Florida recounts engendered the bitterest conflict regarding the election of an American president since Hayes versus Tilden. In 2000 as in 1876, extraconstitutional means were necessary to resolve a bitter dispute, which left an indelible mark on the presidency that followed.

It was different in 2004. Despite legal skirmishing and conspiracy theories over the Ohio outcome, Bush won a small but solid victory in the Buckeye State, and nationwide, he beat Kerry by 3.3 million in the popular vote and by thirty-five electoral votes. Garnering only 50.7 percent of the popular vote, Bush won reelection by the smallest margin of any incumbent except Wilson and Clinton. Likewise, no other reelected president except Wilson had prevailed by fewer electoral votes.[36] Even so, Bush's victory marked the first time in sixteen years that a presidential candidate had won an outright majority of the popular vote. Not since McKinley in 1900 had the reelection of a Republican president coincided with Republican majorities in both houses of Congress. And, unlike 2000, Kerry conceded one day after the election once it became clear that he would not garner enough of the provisional and absentee votes still to be counted to upset Bush in Ohio.[37]

Voters paid a good deal more attention to the 2004 campaigns and attached much greater importance to the outcome than they had in 2000. When asked in preelection polls whether "this year's election" mattered more, less, or about the same than those in "previous years," 47 percent of registered voters in 2000 answered "more," compared with 48 percent who responded "about the same." In all, 72 percent said "more" in 2004.[38] In September 2004, Gallup found interest in national politics running at an "all-time" high, with 81 percent following news of the campaigns "very" or "somewhat" closely. Gallup also reported that 89 percent of Americans had given "quite a lot" of thought to the 2004 election (compared with 72 percent at the same point in 2000).[39] A huge surge in turnout also indicated that Americans regarded the 2004 election as a deciding moment. Nearly 17 million more voters went to the polls than in 2000, and the total vote in excess of 122 million amounted to 59 percent of the eligible population—the highest turnout since 1968.[40]

Contrary to conventional wisdom, massive efforts to register and turn out voters did not make Kerry a winner in Ohio. Despite extraordinary efforts by a coalition of 527 groups, organized labor, and Democratic Party operatives, a Republican drive that relied heavily on volunteers won out.[41] In another departure from conventional wisdom, Bush became the first president since Truman to win reelection with a job approval rating below 50 percent.[42]

THE 2000 ELECTORAL CONTEXT

By most accounts, the Clinton economy should have powered Gore to an easy victory. The White House boasted that unemployment had reached its lowest level in more than three decades, declined steadily for the previous seven years, and remained below 5 percent for thirty-seven months in a row. Moreover, 22.2 million jobs had been created since 1993, the most ever under a single administration.[43] Thanks in no small part to congressional Republicans, the administration projected a surplus of $290 billion. Since 1991, the Dow Jones Industrial Average had risen 7,733 points to a high of 10,662 in July 2000.[44] Spectacular increases also showed up in Standard & Poor's composite index, as well as in the tech-heavy

NASDAQ. At the same time, ordinary Americans had bought into the stock market. Since 1990, one observer noted, "the percentage of Americans owning stocks and mutual funds has doubled, from 23 percent to 46 percent. Factor in the millions whose pension funds are invested in the markets, and for the first time in American history, a majority of citizens have a stake in the public equity and debt markets."[45] Even though the public acknowledged the role of a Republican Congress for bringing this bounty into being, Gore, as Clinton's designated successor, was well positioned to run on a retrospective message of "you never had it so good."

Prior to the Monica Lewinsky scandal and the presidential impeachment that followed, Gore reportedly had devised a plan to put the 1996 fund-raising scandal behind him, strengthen his ties to Democratic constituencies, and emerge from Clinton's shadow.[46] The Lewinsky affair reportedly appalled Gore, who appeared to distance himself from Clinton as the White House waged a campaign of defense, denigration, denial, and deception against the special prosecutor and House Republicans. After the House impeachment vote, however, he stood up for Clinton at a White House rally. Clinton's transgressions, Gore argued, did not rise to the level of impeachment; partisan Republicans had done a great disservice to a man who would be remembered as "one of our greatest presidents."[47]

Polls at the time lent credibility to Gore's argument. Gallup showed that solid majorities of the public opposed Clinton's impeachment and removal from office, a finding tethered to unfortunately worded questions that conflated very different undertakings in the House and Senate. Nor did the public favor a Clinton resignation that would make Gore president. And though most felt that Clinton should suffer some form of public rebuke, 60 percent or more approved of his job performance.[48] Even Republicans who held Clinton in contempt entertained second thoughts about impeachment.[49]

Still, Speaker Gingrich had insisted on making the 1998 midterm elections into a referendum on the Lewinsky scandal. This strategy backfired, resulting in Democratic gains rather than losses in the House. Not since 1934 had the president's party gained House seats in a midterm election. This setback was the last straw for a Republican conference already upset with Gingrich's leadership. Gingrich promptly resigned from Congress. House Republicans received another jolt the following month when word of an extramarital affair forced the resignation of Robert Livingston, Gingrich's replacement as Speaker. Meanwhile, House Judiciary Republicans had proceeded to recommend four counts of impeachment over the heated objections of committee Democrats. Two articles passed the full House on party-line votes, even though few in either party thought that the Senate would convict Clinton on either count.[50] After going through the motions of a trial, the Senate acquitted Clinton.[51]

Ill will over impeachment hardly ended with the Senate vote. Clinton made no secret of his desire to punish the House impeachment managers in the 2000 elections, and Republicans played up Gore's support for Clinton, claiming that they were "joined at the hip."

Signs of "Clinton fatigue" showed up in postimpeachment polls. The Pew Research Center found that nearly three out of every four Americans in 1999 had tired of hearing about "all the problems associated with the Clinton administration."[52] The same poll noted a dip in Gore's ratings.[53] Gore's bitter struggle against former senator Bill Bradley for the 2000 Democratic nomination also led to questions about his partnership with Clinton. When asked about Clinton fatigue during a New Hampshire debate, Gore allowed that continued discussion of the president's "personal mistake" was wearying, yet he insisted that history would regard Clinton as a "great" president.[54]

Unfortunately for Gore, substantially higher percentages of registered voters in 2000 viewed him less favorably than Clinton, even though Clinton fared poorly on evaluations of his character compared with assessments of his job performance (see Figure 7.4).[55] What's more, a 1999 New York Times poll showed that Gore's ratings correlated more with feelings about Clinton's persona than his presidential performance.[56]

As the date of the Democratic convention neared, Gore went to considerable lengths to separate himself from Clinton. Dick Cheney likely reinforced that stratagem by rousing the Republican convention with a line that spoke to Gore's predicament: "Mr. Gore will try to separate himself from his leader's shadow. But somehow we will never see one without thinking of the other."[57]

The first degree of separation occurred when Gore picked Senator Joe Lieberman for a running mate. Although the Gore camp made much of choosing an observant Jew, Lieberman's denunciation of Clinton's behavior in the Lewinsky affair mattered more than his religion.[58]

Next, Gore planted the "eternal kiss" on his wife, Tipper, as millions watched on television. According to one account, Gore had demonstrated that "alpha-male sexuality" could be satisfied within the bonds of matrimony.[59]

The most substantive break with Clinton occurred during Gore's acceptance speech. After briefly lauding the president's economic stewardship, he launched into a populist message that unsettled the Clinton camp and many other Democrats: "This election is not an award for past performance. I'm not asking you to vote for me on the basis of the economy we have. Tonight, I ask for your support on the basis of the better, fairer, more prosperous America we can build together." In yet another rejection of the retrospective strategy that most Democrats had anticipated, Gore called attention to the dark side of the current economy, in which people worked two or more jobs, could not save to put their kids through college, and coped with "skyrocketing" costs of prescription drugs.[60] Pundit Michael Kinsley summarized Gore's message as, "You've never had it so good, and I'm mad as hell about it."[61]

Thereafter, Clinton became a stealth presence, avoided by Gore, banned from must-win Michigan and Pennsylvania, and assigned to raise money at "relatively

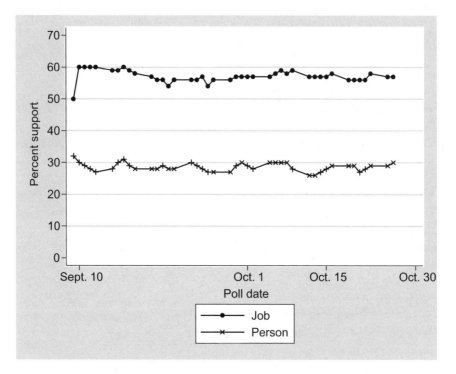

Figure 7.4 Clinton's job and personal approval ratings, fall 2000
Source: Battleground 2000 Poll: Lake, Snell and Perry Associates.

small indoor gatherings."[62] Journalists following Gore interpreted one part of his stump speech as a contrast with Clinton: "I won't always be the most exciting politician, but . . . I will never let you down."[63] Near the end, Gore reminded audiences of his association with Clinton and the strong economy.[64] Republicans pounced whenever the vice president blew on these coals, and polls continued to show that too close a relationship with Clinton would hurt him. One such poll revealed that a joint campaign appearance with Clinton would lessen the chance of a Gore vote among 40 percent of likely voters. Only 17 percent welcomed a reunion.[65]

CHARACTER ISSUES IN 2000

Few of the so-called character issues that dogged Gore in 2000 surprised longtime observers of his political career. Reporters who had followed him since his days in Congress knew about his penchant for inflating his accomplishments while distorting the records of opponents.[66] During the long run-up to the 2000 primaries,

Gore's treatment of Bill Bradley seemed true to form. At one point during a debate, Bradley turned to Gore and uncorked a sound bite replayed repeatedly by the Republicans: "Why should we believe that you will tell the truth as president, if you don't tell the truth as a candidate?"[67] In support of Bradley's attack, the *Boston Globe* dusted off a 1988 memo from an adviser to Gore during his first try for the Democratic nomination. That document admonished Gore to stop making claims that he could not back up.[68]

Thus primed, the press joined the Bush camp in playing up Gore's every misstep in the fall campaign. Unable to conceal his contempt for Bush during their first debate, Gore frequently groaned and grimaced as his opponent fielded questions. He also disputed a Bush claim that he surely knew to be accurate. Media assessments of the first debate made much more of Gore's boorishness and dissembling than his superior grasp of policy issues. A headline in the next day's *New York Post* screamed "Liar! Liar!" The *Post* was hardly an objective source, but even Democrats panned Gore's performance. Asked to account for Gore's behavior, the California Democratic chairman admitted to being at a loss, adding, "I'm not a psychiatrist."[69] Stung by the bad press, Gore complained about hair-trigger coverage. He raised eyebrows again at the next debate by confessing error, promising to do better, and appearing uncharacteristically passive.[70] A more confident and assertive Bush emerged the winner. Still more blunders reinforced doubts about Gore's credibility. By reversing his opposition to tapping the strategic oil reserve, he set himself up for the charge that he would say and do anything to get elected. The vice president's belated opposition to the administration's decision to return a young Cuban refugee to his father in Havana opened him up to charges of trolling for Cuban American votes. His recollection of his mother cooing a certain union lullaby when he was a child backfired when it was learned that the song had not been written until his early adulthood. More scorn followed Gore's claim that his mother-in-law had paid far more for an antiarthritis drug than the pharmaceutical industry charged for the same medicine when administered to pets. Yet another flap arose when he inaccurately claimed that a shortage of desks in the schools of Sarasota, Florida, forced students to stand during class.

Such mishaps enriched the Republican mantra that Gore would "say and do anything to get elected." They also took a toll of his credibility among voters. A *Newsweek* poll showed that Bush enjoyed an eleven-point advantage over Gore on the question of which candidates were "honest and ethical." Likewise, Bush scored nine points higher than Gore in evaluations of which candidate "says what he believes, not just what people want to hear."[71] The VNS exit poll indicated that Bush won 80 percent of the vote from voters most concerned about electing an "honest" and "trustworthy" candidate.[72] By some estimates, doubts about Gore's truthfulness and integrity cost him two or three percentage points on election day.[73]

Rumors of youthful drug use dogged both candidates in 2000, although those swirling around Bush probably got more play in news accounts.[74] They took on new relevance with the 1999 publication of an unfriendly book titled *Fortunate Son*.[75] When confronted by reporters then covering his bid for the Republican nomination, Bush categorically denied allegations, first, that he had been arrested for possession of cocaine in 1972 and, second, that family strings had been pulled to expunge his arrest record. Under further questioning, he avowed that he had not used illegal drugs in the past fifteen years. Reporters soon persuaded him to move the time line back another decade. Beyond that point, however, the governor refused to go. "What you've just heard from me," he declared, "is my answer through the course of the campaign."[76] Bush held his ground, and the news media soon moved on to other matters. At the same time, he freely alluded to a history of alcohol abuse and the religious awakening that restored his self-respect. Ironically, late-breaking news in Maine of a 1976 arrest for driving under the influence may have cost him a point or two in the final preelection polls.[77]

THE 2000 ATTACK PROPENSITIES AND TARGETS

Bush and the GOP waged a more negative campaign against Gore and the Democrats than vice versa. Table 7.1 shows that Republican negativity surpassed Democratic negativity in seven of the nine weeks between Labor Day and election day. The greatest differences between Republican and Democratic attack propensities showed up in the second and third weeks of September, precisely when Bush ran farthest behind Gore. Republicans outattacked Democrats by 23 percent in week two and by nearly 35 percent in week three. Republican negativity rose to 60 percent or higher only in week three. The Democrats waxed most negative in the sixth and seventh weeks of their campaign. Overall, Republicans attacked Democrats in 51 percent of 709 campaign statements, and Democrats assailed Republicans in 44 percent of 770 statements.

Although sparse coverage in the *Times* militates against drawing firm conclusions, Ralph Nader probably attacked Gore and the Democrats more than Bush and the Republicans. The ways in which he labeled Gore—"Pinocchio-nosed," "certified political coward," "identity thief," and "environmental poseur"— suggested that he despised Gore far more than Bush.[78] Indeed, the Republicans replayed one of Nader's toughest lines in one of their attack ads: "Al Gore is suffering from election-year delusion if he thinks his record on the environment is anything to be proud of."[79]

Gore hit back, denying that he had ever backed down on environmental regulation and countering that big oil welcomed every Nader vote.[80] Other Democrats

Table 7.1. Attack Propensities, 2000

Week	Democratic Attacks on Republicans	Democratic Attacks on Nader	Republican Attacks on Democrats	Nader Attacks on Democrats	Nader Attacks on Republicans
1	.442	.001	.486	—	—
2	.288	—	.520	—	.500
3	.281	.016	.627	.143	.095
4	.382	.018	.494	—	—
5	.443	—	.451	.364	.364
6	.600	—	.549	—	—
7	.591	—	.597	—	—
8	.435	.010	.580	.727	.091
9	.432	.062	.384	.439	.293
Overall	.436	.034	.511	.344	.208
N statements	770	770	709	96	96

Notes: Week one: September 4–10; week two, September 11–17; week three, September 18–24; week four, September 25–October 1; week five, October 2–8; week six, October 9–15; week seven, October 16–22; week eight, October 23–29; week nine, October 30–November 7.
— = no cases

urged progressives not to waste their votes on Nader. Indeed, more than half of the Democratic attacks on Nader contended that a vote for him was a vote for Bush, as in a Wisconsin spot on abortion rights: "This year, a five-to-four Supreme Court decision narrowly protected *Roe v. Wade*. A single vote saved a woman's right to choose. As president, George W. Bush would reverse the Court with anti-choice Justices Antonin Scalia and [Clarence] Thomas in control. Bush's goal? Ending legal abortion. Voting for Ralph Nader helps elect George W. Bush. Before voting Nader, consider the risk. It's your choice."[81]

The vast majority of 2000 attacks targeted opposing presidential nominees (see Table 7.2). Nearly nine of every ten shots that the Democrats fired at the Republicans took aim at Bush. Gore targeted Bush in 91 percent of his solo attacks, as did Lieberman in 97 percent of his. Conversely, nine of every ten attacks by Republicans against Democrats singled Gore out. Bush nailed Gore in 95 percent of his solo attacks, as did Cheney in 79 percent of his. Nader figured as the only target of Democratic attacks on Greens, and he accounted for virtually all of the Green attacks on the Democrats and Republicans.[82]

THE 2000 CAMPAIGN TOPICS

Two findings stand out in Table 7.3, which lists the top-ten topics of the 2000 campaigns. First, domestic concerns dominated the agenda of both parties. Second,

Table 7.2. Targeting of 2000 Attacks

	Democratic Targeting of Republicans	Democratic Targeting of Nader	Republican Targeting of Democrats	Green Targeting of Democrats	Green Targeting of Republicans
All attackers					
Presidential nominee	302	26	325	24	17
Other targets	34	—	37	9	4
N attacks	336	26	362	33	21
Nominee targeted	.899	1.00	.898	.727	.809
Solo attacks of presidential nominees	Gore	Gore	Bush	Nader	Nader
Presidential nominee	91	2	168	24	17
Other targets	9	—	9	9	3
N attacks	100	2	177	33	20
Nominee targeted	.910	1.00	.949	.727	.850
Solo attacks of vice presidential nominee	Lieberman	Lieberman	Cheney	LaDuke	LaDuke
Presidential nominee	33	1	22	—	—
Other targets	4	—	6	—	—
N attacks	37	1	28	—	—
Nominee targeted	.971	1.00	.786	—	—

Notes: Some attacks against presidential nominee also targeted others of the same party. The Republicans ignored Nader.

— = no cases

Democrats and Republicans emphasized nine of the same topics, attached identical importance to four, and disagreed slightly on the importance of two more. Social programs and health issues showed up in first place on both agendas, followed by the domestic economy and campaign concerns. Education ranked sixth on both lists. Leadership placed fourth on the Republican agenda, fifth for the Democrats. Likewise, military and defense issues ranked eighth in importance for the GOP and ninth for the Democrats. Nader stressed six of the same topics emphasized by both parties.

The striking convergence just documented carried over to attacks traded between the Democrats and Republicans (see Table 7.4). Disputes over Social Security, prescription-drug benefits, and Medicare constituted the main bones of contention for both parties in 2000; dueling tax plans (punctuated with taunts of "fuzzy math") established the secondary importance of the domestic economy in two-party exchanges. The Democrats and Republicans also clashed on energy and the environment, leadership, education, ideology, dirty campaigning, and national defense, as well as the number, location, and timing of presidential debates. Democratic attackers stressed women's issues (not a top-ten topic for the Republicans), and Republican warriors made much of campaign finance, often by throwing Gore's "no controlling legal authority" utterance from the 1996 race back at him.

METHODS OF ATTACK

All told, just over half of the Democratic attacks on Republican targets appealed to fears of what Bush might do if elected. Gore used this tactic in 61 percent of his attacks, as did Lieberman in 57 percent of his. Democratic attacks on Nader relied chiefly on fear arousal and labeling. Labeling surfaced as the principal method

Table 7.3. Leading Topics of 2000

Democrats	Republicans	Green
Social/health programs (119)	Social/health programs (86)	Ideology/party (14)
Domestic economy (106)	Domestic economy (85)	Leadership (11)
Campaign (78)	Campaign (82)	Campaign finance (9)
Energy/environment (66)	Leadership (64)	Wasted vote (8)
Leadership (46)	Ideology/party (64)	Crime (6)
Education (44)	Education (50)	Domestic economy (5)
Debates (31)	Energy/environment (43)	Social/health programs (5)
Ideology/party (31)	Military/defense (43)	Energy/environment (5)
Military/defense (29)	Debates (42)	Debates (5)
Personal (26)	Women's rights (21)	Women's rights (4)

Note: Top-ten topics accounted for 75 percent of total Democratic statements, 82 percent of total Republican statements, and 75 percent of Green statements.

Table 7.4. Leading Attack Topics of 2000

Democrats Attacking Republicans	Democrats Attacking Nader	Republicans Attacking Democrats	Nader Attacking Democrats	Nader Attacking Republicans
Social/health (80)	Wasted vote (10)	Social/health (56)	Leadership (5)	Leadership (5)
Domestic economy (69)	Women's rights (5)	Domestic economy (53)	Ideology/party (5)	Ideology/party (4)
Energy/environment (33)	Federal judges (4)	Leadership (47)	Wasted vote (3)	Wasted vote (3)
Leadership (29)	Energy/environment (3)	Ideology/party (41)	Federal judges (3)	Campaign finance (3)
Education (18)	Ideology/party (2)	Energy/environment (29)	Energy/environment (3)	Crime (1)
Personal (17)	Crime (1)	Campaign finance (27)	Campaign finance (2)	Social/health (1)
Dirty campaign (11)	Race (1)	Education (25)	Crime (2)	Energy/environment (1)
Ideology/party (10)		Military/defense (20)	Social/health (2)	Domestic economy (1)
Women's rights (10)		Dirty campaign (16)	Domestic economy (1)	Debates (1)
Military/defense (9)		Debates (10)	Women's rights (1)	Foreign policy (1)

Notes: The ten topics most utilized in Democratic attacks on the Republicans accounted for 85 percent of all such attacks; the corresponding figure for Republican attacks on the Democrats was 89 percent. The topics that the Democrats used against the Association of State Green Parties (i.e., Nader) accounted for all such attacks. The topics listed in the table for Nader attacks on the Democrats accounted for 82 percent of the total; the ten topics invoked by Nader against the Republicans accounted for all such attacks.

used by all Republicans against the Democrats. Bush resorted to fear arousal as frequently as labeling. Cheney questioned Gore's veracity in half of his attacks and also relied heavily on fear arousal and labeling. Table 7.5 suggests that Republican attackers saw an opportunity in Gore's credibility problem. In any case, they worked the dishonesty angle far more frequently against the Democrats than vice versa. Nader resorted most to labeling and dishonesty when attacking the Democrats; against Bush, he employed labeling and ridicule most often.

Table 7.5. Attack Methods, 2000

	Presidential Candidate (solo)	Vice-Presidential Candidate (solo)	All Attackers
Democrats attacking Republicans			
Fear arousal	.610	.568	.509
Ridicule	.030	.054	.062
Labeling	.470	.324	.366
Apposition	.420	.405	.271
Dishonesty	.130	.216	.250
Democrats attacking Nader			
Fear arousal	—	—	.654
Ridicule	—	—	—
Labeling	1.00	1.00	.500
Apposition	.500	—	.192
Dishonesty	—	—	.038
Republicans attacking Democrats			
Fear arousal	.497	.393	.398
Ridicule	.102	.214	.108
Labeling	.497	.393	.470
Apposition	.475	.143	.326
Dishonesty	.226	.500	.354
Nader attacking Democrats			
Fear arousal	.273	—	.264
Ridicule	.121	—	.118
Labeling	.515	—	.529
Apposition	.061	—	.059
Dishonesty	.394		.412
Nader attacking Republicans			
Fear arousal	.050	—	—
Ridicule	.200	—	—
Labeling	.600	—	—
Apposition	.100	—	—
Dishonesty	—	—	—

— = no cases

ECHOES FROM CAMPAIGN 2000

When dueling over social programs and health care, the Democrats and Republicans fought over who would do a better job of protecting Medicare, providing a prescription-drug benefit, shoring up Social Security, and fostering health insurance for children. The following narrative captures the exchange of attacks on prescription-drug plans.

In his acceptance speech, Gore had vowed to fight for "a new prescription drug benefit under Medicare for all our seniors." The Republicans, he proclaimed, would give in to the "big drug companies" and would send seniors begging to the health maintenance organizations (HMOs) and insurance companies. "They're for the powerful, and we're for the people. Big tobacco, big oil, the big polluters, the pharmaceutical companies, the HMOs. Sometimes you have to be willing to stand up and say no—so families can have a better life."[83] Gore tirelessly repeated this argument throughout the fall.[84] His plan called for a prescription-drug entitlement to Medicare, to be implemented with a federal subsidy, premiums, and copayments.[85]

Bush unveiled his package on September 5 to an audience of senior citizens in Allentown, Pennsylvania. On the one hand, he called Medicare a "success" as well as an "enduring commitment." On the other, he argued that the program had to be modernized. Gore, he contended, offered only "the same tired, partisan ideas that have led our country nowhere. His is the path of politics, the path of posturing, the path of least resistance. But it is not the path of leadership."[86] Taking his cue from pending legislation on Capitol Hill, Bush laid out what the *Times* described as "the most sweeping overhaul of the federal health insurance program for the elderly since its inception." He called for a system in which private insurers would compete with government to cover 39 million Medicare beneficiaries. Government would subsidize the elderly so that they could purchase insurance with a prescription-drug benefit. Those unwilling to try the market could stay on Medicare, with the option of buying into a subsidized drug plan. In any case, the government would pay for all prescription drugs of elders with incomes of $11,300 or less.[87]

Thus joined, the battle became an ideological debate, with each side warning that the other would harm the welfare of the elderly. Gore wasted no time after the Allentown speech to accuse Bush of leaving "millions of seniors without any prescription drug coverage." Further, he added, "middle-class seniors, nearly half of those who don't have coverage today, would not get coverage." This was all part of Bush's intent to neglect the elderly for the sake of tax cuts for the rich.[88] Speaking at a senior citizens' center in Florida, Bush claimed that his plan, compared to Gore's, provided retirees with greater control over their own care. Indeed, he declared, Gore would permit "only one government-run HMO. You'll be thrown into it. That's where you're going to end up—a government-run HMO."[89]

Republican ads and surrogates supplemented Bush's attacks. Aired in eighteen states, one spot offered the following contrast: "Al Gore's prescription plan forces seniors into a government-run HMO. Governor Bush gives seniors a choice." An RNC ad offered more of the same: "He says he wants to fight for the people against HMOs, but his prescription drug plan forces seniors into one HMO selected by the government. Al Gore: federal HMO. George Bush: seniors choose."

Campaign spokesman Ari Fleischer likened Gore's plan to Clinton's "failed health care effort in 1993." Ralph Reed, the former director of the Christian Coalition and now a Bush campaign official, laid out to reporters the plan for more attacks on Gore: "We'll say he's got bad ideas. Not just that his ideas are not as good as our ideas, but that they could harm people. People might not get the drugs they need because of price controls."[90] Karl Rove attributed Gore's "screechy leftwing populism" to his fear of Nader's appeal; he also added that Gore's running mate had taken big contributions from the insurance and pharmaceutical industries.[91]

Both sides launched new ads in the next few days. The RNC spot showed a notebook comparing the competing prescription-drug plans. The words *Charges Seniors $600 Big Government Access Fee Annually* appeared under the Gore column. *Seniors Choose* showed up under the Bush column. The visual showed Gore silently mouthing something as the words *Gore's Rx Plan?* and *PrescriptionForDisaster.com* showed up on the screen. The Democratic response depicted Gore meeting with senior citizens as the narrator intoned, "Al Gore covers all seniors through Medicare, not an HMO. Bush forces seniors to go to HMOs and insurance companies . . . they have no choice."[92]

Beginning on September 24, Gore dedicated an entire week to pointing up the "real and very significant differences" between his approach and Bush's. "The other side," he avowed, "treats the Medicare surplus as a piggy bank they can use for a tax cut that primarily benefits the wealthiest Americans. I'll veto the use of any money from Medicare for anything other than Medicare." Gore further maintained that Bush would force "many seniors" to show up at welfare offices in order to sign up for state welfare programs. Accordingly, "middle class seniors would be left out completely."[93] Speaking in Florida, he dusted off remarks that Bush had made five years earlier when praising a proposal by Newt Gingrich to cut Medicare: "Elderly people will not suffer as a result of this plan. It's going to make [Medicare] solvent, and Republicans will be heralded not only for saving Medicare, but at the same time for having the political courage to balance the budget." Interviewed by the *Times* after his speech, Gore maintained that Bush still was no friend of Medicare: "He disagrees with its basic premise, and he is looking for any politically viable opportunity to gut it." The Bush plan, he added, was virtually the same as Gingrich's—"raising premiums, taking money out of Medicare for a tax cut that goes mainly to the wealthy, forcing seniors into HMOs, privatizing Medicare."[94]

Bush spokesman Dan Bartlett countered that his candidate had put a genuine proposal on the table: "What is important here is not what Governor Bush said about a plan five years ago that wasn't even his. What's important is what he says about his plan today."[95] Fleischer challenged the notion that seniors would stand in long lines at welfare offices. Rather, the Bush plan would expand on an existing program in twenty-three states where applicants returned forms via the mail. "Al Gore spent last week making things up," Fleischer added, "and now he's continued."[96]

Repeatedly during the first presidential debate, Gore portrayed the Bush tax cuts as a zero-sum game in which lower taxes for "the wealthiest 1 percent" would cost more than "all the spending he proposes for education, health care, prescription drugs, and national defense all combined." Under Bush's Medicare plan, Gore claimed, "95 percent of all seniors" would be without assistance for four or five years. "Big drug companies support Governor Bush's prescription," he added. "They oppose mine."[97]

In response, Bush attacked Gore as part of an administration that had squandered opportunities to make progress on prescription drugs and Social Security reform. "Look," he said, "let's forget all the politics and all the finger-pointing and get some positive things done on Medicare and prescription drugs and Social Security." Bush dismissed a barrage of Gore statistics as "Mediscare," and he also disputed the notion that only Gore opposed the special interests: "I've been standing up to big Hollywood and big trial lawyers."[98]

Speaking at a Florida retirement center, Lieberman warned that Bush's plan would cover only some senior citizens and that insurance companies would balk at selling the kinds of policies needed. "The Bush-Cheney prescription drug plan for seniors, middle-class seniors, comes down to this," he maintained. "Wait four years and then call your HMO in the morning."[99]

Gore pulled out the stops during the third presidential debate, mixing apposition while literally pointing the finger at Bush: "Doctors are giving prescriptions, they're recommending treatment, and then their recommendations are being overruled by HMOs and insurance companies. That's unacceptable. I support a strong national patient's bill of rights. It is actually a disagreement between us." Bush, he charged, was just the man for those on the side of "the big drug companies." After proposing Medicare enrollment for people in their midfifties to early sixties at "reasonable and fair" premiums, Gore fixed his gaze on Bush and said, "We have a big difference on this."[100]

That difference, Bush retorted, was his opposition to a government takeover of health care: "I don't want the federal government making decisions for patients or providers." Earlier in the debate, he had argued that the elderly were entitled to government health insurance to help with the cost of prescription drugs. Such a plan, he added, would only pass after a change of administrations. "There is a lot of bickering in Washington. . . . What I want to do is to call upon Republicans and Democrats to come together and take care of our seniors with prescription drugs." Price controls, however, "would hurt our ability to continue important research and development. The best thing is to reform Medicare."[101] For the rest of the campaign, Bush laced his speeches with references to Gore's "government-run health care system" and "Hillary-Care."[102]

At the end of October, while stumping in Wisconsin and Oregon, Gore lumped Bush with the HMOs, pharmaceutical firms, and insurance companies, noting, "They want to stay in control of the medical decisions, and they're supporting Governor Bush because they want him in control of the medical quality. I want to fight for you."[103]

Bush, too, hit familiar notes, promising choice, drugs, and money for prescription drugs for low- and middle-income seniors. He accused the Democrats of promising but not delivering: "In 1992 they went around the country saying, 'We're going to do something about Medicare and prescription drugs.' In 1996 . . . they said the same thing. And here we are four years later, and they're still saying the same thing. Here's our answer, Mr. Vice President: You had your chance. You have not led and we will."[104]

THE 2004 ELECTORAL CONTEXT

According to Gary Jacobson, George W. Bush ended his first term as "the most divisive and polarizing president in the more than 50 years of public opinion polling."[105] On the one hand, he had garnered "the highest average approval ratings among his own partisans of any president since the question has been polled," and on the other hand, his support among opposing partisans had reached historic lows. The gap in October 2004 reached eighty-three points, the difference between 94 percent satisfaction on the part of Republicans and only 11 percent approval among Democrats.[106] In the same spirit, pundit Michael Barone observed that Bush owed his reelection to the triumph of love over hate.[107]

Evidence of Democratic dissatisfaction with Bush abounded well before election day 2004. A powerful current of anger coursed through Democratic primary electorates in twenty-one states, where exit polls showed that three-fourths or more of the voters disliked Bush.[108] Gallup found that Kerry voters based their choice less on the merits of his candidacy or fondness for him than on their antipathy toward Bush. Conversely, hostility toward Kerry had little to do with voting for Bush.[109]

The Florida Recount

Much of the animosity that Democrats felt for Bush throughout his presidency originated during the intensely litigated recount of the 2000 vote in Florida. After thirty-six days of lawsuits, pregnant and hanging chads, and bellicose rhetoric, the U.S. Supreme Court overruled a pro-Gore ruling by the Florida Supreme

Court, thereby sealing Bush's claim to all of Florida's presidential electors. Only one other American presidential election had been decided by extraconstitutional means, and as in the 1876 election of Republican Rutherford B. Hayes over Democrat Samuel Tilden, the circumstances of Bush's victory polarized the nation. Polls taken during the Florida recount battle and afterward uncovered huge perceptual gaps between Bush and Gore partisans.[110]

Black Antipathy

Ironically, given the animosity that so many African Americans felt toward him, Bush had made more of an effort to win over black voters than any Republican candidate for president since Nixon in 1960. In the end, however, he fared almost as poorly among black voters as Goldwater had in 1964. Parts of his message, most notably his "no child left behind" policy with its voucher provision, should have resonated with parents of minority children trapped in dysfunctional schools. And more than most Republican standard-bearers, Bush stumped in black neighborhoods. He also became the first Republican candidate for president to address an NAACP convention since Reagan in 1980.

During the 2000 contest, however, the NAACP had aired a television ad that condemned his 1999 opposition to a Texas hate-crimes bill. The ad further suggested that Bush, as governor, had been indifferent to the brutal murder of a black man by white thugs.[111] Similar claims issued from Jesse Jackson during the campaign, and he also likened the legal fight over vote recounts in Florida to the 1965 suppression of blacks in Selma, Alabama. Unfazed by the U.S. Supreme Court ruling in *Bush v. Gore,* Jackson called for continued efforts to "delegitimize" and "discredit" Bush—indeed, to "do whatever it takes, but never accept him."[112] Polls showed that African Americans were much more likely than white Democrats to believe that the Florida vote had not been counted fairly, that Bush had stolen the election, and that the outcome had indelibly stained American politics. Blacks were more likely than white Democrats to feel bitter and cheated, and they were also less willing to acknowledge Bush's legitimacy as president (see Table 7.6). Members of the Black Congressional Caucus formally objected to the counting of Florida's electoral votes at a joint session of Congress in January 2001, and Jackson figured prominently in staging a massive protest against Bush's inauguration.

Race-related allegations dogged Bush throughout his first term, including the 2004 contest. In July 2001, NAACP chairman Julian Bond charged that some of Bush's cabinet nominations hailed from "the Taliban wing of American politics."[113] With Jackson looking on during the 2004 campaign, Kerry contended that "a million" black votes had not been counted in 2000.[114] This time joined by Senator Barbara Boxer (D-CA), members of the Black Congressional Caucus challenged the

Table 7.6. Black Discontent with Bush in 2000

	Blacks (%)	White Democrats (%)	All Whites (%)	Blacks – White Democrats
Black votes in Florida not fairly counted	68	47	30	+21
Bush won fair and square	7	21	54	–14
Bush won on a technicality	39	52	31	–13
Bush stole the election	50	26	14	+24
Bitter because Bush declared the winner	37	26	13	+11
Felt cheated because Bush declared winner	68	55	28	+13
2000 election permanently harmed U.S.	68	44	36	+24
Bush not a legitimate president	40	26	13	+14

Source: The Gallup Poll: Public Opinion 2000 (Wilmington, DE: Scholarly Resources, 2001), 424–426.

counting of Ohio's electoral votes in the joint session of Congress after Bush won reelection. "This is a travesty," Senator Rick Santorum (R-PA) said of the Democrats. "They're still not over the 2000 election, let alone the 2004 election." The Ohio challenge lost 268 to 31 in the House and 74 to 1 in the Senate.[115]

No to a National Unity Administration

Owing to the circumstances of his 2000 election, Bush came under considerable pressure to forsake his campaign agenda for a "national unity" program that would satisfy congressional Democrats. "Had Bush moved in this direction after his inauguration," Jacobson asserted, "it is most doubtful that he would have become the most polarizing president in modern history."[116] However, according to Charles O. Jones, budgeting and other realities militated against the idea.[117] In any case, as Vice President Cheney later recalled, "We had an agenda, we ran on that agenda, we won the election—full speed ahead."[118]

The Homeland Security Fight

Yet another source of Democratic anger arose out of the dispute between Bush and congressional Democrats over the creation of a new homeland security department following the terrorist attacks of September 11, 2001. Though he initially opposed the idea, Bush yielded to congressional pressure, even as he insisted on exempting a substantial portion of the department's workforce from civil service rules and union membership. In so doing, Bush created a real predicament for the Democrats. If they refused his terms, failure to establish the department could be blamed on them; and if they went along with Bush, organized labor might revolt. The Democrats chose not to alienate their labor base. By September, the homeland security fight had become a key issue in the midterm election campaigns, with Republicans accusing the Democrats of putting labor's demands ahead of national security. No Republican spoke louder on this subject than President Bush, who infuriated the Democrats by charging, "The Senate is more interested in special interests in Washington, and not interested in the security of the American people." Senate Majority Leader Tom Daschle railed against the charge, but as James Ceaser and Andrew Busch related, the Democrats had been drawn into a fight on homeland security that they could not win.[119]

Bush crisscrossed the nation on behalf of Republican candidates in 2002, exploiting his stratospheric poll standings and playing the national security card. His exertions helped the GOP regain control of the Senate (lost because of the James Jeffords defection) and expand its small majority in the House.[120] Senate Democrats took the defeat of Max Cleland, a disabled veteran of the Vietnam War, especially hard.[121] "Max didn't deserve this fate," Tom Daschle later wrote. "It was gut-wrenching to watch a war hero victimized by a campaign that questioned his patriotism—this man of such courage and honor, who lost an arm and both legs to a grenade in Vietnam, linked to Saddam Hussein and Osama bin Laden by Republican television ads that questioned his commitment to our nation's security."[122]

The Iraq War

Probably no factor figured more prominently in the partisan divide of Bush's presidency than the Iraq War. During late 2003 and early 2004, a series of Gallup Polls revealed that approximately 75 percent of Democrats but only about one Republican in four believed that the Bush administration had intentionally distorted the evidence regarding Iraqi weapons of mass destruction (WMD).[123] Similarly, a June 2004 poll showed that 79 percent of Republicans felt the war had been worth the loss of life, versus 81 percent of Democrats who held the opposite view.[124]

Some context is needed to put such findings in perspective, perhaps beginning with the 1998 enactment of the so-called Iraq Liberation Act, which proclaimed regime change in Iraq to be the official policy of the United States. Specifically, this legislation called on the executive to "seek to remove the regime headed by Saddam Hussein from power in Iraq and to promote the emergence of a democratic government to replace that regime." The means of accomplishing this feat, however, were restricted to propaganda broadcasts and the provision of military "articles and services" to anti-Saddam elements. Underscoring that it was largely an exercise in symbolic politics, the legislation stipulated that "nothing in this Act shall be construed to authorize or otherwise speak to the use of United States Armed Forces (except for aforementioned training of acceptable regime opponents, as well as drawing upon equipment)." Another provision urged establishment of a war crimes tribunal under UN auspices "for the purpose of indicting, prosecuting, and imprisoning Saddam Hussein and other Iraqi officials who are responsible for crimes against humanity, genocide, and other criminal violations of international law."[125]

President Clinton, Secretary of State Madline Albright, and many a Democrat in Congress used the occasion to raise the specter of Saddam reconstituting the arsenal of chemical, biological, and perhaps nuclear weapons that he had possessed or was developing at the outbreak of the First Gulf War. Reacting to Iraq's expulsion of UN weapons inspectors, Senator Robert F. Byrd warned that Saddam had embarked on "a crash course to build up his chemical and biological warfare capabilities." Byrd also alluded to intelligence reports that Hussein was "seeking nuclear weapons."[126]

Perhaps the most detailed assessment of Iraqi WMD capabilities and motives issued from Kenneth Pollack, an expert on the Middle East who served on the National Security Council during the Clinton years.[127] In his considered judgment, Iraq had both motive and means to revive its chemical and biological warfare (CBW) program. According to Pollack, Iraqi officials after the First Gulf War had admitted to producing fifty chemical-warfare missile warheads (filled with the nerve agent sarin) and twenty-five biological warheads (filled with botulinum toxin, anthrax, and aflatoxin). Although UN inspectors had disposed of huge stocks of chemical munitions, supposedly they had not eliminated "any of Iraq's stockpile of VX and filled munitions." Pollack likewise discussed "major dual-use chemical facilities" that masked their CBW capabilities under the guise of producing agricultural or other civilian products; and he credited reports that Iraq had conducted research on *Clostridium perfringens* (which causes gangrene), ricin, and several viruses, including plague. Similarly, he concluded that Iraq possessed "mobile BW labs" that moved around the country "as needed, leaving no trace and virtually no signature that Western intelligence can detect." "The Iraqis have all the equipment and all the agent samples they require," he added, "and it is assumed that they are hard at work."[128] Secretary of State Colin Powell would cite the same or similar intelligence findings when putting the administration's case to the UN Security Council.

The notion that Saddam was close to acquiring a nuclear weapon also loomed large in Pollack's account. By 1991, Iraq had "essentially figured out how to build a nuclear weapon," and the main obstacle to success was "acquiring the necessary fissile material." After the First Gulf War, the International Atomic Energy Agency (IAEA) had concluded that most of this program had been dismantled. Still, "a consensus" existed among experts that Iraq had resumed work on nuclear weapons. Former UN inspectors and other authorities on the Iraqi nuclear program agreed "unanimously" that Iraq was likely working to enrich uranium (probably via centrifuge separation) for nuclear weapons.[129] Citing Senate testimony by the director of the Central Intelligence Agency (CIA), George Tenet, Pollack concluded that it was "only a matter of time before Saddam's regime is able to acquire nuclear weapons if left to its own devices."[130] According to him, U.S. intelligence had estimated that Iraq could have such a weapon as early as 2004; German intelligence had predicted that Iraq would have the bomb within three to six years.[131]

On the subject of Saddam's links to international terrorism, Pollack doubted that the dictator would tolerate a rival power center inside Iraq or hold himself hostage to what terrorists might do without his say-so. Still, Pollack left open the possibility of such an alliance if the United States moved to overthrow Saddam.[132]

Evidently drawing from the same well, the administration began making a case for war against Iraq in the summer of 2002. On August 26, 2002, Vice President Cheney spoke to a Veterans of Foreign Wars (VFW) convention about the likelihood of Saddam acquiring a nuclear device "fairly soon." Cheney expressed certainty that Iraq possessed chemical and biological weapons. He also seconded a recent pronouncement by Henry Kissinger: "The imminence of proliferation of weapons of mass destruction, the huge dangers it involves, the rejection of a viable inspection system, and the demonstrated hostility of Saddam Hussein combined to produce an imperative for preemptive action."[133] President Bush hit many of the same notes during his radio address on September 13: "Today this regime likely maintains stockpiles of chemical and biological agents, and is improving facilities capable of producing chemical and biological weapons. Today Saddam Hussein has the scientists and infrastructure for a nuclear weapons program, and has illicitly sought to purchase the equipment needed to enrich uranium for a nuclear weapon. Should his regime acquire fissile material, it would be able to build a nuclear weapon within a year."[134]

As election day 2002 grew closer, the White House pressed Congress to act on a resolution authorizing presidential use of force against Iraq. "Already," Senate Democratic leader Daschle wrote, "Republicans were laying the predicate for the charge that Democratic senators, up for reelection, were resisting the president's call to arms against Iraq."[135] By his own account, Daschle pressed Bush for assurances that an Iraq war would not detract from the war on terror, that the president would enlist a broad coalition of allies, and that he would consult regularly with Congress after hostilities began.[136] Robert Byrd, Edward Kennedy, Richard Durbin, Paul Wellstone, and other Senate Democrats adamantly opposed such a resolution.[137] At the same time, Senate Foreign Relations chairman Joseph Biden and his Republican colleague Richard Lugar tried to talk the White House into accepting a more restricted resolution with more bipartisan appeal.[138] Their effort collapsed when House Minority Leader Richard Gephardt and Senator Lieberman declared in favor of the White House version on October 2. Byrd, Kennedy, and a few others failed to persuade fellow members of the Senate Democratic caucus to join them in opposing the administration policy. "I made my case," Byrd bitterly recalled, "but it fell on deaf ears."[139]

Meanwhile, Bush stepped up the pressure on congressional Democrats. He thanked Gephardt, Speaker Dennis Hastert, and Senate Republican leader Trent Lott for their backing of a "strong bipartisan resolution" that authorized the use of military force "if necessary to disarm Saddam Hussein." Bush also called the nation's attention to an "important debate" and "historic vote" on Iraq about to take place in the House and Senate.[140]

Among the four Democrats in the Senate running for president at that point, John Kerry appeared to have a better chance of winning the nomination than Lieberman, John Edwards, or Bob Graham.[141] Accordingly, his floor speech on Iraq invited the closest scrutiny. Todd S. Purdum of the *Times* reported that Kerry made a "tortured" and "reluctant" case for disarming Saddam's regime "almost certainly by force."[142] At times, he sounded no less bellicose than Bush or Cheney: "Who among us can say, with any certainty, to anybody, that those weapons might not be used against our troops or against allies in the region? Who can say that this master of miscalculation will not develop a weapon of mass destruction even greater, then reinvade Kuwait, push the Kurds out, attack Israel .... allow those weapons to slide off to one group or another. . . . How do we leave that to chance?" Even though he held that Bush should act "pursuant to" a final UN resolution, as well as work with the United Nations to assemble a multinational force, Kerry also allowed that the lack of such a resolution would not change "the bottom line of what we are voting for." On the one hand, he opposed unilateral action by the United States unless all attempts to assemble a multinational force had failed and the threat was "imminent," and on the other hand, he implied that the threat was indeed imminent:

> According to intelligence, Iraq has chemical and biological weapons as well as missiles with ranges in excess of the 150-kilometer restriction imposed by the United Nations in the ceasefire resolution. Although Iraq's chemical weapons effort was reduced during the UNSCOM inspections, Iraq has maintained its chemical weapons effort over the last four years. Evidence suggests that it has begun renewed production of chemical warfare agents, probably including mustard gas, sarin, cyclosarin, and VX. Intelligence reports show that Iraq has invested

more heavily in its biological weapons programs over the four years, with the result that all key aspects of this program—R&D, production, and weaponization—are active. Most elements of the program are larger and more advanced than they were before the Gulf War. Iraq has some lethal and incapacitating agents and is capable of quickly producing and weaponizing a variety of such agents, including anthrax, for delivery on a range of vehicles such as bombs, missiles, aerial sprayers, and covert operatives, which could bring them to the United States homeland.[143]

On the other side of the Capitol, the administration's version of the resolution (H.J. Res. 114) passed 296 to 133, with all but 6 of the 221 Republicans in favor and 126 Democrats opposed. John Murtha of Pennsylvania voted for the resolution along with eighty other Democrats.[144]

As the House moved to final passage, the Senate took up Democratic amendments that would have imposed substantial limitations on Bush. All failed, including Byrd's attempt to insert a time limit and a congressional veto. To prevent a Byrd filibuster, Lieberman moved and the Senate overwhelmingly supported a cloture motion. Carl Levin offered an amendment to permit presidential use of force only if "pursuant to a new resolution of the United Nations Security Council." It failed. Durbin moved to substitute *imminent* for *continuing* in the threat description. The defeat of his amendment cleared the path for a vote on final passage the next day, October 11. Seventy-two senators voted in favor of H.J. Res. 114 against twenty-three opposed.[145] Kerry, Edwards, and Lieberman voted in favor. Back on the presidential campaign trail, this trio soon learned that Democratic activists and likely primary voters in Iowa and New Hampshire overwhelmingly opposed the conflict they had voted to authorize. Indeed, the winds of antiwar sentiment lofted Howard Dean, a former Vermont governor little known outside of New England, to front-runner status. While Dean raked in the money, picked up endorsements, attracted the media, and surged in the polls, Kerry's stock plunged.[146] Having cornered the antiwar market, Dean banished Kerry, Lieberman, and Edwards from the "Democratic wing of the Democratic Party." "If you're a Democrat and did support the Iraq war," Dean proclaimed, "it calls into question your judgment in one of the most serious questions or actions any president will have to take."[147] At first, Kerry stood by his war vote: "I would have preferred if we had given diplomacy a greater opportunity, but I think it was the right decision to disarm Saddam Hussein. And, when the president made the decision, I supported him, and I support the fact that we did disarm him." Under intense attack from most rivals, however, Kerry tried to distance himself from Bush: "The president and his advisers did not do almost anything correctly in the walk-up to the war. They rushed to war. . . . They did not give legitimacy to the inspections. We could still have been doing inspections even today."[148] Dean's response presaged the "flip-flop" attacks of Republicans: "To this day I don't know what John Kerry's position is. . . . If you agree with the war, then say so, but don't try to wobble around in between."[149]

Owing in no small part to Dean's failings as a candidate, Kerry managed to reposition himself as the electable antiwar alternative.[150] His most important step in this direction occurred in October 2003, when the Senate took up a supplemental appropriation bill totaling $87 billion to pay for the wars in Afghanistan and Iraq. Before the October 17 vote on final passage, Kerry had cosponsored a Biden amendment that would have raised the money by rescinding cuts in the rate for the wealthiest taxpayers. This measure, which was defeated on a party-line vote, formed the basis of Kerry's claim that he had voted for the $87 billion before voting against it.[151]

Although helpful to Kerry in winning the nomination, his vote against final passage of the supplemental appropriation and the convoluted justification that he offered afterward set him up for Republican attacks in the fall. Of all the possible pairings on separate votes to authorize and fund the conflicts in Iraq and Afghanistan, the combination of voting yes to launch the war in 2002 and voting no on money to fund it in 2003 invited the most cynical interpretation of Kerry's motives.[152] The great majority of Democratic senators who had opposed authorizing the war nevertheless voted in favor of the supplemental appropriation. Kerry and his future running mate, John Edwards, were among the four Democrats who acted contrary to the tradition of funding the troops, regardless of how one felt about the conflict itself (see Table 7.7).[153]

Ironically, Kerry's record on Iraq allowed his Republican opponents to have it both ways. On the one hand, they painted him as a weather vane, spinning with every gust of the political wind; on the other, they assailed him as consistently weak on national defense, except for his 2002 vote for war. In 1991, Kerry had voted against authorizing the First Iraq War even though the first President Bush was acting pursuant to UN Security Council resolutions, was advocating a defensive rather than a preemptive war to expel Saddam's forces from Kuwait, and was successful in assembling a multinational force the likes of which had not been seen since World War II. That coalition even included troops from Saudi Arabia, Syria, and other Arab states. Further, no one at the time doubted that Saddam was attempting to develop a nuclear weapon or that he already possessed CBW capabilities.[154]

Bush's Poll Standings

The Second Iraq War would also take a toll on Bush's poll standings, as the net job approval ratings shown in Figure 7.5. Considering the circumstances under which

Table 7.7. Senate Democrats Voting on 2002 Iraq War Resolution and 2003 Supplemental Military Appropriation Bill

	For war resolution	Against war resolution
For supplemental	Baucus, Bayh, Biden, Breaux, Cantwell, Carper, Clinton, Daschle, Dodd, Dorgan, Feinstein, Johnson, Kohl, Landrieu, Lieberman, Lincoln, Miller, Nelson (FL), Nelson (NE), Reid, Rockefeller, Schumer, and Smith	Akaka, Bingaman, Conrad, Corzine, Dayton, Durbin, Feingold, Inouye, Levin, Mikulski, Murray, Reed, Stabenow, and Wyden
Against supplemental	Edwards, Harkin, Hollings, and Kerry	Boxer, Byrd, Graham, Kennedy, Leahy, and Sarbanes

Note: The table lists only the Democratic senators who voted on both measures. It omits Carnahan, Cleland, and Torricelli, who had lost or resigned their seats; the deceased Wellstone; and Lautenberg, elected in 2002 to replace Torricelli.
Source: http://www.senate.gov, 108th Congress, 1st Session, vote 400.

he entered the Oval Office, Bush started off relatively strong with an average net of +35, perhaps reflecting public receptiveness to his "no child left behind" proposal and also his tax-cut plan.[155] Still, consistent with Richard Brody's analysis of honeymoons, a slow but steady falloff occurred in 2001 as uncertainty or reluctance to judge gave way to disapproval and disappointment.[156] The mean of Bush's net approval dropped fifteen points between February and June. The May defection of Senator James Jeffords to the Democrats, which resulted in a Democratic takeover of the Senate, likely contributed to Bush's slide in the Gallup Poll. In any case, his legislative agenda came to a dead stop in the Senate, and as of September 10, 2001, it was still moribund. The terrorist attacks of the following day generated a huge rally of extraordinary duration that lofted Bush's net approval from 21 percent in August to 58 percent in September. He ended the year with net of +76.

Subsequently, Bush's net approval plunged thirty-nine points between January and December 2002. In 2003, his approval tracked developments in Iraq. Bush got a boost when the war commenced on March 19, and another occurred in April, when Baghdad fell to American forces. On May 1, an overconfident White House staged the most premature of victory celebrations in modern history. The president landed on the flight deck of the carrier *Abraham Lincoln* to proclaim "mission accomplished" and to suggest that the democratization of Iraq would soon get under way. Before long, however, events disproved these claims, giving Democrats ample opportunity to make Bush regret his words. His net approval declined from 44 percent in April to a mere 6 percent in October, as the onset of a murderous

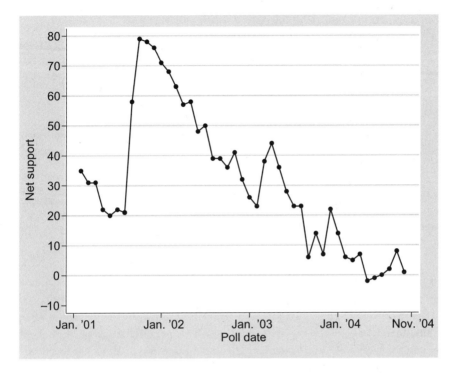

Figure 7.5 Bush's job approval ratings, 2001–2004
Source: Gallup Polls compiled by George C. Edwards III, *Governing by Campaigning* (New York: Pearson-Longman, 2007), 118–121.

insurrection coincided with a spike in American casualties and the collapse of reconstruction efforts. A surprise visit to the troops on Thanksgiving and the capture of Saddam briefly raised the president's net approval to 22 percent. In 2004, escalating casualties, David Kay's report that U.S. intelligence had spectacularly erred about Saddam's WMD, and the Abu Ghraib prison scandal knocked Bush's ratings into negative territory. The year had begun with him at 14 percent in the black, only to fall just below zero in May and June. Net approval inched back to just above zero near the end of his reelection campaign. In view of these setbacks, it was all the more remarkable that Republican support remained steadfast.[157]

THE 2004 ATTACK PROPENSITIES AND TARGETS

Democratic attack propensities exceeded those of the Republicans in every week of the 2004 fall campaign (see Table 7.8). The difference showed up most notably

Table 7.8. 2004 Attack Propensities

Week	Democrats Attacking Republicans	Republicans Attacking Democrats
1	.826	.612
2	.750	.532
3	.576	.535
4	.710	.404
5	.633	.478
6	.625	.600
7	.576	.530
8	.497	.382
Overall	.625	.494
N's	630	540

Note: Week one: September 6–12; week two: September 13–19; week three: September 20–26; week four: September 27–October 3; week five: October 4–10; week six: October 11–17; week seven: October 18–24; week eight: October 25–November 2.

in weeks one, two, and four. More than eight of every ten campaign statements issuing from the Kerry camp in week one attacked the Republican ticket or party, as did 75 percent of all Democratic statements in week two and 70 percent in week four. Indeed, Democratic negativity exceeded 60 percent in five weeks and topped 50 percent every week except the last. The Republicans waged by far the less negative campaign, with negativity scores exceeding 50 percent in five weeks and 60 or higher in only two. Overall, 62 percent of 630 Democratic campaign statements blasted the Republicans, compared with 49 percent of 540 Republican statements flaying the Democrats. The Democrats waged a much more negative race than Gore-Lieberman had in 2000, and despite attacks by the Swift Boat Veterans, the Republicans waxed less negative in 2004 than in 2000.

As usual, the vast majority of attacks by one party targeted the other party's presidential nominee. Eighty-three percent of the 393 attacks launched by Democrats targeted Bush, and 85 percent of 266 Republican attacks fell on Kerry (see Table 7.9). In all, 87 percent of Kerry's solo attacks targeted Bush, whereas 97 percent of Bush's attacks aimed at Kerry. Edwards targeted Bush in nearly 86 percent of his solo attacks, and Cheney drilled Kerry in 81 percent of his.

THE 2004 CAMPAIGN TOPICS

General Campaign Discourse

As in 2000, the Democrats and Republicans converged on nine of the same ten topics that each emphasized the most (see Table 7.10). Military/defense issues

Table 7.9. Targeting of 2004 Attacks

	Democratic Targeting of Republicans	Republican Targeting of Democrats
All attackers		
Presidential nominee	326	225
Other targets	67	42
Total attacks	393	266
Nominee targeted	.829	.846
Solo attacks of		
presidential nominee	Kerry	Bush
Presidential nominee	168	89
Other targets	17	3
Total attacks	184	92
Nominee targeted	.864	.967
Solo attacks of vice-		
presidential nominee	Edwards	Cheney
Presidential nominee	30	22
Other targets	5	5
Total attacks	35	27
Nominee targeted	.857	.815

Note: Some attacks on presidential nominees targeted others of the same party.

easily ranked first on both agendas as a result of 9/11 and the wars in Afghanistan and Iraq. Military service records and related rumblings about patriotism got enough emphasis to rank fifth on both agendas. Near-identical emphasis showed up for the economy, social and health issues, campaign issues, voting and the conduct of elections, leadership, and education. The only topics not part of the top ten for both parties were energy/environment and same-sex marriage. In sum, both sides agreed on the importance of most topics.

Attack Topics

When going negative, both parties made greatest use of military/defense issues, the domestic economy, and social/health concerns. Likewise, each candidate's military service record during the Vietnam War provoked attacks and counterattacks, as did the topic of leadership. Republicans appeared less inclined than Democrats to clash on education, disputes over voter registration,[158] crime, and foreign policy, whereas Democratic attackers appeared less willing than Republicans to fight over same-sex marriage. Still, the battle was joined on the most vital issues of the day.

With ongoing wars in Afghanistan and Iraq as well as the broader struggle against terrorism, military and national security concerns understandably

Table 7.10. Leading Topics in 2004

All Campaign Statements		Attack Statements	
Democrats	Republicans	Democrats	Republicans
Military/defense (166)	Military/defense (163)	Military/defense (136)	Military/defense (97)
Domestic economy (83)	Domestic economy (55)	Domestic economy (59)	Domestic economy (27)
Social/health (77)	Campaign (55)	Social/health (55)	Social/health (27)
Campaign (58)	Social/health (46)	Energy/environment (18)	Patriotism, war record (25)
Patriotism, war record (28)	Patriotism, war record (35)	Patriotism, war record (17)	Leadership (19)
Voting issues (25)	Leadership (23)	Leadership (15)	Dirty campaign (9)
Energy/environment (24)	Debates (23)	Education (12)	Gay marriage (9)
Leadership (20)	Voting issues (14)	Voting issues (9)	Ideology/party (6)
Education (17)	Gay marriage (14)	Crime (8)	Women's rights (6)
Debates (16)	Education (11), Ideology/party (11)	Foreign policy (8)	Stem-cell research (4)

Notes: The topics most stressed by the Democrats accounted for 82 percent of all their campaign statements; the corresponding figure for the Republicans was 82 percent. The ten topics most utilized in Democratic attacks on the Republicans accounted for 84 percent of all such attacks; the corresponding figure for Republican attacks on the Democrats was 86 percent.

dominated the 2004 attack agendas. The Kerry-Edwards ticket and allied groups raised such issues in 34 percent of their attacks, as did the Republicans in 36 percent of theirs. Iraq figured more frequently in the attacks of both parties than Afghanistan, the war on terror, or the potential of hostilities with North Korea or Iran. Still, as Table 7.11 shows, the Democrats invoked the war in Iraq substantially more than the Republicans. Conversely, the Republicans outattacked the Democrats on the broader war against terrorism. All told, the Iraq War figured in 78 percent of Democratic attacks pertaining to military/defense matters and in two-thirds of all such Republican attacks. Conversely, the war on terror showed up as a topic in one-third of Democratic attacks and in 41 percent of all Republican attacks.

Both sides saw parallels between the new war in Iraq and an old one in Vietnam. Part of that debate centered on whether Iraq was becoming another "quagmire" of Vietnam proportions. Another part pertained to each candidate's Vietnam service record in regard to his fitness as a twenty-first-century commander-in-chief. Although much of the assault on Bush's stint in the Texas Air National Guard took place before Kerry's nomination, the Democrats continued to contrast the combat decorations of their man with the "special treatment" that allegedly allowed Bush to evade his obligation to the National Guard. This approach was most in evidence

Table 7.11. Party Emphasis on 2004 Military and Defense Issues

Issue	Democratic (%)	Republican (%)
Iraq War only	49.3	36.1
War on terror only	17.9	26.8
Iraq + war on terror	14.9	14.4
Iraq + Afghanistan	2.2	6.2
Iraq + two other conflicts	11.9	10.3
Other	3.8	6.2

Note: The "two other conflicts" for the fifth entry include any combination of Afghanistan, the war on terror, the potential of war with North Korea, or some other recent undertaking by U.S. forces in Bosnia, Kosovo, Haiti, or Somalia.

at the Boston convention, where Kerry appeared awash in flags and uniforms and where old footage of the determined, helmeted, flak-jacketed, and rifle-toting Kerry extolled his warrior experience. A pro-Kerry group dubbed Texas for Truth soon aired a TV ad charging that Bush's lax service in the Air National Guard had bordered on desertion.[159] The DNC dispatched Senator Tom Harkin and others to accuse Bush of lying about his service record. Kerry operative Howard Wolfson branded Bush "a son of privilege, a fortunate son, who has had strings pulled for him, who used his connections to avoid service."[160]

CBS News weighed in with a *60 Minutes* story that purportedly confirmed charges that the young George W. Bush had been given VIP treatment. Bush supporters hit back, accusing the network of throwing in with the Kerry campaign. The latter charge gained credibility once it became clear that Dan Rather and his producer, Mary Mapes, had based the story largely on bogus documents provided by a partisan Democrat. Bloggers dealt a mortal blow to the CBS story by questioning the type font of documents that supposedly dated back to the 1970s. Further investigation showed that the documents on which CBS based the story had been forged. Black Rock was further discomfited when rival networks reported that Mapes had put her source in contact with the Kerry camp.[161] At this point, CBS officials disavowed the story, thereby forcing a hitherto defiant Rather into making an abject apology on air. Mapes lost her job as a result of this fiasco, and the independent postmortem that CBS commissioned to investigate the affair reflected poorly both on her and on Rather.[162]

About the same time, the Pentagon released documents pertaining to Bush's service record, papers that were earlier said to have been lost. Although the timing of this release raised eyebrows at the *Times* and other major news organizations, no one disputed the authenticity of the documents. And they revealed that Lieutenant Bush had flown 336 hours in *F102A* fighter jets, had ranked in the middle of his flight training class, had scored high on airmanship and flying without navigational instruments, and had last piloted a military aircraft in April 1972. The

1972 date coincided with the timing of his leave to manage an Alabama election campaign.[163]

Seemingly unfazed by the CBS debacle, DNC chairman Terry McAuliffe vowed to pursue the National Guard issue. "Why," he asked, "can't George Bush tell us unequivocally why he skipped that flight exam, or why he leapfrogged over 150 people waiting to get into the National Guard, or why he, the son of a congressman, managed to get an honorable discharge when he did not get enough credits?"[164] By that time, however, the unwelcome spotlight on what the candidates had done during the Vietnam War had shifted to Kerry.

Kerry's Vietnam story consisted of two parts—four months spent in Vietnam, punctuated by combat and hazardous missions, and a much longer stint back home as an outspoken opponent of the war. In his latter capacity, the youthful Kerry courted publicity for his antiwar activities, as in a television interview with ABC News in which he spoke freely of "giving back" (i.e., throwing away) seven or more of his military decorations to protest the war. Other film showed him and other demonstrators tossing medals or ribbons over a fence. Every word of his 1971 testimony to the Senate Foreign Relations Committee was reprinted verbatim as part of the hearings transcript, and at least some of what he said was filmed. A widely circulated photo showed him sitting not far behind actress Jane Fonda at an antiwar function.[165]

The White House and the Bush-Cheney campaign made a show of respect for Kerry's combat experience even as they declared his antiwar activities fair game for criticism. However, the Swift Boat Veterans and POWs for Truth, a pro-Bush 527 group, made no such distinction. Their TV ads attacked Kerry's record as a combat veteran as well as his antiwar activism. The group justified its attacks as follows:

> Senator John Kerry has made his 4-month combat tour in Vietnam the center-piece of his bid for the presidency. . . . We speak from personal experience—our group includes men who served beside Kerry in combat as well as his commanders. Though we come from different backgrounds and hold varying political opinions, we agree on one thing: John Kerry misrepresented his record and ours in Vietnam and therefore exhibits serious flaws in character and lacks the potential to lead. . . . For more than thirty years, most Vietnam veterans kept silent as we were maligned as misfits, drug addicts, and baby killers. Now that a key creator of that poisonous image is seeking the Presidency we have resolved to end our silence.[166]

Their first ad ("Any Questions?") aired just after the Democratic convention in relatively few media markets. Playing off a recent speech by John Edwards—who had declared that anyone wanting to know what Kerry was made of should talk to the men he served with in Vietnam—this spot consisted almost entirely of sound bites from thirteen veterans who accused Kerry of lying about two of his medals and of betraying his comrades. Kerry, the voice-over concluded, could not be trusted. Because of coverage on the evening news and via the Internet, the ad's audience expanded exponentially. The National Annenberg Election Survey (NAES) found that more than half of the public had either viewed the ad or heard of it within two weeks of its airing. Nearly half of those who regularly watched cable news programs had seen it, and worse for Kerry, 46 percent of such viewers deemed it believable.[167] To the consternation of Democrats, Kerry kept silent for two weeks before accusing Bush of using the Swift Boat Vets to do his "dirty work." By that time, however, 30 percent of the public doubted that Kerry had earned all of his medals.[168]

Hard on the heels of Kerry's belated response, the Swift Boat Vets struck again with their "Sellout" ad, nearly all of which consisted of old film and audio of Kerry's 1971 testimony before the Senate Foreign Relations Committee. A youthful Kerry appeared on screen reciting a litany of atrocities supposedly committed by American troops against the Vietnamese population. His voice mechanically slowed in the attack ad, Kerry averred that such crimes had been "committed on a day-to-day basis with the full awareness of officers at all levels of command." Specifically, American soldiers were said to have "raped, cut off ears, cut off heads, taped wires from portable telephones to human genitals and turned up the power, cut off limbs, blown up bodies, randomly shot at civilians, razed villages in a fashion reminiscent of Genghis Khan, shot cattle and dogs for fun, poisoned food stocks, and generally ravaged the countryside of South Vietnam."[169] By giving such testimony, the ad charged, Kerry had betrayed fellow Americans still fighting in Vietnam.[170]

The Swift Boat Vets fired another salvo on August 26 with the ad "Gunner," in which a former crewmate disputed Kerry's claim to have taken their swift boat into Cambodian waters. "Medals" soon followed with footage of Kerry and other "winter soldiers" throwing somebody's decorations over a fence. The same spot showed the ABC segment in which Kerry justified this activity as a symbolic protest of an illegitimate war.[171] Sorely provoked by the "Medals" ad, Kerry hit back on September 16, accusing the Swift Boat Vets of lying. One day later, a new ad, "Dazed and Confused," juxtaposed Kerry's denials with the same footage of his ABC interview shown in "Medals."

Five days later, the Swift Boat Vets aired "Friends," which accused Kerry of consorting with enemy envoys in Paris while American troops were fighting in Vietnam. Nine days after that, "Never Forget" aired, in which the wives of two former POWs appeared on camera to talk about how Kerry's testimony before the Senate Foreign Relations Committee had affected the morale of their husbands, who at the time were prisoners of war in North Vietnam. Kerry's testimony, they charged, had given "aid and comfort to the enemy by advocating their negotiating points to our government." Another spot, entitled "Why?" repeated these allegations on October 13. Also launched on October 13, "They Served" showed aging veterans looking somberly at the camera while the voice-over intoned that each had been decorated for valor in the Vietnam conflict. Unlike Kerry, the narrator added, they had kept their medals. "Honesty and character still matter," the ad concluded, "especially in time of war."[172]

On balance, it appears that the fight over Vietnam War records inflicted more damage on Kerry than on Bush. A CBS/*New York Times* poll released before the unraveling of the *60 Minutes* story showed that only 20 percent of voters believed that Bush had told the whole truth about his National Guard service. Similarly, only 29 percent thought that Kerry had been completely honest about his Vietnam medals. However, except for claims that Kerry was not entitled to his medals, the charges against him were far more serious than those against Bush. Moreover, some Swift Boat Vets attacks were well documented, with Kerry as the chief witness for the prosecution. The record of his Senate testimony left no doubt that Kerry had met with two enemy delegations in 1970, as charged by the Swift Boat Vets,[173] or that he had advocated their negotiating points when appearing before the Senate Foreign Relations Committee.[174] As for the claim that his testimony had gotten back to American POWs and lowered their morale, the best judges of how they felt at the time clearly were the imprisoned men and the wives in whom they later confided. The tossing of medals and ribbons had been captured on film, along with the Kerry interview. Whether Kerry had thrown away his medals, his ribbons, or, as he claimed years later, decorations belonging to other disgruntled veterans was of no consequence.

ATTACK METHODS

Charges of dishonesty filled the air in 2004. Table 7.12 shows that the Republicans used this tactic more than any other. Bush ripped and tore at Kerry's truthfulness in nearly 55 percent of his solo attacks, as did 47 percent of all Republican attacks. Kerry and Democrats in general resorted most to fear arousal and accusing Bush of lying. The dishonesty charge ranked first among tactics used by Bush and all Republicans when assailing the Democrats, and it tied for first with fear arousal in Cheney's attacks. Typically, Republican attackers embellished the dishonesty charge by labeling Kerry a flip-flopper. Bush often supplemented these methods with apposition, that is, by comparing his steadiness on the war with Kerry's inconsistency. Bush also made greater use of ridicule than Cheney, Kerry, and Edwards.

Table 7.12. Attack Methods, 2004

	Presidential Candidate (solo)	Vice-Presidential Candidate (solo)	All Attackers
Democrats attacking Republicans			
Fear arousal	.659	.486	.541
Ridicule	.065	.086	.061
Labeling	.265	.229	.297
Apposition	.324	.400	.269
Dishonesty	.357	.229	.381
Republicans attacking Democrats			
Fear arousal	.419	.444	.367
Ridicule	.237	.074	.142
Labeling	.419	.296	.371
Apposition	.452	.296	.273
Dishonesty	.548	.444	.468

ECHOES FROM THE CAMPAIGN TRAIL

Owing to the importance of the war in the rhetoric of the 2004 campaigns, this section focuses on exchanges over the country's Iraq policy. Both sides sought this confrontation and willingly engaged in a ferocious exchange. Because of the sheer volume of material, this section draws entirely from clashes that took place in the period from Labor Day to just before the first presidential debate.

Democratic Attacks on Bush and Cheney

Kerry's fall campaign began on a note of gloom brought about by the first of the Swift Boat Vets ads, the disappearance of his lead in the polls, and a successful convention for Bush. The *Times* reported infighting among members of Kerry's "high command" and "the Kennedy camp," which had been enlisted to save the campaign. The slowness of Kerry's response to the initial Swift Boat Vets ad was one point of contention, and disagreement over the campaign theme was another. Joel Johnson, formerly of the Clinton White House, announced that the campaign would make the case that "Bush has taken us in the wrong direction. If you want more of the same for the next four years, vote for President Bush. If you want a new direction, John Kerry and John Edwards." A former member of the high command demurred: "I think our negative frame should be that George Bush is a liar. He misled the country on Iraq. And then everything else that he lies about— bring it back to that."[175]

In fact, as Kerry demonstrated while stumping in Ohio, West Virginia, and Pennsylvania, the Democrats could combine criticism of the Iraq War with claims that Bush had neglected domestic problems, as well as the war on terror. Cleveland voters got a taste of this argument when Kerry offered a zero-sum view of the cost of fighting in Iraq against the funding of social programs: "George Bush's wrong-headed, go-it-alone Iraq policy has cost you . . . over $200 billion. That's $200 billion we're not investing in Cleveland. That's $200 billion we're not investing in our schools and in No Child Left Behind. That's $200 billion we're not investing in health care for all Americans and prescription drugs that are affordable." In what became a staple of his stump speech, he proclaimed, "When it comes to Iraq, I would not have done just one thing differently. I would have done everything differently from this president."[176] In Cincinnati two days later, Kerry lamented "a catastrophic choice that has cost us $200 billion because we went it alone, and we've paid an even more unbearable price in young American lives and the risks our soldiers take." Bush, he avowed, had made "the wrong choices," adding, "He himself now admits he miscalculated in Iraq, but, in truth, his miscalculation was ignoring the advice he was given, including the very best advice of America's own military."[177] On September 12, Kerry assailed the administration's concentration on Iraq as harmful to its ability to cope with other national security threats: "They have taken their eye off the real ball. They took it off in Afghanistan and shifted it to Iraq. They took it off in North Korea and shifted it to Iraq. They took it off in Russia and the nuclear materials there, and shifted it to Iraq."[178]

Such attacks did not always go down well. Speaking to a National Guard convention on September 14, Kerry declared that the president "just glosses over Iraq as if everything is fine. But you and I know . . . that whole parts of Iraq are in control of terrorists, or jihadists and insurgents that weren't before. That our troops are overextended, our National Guard and Reserve troops are overextended, and this president has not done what is necessary to fight the most effective war on terror."[179] In the same speech, Kerry accused Bush of operating in a "fantasy world of spin" and of lying about how precarious the American mission had become. "No!" a colonel in the Louisiana Guard shouted before storming out. Others pointedly withheld applause when Kerry finished.[180]

Kerry embellished his Iraq message three days later by accusing the administration of planning to mobilize the army reserves and National Guard units immediately after the election. "Hide it from the people, then make the move," he charged in Albuquerque. Evidently, this rumor originated with Representative John Murtha (D-PA), and in any case, the Pentagon promptly denied it. Kerry also seized on Cheney's association with Halliburton to accuse him of war profiteer-ing: "We need a president and a vice president who aren't going to sacrifice the taxpayers' money on the altar of no-bid cronyism while our fighting men and women go without the armor and the equipment they need."[181]

On September 20, Kerry used a New York University speech to warn of an Iraq war that would never end without a change of U.S. policy. "Today," he declared, "President Bush tells us that he would do everything all over again, the same way. How can he possibly be serious? Is he really saying that if we knew there were no imminent threat, no weapons of mass destruction, no ties to Al Qaeda, the United States should have invaded Iraq?" As for Saddam Hussein, he said that "we have traded a dictator for a chaos that has left America less secure."[182]

One *Times* reporter opined that the "last hope" of the Kerry camp to undercut "the image of Mr. Bush as a competent war leader" was to pound away on "why 'terrorists are pouring across the border' into Iraq, why so few of America's al-lies have joined the effort, and why Iran and North Korea have advocated their nuclear programs while the administration has been preoccupied with Iraq."[183] Former president Carter agreed: "The overwhelming issue . . . is the Iraqi war and the war against terrorism, and who can address these problems more wisely and more honestly. I think that's the issue that Kerry has to pursue, because . . . President Bush has not been honest with the American people, and certainly has failed in almost everything he professes to be doing in Iraq and in Afghanistan, unfortunately."[184]

Already on record as being doubtful about holding January elections in Iraq, Kerry assailed the interim Iraqi prime minister, Ayad Allawi, when he met with Bush in Washington on September 23. At that meeting, Allawi, Bush, and Secre-tary of Defense Donald Rumsfeld had acknowledged that conditions were "less than perfect" in some parts of the country. Nonetheless, they agreed that the vote should proceed on schedule. Kerry accused Allawi of spreading disinformation: "I think the prime minister is, obviously, contradicting his own statement of a few days ago, where he said the terrorists were pouring into the country. The prime minister and the president are here, obviously, to put their best face on the policy. But the fact is that the CIA estimates, the reporting, the ground operations, and the troops all tell a different story." Noting that "no-go zones" had been established in Iraq, Kerry declared, "You can't hold an election in a no-go zone."[185]

A day later, the Democratic candidate embellished his "wrong war" argument in a speech at Temple University:

The invasion of Iraq was a profound diversion from the battle against our great-est enemy, Al Qaeda, which killed more than 3,000 people on 9/11 and which still plots our destruction today. And there's no question about it. The president's misjudgment, miscalculation, and mismanagement of the war in Iraq all make the war on terror harder to win. Iraq is now what it was not before the war—a haven for terrorists. George Bush has made Saddam Hussein the priority. I would have made Osama bin Laden the priority. As president, I will finish the job in Iraq and refocus our energies on the real war on terror.[186]

Stumping in Wisconsin just before the first presidential debate, Kerry pounced on a Bush statement that invading Iraq had been the right call and that it was still the right decision. He exclaimed:

It is unbelievable that just this morning we learned that the president had said he would do it all over again, and dress up in a flight suit, and landing on an aircraft carrier, and say "mission accomplished" again. Well, my friends, when the president landed on that aircraft carrier, 150 of our young sons and daughters had given their lives. Since then, tragically, since he said mission accomplished, tragically over 900 have now died.[187]

Although some Democrats saw Edwards as a reluctant warrior, the record shows that he frequently lambasted Bush and Cheney. On September 12, for example, he charged that Bush had created a "mess" in Iraq (a contention uttered by Kerry three days earlier) and thereby had diverted attention from domestic problems, as well as the threats posed by Iran and North Korea. He also accused Cheney of peddling false information about Saddam's links to Al Qaeda.[188] One week later, Edwards repeated a Kerry accusation that the administration had concealed plans for a massive call-up of reserve and National Guard troops after the election.[189] On September 22, he responded to a Cheney attack on Kerry by labeling the vice president "a chief architect of the Iraq quagmire."[190] Eight days later, Edwards read aloud from a 1992 speech that Cheney had delivered in Seattle when he was the secretary of defense. Responding to criticism of the first President Bush for not going all the way to depose Saddam in the First Gulf War, Cheney had offered the following rationale: "Once we had rounded him up and gotten rid of his government, then the question is what do you put in its place? You know, you then have accepted the responsibility for governing Iraq." "He knew!" Edwards exclaimed in Weirton, West Virginia. "That's the worst part of this—he knew how dangerous this was."[191]

No Kerry surrogate took the fight to Bush more passionately than Ted Kennedy. On September 10, for instance, the senior senator from Massachusetts inveighed against the war as "a catastrophe for our soldiers, who were foolishly sent to war with no place to win the peace."[192] Sixteen days later—"his voice ever rising, his face ever reddening, his arms ever swirling"—Kennedy roused students at George Washington University by excoriating Bush as "the world record-holder for flip-flops" and as "catastrophically wrong." The *Times* account characterized this speech as the most acerbic of the many on this subject that Kennedy had uncorked in the previous eighteen months.[193] Senator Biden offered a milder reproach when disputing Bush's characterization of Iraq as the central front in the war on terror: "Well, by that . . . measure, I think the war on terror is in trouble."[194]

The Democrats and their 527 groups fired off a flurry of television and radio ads, such as "Wrong Choices," which aired in week one of the fall campaign and declared, "George Bush: $200 billion for Iraq. In America, lost jobs and rising health care costs. George Bush's wrong choices have weakened us here at home."[195] On September 16, MoveOn.org ran "Quagmire," a spot that showed a soldier sinking deep into desert sand while holding his rifle in a gesture of surrender. The audio accused Bush of "misleading us into war with Iraq," of "sending poorly equipped soldiers into battle," and of falsely proclaiming "mission accomplished." The words *Over 1,000 U.S. soldiers killed* appeared on screen, while the audio blasted Bush for spending $150 billion needed for schools and health care. The voice-over continued, "Now, facing a growing insurgency, he has no real plan to end the war."[196] Three days later, Kerry appeared in one of his ads to reiterate a familiar charge: "Two hundred billion dollars. That is what we are spending in Iraq because George Bush chose to go it alone. Now the president tells us that we don't have the resources to take care of health care and education here at home. That's wrong."[197] Stung by a windsurfing ad that ridiculed inconsistencies in Kerry's rhetoric, the Democrats hit back: "One thousand U.S. casualties. Two Americans beheaded just this week. The Pentagon admits terrorists are pouring into Iraq. In the face of the Iraq quagmire, George Bush's answer is to run a juvenile and tasteless attack ad."[198] Another ad sought to counter a positive take on the Allawi visit: "Terrorists are pouring into the country. Attacks on U.S. forces are increasing every month. A thousand American soldiers have died. We need a fresh start to fix the mess in Iraq."[199] Real Voices, a Kerry support group, announced plans on September 24 to bring out an ad the next week that featured relatives of slain soldiers questioning Bush's handling of the Iraq war.[200] Three days later, the Kerry camp announced that a new spot would run in the same media markets targeted by the Bush-Cheney campaign. The new ad repeated themes of quagmire and inadequate planning: "George Bush said Iraq was 'mission accomplished.' Sixteen months later, he still doesn't get it. Today, over 1,000 soldiers dead, kidnappings, even beheadings of Americans. Still, Bush has no plan what to do in Iraq. How can you solve a problem when you can't see it?"[201]

Republican Attacks on Kerry

Since the 2003 vote against providing another $87 billion to fund the troops in Iraq and Afghanistan, Kerry had given his adversaries additional openings to cry "flip-flop." One such lapse occurred in July 2004, when he and his temperamental spouse showed up at the Grand Canyon for a photo opportunity. Hoping that the gaggle of accompanying reporters would ask him about the environment, Kerry instead had to contend with questions regarding a recent challenge from Bush. If the Democratic nominee had to do it all over again—knowing what he now knew—would he have voted in support of the Iraq War? "Yes," Kerry told reporters, "I would have voted for the authority. I believe it was the right authority for the president to have."[202] In mid-September, however, Kerry gave a very different answer. When asked by radio host Don Imus whether he knew of "any circumstances" that warranted going to war with Iraq, Kerry answered, "No, none that I see."[203] This disparity set him up for the windsurfing ad that ridiculed his inconsistency on the war.[204]

On the campaign trail, Bush seldom missed an opportunity to paint Kerry as a flip-flopper. On September 7, to cite one example, he suggested that Kerry had difficulty making up his mind. "After saying he would have voted for the war, even knowing everything we know today," Bush deadpanned to a Missouri crowd, "my opponent woke up this morning with new campaign advisors and yet another new position." Delighted supporters chanted "flip-flop, flip-flop."[205] Still in the Show-Me State the next morning, Bush took aim at Kerry's "wrong war" charge. "He woke up yesterday morning with yet another new position," Bush chortled to a crowd of 10,000. "And this one is not even his own. It is that of his one-time rival, Howard Dean. He even used the same words that Howard Dean did, back when he supposedly disagreed with him. No matter how many times Senator Kerry flip-flops, we were right to make America safer by removing Saddam Hussein from power."[206] Stumping with Bush Democrat Zell Miller in Ohio and West Virginia on September 10, the president contrasted Kerry's language on Iraq expenditures that should have gone to meet domestic needs with an earlier Kerry pronouncement that the U.S. should spend whatever was necessary to succeed in Iraq. "When it comes to Iraq," Bush exclaimed to a West Virginia crowd, "my opponent has more different positions than all of his colleagues in the Senate combined." On one point, the president continued, Kerry was quite clear: "If he had his way, Saddam Hussein would still be in power and would still be a threat to the security of America and the world."[207]

The president elaborated on the spending issue when addressing a receptive National Guard convention on September 14:

> Last week, my opponent questioned the cost of our operations in Iraq, and said that the money could have been better spent elsewhere. The problem is, just last summer he had a completely different view. Asked whether he believed we should reduce funding for operations in Iraq, my opponent at the time replied: "No. I

think we should increase it." Asked by how much, he said, "By whatever number of billions of dollars it takes to win. It is critical that the United States of America be successful in Iraq."

For the first time, the *Times* reported, this particular attack ignited a standing ovation, which, in turn, evoked a "tight smile" from Bush. "The President of the United States [must] speak clearly and consistently," Bush added, "and not change positions because of expediency or pressure."[208]

Following Kerry's address at New York University—where the Democratic candidate spoke of trading a dictator for chaos and unending war and also hinted at a plan to bring American troops home "within the next four years"—Bush hit back during a New Hampshire stop:

> Forty-three days before the election, my opponent has now settled on a proposal for what to do next, and it's exactly what we're currently doing.

Later, at a Manhattan fund-raiser (only blocks from a similar event featuring Kerry), Bush flayed Kerry's pattern of

> twisting in the wind with new contradictions on old positions on Iraq. Incredibly, he now believes our national security would be stronger with Saddam Hussein in power, not in prison. He's saying he prefers the stability of dictatorship to the hope and security of democracy. I couldn't disagree more, and, not so long ago, neither did my opponent.[209]

In Pennsylvania the next day, Bush proclaimed, "You can't lead the war on terror if you wilt or waver when times are tough." After ticking off the usual examples, he brought up Kerry's vote against the 2003 supplemental: "He said, 'I actually voted for the $87 billion before I voted against it.' Nobody talks like that in Latrobe."[210] In Colorado, he observed that Kerry had described his 2003 vote as "a complicated matter." Bush roused his audience with what had become a staple of his stump speech: "There is nothing complicated about supporting our troops in combat!"[211]

The Allawi visit on September 23 provided yet another platform for Republican attacks. Standing in the Rose Garden with the interim prime minister, Bush slapped at his rival without naming him:

> I think it is very important for the American president to mean what he says. That's why I understand that the enemy could misread what I say. I don't want them to be emboldened by any confusion or doubt. I don't want them to think that, well, maybe all they got to do is attack and we'll shirk our duty.[212]

Stumping the next day in Wisconsin, Bush took Kerry to task for sniping at Allawi:

> This great man came to our country to talk about how he's risking his life for a free Iraq . . . and Senator Kerry held a press conference and questioned Prime Minister Allawi's credibility. You can't lead this country if your ally in Iraq feels like you question his credibility. The message ought to be to the Iraqi people: "We support you." The message ought to be loud and clear: "We'll stand by you if you do the hard work."

In Wisconsin, Bush seized another opportunity to challenge Kerry assertions that the Iraq War had endangered rather than enhanced national security. "Earlier this week," he stated, "my opponent said he would prefer the dictatorship of Saddam Hussein to the situation in Iraq today. . . . I just strongly disagree. It's tough work, no question about it. . . . But, if Saddam Hussein were in power, our security would be threatened."[213]

Vice President Cheney routinely linked Iraq to the war on terror when attacking Kerry and the Democrats. Because Cheney generally gave the same speech at every event, the *Times* record of his campaign statements likely understates his contribution.[214] Still, he made the headlines on occasion, as on September 7, when he resorted to an extreme version of fear arousal: "It's absolutely essential that eight weeks from today, on November 2, we make the right choice. Because if we make the wrong choice, then the danger is that we'll get hit again, and we'll be hit in a way that will be devastating from the standpoint of the United States."[215] Cheney later backed away from this claim, which the *Times* judged to be "one of the toughest attacks launched in a presidential election in 40 years."[216]

Cheney proved more adept when rapidly responding to Kerry charges. When Kerry contended that Bush's coalition of the willing in Iraq was "phony," for example, Cheney quickly accused the Democrat of "demeaning our allies." Then, he gave a twist of the knife: "When it comes to diplomacy, it looks like John Kerry should stick to windsurfing."[217] Cheney also promptly responded to Kerry's National Guard speech: "Senator Kerry today said he would always be straight with the American people on the good days and on the bad days. In Senator Kerry's case, that means when the headlines are good, he's for the war; and, when his poll numbers are bad, he's against it."[218]

The vice president tirelessly portrayed Kerry as a flip-flopper. Stumping in Arkansas on September 14, he read aloud, "in a slow, scornful monologue," a criticism of Howard Dean that Kerry had uttered during the Democratic primary contest: "Those who doubted whether Iraq or the world would be better off without Saddam Hussein and those who believe today we are not safer with his capture don't have the judgment to be president or the credibility to be elected president." "In the spirit of bipartisanship," Cheney quipped, "this is one position of Senator Kerry's that I do agree with."[219] In Albuquerque, Cheney characterized Kerry's position on Iraq as "absolutely incoherent." "He has been unable to come to grips with one of the fundamental issues of the day, come up with a policy and stick to it," he stated. "In all my years in politics, I have never seen a candidate with so many different positions on one issue." Kerry, he added, "seems to change with the political pressures of the moment, or [referring to the latest shakeup in Kerry's staff] when he gets a new team of advisors."[220] Still, Cheney saw enough consistency in Kerry's rhetoric to condemn it as defeatist: "John Kerry is trying to tear down all the good that has been accomplished, and his words are destructive to our effort in Iraq and the global war on terror."[221]

Operatives in and outside of the White House pummeled Kerry as well. Campaign spokesman Steve Schmidt emerged as a leading surrogate, one prone to characterize the Democratic standard-bearer as "completely incoherent on Iraq." In the first week of the fall campaign, Schmidt came out swinging:

He said we are wasting money after previously saying we need to spend more. He said he will stand by our troops after voting against funding to support them. This week, he echoed Howard Dean, saying it was the wrong war at the wrong time, but he voted for the war and said he would vote for it again. John Kerry has given twelve major speeches on Iraq, and the American people still have no idea where he stands.[222]

Schmidt struck again after the Temple University speech, contending that Kerry had embraced

initiatives that the president is already implementing, even as he cynically attacks the president with defeatist rhetoric and talk of retreat. John Kerry will say anything he thinks benefits him politically, regardless of its effect on our troops in the field and our allies fighting alongside them.[223]

Just before the first debate, Bush's communications director, Nicole Devenish, also got in a lick or two:

This guy seems to have this belief that every time he speaks . . . he doesn't have to worry about contradictory things he's said in recent days, weeks, and months.[224]

One day before the first debate, Kerry still struggled to counter the flip-flop attacks (which would follow him for the rest of the race). According to the *Times*, his "I voted for the $87 billion before I voted against it" gaffe was "Exhibit A" in the Republican indictment. "It was just a very inarticulate way of saying something," he allowed on *Good Morning America*, "and I had one of those inarticulate moments late in the evening when I was dead tired in the primaries, and I didn't say something very clearly." Kerry added that he had voted no on final passage because he wanted the wealthiest to "share the burden of paying for the war." The defeat of the tax-cut rollback had rendered the final version unacceptable. "It was a protest," he contended. "Sometimes you have to stand up and be counted, and that's what I did." Grudgingly, he acknowledged that the flip-flop attacks had been effective: "See, what the Republicans do—and they love to do it, and they're very good at it, and they've spent millions of dollars doing it—is just find a little sentence here and find a little sentence there and take it out of context." A Republican response went out to reporters via e-mail, claiming that Kerry had offered his rationale in the afternoon rather than late at night, that he had done so at the first campaign event of his day rather than the last, and that he said these words on March 16—"two weeks" after the nomination had been secured. "Perhaps his watch was on Paris time," the message ended.[225]

CONCLUSION

Although the Republicans waged a less negative campaign than they had in 2000, the surge in the attack propensities of Democrats made for a much more negative race in 2004. Though not on the ballot, Clinton had polarized the electorate in 2000 and complicated Gore's candidacy. Bush proved to be an even more divisive presence in 2004, and the bitter exchanges charging deception and malfeasance, on the one hand, and flip-flopping as well as defeatism, on the other, underscored the intense polarization of the times. By the fall of 2004, the limits and shortcomings of the administration's war policy had become obvious, as had the failure to find the WMD that served as the principal justification for invading Iraq. More than a few congressional Democrats who had voted for the war in 2002 claimed that the administration had lied to them. Yet for all of his difficulties over Iraq, as well as questions about the administration's antiterrorism efforts before 9/11, Bush still held higher cards than Kerry on the war against terror. The duel over Vietnam service records had wounded Kerry's credibility as commander-in-chief more seriously than Bush's. In the second of the back-to-back dead heats between two evenly matched and ideologically cohesive parties, Bush emerged with modest but solid wins in both the popular vote and the Electoral College. Nonetheless, Iraq, Hurricane Katrina, Republican lobbying scandals, and a legion of other difficulties presaged the Republican loss of both houses of Congress in 2006. Both parties geared up for open nominating races in 2008 and a new battle for the White House.

8. Summary and Synthesis: Have Presidential Campaigns Become More Negative?

We began this book by posing the question of whether presidential campaigns in the United States have become progressively more negative since 1960. The simple answer to this complex question is that they have not.

We measured the negativity of entire contests by summing the attack statements of every participant in a contest and dividing that result by the grand total of campaign statements. A score close to 100 would indicate that almost every statement took the form of an attack, whereas a score close to 0 would reflect the virtual absence of attacks. The average negativity score across all twelve contests was 56.9 percent, and of the six above-average races, five took place before 1992. All three of the most recent races scored below average, although by only a whisker in 2004. (See Figure 8.1.)

It is widely held that negativity levels have been driven ever upward by an increase of polarization along party and ideological lines. Yet even though voting choices in 2000 reflected the highest degree of polarization up to that point in recorded American electoral history, the overall negativity of the 2000 contest ranked lower than that of any other race in our study except the one in 1976. Even the 2004 election, in which the link between party label and vote choice was phenomenal, ranked seventh out of twelve in overall negativity. The implication that we derive from Figure 8.1 is, first, that situational factors that range from electoral context to candidate predilections figure more importantly in negative campaigning than has generally been acknowledged and, second, that polarization is less important than originally thought.

Of course, the negativity score of an entire contest can mask a significant difference in the negativity of the competing sides. Moreover, to capture the complexity of campaign negativity, we must take account of the contributions made by minor parties in nearly half of the twelve races. Accordingly, the "all-opposing parties" measure in Table 8.1 indicates the propensity of one party to assail the other two. We also note "main opposition" negativity—that is, the propensity of one party to attack the more formidable or objectionable of the other two. In 1968, for instance,

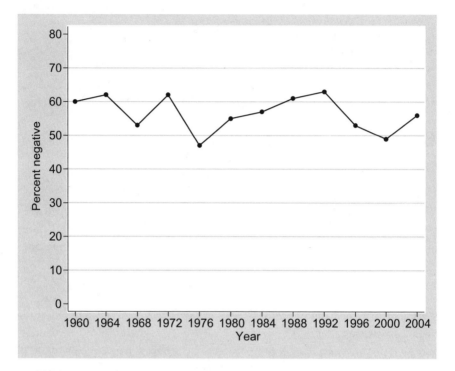

Figure 8.1 The negativity of presidential races, 1960–2004

the Democrats scored 57 on "all-opposition" negativity (against the AIP as well as the GOP), compared with 42 percent against just the Republicans. Naturally, the all- and main-opposition scores of a major party were essentially identical in two-way races. They were also essentially identical in three-way races whenever a major party refused to exchange attacks with a minor party. In any case, the Democrats and Republicans invariably went after each other more than after any third party, and even when playing the spoiler, a minor party always attacked both major parties.

The most negative campaign of all took place in 1960, a two-way race in which the Democrats went all out to regain the White House. (This finding will take on added importance when we compare our results to those from studies that focus entirely on campaign ads made for television.) Altogether, eight campaigns registered higher than 60 percent on all-opposition negativity, and five of these eight took place before 1992. Conversely, seven campaigns scored less than 50 percent, including those of the Democrats in 1996 and 2000 and the Republicans in 2004.

Examining the now familiar measures for the twenty-nine presidential candidates (see Table 8.2), we see further evidence that negativity has not risen steadily

Table 8.1. Two Measures of Party Negativity

Party	Campaign	Against All Opposing Parties	Against Main Party in Opposition
Democratic	1960	.713	.713
Reform	1996	.703	.418
Democratic	1972	.697	.697
Republican	1992	.688	.637
Democratic	1984	.664	.664
Republican	1964	.654	.654
Democratic	1988	.650	.650
Democratic	2004	.633	.625
Democratic	1992	.597	.564
Democratic	1964	.595	.595
Republican	1988	.578	.578
Green	2000	.573	.354
National Unity	1980	.572	.353
Democratic	1968	.570	.417
Democratic	1980	.564	.533
Republican	1996	.555	.550
Republican	1980	.547	.545
Republican	1968	.536	.440
Perot	1992	.527	.353
Democratic	1976	.512	.505
Republican	2000	.512	.511
Republican	1960	.511	.511
Republican	2004	.494	.494
Republican	1972	.489	.489
Democratic	2000	.470	.436
Democratic	1996	.460	.455
Republican	1984	.441	.441
Republican	1976	.440	.440
AIP	1968	.407	.215

Notes: The party campaigns are listed from highest to lowest according to their all-opposition negativity. The Democrats were the main opposition (most attacked) party for all third parties except Perot's 1992 one.

over time. Of the nine nominees who scored highest on both negativity scales, only Mondale, McGovern, and Kennedy exceeded 70 percent. Thus, for all his ferocity in 2004, Kerry was actually less negative than Mondale, McGovern, Kennedy, and Goldwater. At the other extreme, Clinton in 1996 and Gore in 2000 rated near the bottom of both negativity scales.

For vice-presidential candidates, the traditional "attack dogs" in presidential contests, more than half of the Democrats and Republicans scored above 60 percent on both measures; of the fourteen highest on main-opposition negativity, ten trod the campaign trail in the sixties, seventies, and eighties. Miller, Goldwater's running mate in 1964, topped this list (see Table 8.3).

Table 8.2. Negativity of the Presidential Candidates

Candidate (Party)	Campaign	Against All Opposing Parties	Against Main Party in Opposition
Mondale (D)	1984	.796	.796
McGovern (D)	1972	.781	.781
Perot (Reform)	1996	.757	.418
Kennedy (D)	1960	.755	.755
Goldwater (R)	1964	.685	.685
G. H. W. Bush (R)	1992	.674	.631
Perot (I)	1992	.666	.396
Kerry (D)	2004	.663	.663
Dukakis (D)	1988	.627	.627
Carter (D)	1980	.627	.609
Humphrey (D)	1968	.621	.475
Nixon (R)	1960	.604	.604
Nader (G)	2000	.602	.375
Dole (R)	1996	.593	.590
Anderson (NU)	1980	.575	.343
Nixon (R)	1968	.562	.502
G. H. W. Bush (R)	1988	.547	.547
Reagan (R)	1980	.544	.541
Carter (D)	1976	.536	.536
Clinton (D)	1992	.520	.505
G. W. Bush (R)	2000	.490	.490
Reagan (R)	1984	.481	.481
G. W. Bush (R)	2004	.463	.463
Johnson (D)	1964	.435	.435
Wallace (AIP)	1968	.418	.212
Ford (R)	1976	.393	.393
Gore (D)	2000	.313	.307
Clinton (D)	1996	.302	.295
Nixon (R)	1972	.287	.287

Note: The candidates are listed from highest to lowest on their all-opposition negativity. (Wallace attacked the Republicans more than the Democrats, albeit not by much.)

In sum, we uncovered no support for the idea that negativity in presidential races has steadily escalated since 1960. Three of the five most negative contests took place before 1976, five of the eight most negative campaigns waged by a party predated 1992, eight of the thirteen presidential candidates who scored higher than 60 percent on all-opposition negativity ran before 1992, six of the nine who topped the main-opposition list ran before 1992, and ten of the fourteen vice-presidential candidates who scored higher than 60 percent on both measures ran before 1992.

Table 8.3. The Negativity of the Vice-Presidential Candidates

Candidate (party)	Campaign	Against All Opposing Parties	Against Main Party in Opposition
Miller (R)	1964	.813	.813
Gore (D)	1992	.770	.744
Bentsen (D)	1988	.726	.726
Humphrey (D)	1964	.718	.718
Johnson (D)	1960	.710	.710
Cheney (R)	2004	.710	.710
Mondale (D)	1976	.687	.687
Dole (R)	1976	.675	.675
Shriver (D)	1972	.658	.658
Bush (R)	1980	.657	.657
Mondale (D)	1980	.651	.651
Edwards (D)	2004	.636	.636
Quayle (R)	1992	.632	.632
Quayle (R)	1988	.627	.627
Gore (D)	1996	.591	.591
Agnew (R)	1968	.588	.493
Cheney (R)	2000	.538	.538
Ferraro (D)	1984	.536	.536
Agnew (R)	1972	.528	.528
Muskie (D)	1968	.518	.323
Lieberman (D)	2000	.469	.457
Bush (R)	1984	.442	.442
Kemp (R)	1996	.258	.258
Lodge (R)	1960	.185	.185

Note: The vice-presidential nominees of the minor parties are omitted owing to their small number of reported attacks; the major-party candidates are listed from highest to lowest according to their all-opposition negativity.

HOW AND WHY OUR FINDINGS DIFFER FROM THOSE OF OTHER STUDIES

These findings run counter to those reported in studies based entirely on television ads. Why is this the case? Such differences stem from the use of different data sources, different samples, different decision rules, and, in some instances, different units of analysis. Recently, John Geer reported that the percentage of negative appeals in his sample of TV ads increased fourfold from 1960 to 1996, and he projected a fivefold increase in 2004.[1] Earlier studies by Benoit, West, Kaid and Johnston, and Jamieson and colleagues also pinpointed 1960 as the contest they considered the least negative. In our study, however, 1960 ranked fifth-highest in overall negativity, and the 1960 Democratic campaign scored highest of all;

Kennedy ranked among the most negative of all the presidential candidates, and his running mate was also more negative than most other vice-presidential candidates. We deem ad-based assessments of the 1960 race problematic because attack ads—indeed, all campaign ads—were in their infancy then. No one, however, would claim that negative campaigning was in its infancy in 1960, and our analysis, unlike those based on TV ads, captures the negativity of that race.

As noted in Chapter 1, we drew our information from a leading print source, an exemplar of what campaign practitioners call the "free media." By contrast, studies of television ads draw wholly from the "paid media," in which sponsors exercise complete control of content. This difference has too many ramifications for us to consider here, but one example underscores its importance. Candidates seldom, if ever, air ads that discuss their standing in the polls or other aspects of the horse race. The prodigious cost of advertising alone is enough to render such appeals infeasible. In fact, though, trailing candidates almost always question the polls ("The only poll that counts is the one on election day"), and more than a few evoke the memory of Harry Truman's 1948 comeback. Also, candidates and campaign spokespersons must field many questions about various aspects of the horse race. Although they are generally devoid of attacks on the opposition, such statements are integral components of campaign discourse and certainly are material to the computation of attack propensities, typically as components of the denominator. Studies based on TV ads leave them out of consideration.

Another major difference pertains to sample designs. Our analysis is based on every campaign statement published between Labor Day and election day in every news item of the *Times* about each of the twelve contests. As noted in Chapter 1, studies based on TV ads have varied in the samples they have drawn and the ad collections from which they have drawn them. For example, Geer restricted his sample in various ways.[2] Two of those restrictions contrast starkly with ours, and we deem these differences significant. First, by selecting only ads sponsored or authorized by a presidential campaign, Geer omitted such hard-hitting spots as the ones that showed a glowering Willie Horton in 1988 or the Swift Boat Vets attacks on Kerry in 2004. These attacks were undeniably important, and whenever the *Times* linked them to the fortunes of a presidential candidate, we counted them. Second, by counting each ad only once, no matter how often it was aired, Geer ignored an axiom of negative campaigning—exploit an opponent's weakness by hammering away at it again and again. In 1988, for instance, Dukakis and Bentsen repeatedly attacked Quayle as far too callow a choice to be a heartbeat away from the presidency. To undercount such a drumbeat risks significantly understating the attacker's negativity.

Aside from questions about the merits of ad-based versus print-based research, critics of our approach may argue that we have ignored important changes in the conventions of campaign journalism. Given the journalistic paradigm shift that is said to have begun during the 1960s and well before 2000, how can we view coverage of the 1960 and 2000 contests (both dead heats) as comparable?

A leading exponent of the paradigm shift thesis, Thomas Patterson, has criticized news media coverage of presidential campaigns.[3] In his account, journalists have moved decisively away from a descriptive mode of reporting in which candidates spoke for themselves to an interpretative and profoundly cynical framing of the news in which gamesmanship and strategy regularly trump policy substance.[4] One consequence of this shift is the presumption on the part of reporters that "candidates are in the game to win and will do almost anything to accomplish that goal." Another is to hype candidates with momentum while panning those who lag behind.[5]

Patterson never directly linked the paradigm shift that he perceived to coverage of negative campaigning. The closest he came was in the following passage: "For reporters, controversy is the real issue of campaign politics. The press deals with charges and countercharges, rarely digging into the details of the candidates' positions or the social conditions of underlying policy problems. It is not simply that the press neglects issues in favor of the strategic game; issues, even when covered, are subordinated to the drama of the conflict generated between the opposing sides."[6] Importantly, that passage rings no less true for campaign coverage in the 1960s and earlier, when reporters were less inclined to place their personal gloss on a candidate's words, than for coverage of later campaigns.

In short, we put 1960 in the same category with 1980, 2000, and 2004 because the polls showed that each contest was close, the lead changed hands one or more times between Labor Day and election day, and each race ended in a dead heat. Paradigm shifts notwithstanding, we know of no reason to assume that the *Times* was less prone to cover attacks exchanged between the Democrats and Republicans in 1960 than it was in 2004—and bear in mind that by our count, the Democratic campaign of 1960 was the *most* negative of all those considered here.

THE SKAPERDAS-GROFMAN MODEL

The Skaperdas-Grofman model treats decisions to go negative as both rational and contingent on candidate standings in the race. Such decisions rely on a cost-benefit analysis of the consequences of attacking a rival. The more settled the race, the easier the calculation is for leaders and trailers alike. The core prediction of the model is that in a two-party contest, the trailing candidate should always wage the more negative campaign. This prediction is most applicable in runaway and somewhat competitive contests, for the lead never changes in such races and is substantial all or most of the time. Comeback races present more of a challenge to the model as the gap narrows to the point of disappearance, and dead heats are, by definition, the hardest to read.

To summarize the differences between Democratic and Republican attack propensities, we can simply subtract the Republican propensity from the Democratic one; a positive sign indicates that the Democrats outattacked the Republicans, a negative sign indicates the opposite, and higher scores indicate a larger interparty gap.

For the runaway races, the sign of each propensity difference runs in the expected direction—negative for 1964, when the underdog Republicans outattacked the Democrats (albeit not by very much), and positive for 1972 and 1984, when the trailing Democrats waged by far the more negative campaign. However, when these differences are disaggregated on a week-by-week basis, the prohibitively favored side outattacked the hopelessly trailing side in nearly half of the weeks in these runaway campaigns. Even Lyndon Johnson, who had delegated so much attack responsibility to Humphrey and others, outattacked Goldwater in the final week.

As for the somewhat competitive races (1988, 1992, and 1996), the overall scores all upheld the model's core prediction. Some contrary findings did show up among the weekly scores; for example, in 1988, Bush beat up on Dukakis more than vice versa in nearly half of the weeks. Similarly, Democratic negativity slightly surpassed that of the GOP in week three of 1992, when Clinton led Bush by nine points. More anomalies cropped up in 1996, with the Democrats outattacking the Republicans in the second and third weeks. Clinton's negativity likewise topped Dole's in week three.

By definition, the trailer in a comeback race erases a gap once deemed insuperable. However, the timing and dynamics of such comebacks have differed notably. Signs of Humphrey's resurrection in 1968 did not appear until the end of September. Ford's comeback became evident much earlier in 1976. Despite the differences in timing, the model suggests that Humphrey and the Democrats should always have outattacked Nixon and the Republicans. After all, Nixon never lost his lead in the Gallup Poll, although Humphrey's late surge rendered that lead nominal. Similarly, the GOP and Ford should have outattacked the Democrats and Carter until very late in the contest. Instead, Nixon and the Republicans waged the more negative campaign overall, as well as in more than half of the nine weeks of electioneering. Indeed, the negativity of the Republicans in week one topped that of the Democrats by more than eighteen points. In a further contradiction of the model, this huge disparity occurred at the nadir of Humphrey's poll ratings. Somewhat more consistent with the model, the Republicans outattacked the Democrats near the end of the race, at which point the gap had nearly closed. At the very end, when Humphrey may have sensed a loss of momentum owing to developments in Vietnam, he and the revitalized Democrats outattacked Nixon and the Republicans.

The model fared more poorly still in the context of the 1976 contest. Contrary to the core prediction, the favored Democrats outattacked the underdog Republicans week after week. For example, during the campaign's second week, when Carter still enjoyed a big lead, his negativity topped Ford's by a whopping thirty-three points.

In dead heats, each side has little basis on which to calculate the costs and benefits of going negative. Moreover, the cost of a bad call, like the fallout from a blunder or some other "campaign event," can be very high in so close a race. Thus, from the model's perspective, each side should be motivated to play it safe, engaging in some attacking but hardly waging the fight one expects of the desperate trailer in a runaway contest. That, however, was precisely what the former commander of *PT 109* chose to do in 1960. Kennedy outattacked Nixon by fifteen points, and the Democratic score surpassed that of the Republicans by twenty points. Kennedy even eclipsed Nixon in the campaign's opening week by seventy points.

Another former naval person with experience in small-boat warfare waged a similarly ferocious campaign for president in 2004: Kerry outattacked Bush by twenty points and surpassed Bush's negativity in every week. At the same time, the Democratic Party waxed far more negative against the Republican Party than vice versa. Unlike 1960, however, Kerry's behavior resembled one suggestion of the Skaperdas-Grofman model: Kerry outattacked Bush by much bigger margins during the first half of the campaign, when he trailed in the polls, than during the second, after regaining the lead.

In 2000, Bush waged a more negative campaign than Gore in every week except the very first, and the Republicans outattacked the Democrats seven weeks out of nine. Republican negativity varied according to Bush's standing in the race. A surge in Republican negativity coincided with other efforts to overcome Gore's lead after the Democratic convention; subsequently, a net decline occurred around the time that Bush regained the lead; and yet another surge occurred in the closing weeks as Gore appeared to be moving up in the polls.

In 1980, the Republicans waged a slightly more negative race overall, even though Carter outattacked Reagan most of the time. As the model predicts, shifts in the direction of candidate and party net negativity coincided with changes in the lead.

The Skaperdas-Grofman model also suggests that the candidate in third place in a three-way race should be expected to concentrate on the front-runner rather than runner-up. However, because it is difficult to distinguish between the first- and second-place candidates in a close race, the model becomes problematic. Although minor-party candidates ran last in every three-way race that we studied, only in the somewhat competitive races of 1992 and 1996 did the hierarchy of candidate standings permit a clear test of the model's prediction. From Labor Day on in both races, Clinton always led, the Republican always ran second, and

Perot always ran third. Therefore, Perot should have concentrated his attacks on Clinton while sparing Bush and Dole. Instead, however, he concentrated his 1992 attacks on Bush rather than Clinton. The *Times*'s spotty coverage of Perot's 1996 campaign cautions against drawing any firm conclusion about which side felt his lash more.

In sum, in the contest most conducive to a test of the model-based proposition, Perot concentrated his attacks on the weaker, not the stronger, of the two opponents. Many accounts of the 1992 race have suggested that Perot wanted Clinton to win and that he ran in large part to prevent a Bush comeback, acting out of a deep loathing of Bush. The model makes no allowance for the Perot kind of spoiler.

What about major-party attacks against third-ranked candidates? According to the model, the Democrats and Republicans should have directed their attacks at each other, taking little or no notice of the minor party. Instead, the propensity of a major party to attack a minor party appears to have been a function of the perceived threat posed by the minor party. The Democratic and Republican offensives against the AIP in 1968 reflected Wallace's threat to both parties. Because of the problems that Anderson posed in Carter's must-win states in 1980, the Republicans gave him a pass. Not surprisingly, the Democrats attacked Anderson almost every week. Due to Perot's hostility to Bush in 1992, the Republicans attacked him more frequently than the Democrats did. In 2000, Nader, who threatened Gore in a handful of Gore's must-win states, drew fire only from Democrats. The Republicans had no interest whatever in tearing Nader down. Only in 1996 did both major parties act consistently with the model-based expectation that they would ignore minor-party challengers.

THE DIVISION OF LABOR AMONG ATTACK SOURCES

The Democrats Attacking the Republicans

Among the Democrats, presidential candidates were featured in the *Times* as the most prolific attackers. Most of their attacks were made solo, and these solo attacks amounted to 40 percent or more of the Democratic attacks in nine of the twelve campaigns. Carter assumed the heaviest burden by personally launching 57 percent of all Democratic attacks against the Republicans in 1976, and he essentially repeated this performance in 1980. At the opposite extreme, Johnson, Clinton, and Gore stand out for having delegated so much of the attack duties to others. Vice-presidential candidates generally contributed much less to attacks against Republicans, but of course, they usually received much less coverage in the *Times* than their running mates. Of all the Democrats, only Humphrey was reported to have delivered more solo attacks than his running mate.

Whereas operatives of varying responsibilities and prominence made their big-gest contributions in 1996 and 2000, surrogates' contributions to the Democratic total fell off notably after the 1964 campaign. The contributions of labor leaders, trial lawyers, and members of other groups that regularly bolstered Democratic campaigns loomed largest not only in the 1960s but also in 1980, 2000, and 2004. In no instance, though, did such groups make as much as 10 percent of all the re-ported Democratic attacks on the Republicans. The thinning of labor's ranks may have had a deleterious effect, but at the same time, changes in campaign finance laws have facilitated the rise of 527 groups. In 2004, a coalition of liberal and anti-war 527s is said to have functioned as a second party that not only aired attack ads against Bush but also mobilized the Democratic vote.[7]

The Republicans Attacking the Democrats

Of all the Republican presidential candidates, only Dole made enough solo at-tacks to account for more than half of his party's total. Nixon, the only three-time nominee of a major party for president since Franklin D. Roosevelt, took on greater responsibility as an attacker in his 1960 and 1968 campaigns than in 1972, when he did very little.

Among the Republicans nominated for vice president, Miller, Agnew, Dole, and Bush stood out as particularly active attackers, with each reported as deliv-ering more than a fifth of the total. Conversely, Kemp and Lodge showed up as remarkably conflict-averse candidates.[8]

As was also true of attacks by Democratic campaign operatives, we observed no relationship between the proportion of solo attacks by presidential candidates and attacks by Republican operatives. Republican surrogates made by far the larg-est percentage of their attacks in the 1960, 1968, and 1972 campaigns, after which they played a much reduced role. A plausible explanation centers on Nixon's ef-forts over the years to elect fellow Republicans and the resulting debt that the beneficiaries of his commitment owed him. As vice president, he had stumped for his party's candidates for Congress, as well as candidates for governor and other statewide offices. Following the devastation of the Republican ranks wreaked by Goldwater's defeat, Nixon set out to rebuild the party as well as position himself for another presidential nomination.[9] He went all out in 1966 to elect Republicans to Congress and was credited for much of the success that followed.[10] Evidently, the countless speeches, photo opportunities, and party dinners on behalf of Re-publican aspirants paid off.

Longtime organizations and associations, as well as ad hoc groups, have of-ten helped the Republicans take on the Democrats. The usual suspects include the National Rifle Association, business groups, and the Christian Right, most notably pro-life groups. Anti-Catholic groups and others mobilized by religious concerns figured importantly in Nixon's 1960 campaign. By calling for immediate and unconditional withdrawal from South Vietnam in 1972, McGovern attracted the opposition not only of pro-Nixon groups but also of the governing boards of unions that normally backed Democrats for president. In 1988, ad hoc organizations went beyond party attacks to familiarize millions with Willie Horton's mugshot. But no pro-Republican group made as big a splash as the Swift Boat Vets in 2004. Bankrolled by Bush supporters, this 527 group unleashed one of the most sustained, devastating, and publicized air wars in the history of modern presidential campaigns. All told, it accounted for roughly one in ten of all the Republican attacks reported in the *Times*.

Table 8.4 compares the efforts of Democratic attackers with their opposite numbers on the Republican side, again with a positive figure indicating a greater effort by Democrats. Goldwater, McGovern, Carter in 1976, Dole, Bush in 2000, and Kerry exhibited a much greater affinity for solo attacks than did their opponents. Among vice-presidential candidates, the difference was less pronounced, although Agnew notably outgunned his opposite numbers in 1968 and 1972, as did Bush when up against Ferraro in 1984. Republican operatives fired many more volleys on behalf of the Nixon-Agnew ticket in 1972 than their Democratic counterparts did, and Democratic aides outattacked Dole's operatives in 1996. The biggest difference in shares of attacks made by surrogates turned up in 1964, when a legion of Democratic officeholders added their voices to the assault on Goldwater.

THE TARGETING OF ATTACKS

Major Party Targeting of Major Parties

Almost invariably, the principal object of one party's attacks was the other party's presidential candidate. On average, the Democrats targeted the Republican nominee in 83 percent of their attacks on the other major party, and the Republicans followed suit 82 percent of the time. In Table 8.5, we provide an accounting of these targeting strategies. Goldwater figured as a target in virtually every 1964 Democratic attack, Reagan came in for very similar treatment in 1980, and all but three of the other Republican candidates came under fire in no less than 82 percent of the Democrats' attacks. Ripped in only 61 percent of Democratic attacks, Nixon got off relatively lightly in 1960. Similarly, the Republicans riddled Dukakis and Clinton in more than 90 percent of their attacks, and they blasted Carter and Gore in nearly 90 percent. Almost all of the other Democratic candidates came under fire in more than 80 percent of the attacks.

During the 1960s, the parties differed substantially in the degree to which they concentrated their attacks on the opposing presidential candidate. The

Table 8.4. Net Differences in Contributions of Major-Party Attackers, 1960–2004

Year	Presidential Candidate, Solo	Presidential Candidate, Total	Vice-Presidential Candidate, Solo	Campaign Operatives	Surrogates	Groups
1960	3.3	5.0	7.0	-3.4	-1.7	-4.6
1964	-19.0	-20.7	1.6	-0.3	11.2	7.9
1968	1.4	4.1	-10.3	2.2	-6.4	5.4
1972	35.7	36.3	-8.9	-13.8	-5.7	-1.8
1976	15.8	14.1	-6.7	0.5	-3.8	0.4
1980	2.5	-0.9	-2.0	-0.8	2.1	2.2
1984	9.2	8.7	-9.0	-3.9	2.4	1.7
1988	0.1	1.0	2.9	1.0	3.1	-1.8
1992	-2.0	-8.1	1.3	3.1	1.0	-1.0
1996	-29.9	-32.7	5.5	13.7	1.0	-1.6
2000	-19.0	-19.1	3.3	3.5	3.3	2.9
2004	12.1	11.0	-1.3	-5.3	-2.3	-5.3

Note: The net negativity differences reported in this table were calculated by subtracting the attack percentages of Republican sources from the attack percentages of counterpart Democratic sources; a minus sign in each instance indicates that the Republican source out-attacked the Democratic source.

Republicans criticized Kennedy much more than the Democrats homed in on Nixon, a difference consistent with the divergent strategies we discussed in Chapter 5. Nixon sought to frame the election as a choice for the more experienced candidate, whereas Kennedy wanted a clash of party traditions. Hoping to build on the split between Goldwater conservatives and the northeastern liberals in the GOP, the Democrats demonized Goldwater and wept crocodile tears for Rockefeller-Scranton Republicans. Goldwater wanted to focus the fight on ideology rather than the candidates; unfortunately for him, the fight featured both. Humphrey desperately needed the votes of Democrats who opposed the war and who had backed Robert Kennedy or Eugene McCarthy for the nomination. One way to win them back was to rekindle the animosity that so many liberal Democrats had long felt toward Nixon.

Major Party Targeting of Minor Parties

Nearly every attack by a major party against a minor one fell on the presidential standard-bearer. Only LeMay among the running mates of minor presidential candidates came under heavy fire.

Table 8.5. Targeting of Presidential Nominees by Major Parties, 1960–2004

Year	Targeted by Democrats			Targeted by Republicans			Difference
	Presidential Candidate Only	Presidential Candidate Plus Others	Presidential Candidate Total	Presidential Candidate Only	Presidential Candidate Plus Others	Presidential Candidate Total	
1960	41.0	20.1	61.1	62.6	18.7	81.3	-20.2
1964	67.4	31.3	98.7	23.1	32.8	55.9	42.8
1968	61.9	26.7	88.6	33.3	35.4	68.9	19.7
1972	37.0	37.7	74.4	70.5	13.7	84.2	-9.8
1976	47.3	37.2	84.5	69.1	20.3	89.3	-4.8
1980	85.3	10.0	95.3	70.2	19.4	89.6	5.7
1984	52.6	35.2	87.8	36.7	44.4	81.1	6.7
1988	39.0	43.6	82.6	77.4	14.1	91.5	-8.9
1992	68.1	21.6	89.7	75.0	16.1	91.1	-1.4
1996	38.5	24.2	62.7	67.8	15.1	82.9	-20.2
2000	81.8	8.0	89.8	72.9	16.8	89.7	0.1
2004	76.3	6.9	83.2	79.4	4.9	84.3	-1.1

Note: A negative difference in the righthand column indicates that the Republicans attacked the Democratic presidential candidate more than the Democrats attacked a Republican presidential nominee; a positive difference indicates a higher percentage of Democratic attacks.

Minor Party Targeting of Major Parties

At times, the targeting strategies employed in exchanges between major and minor parties amounted to asymmetrical warfare. Nearly every missile launched by a major party against a minor one zeroed in on the presidential standard-bearer. Indeed, the pattern exhibited so little variation that we saw no need to elaborate upon it in a table. Minor-party attacks, however, varied substantially in the degree to which they targeted Democratic and Republican standard-bearers. Only in 1980 did minor-party attackers aim virtually all of their attacks at the major-party nominees (see Table 8.6). This targeting strategy manifested Anderson's attempt to peel off Democrats as well as Republicans who were unhappy with their respective nominees. In other words, attack the nominee, not his party. In 1968, Wallace singled Nixon out for criticism much more frequently than Humphrey. This disparity likely reflected Wallace's concern to counter Nixon's southern strategy. In any case, Humphrey figured as a target in only 37 percent of Wallace-LeMay attacks, compared with the 59 percent directed at Nixon.

METHODS OF ATTACK

To attack the Republicans, the Democrats relied most of all on arousing fear. Nine of the party's twelve candidates for president and eight who sought the vice presidency resorted to this tactic more often than to any other. Labeling usually was the next-most-utilized method, and apposition and dishonesty vied for third place in the order of attack methods. With few exceptions, ridicule showed up as the Democrats' method of last resort. Evidently, personal style, experience, habit, and instinct had more to do with the candidates' choice of attack methods than their poll standings and other contextual factors. Humphrey, for example, relied most heavily on labeling, not only as Johnson's running mate in 1964, but also as the presidential nominee in 1968.

Fear arousal also stood out as the principal attack method of nine Republican presidential candidates. However, only three nominees for vice president on Republican tickets appealed most to voter fears. Among presidential candidates, the tactic of pejorative labeling ranked first in use for Goldwater and for the elder Bush in 1988; it showed up as the second-most-utilized method of attack in all three of Nixon's campaigns and in both of Reagan's races, as well as in the efforts of Dole and George W. Bush in 2000. The younger Bush stood out in 2004 as the only Republican presidential candidate who relied more on charges of dishonesty than any other attack method. Among Republicans running for vice president, Lodge, Quayle, and Cheney (in 2000 as well as 2004) played the dishonesty card more than any other. Ridicule almost always lagged behind all other methods employed by presidential and vice-presidential candidates alike.

Table 8.6. Third-Party Targeting of Major-Party Presidential Candidates

| Year | Attacks against Democrats | | | Attacks against Republicans | | |
	Presidential Candidate Alone	Presidential Candidate Plus Others	Total	Presidential Candidate Alone	Presidential Candidate Plus Others	Total
1968	16.3	20.4	36.7	34.1	25.0	59.1
1980	89.0	4.0	93.0	88.7	4.8	93.5
1992	69.0	2.4	71.4	46.5	15.3	61.8
1996	52.6	10.5	63.1	50.0	23.1	73.1
2000	61.8	8.8	70.6	76.2	4.8	81.0

Again, we suspect that candidates used the attack methods that best suited their particular blend of experience, style, and political instinct. In some cases, such as all three of the campaigns waged by Nixon, variations in electoral context appear not to have affected his principal reliance on fear arousal. The same was true in both of Reagan's campaigns, as well as of those waged both times by Agnew, Bush, and Cheney.

Republicans usually played on the fears of voters more than Democrats did, and this difference loomed largest in the 1988 and 1992 contests. The Republicans also outlabeled the Democrats in every contest except Carter versus Ford in 1976. Not surprisingly, the biggest difference occurred in 1988, when the Republicans rarely missed an opportunity to invoke the "L word" against Dukakis. Charges of dishonesty or gross inconsistency figured importantly in both Republican campaigns waged against Carter, in the exchanges between Clinton-Gore and Bush-Quayle in 1992, and in the thrust and parry between Gore-Lieberman and Bush-Cheney in 2000, as well as in the 2004 donnybrook. And in 2004, for instance, nearly half of all Republican attacks depicted Kerry as a serial flip-flopper, compared with 38 percent of Democratic attacks that accused Bush of lying about Iraqi WMD and other things.

In sum, the Republicans generally have made greater use of fear arousal and labeling than the Democrats, with no major differences showing up in the use of ridicule and apposition. Neither party has cornered the market on charging dishonesty. The rising chorus of fear arousal and dishonesty charges since 1984 likely has contributed to the perception that presidential campaigns have become more negative.

CAMPAIGN TOPICS AND THE ISSUE-AVOIDANCE THESIS

According to the selective-emphasis/issue-avoidance thesis, each party showcases the issues it "owns" while avoiding those staked out by the other party. In previous chapters, we reported numerous instances that contradicted the notion that an issue owned by one party was an issue avoided by the other. We consider the concept of issue ownership both brittle and misleading—brittle because it posits that possession by one party means avoidance by the other and misleading in the races that we studied because each major party repeatedly discussed issues that were more favorable to the other party. This is not to deny that topics or issues may well confer an advantage on one side. Clearly, the Republicans enjoyed an advantage on military and national security issues during the 1980s and again in 2004; likewise, the Democrats have recently benefited from making issues of Social Security and health care. But defense and social/health issues are perennials in presidential campaigns—topics too salient for either party to avoid. Carter simply had to discuss the economy in 1980, and the same was true of Bush in 1992. And in any case, the Democrats and Republicans more often addressed rather than ducked the same concerns. Moreover, as the economy issue illustrates, a topic presumably owned by one party can be turned to the other's advantage when circumstances warrant. Some topics (for instance, the domestic economy and national defense) normally are too salient for either side to avoid.

We hasten to emphasize that the high degree of interparty issue convergence that we observed should not be confused with the Downsian game of gravitating toward the other party's issue positions when those positions are favored by most of the electorate.[11] Rather, in the process of addressing the same problems, the two sides may or may not agree on solutions.

One powerful impetus to such convergence is both parties' acceptance of the idea that their presidential nominees must debate issues on national television. Initiated by Kennedy and Nixon in 1960, presidential debates did not become an integral part of the process until resurrected by Carter and Ford in 1976. Every pair of presidential candidates since has participated in at least one televised debate, and so has every pair of vice-presidential candidates except one (in 1980). Despite their obvious limitations, the debates are engines of issue convergence.

This is not to suggest that debates are necessary for substantial convergence to occur. Consider presidential contests in which no debates took place. Despite Johnson's disinclination to debate Goldwater in 1964, both parties highlighted military and defense matters more than any other topic, and they likewise put identical stress on ideology/party tradition, race, and foreign policy. When all was said and done, the Democrats had allocated nearly all of their campaign statements to the same eight topics most emphasized by the Republicans. In 1968, despite Nixon's refusal to debate Humphrey, a similar pattern of convergence played out. Both sides attached precisely the same importance to military and defense issues (foremost on both agendas), leadership (second on both), the domestic economy (seventh), and social and health policies (eighth). Although less convergence took place in 1972, both parties addressed seven of the same topics in that race.

To provide a different perspective on the relationship between the regularity of topical importance and the degree of convergence, we distinguished among "perennial" topics (which placed in the top ten of one or both parties in at least ten races), "occasional" topics (which surfaced no fewer than four times), and "rare" topics (which turned up on a party agenda three times or less).

The list of perennial topics consisted of leadership, campaign matters, the domestic economy, military/defense, social/health programs, ideology and party tradition, and foreign policy. Leadership always showed up as a top-ten topic for both parties, as did discussion of diverse aspects of campaigning, such as poll standings and strategy. Only in 1964 did one party opt not to put major emphasis on the domestic economy. Further, the economy ranked exactly the same for both parties in six of the twelve races. Similarly, only in 1996 did a major party fail to emphasize military/defense matters as one of its foremost concerns. Indeed, war and defense ranked number one on both party agendas in 1960, 1964, 1968, and 2004; it ranked fourth among the top ten of both parties in 1976. Because the Democrats are generally thought to "own" issues pertaining to social programs and health care, we were not surprised to find that this topic always rated high on their agenda. But we also discovered that such issues ranked among the Republicans' top-ten concerns in nine of the twelve races. Moreover, Republican tickets put no less emphasis on the social/health topic than the Democrats did in 1968, 1972, and 2000. Both sides converged on ideology and party traditions in nine instances and gave the topic equal or nearly equal emphasis in four. The Democrats and Republicans alike regarded foreign policy as a topic worthy of major emphasis in half of the presidential contests. All told, convergence dominated campaign discourse on perennial topics. Out of a possible 80 pairings, convergence occurred 87 percent of the time, and the Democrats and Republicans attached identical importance to the same topic in 22 pairings.

Occasional topics (those showing up as a top-ten item on a major-party agenda in at least one-third of the presidential races) consisted of race, debates, patriotism/war record, crime, corruption/abuse of power, energy/environment, women's issues and rights (including abortion), and education. High levels of two-party convergence occurred on discussion of racial issues, which figured importantly in the 1960, 1964, 1968, 1976, and 1980 contests. Only in 1972 did one party appear to duck race when the other party chose to make it a top-ten concern. Similarly, when one party chose to highlight crime, the other did so as well; the same held for discussion of presidential debates and for major concerns on gender. Less convergence took place when one emphasized issues pertaining to patriotism or the military service records of presidential or vice-presidential candidates, and the same can be said of the emphasis placed on education and on corruption. All told, the parties converged in 27 out of 50 possible pairings (54 percent) on topics of occasional salience.

Convergence sometimes happened when one party embraced a topic that, in retrospect, rarely achieved top-ten status. Religion showed up as highly salient in 1960 and again in 1984, and both parties on both occasions emphasized it. Similarly, both parties emphasized Iran's taking of American hostages in 1976, and both parties addressed issues pertaining to the administration of elections in 2004, such as the potential for fraudulent voting or suppression of the vote. Farm policy showed up as a major topic of emphasis on at least one party's agenda in 1960, 1964, and 1976, but only in 1960 did both parties emphasize it. No convergence whatever occurred on the labor topic (last among the Democrats' top ten in 1968 and 1972 and likewise tenth on the 1984 Republican agenda), campaign finance in two races, Republican characterizations of Johnson's moral character in 1964, or Republican emphasis of gay marriage in 2004. Overall, convergence occurred in only 5 of 14 possible pairings of rare salience.

LEADING TOPICS OF MINOR PARTIES

The same tug felt by the Democrats and Republicans evidently operated as well on the independents and minor-party candidates. Wallace and the AIP showcased six of the same topics highlighted by the Democrats, while emphasizing eight on the Republican agenda. Even greater convergence occurred in 1980, when Anderson stressed nine of the ten themes that made the top-ten list of both parties. Perot in 1992 stressed seven that were important to the Democrats, five of which also ranked high on the Republican list. In 1996, Perot again converged on five of the same topics that the major parties highlighted. Nader played up six such concerns in 2000. On the debit side, Wallace said little or nothing about the economy or social and health programs. Nor did he join Humphrey in making a big issue of Nixon's refusal to debate. No other minor or independent candidate notably emphasized social and health programs except Nader, who said next to nothing on national defense.

CONCLUSION

Amid all the general and specific findings reported here, three broad conclusions stand out, each of which poses a stark contrast to prominent and widely accepted understandings of campaign strategy. First, the negativity of presidential contests has not increased progressively over time. Second, parties and candidates in varying strategic environments did not, for the most part, implement attack strategies that would have been anticipated for them based on a prominent "rational" model of campaigning. And third, the parties did not avoid discussing issues "owned" by the other side. A much-compressed summary of the key points of evidence that led us to these conclusions appears in Table 8.7.

As for the first conclusion, the negativity of the last twelve presidential races has varied in ways that repeatedly contradicted the steady-increase thesis. By whatever measure, the Democrats waged their most negative campaigns in 1960, 1972, and 1984, and two of their least negative efforts took place in 1996 and 2000. Similarly, the fiercest Republican campaigns played out in 1964, 1988, and 1992, and two of their least combative races occurred in 1972 and 1984.

Although the Skaperdas-Grofman model proved to be a useful organizing framework for analyzing campaign negativity, it served primarily as a foil for one contrary finding after another. In 1964, for example, the prohibitively favored Democrats defied the model's foremost assumption by waging a ferocious campaign against a hapless foe. Further contradictions showed up in the weekly attack scores of various campaigns. Then, too, the model's predictions were directly contravened by the attack dynamics of both comeback races. Nor did the model shed much light on the behavior of dead heat contestants. As for the attack strategies of minor or independent candidates, their standing in the race had no discernible bearing on Anderson's treatment of Carter, Perot's vendetta against the elder Bush, or Nader's assault on Gore.

Although the elegant abstractions of a model such as Skaperdas and Grofman's serve a useful heuristic function, this particular model abstracts away too much and thereby ignores a multitude of factors that figure importantly in candidates' decisions to go negative. Candidates act strategically in ways not recognized by the model, and their game plans usually incorporate personal style, habits gained over the course of a political career, dislike or admiration of a rival, and commitment to issues or causes.

Beyond that, the model makes no allowance for crises that spring from political blunders or personal failings on the part of a candidate or some other prominent member of the team. Such episodes often knock campaigns off course. Similarly, campaign strategies are often products of compromise between warring advisers who ostensibly work for the same candidate, or they may represent the triumph of one such faction over another; key operatives may leave a candidate's entourage and be replaced by others with very different ideas; and the short-term need to appease different subsets of the campaign team or to hold the candidate's coalition together may become a more decisive consideration than any longer-term, "rational" strategy aimed at defeating the opposing party.

Finally, issue convergence—the tendency of the competitors in a presidential campaign to discuss the same issues rather than staking out their own issue turf and avoiding that of the opposition—has been the rule rather than the exception. Whatever their failings, the contenders in modern presidential campaigns deserve credit for engaging with one another on the issues.

Table 8.7. Overview of Key Results

Year	Type of Race	Attack Propensity Rank of Campaign			Leading Topic		% Major Party Issue Convergence
		Democratic Party	Republican Party	Minor Parties	Democratic	Republican	
1960	Dead heat	1	9		Defense	Defense	90
1964	Runaway	7	2		Defense	Defense	80
1968	Comeback	8	6	5	Defense	Defense	80
1972	Runaway	2	11		Campaign	Defense	70
1976	Comeback	10	7.5		Economy	Economy	80
1980	Dead heat	9	5	3	Defense	Economy	100
1984	Runaway	3	12		Defense	Economy	90
1988	Somewhat competitive	4	3		Leadership	Defense	80
1992	Somewhat competitive	6	1	4	Economy	Economy	90
1996	Somewhat competitive	12	4	1	Economy	Economy	80
2000	Dead heat	11	7.5	2	Social Security/ health	Social Security/ health	90
2004	Dead heat	5	10		Defense	Defense	90

Notes: The attack propensity ranks are within each party; thus, each Democratic campaign is ranked only in comparison with the other Democratic campaigns, and the same holds for the Republicans. The convergence figures reflect the degree to which both parties addressed the same top-ten topics in a given campaign.

APPENDIX: COLD WAR BACKGROUND TO 1960 PRESIDENTIAL CONTEST

Date	Event
January 1954	Secretary of State John Foster Dulles announces a new policy of deterring aggression against the free world — the doctrine of massive retaliation "by means and at places of our choosing."
January 1955	Eisenhower requests and receives congressional authorization to defend Formosa (Taiwan) and "closely related localities." Kennedy and other senators fail in an attempt to exclude Quemoy and Matsu islands from the resolution. The administration had argued that the commitment must remain ambiguous to deter Communist seizure of potential staging areas for invasion of Formosa.
January 1956	In a *Life* magazine interview, Dulles claims that the massive-retaliation doctrine prevented the outbreak of wider wars in Asia. His claim ignites a partisan debate over the risks and efficacy of massive retaliation.
October 1957	The USSR launches Sputnik, the first satellite to orbit the globe, creating great concern in the United States about Soviet missile capabilities.
May 1958	A mob attacks Vice President Nixon's limousine in Caracas; Marines prepare to rescue the vice-presidential party if necessary; Nixon returns home to a hero's welcome.
July 1958	After a Baathist coup in Iraq, Eisenhower orders Marines ashore in Beirut to prevent the overthrow of Lebanon's pro-Western government; Soviet premier Nikita Khrushchev reacts angrily and calls for a great-power summit on the Middle East; Eisenhower says the United Nations is the proper forum for such discussions; U.S. negotiators eventually negotiate a peaceful resolution of the crisis and American troops depart.
August 1958	Eisenhower offers to suspend nuclear tests in the atmosphere for one year, starting October 31, if the Soviets follow suit; the Soviet tests end in November, though without a formal agreement; the People's Republic of China (PRC) begins bombarding the nearby islands of Quemoy and Matsu occupied by Nationalist troops; Eisenhower augments the Seventh Fleet, ponders the

use of nuclear weapons in the event of a Communist assault on Quemoy or Matsu; the British make clear their unwillingness to go to war over these tiny islands; the crisis lingers into October, by which time Eisenhower's policy has evoked a preponderantly negative reaction from leaders of both parties, albeit for different reasons.

November 1958   Khrushchev threatens to turn Berlin over to East Germany unless the British, French, and Americans withdraw their troops from West Berlin; the White House rejects the demand and vows that military force will be used if necessary to maintain its presence.

January 1959   Fidel Castro overthrows Cuban strongman Fulgencio Batista.

July 1959   Eisenhower invites Khrushchev to visit the United States, then goes abroad to consult with European allies; Nixon and Khrushchev tangle in the famous "kitchen debate" at an American trade fair in Moscow; Nixon receives a warm welcome in Poland.

September 1959   Khrushchev tours United States, meets with Eisenhower at Camp David, invites Eisenhower to visit the USSR, and backs off setting a deadline for a Berlin settlement. Eisenhower pledges to attend a Paris summit with the other occupying powers in the spring of 1960.

February 1960   Following discussions of a ban on atmospheric testing of nuclear weapons, the Soviets indicate a willingness to negotiate a treaty provided that the Americans and British cease underground testing for the next four to five years.

March 1960   Eisenhower and British prime minister Harold Macmillan accept the Soviet offer; Eisenhower calls for a test ban treaty before the May summit in Paris; Eisenhower also orders the CIA to begin training Cuban exiles for a possible invasion of the island.

May 1960   The Soviets shoot down a U-2 spy plane over Russia and capture the pilot, Gary Powers; assuming that Powers did not survive, the CIA and State Department deny Khrushchev's claim that the plane was on a spy mission; Khrushchev reveals that Powers is alive and that he admitted spying; the Russians put photos of Soviet installations taken by Powers and parts of the plane on exhibit; Khrushchev says that Eisenhower must not have known about what the militarists in his government had done; Secretary of State Christian Herter defends the U-2 mission as necessary to protect against a Soviet sneak attack; Eisenhower assumes full responsibility for the flight; Khrushchev boycotts the first session of the summit and demands that Eisenhower apologize for violating Soviet airspace, and that he cancel all future missions; Eisenhower reveals that he had already suspended U-2 flights, but refuses to apologize; sensing allied unity on Berlin, Khrushchev declares the summit a failure, denounces Eisenhower, and vows to revisit the Berlin problem with the next American president in six to eight months; Eisenhower addresses the nation on television, defending the U-2 flights on national security grounds, blaming Khrushchev for scuttling the summit, and citing the support of U.S. allies.

June 1960   Khrushchev blames the summit failure on a "spineless" Eisenhower, hints of another Berlin crisis unless the United States agrees to a new summit in six to eight months; Khrushchev also intimates that he wants a Democrat to win the 1960 election.

July 1960   Following Castro's seizure of American-owned oil refineries, Eisenhower obtains congressional authority to end importation of sugar from Cuba; Castro's government seizes more American-owned properties; in Moscow, Khrushchev promises economic aid to Cuba and warns that Soviet rockets will defend Cuba against any U.S. intervention; Eisenhower declares that the United States will not permit a Communist regime in the Western Hemisphere; two days later, the Kremlin announces the downing of a U.S. reconnaissance plane over the Barents Sea; Eisenhower denounces this "wanton act of aggression" over international waters; at the United Nations, ambassador Lodge defends the U.S. position; Belgian troops intervene in the Congo, formerly a Belgian colony, to protect European nationals against rampaging Congolese troops; Congo premier Patrice Lumumba demands an immediate withdrawal of the Belgians and appeals to Khrushchev for military assistance if they do not; Lodge declares that the United States will do "whatever may be necessary" to stop any military intervention not authorized by the United Nations; Khrushchev tells journalists in Moscow that the Monroe Doctrine is dead; Lodge responds, saying "Don't touch us; don't touch those with whom we are tied; don't seek to extend Communist imperialism"; Japanese prime minister Nobusuke Kishi cancels an Eisenhower visit, claiming that he cannot guarantee the President's safety.

August 1960   UN troops replace Belgian forces in the Congo, thus bringing a brief calm even as Lumumba courts Soviet aid and rival Moise

Tsombe moves his Katanga province toward secession; Castro's brother Raoul returns from a Moscow trip and reiterates Soviet willingness to defend Cuba against the United States with "rockets"; Castro seizes all remaining properties owned by Americans in Cuba; the United States calls on the Organization of American States to condemn Cuba for allowing Soviet penetration of the hemisphere but settles for a "bland resolution open to many possible interpretations"; Castro establishes formal diplomatic ties with Communist China.

September 1960   Khrushchev and Castro attend meetings of the UN General Assembly; the Soviet leader stays for two weeks before departing October 3.

Sources: Robert A. Divine, *Foreign Policy and US Presidential Elections 1952–1960* (New York: New Viewpoints, 1974); Chester J. Pach Jr. and Elmo Richardson, *The Presidency of Dwight D. Eisenhower*, rev. ed. (Lawrence: University Press of Kansas, 1991), 187–210; *Congress and the Nation 1945–1964: A Review of Government and Politics in the Postwar Years* (Washington, D.C.: Congressional Quarterly Press, 1965), 285.

NOTES

PREFACE AND ACKNOWLEDGMENTS

1. Buell notes of the October 29, 2004, rally.

2. All direct quotes are from the text released by the White House and posted on its Web site at http://www.whitehouse.gov/news/releases/2004/10/20041029-24.html.

3. For a collection of such materials, see Joel H. Silbey, ed., *The American Party Battle: Election Campaign Pamphlets, 1828–1876* (Cambridge, MA: Harvard University Press, 1999).

CHAPTER I. NEGATIVITY AND PRESIDENTIAL CAMPAIGNS

1. This literature is vast, as reviewed by Richard R. Lau and Lee Sigelman, "The Effectiveness of Negative Political Advertising: A Literature Review," in James Thurber, Candice Nelson, and David Dulio, eds., *Crowded Airwaves: Campaign Advertising in Modern Elections* (Washington, DC: Brookings, 2000), 10–43. See also William G. Mayer, "In Defense of Negative Campaigning," *Political Science Quarterly* 111 (November 1996): 437–455; Stephen Ansolabehere, Shanto Iyengar, Adam Simon, and Nicholas Valentino, "Does Attack Advertising Demobilize the Electorate?" *American Political Science Review* 88 (December 1994): 829–838; Michael Pfau and Henry C. Kenski, *Attack Politics: Strategy and Defense* (New York: Praeger, 1990).

2. Martin P. Wattenberg and Craig Leonard Brians, "Negative Campaign Advertising: Demobilizer or Mobilizer?" *American Political Science Review* 93 (December 1999): 891–899. For early studies of attack politics on the Internet, see Robert H. Wicks and Boubacar Souley, "Going Negative: Candidate Usage of Internet Web Sites during the 2000 Presidential Campaign," *Journalism and Mass Communication Quarterly* 80 (Spring 2003): 128–143; also Souley and Wicks, "Tracking the 2004 Presidential Campaign Web Sites," *American Behavioral Scientist* 49 (December 2005): 535–547.

3. Tom Curry, "'527' Groups Rewrite Campaign Rules," August 18, 2004, available at http://www.msnbc.com. For an early argument against exaggerating the impact of admittedly important 527 groups, see Steve Weisman and Rush Hassan, "BCRA and the 527 Groups," draft chapter released by the Campaign Finance Institute on February 9, 2005, and published in Michael J. Malbin, ed., *The Election after Reform: Money, Politics and the Bipartisan Campaign Finance Reform Act* (Lanham, MD: Rowman & Littlefield, 2006).

4. *Fahrenheit 9/11* was hardly Hollywood's first effort to sink a candidacy. In 1934, motion picture moguls made a major effort to defeat Upton Sinclair—the well-known radical and Democratic nominee for governor of California. Like *Fahrenheit*, this film, *California Election News*, injected a major dose of conspiracy theory into the attack on Sinclair and his End Poverty in California (EPIC) movement. See Greg Mitchell, *The Campaign of the Century: Upton Sinclair's Race for Governor of California and the Birth of Media Politics* (New York: Random House, 1992).

5. Probably the most outlandish hatchet job prior to 2004 was Haley J. Evetts, *A Texan Looks at Lyndon: A Study in Illegitimate Power* (Canyon, TX: Palo Duro Press, 1964). Among other things, the book implicated Johnson in a murder. Goldwater supporters saw to its wide distribution. A search of the Barnes and Noble Web site revealed that books denigrating George W. Bush greatly outnumbered those hostile to John Kerry. The most notable anti-Kerry tracts were John E. O'Neill and Jerome R. Corsi, *Unfit for Command* (Washington, DC: Regnery, 2004), and David N. Bossie, *The Many Faces of John Kerry* (Nashville, TN: WND Books, 2004). As of late October 2004, Barnes and Noble listed more than fifty anti-Bush books published in time for the Bush-Kerry set-to. The following titles suffice to illustrate the tone of these offerings: Jack Huberman, *The Bush-Hater's Handbook: A Guide to the Most Appalling President of the Past 100 Years* (New York: Nation Books, 2003); David Corn, *The Lies of George W. Bush* (New York: Crown, 2003); Bill Press, *Bush Must Go: The Top Ten Reasons Why George W. Bush Doesn't Deserve a Second Term* (New York: Dutton, 2004); John W. Dean, *Worse Than Watergate: The Secret Presidency of George W. Bush* (Boston: Little, Brown, 2004); Robert C. Byrd, *Losing America: Confronting a Reckless and Arrogant Presidency* (New York: W. W. Norton, 2004); James Bovard, *The Bush Betrayal* (New York: Palgrave, 2004); Maureen Dowd, *Bushworld: Enter at Your Own Risk* (New York: G. P. Putnam's Sons, 2004); Eric Alterman and Mark J. Green, *The Book on Bush: How George W. (Mis) leads America* (New York: Viking Press, 2004); John O'Farrell, *Global Village Idiot: Dubya, Dumb Jokes and One Last Word before You Vote* (New York: Grove/Atlantic, 2004); Willis Clint, ed., *The I Hate George W. Bush Reader: Why Dubya Is Wrong about Absolutely Everything* (New York: Nation Books, 2004); Molly Ivins and Lou Dubose, *Bushwhacked: Life in George W. Bush's America* (New York: Random House, 2004); Jim Hightower, *Let's Stop Beating around the Bush* (New York: Viking, 2004). Equally vitriolic though less suggestively titled are Michael Moore, *Dude, Where's My Country?* (New York: Warner Books, 2003); George Soros, *The Bubble of American Supremacy: Correcting the Misuse of American Power* (New York: Public Affairs, 2004); and Kitty Kelley, *The Family: The Real Story of the Bush Dynasty* (New York: Doubleday, 2004).

6. Stephen Ansolabehere and Shanto Iyengar, *Going Negative: How Political Advertisements Shrink and Polarize the Electorate* (New York: Free Press, 1995), 115–116. For a straightforward if self-serving justification of very early attacks by the 1996 Clinton campaign, see Dick Morris, *Behind the Oval Office: Getting Reelected against All Odds* (Los Angeles: Renaissance Books, 1999), 148–149.

7. Darrell M. West, *Air Wars: Television Advertising in Election Campaigns, 1952–1992* (Washington, DC: Congressional Quarterly Press, 1993), 13.

8. West, *Air Wars: Television Advertising in Election Campaigns, 1952–1996*, 3rd ed. (Washington, DC: Congressional Quarterly Press, 2001), 45.

9. The Pew Research Center for the People and the Press, "Voters Liked Campaign 2004, but Too Much 'Mudslinging,'" released November 11, 2004, available at http://www.people-press.org.

10. Stuart H. Surlin and Thomas F. Gordon, "How Values Affect Attitudes toward Direct Reference Political Advertising," *Journalism Quarterly* 54 (1997): 84–98, at 93. Stergios Skaperdas and Bernard Grofman adopted this definition in "Modeling Negative Campaigning," *American Political Science Review* 89 (March 1995): 49–61. Ansolabehere and Iyengar used the terms *negative advertising* and *attack advertising* synonymously in *Going Negative*.

11. Mayer, "In Defense of Negative Campaigning," 440–441.

12. Ibid.

13. Richard R. Lau and Gerald M. Pomper, *Negative Campaigning: An Analysis of U.S. Senate Elections* (Lanham, MD: Rowman & Littlefield, 2004), 4. Their definition of *positive campaigning* closely resembles Benoit's *acclaiming*. See William L. Benoit, *Seeing Spots: A Functional Analysis of Presidential Television Advertisements, 1952–1996* (Westport, CT: Praeger, 1998).

14. Lau and Pomper, *Negative Campaigning*, 25.

15. Kathleen Hall Jamieson, Paul Waldman, and Susan Sherr, "Eliminate the Negative? Categories of Analysis for Political Advertisements," in James A. Thurber, Candice J. Nelson, and David A. Dulio, eds., *Crowded Airwaves: Campaign Advertising in Elections* (Washington, DC: Brookings, 2000), 44–64.

16. William Safire, *Safire's Political Dictionary: An Enlarged, Up-to-Date Edition of The New Language of Politics* (New York: Random House, 1978), 435–436.

17. Quoted in Howell Raines, "Reagan's Camp Sees Carter as His Own Worst Enemy," *NYT*, October 12, 1980, A32.

18. Kathleen Hall Jamieson, *Dirty Politics: Deception, Distraction, and Democracy* (New York: Oxford University Press, 1992), 45.

19. John G. Geer, "The Rise of Negativity in Presidential Campaigns: Causes and Consequences," paper delivered at the annual meeting of the American Political Science Association, Chicago, September 2–5, 2004, 7.

20. Richard Armstrong, a direct-marketing executive, has maintained that "today's attack ads must be scrupulously researched and fairly presented. A scurrilous attack on television runs the risk of sparking backlash from the opponent, the press, and the public itself that is potentially devastating to the candidate who airs it. So television actually has been a kind of built-in self-correction mechanism that prevents politics from getting too dirty or too dishonest." See his *The Next Hurrah: The Communications Revolution in American Politics* (New York: William Morrow, 1988), 25–26. See also Jamieson, *Dirty Politics*, 103, for a discussion of the relationship between the intensity of attacks and their factual content.

21. For an example of just how complex and yet incomplete the effort to separate fact from fiction in campaign attacks can be, see Jamieson's lengthy discussion of the Willie Horton ads in *Dirty Politics*, 3–42. Although painstaking in pointing up distortions in both Republican and media accounts of Horton's murder conviction and subsequent crimes after violating his furlough, Jamieson glossed over Horton's criminal acts *before* his murder conviction, such as assault with intent to kill, other assaults, and breaking and entering. See David C. Anderson, *Crime and the Politics of Hysteria: How the Willie Horton Story Changed American Justice* (New York: Times Books, 1995), 58–62. For a valiant effort to expose factual errors on both sides in the 2004 presidential campaign, see the Web site of the Fact Check Project at the University of Pennsylvania, http://www.FactCheck.org. In an October 31, 2004, posting, the fact checkers prefaced their summary of distortions with the following acknowledgment: "We haven't addressed every false or misleading statement in the campaign—there were too many of them and our resources are too limited for that." We make limited use of FactCheck in Chapter 6 when discussing Swift Boat Vets attacks against John Kerry.

22. Lau and Pomper, *Negative Campaigning*; see also Mayer, "In Defense of Negative Campaigning"; Jamieson, *Dirty Politics*, 102–103.

23. Here, we take issue with Benoit, who in several works distinguished between "attacks" that portray the opposing candidate in an unfavorable light and "defenses" that "respond to" or "refute" an attack on the candidate. In our view, the defense can be as negative as the attack, as Benoit's own examples of defense statements reveal. Consider the way Al Gore ended his response to Bill Bradley's accusation in 2000 that he had supported tax-exempt status for Bob Jones University: "So that is a phony and scurrilous charge." See William L. Benoit, P. M. Pier, LeAnn M. Brazeal, and John P. McHale, *The Primary Decision: A Functional Analysis of Debates in Presidential Primaries* (Westport, CT: Praeger, 2002), 116.

24. Turner Catledge, "The ABC's of Political Campaigning," *New York Times Magazine*, September 22, 1940, 9.

25. Evan Thomas asserted that all major campaigns now have rapid-response units: "The 24/7 media and the technology of the Internet demand it. . . . Technology has quickened the pace and provided new weapons for hitting back. Digital video-recording devices can 'capture' an image of a candidate making a speech and immediately pass it around via email and the Internet. Admen can cut a response ad overnight if not sooner." See his book *Election 2004: How Bush Won and What You Can Expect for the Future* (New York: Public Affairs, 2004), 59.

26. For a close comparison of these studies, see Jamieson, Waldman, and Sherr, "Eliminate the Negative?" 44–64; this is also the source for the CDMP findings. Jamieson and her associates contrasted their CDMP findings with those reported by West in his second edition of *Air Wars: Television Advertising in Election Campaigns, 1952–1996* (Washington, DC: Congressional Quarterly Press, 1997), as well as with those of Linda Lee Kaid and Anne Johnston, "Negative versus Positive Television Advertising in U.S. Presidential Campaigns 1960–1968," *Journal of Communication* 41 (Summer 1991): 53–64. To update the Kaid-Johnston analysis, Jamieson, Waldman, and Sherr included Kaid's 1997 note, "The 1996 Presidential Campaign Spots," in *Political Advertising Research Reports* 3 (1997): 1. Correlating his negativity readings with the other studies mentioned in this paragraph, Geer reported coefficients of .78 with Jamieson, .93 with Kaid and Johnston, "a staggering .97" with Benoit, and a mere .59 with West. Like other scholars, Geer regards West as an outlier. See his book *In Defense of Negativity: Attack Ads in Presidential Campaigns* (Chicago: University of Chicago Press, 2006), 37–39.

27. Physical violence against and intimidation of voters occurred frequently on nineteenth-century election days, when voters occasionally had to force their way through tense and often hostile crowds to reach the polling place. For a detailed account of these conditions, see Richard Franklin Bensel, *The American Ballot Box in the Mid-nineteenth Century* (New York: Cambridge University Press, 2004), 8–21. The secret ballot and regulation of public space near polling places reduced the potential for intimidation and violence in the twentieth century. Still, almost every race in our study inspired the odd act of vandalism or intimidation, although acts of physical intimidation may have surged in 2004 compared with other contests going back to 1960.

28. John J. Pitney, *The Art of Political Warfare* (Norman: University of Oklahoma Press, 2000), 9.

29. Nancy C. Unger, *Fighting Bob La Follette: The Righteous Reformer* (Chapel Hill: University of North Carolina Press, 2000), 295.

30. For an extensive application of boxing metaphors to campaigns, see Armstrong's account of the 1986 U.S. Senate race in South Dakota in his *Next Hurrah*, 23.

31. See Richard P. McCormick, *The Presidential Game: The Origins of American Presidential Politics* (New York: Oxford University Press, 1982), 27–30, 33–34.

32. Quoted in Michael A. Bellesiles, "'The Soil Will Be Soaked with Blood': Taking the Revolution of 1800 Seriously," in James Horn, Jan Ellen Lewis, and Peter S. Onuf, eds., *The Revolution of 1800: Democracy, Race, and the New Republic* (Charlottesville: University of Virginia Press, 2002), 59.

33. John Ferling, "Cliffhanger: The Election of 1800," *Smithsonian* 35, no. 8 (November 2003): 48. For more on the 1800 campaign, see Ferling, *Adams vs. Jefferson: The Tumultuous Election of 1800* (New York: Oxford University Press, 2004); also Bernard A. Weisberger, *America Afire: Jefferson, Adams, and the Revolutionary Election of 1800* (New York: William Morrow, 2000).

34. David C. Coyle, *Ordeal of the Presidency* (Washington, DC: Public Affairs Press, 1960), 127.

35. Jamieson, *Dirty Politics*, 77.

36. Ibid., 199.

37. John C. Waugh, *Reelecting Lincoln: The Battle for the 1864 Presidency* (New York: Crown, 1997), 315. See also Mark E. Neely, *The Union Divided: Party Conflict in the Civil War North* (Cambridge, MA: Harvard University Press, 2002).

38. Mark Wahlgren Summers, *Rum, Romanism & Rebellion: The Making of a President 1884* (Chapel Hill: University of North Carolina Press, 2000), 190–191.

39. James Bryce, *The American Commonwealth*, vol. 2 (New York: Macmillan, 1900), 216.

40. See Gil Troy, *See How They Run: The Changing Role of the Presidential Candidate*, rev. ed. (Cambridge, MA: Harvard University Press, 1996).

41. Thomas Fleming, *The Illusion of Victory: America in World War I* (New York: Basic Books, 2003), 464–465.

42. V. O. Key Jr., *Politics, Parties, and Pressure Groups* (New York: Thomas Y. Crowell, 1944), 599–600.

43. Richard Norton Smith, *Thomas E. Dewey and His Times* (New York: Simon & Schuster, 182), 514–517.

44. Polsby and Wildavsky accounted for Dewey's reticence as follows: "A vigorous campaign on Dewey's part, it was said, would have taken the steam out of Harry Truman's charges and would thus have brought him victory. Perhaps. What we know of the 1948 election suggests that it provoked a higher degree of voting on the basis of economic class than any of the elections that succeeded it. A slashing attack by Dewey, therefore, might have polarized the voters even further. This would have increased Truman's margin. . . . Had the election gone the other way—and a handful of votes in a few states would have done it—we would have heard much less about Dewey's blunder and much more about how unpopular Truman was in 1948." See Nelson W. Polsby and Aaron B. Wildavsky, *Presidential Elections: Strategies and Structures of American Politics*, 11th ed. (Lanham, MD: Rowman & Littlefield, 2004), 179.

45. David McCullough, *Truman* (New York: Simon & Schuster, 1992), 661.

46. Ibid., 701, emphasis added. For case studies of the 1948 campaign, see Jules Abels, *Out of the Jaws of Victory: The Astounding Election of 1948* (New York: Henry Holt, 1959); Gary A. Donaldson, *Truman Defeats Dewey* (Lexington: University Press of Kentucky, 1999); and Zachary Karabell, *The Last Campaign: How Harry Truman Won the 1948 Election* (New York: Alfred A. Knopf, 2000).

47. Glen W. Richardson, *Pulp Politics: How Political Advertising Tells the Stories of American Politics* (Lanham, MD: Rowman & Littlefield, 2003), 7.

48. Mayer, "In Defense of Negative Campaigning," 442.

49. Geer, *In Defense of Negativity*, 6.

50. Jamieson, Waldman, and Sherr, "Eliminate the Negative?" 45.

51. Bruce L. Felknor, *Dirty Politics* (New York: W. W. Norton, 1966), 40–41.

52. A. B. Norton, *The Great Revolution of 1840: Reminiscences of the Log Cabin and Hard Cider Campaign* (Mount Vernon, OH: A. B. Norton, 1888), 8.

53. Waugh, *Reelecting Lincoln*, 315.

54. Robert A. Slayton, *Empire Statesman: The Rise and Redemption of Al Smith* (New York: Free Press, 2001), 316–317.

55. Stephen E. Ambrose, *Nixon: The Education of a Politician, 1913–1962* (New York: Simon & Schuster, 1987), 298 and 289.

56. For example, see Bruce Buchanan, *Electing a President: The Markle Commission Research on Campaign '88* (Austin: University of Texas Press, 1991).

57. E. J. Dionne, "The Clinton Enigma: Seeking Consensus, Breeding Discord," in Gerald M. Pomper, ed., *The Election of 2000* (Chatham, NJ: Chatham House, 2001), 2.

58. Jamieson, Waldman, and Sherr, "Eliminate the Negative?" 46–47; see Richard R. Lau, Lee Sigelman, Caroline Heldman, and Paul Babbitt, "The Effects of Negative Political Advertisements: A Meta-analytic Assessment," *American Political Science Review* 93 (December 1999): 851–875, for another inventory of this research.

59. For example, see Gina M. Garramone, Charles T. Atkin, Bruce E. Pinkleton, and Richard T. Cole, "Effects of Negative Political Advertising on the Political Process," *Journal of Broadcasting and Electronic Media* 34 (Summer 1990): 299–311; Michael Basil, Caroline Schooler, and Byron Reeves, "Positive and Negative Political Advertising: Effectiveness of Ads and Perceptions of Candidates," in Frank Biocca, ed., *Television and Political Advertising*, vol. 1 (Hillsdale, NJ: Lawrence Erlbaum, 1991), 245–262.

60. Kaid and Johnston, "Negative versus Positive Television Advertising."

61. Jon F. Hale, Jeffrey C. Fox, and Rick Farmer, "Negative Advertisements in U.S. Senate Campaigns: The Influence of Campaign Content," *Social Science Quarterly* 77 (June 1996): 329–343.

62. West, *Air Wars,* 3rd ed., 65.

63. See, for example, Ronald P. Hill, "An Exploration of Voter Responses to Political Advertisements," *Journal of Advertising* 18 (Winter 1989): 14–22; Kenneth M. Goldstein, "Political Advertising and Political Persuasion in the 1996 Presidential Campaign," paper presented at the 1997 meeting of the American Political Science Association, August 28–31, Washington, DC.

64. Jamieson, *Dirty Campaigning,* 45.

65. John G. Geer, "Assessing Attack Advertising: A Silver Lining," in Larry M. Bartels and Lynn Vavreck, eds., *Campaign Reform: Insights and Evidence* (Ann Arbor: University of Michigan Press, 2000), 62–78.

66. See William L. Benoit, Joseph R. Blaney, and P. M. Pier, *Campaign '96: A Functional Analysis of Acclaiming, Attacking, and Defending* (Westport, CT: Praeger, 1998); Benoit, *Seeing Spots;* Jamieson, Waldman, and Sherr, "Eliminate the Negative?"; and Benoit et al., *Primary Decision.*

67. For example, the Oklahoma archive reportedly possesses 97 ads from the 1960 campaign, when 122 actually aired, and includes spots never shown. See Jamieson, Waldman, and Sherr, "Eliminate the Negative?" 50.

68. When comparing his findings with those of Kaid and Johnston, for instance, Benoit noted that his sample included 191 fewer ads from the 1976 and 1980 campaigns. See his *Seeing Spots,* 166.

69. Geer, "Assessing Attack Advertising," 67; Jamieson, Waldman, and Sherr, "Eliminate the Negative?" 52.

70. West, *Air Wars,* 3rd ed., 46–47. For criticism of his generalizing from prominent ads only, see Jamieson, Waldman, and Sherr, "Eliminate the Negative?" 45; also Benoit, *Seeing Spots.* West cited Jamieson's *Packaging the Presidency,* 2nd ed. (New York: Oxford University Press, 1992).

71. For an exhaustive review of the literature up to the 1990s, see Lau et al., "Effectiveness of Negative Political Advertisements," 851–876; see also Lau and Sigelman, "Effectiveness of Negative Political Advertising."

72. On the tactical division of labor between presidential and vice-presidential candidates, see Lee Sigelman and Emmett H. Buell Jr., "You Take the High Road and I'll Take the Low Road? The Interplay of Attack Strategies and Tactics in Presidential Campaigns," *Journal of Politics* 65 (May 2003): 518–531.

73. Words such as *issues, topics,* and *themes* are used interchangeably in the issue-ownership literature. Some issues exhibit greater complexity and breadth than others, and researchers typically combine two or more closely related issues under the same heading, such as taxes and

government spending. For example, one finds the designation of "jobs/labor" as a Democratic issue, "taxes" as a Republican issue, and "the economy" as a performance issue in John R. Petrocik, William L. Benoit, and Glenn J. Hansen, "Issue Ownership and Presidential Campaigning, 1952–2000," *Political Science Quarterly* 118, no. 4 (2003–2004): 599–626. But taxes and jobs are key aspects of the economy, and to avoid such confusion, we distinguish between issues and topics. Thus, e.g., we have coded employment as one of several issues that fall under the heading of the U.S. economy.

74. Key, *Politics, Parties, and Pressure Groups*, 1944 ed., 601.

75. Our choice draws upon scholarly sources as well as personal observation. V. O. Key Jr. pointed up the importance of ridicule as a method of attacking or counterattacking in his classic text, *Politics, Parties, & Pressure Groups*, 5th ed. (New York: Thomas Y. Crowell, 1964), 474; Kaid and Johnston also emphasized ridicule along with fear arousal and labeling in "Negative versus Positive Television Advertising"; Jamieson stressed apposition in *Dirty Politics*, 47; and V. Lance Tarrance made much of lying and dishonesty charges in *Negative Campaigning and Negative Votes: The 1980 Elections* (Washington, DC: Free Congress Research and Education Foundation, 1982).

76. Occasionally, we came across statements that literally did not attack an electoral opponent but were nonetheless described as attacks. We coded such statements as negative. The 1964 "Daisy Ad," for example, never mentioned Goldwater or the GOP, but Goldwater, Johnson, television news commentators, and everybody else saw the ad for what it was.

77. News coverage of presidential statements, bill signings, and foreign policy decisions hardly ceases during a presidential campaign. Rather than code every news item about the words and deeds of incumbents seeking reelection, we accepted only those explicitly linking a given statement or action to the campaign. Similarly, a story about upcoming congressional elections counted when linked to the presidential race. Reporters writing these stories generally made the necessary connection. With respect to Labor Day as our starting point, we fully appreciate that this holiday has lost most of its significance to presidential campaigning. Major changes in the system of presidential nominations, most notably dramatic increases in the number and "front loading" of primaries, has opened up a lengthy interregnum between early resolution of the nominating race and the national convention months later. Nominees-apparent now use this interval to launch an early version of the general-election campaign. These changes are sufficiently recent, however, for us to defend Labor Day as the start of a standard observation period. Moreover, starting dates of interregnums in recent election cycles have varied. And one could argue à la 2004 that presidential primaries have become a key part of the general election campaign.

78. We photocopied news items for the 1960–1988 races from *New York Times* microfilm obtained from the Denison University Library, and we derived subsequent campaign statements from printed copies of the *Times*'s national edition, sold in Ohio.

79. On kappa, see Jacob Cohen, "A Coefficient of Agreement for Nominal Scales," *Educational and Psychological Measurement* 20 (1960): 37–46. See also Donald P. Hartmann, "Consideration in the Choice of Interobserver Reliability Estimates," *Journal of Applied Behavior Analysis* 10 (1977): 103–116.

80. Jamieson, *Dirty Politics*, 138.

81. Benjamin I. Page, *Choices and Echoes in Presidential Elections: Rational Man and Electoral Democracy* (Chicago: University of Chicago Press, 1978), 111–112.

82. Peter Applebombe, "'Vintage' Reagan Stumps in the South," *NYT*, November 1, 1992, A17.

83. Glen Justice, "In Final Days, Attacks Are in the Mail and below the Radar," *NYT*, October 31, 2004, A21.

84. As a check on the comprehensiveness of campaign coverage in the *New York Times*, we also coded the *Washington Post*'s reporting of the 1992 race. Although the *Times* noted 31 percent more attacks than did the *Post*, the patterns of coverage in both newspapers closely paralleled one another. For example, 47.3 percent of all attacks reported in the *Times* were made by Republicans and directed against Democrats. In the *Post*, this figure was 46 percent.

85. For the most profound statement on the selectivity of the news, see Walter Lippmann, *Public Opinion* (New York: Free Press, 1965). Contemporary studies uphold Lippmann's insight. See, for instance, Michael J. Robinson and Margaret A. Sheehan, *Over the Wire and on TV: CBS and UPI in Campaign '80* (New York: Russell Sage, 1983); Richard Joslyn, *Mass Media and Elections* (Reading, MA: Addison-Wesley, 1984); Tom Rosensteil, *Strange Bedfellows: How Television and the Presidential Candidates Changed American Politics* (New York: Hyperion, 1993).

86. Diana Owen, *Media Messages in American Presidential Elections* (Westport, CT: Greenwood Press, 1991).

87. Louis W. Liebovich, *The Press and the Modern Presidency: Myths and Mindsets from Kennedy to Election 2000*, rev. ed. (Westport, CT: Praeger, 2001), 5.

88. Jamieson, *Dirty Politics*, 136–199.

89. Edwin R. Bayley maintained that interpretative reporting had become standard practice by 1954: "McCarthy's tactics produced lasting changes in the media. Newspaper people realized that it was not enough simply to tell what had happened or what had been said, but that they had to tell what it meant and whether or not it was true. See his *Joe McCarthy and the Press* (New York: Pantheon Books, 1982), 219.

90. For example, see S. Robert Lichter and Richard E. Noyes, *Good Intentions Make Bad News* (Lanham, MD: Rowman & Littlefield, 1995); Thomas E. Patterson, *Out of Order* (New York: Vintage, 1994).

91. E. O. Stene, "Newspapers in the Campaign," *Social Sciences* 12 (1937): 213–215.

92. Our typology closely resembles that of James E. Campbell in *The American Campaign: U.S. Presidential Campaigns and the National Vote* (College Station: Texas A&M University Press, 2000). Elsewhere, we classified these races differently, consigning 1988, 1992, and 1996 to the same "runaway" category as 1964, 1972, and 1984—all campaigns in which one ticket consistently led by a wide margin in the polls from Labor Day to election day. We categorized 1960, 1968, 1976, 1980, and 2000 as "fluid" campaigns. See Sigelman and Buell, "You Take the High Road," 518–531.

93. On 1960, see Lawrence D. Longley and Neal R. Peirce, *The People's President: The Electoral College in American History and the Direct Vote Alternative*, rev. ed. (New Haven, CT: Yale University Press, 1981), 63–73; also by the same authors, *The Electoral College Primer 2000* (New Haven, CT: Yale University Press, 1999), 46–59.

94. Jack W. Germond and Jules Witcover, *Blue Smoke and Mirrors: How Reagan Won and Why Carter Lost the Election of 1980* (New York: Viking Press, 1981), 286–306.

95. "Trial Heat: Bush vs. Kerry vs. Nader," October 31, 2004, posted on the Gallup Poll Web site at http://www.gallup.com.

96. More than 200 third-party candidates and independents got on the ballot in more than one state from 1840 to 2004. Among these, Perot ranked third for his share of the popular vote in 1992 (surpassed only by two former presidents, Theodore Roosevelt in 1912 and Millard Fillmore in 1856). George Wallace ranked sixth. Perot was put in eleventh place by his 1996 showing, and Ralph Nader in 2000 ranked seventeenth, far better than in his 1996 and 2004 showings.

97. James W. Ceaser and Andrew E. Busch maintained that Pat Buchanan had an equally negative impact on Bush support in states narrowly won by Gore. See their *Perfect Tie: The True Story of the 2000 Election* (Lanham, MD: Rowman & Littlefield, 2001), 158.

98. Skaperdas and Grofman, "Modeling Negative Campaigning."

99. Damore argued that this calculation is more complicated than suggested by Skaperdas and Grofman because positive campaigning also entails risk as well as benefit. He cited Dole's 1996 pitch for a big tax cut as a case in point. This message appealed to fewer voters than those favoring Clinton proposals to pay down the debt and shore up Social Security. Candidates making an unpopular if positive issue appeal must consider the cost of not staying on message. Changing the message confuses voters and creates an impression that the candidate lacks focus or conviction, perceptions that dogged Dole's candidacy. Altered or not, "positive appeals also may be costly because such messages allow the opposition to produce its message without interference"; see David E. Damore, "Candidate Strategy and the Decision to Go Negative," *Political Research Quarterly* 55 (September 2002): 671.

100. Skaperdas and Grofman, "Modeling Negative Campaigning," 53.

101. Ibid.

102. Our definition adheres to the one in Safire, *Safire's Political Dictionary*, 678.

103. Linda Charlton, "McCarthy, Riding in Tourist Class, May Spoil Races of Men Up Front," *NYT*, October 28, 1976, A49.

104. Skaperdas and Grofman, "Modeling Negative Campaigning," 55.

105. Ibid.: "Most obviously, if a candidate were more vulnerable to negative campaigning on some aspect of his history or issue position than others, then we could have negative attacks against a weaker candidate with a comparatively larger vulnerability."

106. Key mentioned this possibility in the 1944 edition of *Politics, Parties, and Pressure Groups*, arguing on p. 588 that intense Republican criticism of FDR in 1940 probably hurt the Republican cause: "That would be the deduction if there is any validity in the theory that relentless and untempered criticism may redound to the benefit of its victim."

107. Key, 1965 ed. of *Politics, Parties, and Pressure Groups*, 473.

108. Ian Budge and Dennis J. Fairlie, *Explaining and Predicting Elections: Issue Effects and Party Strategies in Twenty-three Democracies* (London: George Allen & Unwin, 1983), 41.

109. Ibid., 52; see pp. 26–41 for grouping of specific issues.

110. John R. Petrocik, "Issue Ownership in Presidential Elections, with a 1980 Case Study," *American Journal of Political Science* 40 (August 1996): 825–850.

111. Petrocik, Benoit, and Hansen, "Issue Ownership and Presidential Campaigning," 599–626.

112. We note, however, that performance issues often carry over to the next campaign, thereby raising the possibility that some are no less durable than "owned" issues. The fund-raising irregularities that likely prevented Clinton from winning a popular-vote majority in 1996 clearly fall under the "conduct of government officials," a performance issue. Yet this scandal came back to bite Gore in 2000, undermining his position as a reformer. Similarly, partisan differences over Clinton's character that showed up in 1992 still divided the electorate in 2000.

113. Adam F. Simon, *The Winning Message: Candidate Behavior, Campaign Discourse, and Democracy* (New York: Cambridge University Press, 2002). William Riker came up with similar propositions in his analysis of state debates in 1787 and 1788 over ratification of the U.S. Constitution: "When one side has an advantage on an issue, the other side ignores it, but when neither side has an advantage, both seek new and advantageous issues." See Riker, *The Strategy of Rhetoric: Campaigning for the American Constitution* (New Haven, CT: Yale University Press, 1996), 105–106. In framing his "dominance/dispersion principle," Riker reported that "most of the time opponents do not talk about the same things." See his "Rhetorical Interaction in the Ratification Campaigns," in William H. Riker, ed., *Agenda Formation* (Ann Arbor: University of Michigan Press, 1993), 81–123.

114. Budge and Fairlie, *Explaining and Predicting Elections,* 129.

115. Petrocik, Benoit, and Hansen, "Issue Ownership and Presidential Campaigning, 1952–2000," 602.

116. Ibid., 609–613.

117. John H. Aldrich and John D. Griffin, "The Presidency and the Campaign: Creating Voter Priorities in the 2000 Election," in Michael Nelson, ed., *The Presidency and the Political System,* 7th ed. (Washington, DC: Congressional Quarterly Press, 2003), 239–256.

118. Ibid., 242.

119. David E. Damore, "The Dynamics of Issue Ownership in Presidential Campaigns," *Political Research Quarterly* 57 (September 2004): 391–398.

120. Ibid., 394.

121. See Lee Sigelman and Emmett H. Buell Jr., "Avoidance or Engagement? Issue Convergence in U.S. Presidential Campaigns," *American Journal of Political Science* 48 (October 2004): 650–661.

122. Anthony Downs, *An Economic Theory of Democracy* (New York: Harper & Row, 1957).

123. Ibid., 28.

CHAPTER 2. THE RUNAWAY RACES OF 1964, 1972, AND 1984

1. Dewey B. Martin wrote of the 1964 campaign, "From the moment it began to the end, with a single brief interruption in mid-October, just about everybody knew who would win." See his "Election of 1964," in Arthur M. Schlesinger Jr. and Fred Israel, eds., *History of American Presidential Elections,* vol. 4 (New York: Chelsea House, 1971), 3588. Herbert S. Parmet took a similar view of the 1972 contest: "The McGovern failure was readily predictable. He never had a chance." See Parmet, *The Democrats: The Years after FDR* (New York: Oxford University Press, 1976), 303. Paul C. Light and Celinda Lake were hardly alone in concluding that it was difficult to imagine any scenario in which a Democrat could win in 1984. See their chapter "The Elections: Candidates, Strategies, and Decisions" in Michael Nelson, ed., *The Elections of 1984* (Washington, DC: Congressional Quarterly Press, 1985), 93.

2. This is not to deny that individual preferences change even during a runaway campaign. For an analysis of such shifts in 1972, see Clifford W. Brown Jr., *Jaws of Victory: The Great-Game Politics of 1972* (Boston: Little, Brown, 1974), 156–157.

3. Goldwater later wrote that he had looked forward to running against John F. Kennedy in 1964. Within days of Kennedy's assassination, however, he concluded that he had little chance of defeating Johnson, whom he regarded as unprincipled and corrupt. Conservative supporters convinced him to seek the nomination anyway. Goldwater later described his rationale for running: "In my gut there never was a burning desire to be president. I just wanted the conservatives to have a real voice in the country. . . . Someone had to rally the Republican Party and turn the direction of the GOP around. There was no one to do it but me. We'd lose the election but win the party." See Barry M. Goldwater, with Jack Casserly, *Goldwater* (New York: St. Martin's Press, 1988), 195.

4. Scott offered three amendments to the 1964 platform—a denunciation of the John Birch Society, the Ku Klux Klan, and the Communist Party; a plank committing the GOP to support vigorous enforcement of the Civil Rights Act; and a declaration that the president would exercise sole authority over the use of nuclear weapons—all of which lost on voice votes. Romney offered two amendments, one condemning unnamed extremist groups and another pledging the GOP

to fight against discrimination in local and state government as well as in the private sector. Again, the nays drowned out the yeas. See *National Party Conventions, 1831–2000* (Washington, DC: Congressional Quarterly Press, 2001), 121–122.

5. Richard M. Nixon, *RN: The Memoirs of Richard Nixon*, vol. 1 (New York: Warner Books, 1978), 321.

6. For an insider's account of how Goldwater came by the extremism-is-no-vice language, see J. William Middendorf II, *A Glorious Disaster: Barry Goldwater's Presidential Campaign and the Origins of the Conservative Movement* (New York: Basic Books, 2006), 127–136.

7. John H. Kessel, *The Goldwater Coalition: Republican Strategies in 1964* (Indianapolis, IN: Bobbs-Merrill, 1965), 191; Harold Faber, *The Road to the White House: The Story of the 1964 Election by the Staff of the "New York Times"* (New York: McGraw-Hill, 1965), 141–142.

8. See Rick Perlstein, *Before the Storm: Barry Goldwater and the Unmaking of the American Consensus* (New York: Hill and Wang, 2001).

9. Barry Goldwater, *The Conscience of a Conservative* (Shepherdsville, KY: Victor Publishing, 1960).

10. For the full text of Goldwater's Senate speech opposing the test ban, see F. Clifton White, *Suite 3505: The Story of the Draft Goldwater Movement* (Ashland, OH: Ashbrook Press, 1992), 397–400.

11. For the full text of his Senate speech against Titles II and VII of the Civil Rights Act, see ibid., 401–403.

12. Kessel, *Goldwater Coalition*, 199.

13. Theodore H. White, *The Making of the President, 1964* (New York: Atheneum, 1965), 324; Perlstein, *Before the Storm*, 49.

14. *Presidential Elections, 1789–1996* (Washington, DC: Congressional Quarterly Press, 1997), 67 and 191.

15. In 1960, 95 percent of all Republican voters had cast their ballots for Nixon, along with 57 percent of the independents. See Harold Stanley and Richard Niemi, *Vital Statistics on American Politics*, 4th ed. (Washington, DC: Congressional Quarterly Press, 1994), 106.

16. Theodore H. White, *The Making of the President, 1972* (New York: Atheneum, 1973), 340.

17. Scott Stossel, *Sarge: The Life and Times of Sargent Shriver* (New York: Atheneum, 1973), 340.

18. For accounts of the Eagleton affair and its consequences for McGovern's campaign, see Nixon, *RN*, 155–160; White, *Making of the President, 1972*, 197–207; and Gary Hart, *Right from the Start: A Chronicle of the McGovern Campaign* (New York: Quadrangle, 1973), 262–264. Post-Eagleton polls indicated that the affair had lasting ill effects for McGovern. See Brown, *Jaws of Victory*, 137–140. Anecdotal evidence of damage wrought by the Eagleton episode surfaced in the *Times*. Correspondent James M. Naughton quoted one "distressed" spokesman for the Democrats as saying, "I think there are still 10 to 12 million people who are mad at George McGovern because of the Eagleton affair. What I don't know is if, when they go into that voting booth, they're still going to be mad enough to vote for Richard Nixon." See Naughton, "The Eagleton Impact," *NYT*, October 7, 1972, A18. McGovern's New Jersey campaign manager said that "the whole thing comes down to one word, Eagleton. I find the same thing all over the state." See Naughton, "Eagleton Joins McGovern in Campaign Effort to Confront the Credibility Issue," *NYT*, October 8, 1972, A50.

19. Hart, *Right from the Start*, 264.

20. George McGovern, *Grassroots: The Autobiography of George McGovern* (New York: Random House, 1977), 218.

21. Ibid., 219–231.

22. William Crotty, *Party Reform* (New York: Longman, 1983), 155–202. Soon, however, Daley realized that repudiating McGovern might hurt his machine and the state Democratic Party on election day. Accordingly, McGovern met with Daley and other machine politicians in Chicago. "This has been an unusual election," Daley informed the gathering. "But that's all behind us now. Today we're interested in electing the ticket." See Seth King, "Daley Calls on Chicago to Back McGovern, 'the Next President,'" *NYT,* September 12, 1972, A32.

23. Philip Shabecoff, "Meany Criticizes 'Elite' Democrats," *NYT,* September 19, 1972, A38.

24. Philip Shabecoff, "9 Heads of Building Unions Back Nixon for Re-election," *NYT,* September 27, 1972, A34. This is not to say that all labor leaders abandoned McGovern. Shortly after the AFL-CIO vote, McGovern supporters formed the National Labor Committee for the Election of McGovern-Shriver. See Shabecoff, "Labor Panel Aiding McGovern," *NYT,* September 5, 1972, A28.

25. Robert Dallek, *Flawed Giant: Lyndon Johnson and His Times, 1961–1973* (New York: Oxford University Press, 1998), 617; Nixon, *RN,* 167–168; Stephen E. Ambrose, *Nixon: The Triumph of a Politician, 1962–1972* (New York: Simon & Schuster, 1989), 586. For McGovern's account of relations with Johnson, see his *Grassroots,* 227–230.

26. White, *Making of the President 1972,* 216–217.

27. Jack Rosenthal, "New Survey Finds Nixon Is Leading McGovern 62–23%," *NYT,* September 25, 1972, A1.

28. White, *Making of the President, 1972,* 335–336. Before the Eagleton debacle, the ratio had been three favorable to one unfavorable.

29. McGovern, *Grassroots,* 225.

30. Ibid., 235.

31. Hart, *Right from the Start,* 318.

32. McGovern, *Grassroots,* 233.

33. Ibid., 245.

34. *Presidential Elections, 1789–1996,* 69, 121; Stanley and Niemi, *Vital Statistics,* 106.

35. Thomas E. Mann, "Elected Officials and the Politics of Presidential Selection," in Austin Ranney, ed., *The American Elections of 1984* (Durham, NC: Duke University Press, 1985), 116; Jack W. Germond and Jules Witcover, *Wake Us When It's Over: Presidential Politics of 1984* (New York: Macmillan, 1985), 345; Gary Orren, "The Nomination Process: Vicissitudes of Candidate Selection," in Nelson, ed., *The Elections of 1984,* 67.

36. Gerald M. Pomper, "The Presidential Elections," in Gerald M. Pomper, ed., *The Election of 1984: Reports and Interpretations* (Chatham, NJ: Chatham House, 1985), 71; Germond and Witcover, *Wake Us,* 345.

37. Germond and Witcover, *Wake Us,* 358–359.

38. Steven M. Gillon, *The Democrats' Dilemma: Walter F. Mondale and the Liberal Legacy* (New York: Columbia University Press, 1992), 363.

39. Lance had been forced to resign as Carter's budget director in 1977 after charges of banking irregularities. An indictment followed in 1979. Lance was acquitted on most charges, and the Justice Department dropped the others in 1980. Lance went on to become chairman of the Georgia Democratic Party and helped Mondale eke out a narrow victory in the 1984 Georgia primary. See Germond and Witcover, *Wake Us,* 386.

40. For a detailed account of Mondale's difficulty in working with Ferraro, his dismay over her tax problems, and the strains that developed, see Gillon, *Democrats' Dilemma,* 365–370.

41. *National Party Conventions, 1831–2000,* 144.

42. Francis X. Clines, "Confident Reagan Vows to 'Make America Great Again,'" *NYT*, September 4, 1984, A1.

43. David E. Rosenbaum, "Poll Shows Many Chose Reagan Even If They Disagree with Him," *NYT*, September 19, 1984, A1.

44. Francis X. Clines, "Mondale Seen Ahead in Only 4 States," *NYT*, October 26, 1984, A7.

45. Bernard Weinraub, "Aides Reported to Say Mondale Support Ebbs," *NYT*, October 27, 1984, A30.

46. *Presidential Elections, 1789–1996*, 69, 72, and 124.

47. Stanley and Niemi, *Vital Statistics*, 106.

48. Fendall W. Yerka, "Goldwater Says President Avoids Campaign Issues," *NYT*, September 22, 1964, A1.

49. Nixon, *RN*, 161.

50. James A. Wooten, "President's Surrogates to Step Up Campaign Tempo," *NYT*, September 6, 1972, A32.

51. As noted in Chapter 1, we did not code intraparty criticism as attacks, e.g., when a liberal Republican senator criticized Goldwater or a conservative Democrat expressed a low opinion of McGovern. We did code attacks by partisans who defected to the other party and worked for its ticket, such as John Connally and other Democrats who were for Nixon in 1972.

52. See Gillon, *Democrats' Dilemma*, 372–390.

53. We should also note John R. Petrocik, William L. Benoit, and Glenn J. Hansen's claim that the *New York Times* consistently understated the degree of convergence in presidential campaigns. See their "Issue Ownership and Presidential Campaigning," *Political Science Quarterly* 118, no. 4 (2003–2004): 615. Having relied solely on the *Times* for data on campaign statements, we cannot disprove this claim outright, but we can determine whether convergence was rare or common in campaigns. Obviously, a great deal of convergence occurred during the three runaway races.

54. The difference in 1972 in the propensity of competing vice-presidential nominees to use apposition was negligible.

55. Charles Mohr, "Goldwater Calls Tax Cut Cynical," *NYT*, September 9, 1964, A27.

56. Yerka, "Goldwater Says President Avoids Campaign Issues."

57. Charles Mohr, "Goldwater Calls Rivals 'Fascists,'" *NYT*, October 14, 1964, A1; Mohr, "Goldwater Asserts Johnson's Integrity Is the Main Issue," *NYT*, October 19, 1964, A1.

58. E. W. Kenworthy, "Fulbright Scorns G.O.P. Candidates," *NYT*, September 9, 1964, A25.

59. Joseph A. Loftus, "Miller Deplores Johnson's TV Link," *NYT*, September 11, 1964, A19. Earlier, Miller had assailed Humphrey's voting record as "one of the most radical in Congress," and he denounced the ADA as "unquestionably the most influential of the radical leftist groups in Washington today." Senator Fulbright vigorously defended Humphrey and attacked Miller in a September 8 speech on the Senate floor. "The statements by Representative Miller," Fulbright declared, "confirm . . . that he was chosen for the job of hatchet man, not because he is well known or a man of stature, but because he is capable of the most foul-mouthed vituperation and unrestrained misrepresentation of any man in public life." See E. W. Kenworthy, "Fulbright Scorns G.O.P. Candidates," *NYT*, September 9, 1964, A25. Miller promptly denounced Fulbright as "an apostle of retreat" who had never understood the Communist threat. See Loftus, "Fulbright Focus of Miller Attack," *NYT*, September 10, 1964, A16.

60. Charles Mohr, "Johnson Sees U.S. Choice: Either 'Center' or 'Fringe,'" *NYT*, September 24, 1964, A1.

61. "Nixon Denounces 'Radical' Humphrey," *NYT*, October 27, 1964, A21.

62. Lyndon Baines Johnson, *The Vantage Point: Perspectives on the Presidency, 1963–1969* (New York: Holt, Rinehart, and Winston, 1971), 103.

63. Carl Solberg, *Hubert Humphrey: A Biography* (New York: W. W. Norton, 1984), 259.

64. Mohr, "Johnson Sees U.S. Choice."

65. Fendall W. Yerka, "Johnson Invites Republicans' Aid," *NYT,* September 29, 1964, A1.

66. Yerka, "Johnson Alters Campaign Style," *NYT,* October 15, 1964, A30.

67. Earl Mazo, "Bold Democratic Goal," *NYT,* September 14, 1964, A28.

68. E. W. Kenworthy, "Humphrey Scores G.O.P. Birch Stand," *NYT,* September 24, 1964, A34.

69. Kenworthy, "Appalachia Area Cheers Humphrey," *NYT,* September 27, 1964, A65.

70. Joseph A. Loftus, "Humphrey Scores Attacks by G.O.P.," *NYT,* October 8, 1964, A58.

71. Fendall W. Yerka, "Humphrey Extols George Marshall," *NYT,* October 29, 1964, A22.

72. Damon Stetson, "President Backed by Steelworkers," *NYT,* September 23, 1964, A27.

73. Homer Bigart, "Humphrey Joins Kennedy on Campaign Swing Here," *NYT,* September 25, 1964, A1.

74. Kenworthy, "Fulbright Scorns G.O.P. Candidates."

75. Douglas E. Kneeland, "Kennedy Helps McGovern Stir Big Minneapolis Rally," *NYT,* September 12, 1972, A32.

76. Kneeland, "McGovern Assails Nixon Administration as 'Scandal Ridden,'" *NYT,* October 1, 1972, A46; "Transcript of Senator McGovern's Speech Offering a Plan for Peace in Indochina," *NYT,* October 11, 1972, A29.

77. McGovern's interest in freeing American POWs dated back at least to September 1971, when he met personally with a North Vietnamese official in Paris. For Nixon's version of this episode, in which he claimed that Hanoi had manipulated McGovern, see Nixon, *RN,* 56–57.

78. "McGovern Hints Politics Delays P.O.W.'s Release," *NYT,* September 25, 1972, A42; James M. Naughton, "Humphrey Stumps Coast for Old Rival, McGovern," *NYT,* September 27, 1972, A1.

79. Kneeland, "McGovern Assails Nixon Administration."

80. Kneeland, "McGovern, in Jersey, Calls for $6 Billion to Aged," *NYT,* September 21, 1972, A1.

81. Warren Weaver, "Charges Traded by Party Heads," *NYT,* September 20, 1972, A34.

82. "Transcript of Senator McGovern's Speech Offering a Plan for Peace in Indochina," *NYT,* October 11, 1972, A29.

83. Christopher Lydon, "G.I.'s Regret Stuns a McGovern Rally," *NYT,* October 13, 1972, A20.

84. "McGovern Bars Unity Drive If Beaten," *NYT,* October 29, 1972, A48.

85. "Transcript of Senator McGovern's Speech."

86. Douglas E. Kneeland, "McGovern Says He Hopes Nixon View Is Confirmed," *NYT,* October 27, 1972, A1.

87. James M. Naughton, "McGovern Asserts Nixon Pretended to Be Near Peace," *NYT,* November 4, 1972, A1.

88. Douglas E. Kneeland, "McGovern Warns Nixon Lacks Plan to Quit Vietnam," *NYT,* November 5, 1972, A1.

89. James M. Naughton, "McGovern Asserts Nixon Misleads Nation on Peace," *NYT,* November 6, 1972, A1.

90. See Stossel, *Sarge,* 529–536, and also Chapter 4 in this book for more on Nixon's possible role in aborting the talks.

91. Christopher Lydon, "Shriver Criticizes Proposal for Coalition in Vietnam," *NYT,* November 1, 1972, A26.

92. Lydon, "Shriver's Mother Honored at Party," *NYT*, November 3, 1972, A21.

93. Nixon, *RN*, 200. Nixon read the polls correctly. See Brown, *Jaws of Victory*, 200; also Jack Rosenthal, "Poll Finds Issues Not at Issue in 1972," *NYT*, October 8, 1972, A54.

94. Ambrose, *Nixon*, 580.

95. Ibid., 582. Early in October, without using the word *amnesty*, McGovern promised to let deserters and draft evaders "come home." He also lashed out at Nixon for making draft evaders "scapegoats for his murderous policy in Vietnam." See Christopher Lydon, "Shriver Assails 'Lies and Smears,'" *NYT*, October 25, 1972, A33.

96. Tad Szulc, "President Says 'Opinion Leaders' Failed Him on War," *NYT*, October 16, 1972, A29.

97. Linda Charlton, "President Praises Returning G.I.'s," *NYT*, October 23, 1972, A1.

98. "McGovern Accused of Parroting Hanoi," *NYT*, September 22, 1972, A31; James Wooten, "Agnew's Attacks Growing Tougher," *NYT*, September 22, 1972, A14; Wooten, "Agnew Criticizes Dakotan on Arms," *NYT*, September 26, 1972, A36.

99. Robert Semple, "Agnew Denies That Nixon Hides from the Electorate," *NYT*, October 3, 1972, A32.

100. James Wooten, "Agnew Asserts Dakotan Uses Smear and Offers 'Philosophy of Defeat,'" *NYT*, October 5, 1972, A1.

101. "Agnew Excoriates McGovern on Accord," *NYT*, October 31, 1972, A36.

102. "McGovern Hints Politics Delays P.O.W. Release."

103. Ibid. The same story contained George Meany's reaction to the McGovern plan: "Instead of emphasizing Hanoi's responsibility for continuing the bloodshed, the opponents of our country's policy do nothing but blame the United States." See also William A. Beecher, "G.O.P. Leaders Criticize McGovern's Peace Plan," *NYT*, October 12, 1972, A40.

104. James Wooten, "Agnew Says McGovern Would Crimp Defenses," *NYT*, September 21, 1972, A40.

105. Robert Semple, "McGovern Unit Says Defense Can Be Cut," *NYT*, September 22, 1972, A30.

106. Semple, "Nixon Views Rival As Left's Captive," *NYT*, September 28, 1972, A52.

107. Warren Weaver, "G.O.P. Switches TV Campaign to Attack on McGovern," *NYT*, October 4, 1972, A30.

108. Bernard Weinraub, "Mondale Plans to Focus on Issues Where He Says Reagan Is Weak," *NYT*, September 9, 1984, A1.

109. Weinraub, "Democrats Press Challenge," *NYT*, September 4, 1984, A1.

110. Weinraub, "Mondale Says Reagan Raised Taxes of the Poor," *NYT*, September 5, 1984, A20.

111. Fay S. Joyce, "Mondale Program Would Raise Taxes $85 Billion by '89," *NYT*, September 11, 1984, A1.

112. Joyce, "Mondale Tells President He 'Can't Hide' on Deficit," *NYT*, September 12, 1984, B8.

113. Joyce, "Mondale Depicts President as Cruel to the Needy," *NYT*, September 13, 1984, B13.

114. Hedrick Smith, "Mondale Tactics: Shift to New Area," *NYT*, October 3, 1984, B17.

115. Bernard Weinraub, "Mondale Shifting Focus from Deficit," *NYT*, October 18, 1984, D27.

116. Ronald Reagan, *An American Life* (New York: Pocket Books, 1992), 225.

117. Reagan biographer Lou Cannon wrote that Mondale's promise to raise taxes elated Reagan's advisers. "I was in ecstasy," said one. "The political graveyard is full of tax increasers." See Cannon, *President Reagan: The Role of a Lifetime* (New York: Touchstone Books, 1992), 511. A

CBS/*New York Times* poll taken from October 23 to 25 and published on October 28, 1984, confirmed that domestic economic issues worked to Reagan's advantage. Fifty-five percent of the entire sample of respondents said that the economy was more important than any other issue. Given a choice between "will get worse" and "will not get worse," 86 percent of Reagan supporters, 70 percent of independents, and 31 percent of Mondale supporters said the economy would not get worse if Reagan won. Asked what would happen if Mondale won, 14 percent of Reagan supporters, 27 percent of independents, and 79 percent of Mondale supporters said the economy would not get worse. This poll further underscored Mondale's "striking difficulties" in winning support from the "political center." See Hedrick Smith, "Failure to Win Independents Hurting Mondale, Poll Finds," *NYT*, October 28, 1984, A1.

118. Francis X. Clines, "Confident Reagan Vows to 'Make America Great Again,'" *NYT*, September 4, 1984, A1.

119. Clines, "Reagan Would Tell Gromyko 'The U.S. Marines Mean No Harm,'" *NYT*, September 12, 1984, A1.

120. Steven R. Weisman, "Reagan Attacks Mondale Tax Plan," *NYT*, September 13, 1984, B14.

121. Francis X. Clines, "President Heaps Praise on Voters in the Northeast," *NYT*, September 20, 1984, B20.

122. Bernard Weinraub, "Making Campaign Crowds Feel Good," *NYT*, October 5, 1984, D19.

123. "Reagan Presses Attack on Mondale Tax Views," *NYT*, October 14, 1984, A28.

124. Francis X. Clines, "Reagan Goes on Attack by Quoting Democrats," *NYT*, October 16, 1984, A24.

125. Clines, "Reagan at Ohio Rally Attacks Mondale Anew," *NYT*, October 24, 1984, B19.

126. Howell Raines, "Candidates Focus on Closest States in Final Weekend," *NYT*, November 4, 1984, A1.

127. Maureen Dowd, "Ferraro-Jackson Team Rouses Memphis Rally," *NYT*, October 4, 1984, B17.

128. Gerald M. Boyd, "Ferraro Assails Reagan as Captive of 'the Powerful and the Greedy,'" *NYT*, October 17, 1984, A24.

129. Boyd, "Bush Says Mondale Proposal Is One of 'Economic Gloom,'" *NYT*, September 11, 1984, A25; Boyd, "Bush Takes on Audience Questions at Campaign Rally in Syracuse," *NYT*, October 26, 1984, A17.

130. Jane Perlez, "Bush Says Ford Made 'Sense' of Beirut Blast," *NYT*, October 1, 1984, B10.

CHAPTER 3. THE SOMEWHAT COMPETITIVE RACES OF 1988, 1992, AND 1996

1. The average margin of victory in runaway races was 21.3 percent, whereas in somewhat competitive contests, it was 7.3 percent.

2. Other polls also showed Bush leading Dukakis during the fall but sometimes by a lesser margin than reported by Gallup. Several polls, including one taken by the Bush organization, indicated that Dukakis had all but erased the gap in September. See Peter Goldman and Tom Matthews, *The Quest for the Presidency: The 1988 Campaign* (New York: Simon & Schuster/Touchstone, 1989), 368; also Barbara G. Farah and Ethel Klein, "Public Opinion Trends," in Gerald M. Pomper, ed., *The Election of 1988: Reports and Interpretations* (Chatham, NJ: Chatham House, 1989), 105.

3. *Presidential Elections, 1789–1996* (Washington, DC: Congressional Quarterly Press, 1997), 73 and 125.

4. See, for example, Christine Black and Thomas Oliphant, *All by Myself: The Unmaking of a Presidential Campaign* (Chester, CT: Globe Pequot Press, 1989); Jack W. Germond and Jules Witcover, *Whose Broad Stripes and Bright Stars? The Trivial Pursuit of the Presidency, 1988* (New York: Warner Books, 1989); Herbert S. Parmet, *George Bush: The Life of a Lone-Star Yankee* (New York: Scribner, 1997); Goldman and Matthews, *Quest for the Presidency.*

5. Goldman and Matthews, *Quest for the Presidency*, 297–308.

6. After hearing these discussions, Lee Atwater later told reporters, he had immediately realized "that the sky was the limit on Dukakis's negatives." See Parmet, *George Bush*, 336. In the same place, Parmet referred to two focus groups of Reagan Democrats, each consisting of fifteen participants. Goldman and Matthews mentioned only one group, consisting of a dozen members, in their *Quest for the Presidency*, 300.

7. Ibid., 307–308.

8. Black and Oliphant, *All by Myself*, 232–253; Germond and Witcover, *Whose Broad Stripes*, 351–362; Goldman and Matthews, *Quest for the Presidency*, 333–353.

9. Black and Oliphant, *All by Myself*, 235.

10. Richard L. Berke, "Independent Groups Putting 11th Hour Millions in Races," *NYT*, October 26, 1984, A23. At least one showed a picture of Willie Horton, a black man with a long criminal record who had been frequently released on weekend passes from prison—despite a murder conviction that rendered him ineligible for parole. While on furlough, he fled to Maryland, where he brutalized a couple, raping the woman. A Maryland court sentenced him to serve a minimum of eighty-five years under consecutive rather than concurrent sentences. The Maryland judge refused to let Horton serve this extra time in Massachusetts: "I'm not prepared to take the chance that Mr. Horton might again be furloughed or otherwise released." Largely because of his initial reaction to the affair—refusing to meet with the victims and seemingly dismissing the episode as a statistical anomaly in a generally successful program—Dukakis would pay a heavy political cost. Prodded by lavish coverage in the *Lowell (Massachusetts) Eagle-Tribune*, state legislators introduced a bill to end weekend passes for convicted murderers. After apparently helping to stall this legislation, Dukakis signed it in April 1988 and later claimed credit for its demise. See David C. Anderson, *Crime and the Politics of Hysteria: How the Willie Horton Story Changed American Justice* (New York: Times Books–Random House, 1995); see also "A *Reader's Digest* Exclusive," *NYT*, September 16, 1988, A18.

11. Black and Oliphant, *All by Myself*, 282–296; Germond and Witcover, *Whose Bright Stars*, 6–9.

12. The others were Taft in 1912, Hoover in 1932, Ford in 1976, and Carter in 1980.

13. Lincoln won only 39.9 percent in 1860; Wilson garnered only 41.8 percent in 1912. See *Presidential Elections, 1789–1996*, 93 and 106.

14. Ibid., 74, 92, and 106.

15. David E. Rosenbaum, "Two Points of View on Creating New Jobs," *NYT*, September 27, 1992, A16.

16. Emmett H. Buell Jr., "The Invisible Primary," in William G. Mayer, ed., *In Pursuit of the White House: How We Choose Our Presidential Nominees* (Chatham, NJ: Chatham House, 1996), 3.

17. George Gallup Jr., *The Gallup Poll: Public Opinion in 1992* (Wilmington, DE: Scholarly Resources, 1993); Kathleen A. Frankovic, "Public Opinion in the 1992 Campaign," in Gerald M. Pomper, ed., *The Election of 1992* (Chatham, NJ: Chatham House, 1993), 110–131.

18. Walter Dean Burnham, "The Legacy of George Bush," in Pomper, ed., *The Election of 1992*, 1–38.

19. The economy eventually did improve, but news of this came too late to save Bush. Indeed, the best news for Bush—2.7 percent growth in the third quarter—appeared in the *Times* on October 28; see Robert D. Hershey, "U.S. Economy Grew at a Rate of 2.7% during 3d Quarter," *NYT*, October 28, 1992, A1.

20. Charles Kolb, *White House Daze: The Unmaking of Domestic Policy in the Bush Years* (New York: Free Press, 1994).

21. Gallup, *The Gallup Poll: Public Opinion in 1992*; Peter Goldman, Thomas M. DeFrank, Mark Miller, Andrew Murr, and Tom Matthews, *Quest for the Presidency, 1992* (College Station: Texas A&M University Press, 1994), 249.

22. James W. Ceaser and Andrew E. Busch, *Upside Down and Inside Out: The 1992 Elections and American Politics* (Lanham, MD: Littlefield Adams Quality Paperbacks, 1993), 87–88; Jack Germond and Jules Witcover, *Mad as Hell: Revolt at the Ballot Box* (New York: Warner Books, 1993), 492. Exit polls also showed strong support for Perot among Democratic and Republican voters in the 1992 presidential primaries. See Gerald Posner, *Citizen Perot: His Life and Times* (New York: Random House, 1996), 256 and 261; also Ross K. Baker, "The Presidential Nominations," in Pomper, ed., *The Election of 1992*, 58.

23. Gallup, *The Gallup Poll: Public Opinion in 1992*.

24. Goldman et al., *Quest for the Presidency, 1992*, 449–451.

25. Dan Quayle, *Standing Firm: A Vice-Presidential Memoir* (New York: HarperCollins, 1994), 311.

26. Marlin Fitzwater, *Call the Briefing! Reagan and Bush, Sam and Helen: A Decade with Presidents and the Press* (Holbrook, MA: Adams Media, 1995), 347.

27. "When Perot Said He Wouldn't Run," *NYT*, October 2, A12 (excerpts from Perot's July 16 statement).

28. Perot signaled his likely intent on September 18. See Richard L. Berke, "Perot Says He May Rejoin Race to Publicize His Economic Plan," *NYT*, September 19, 1992, A1. Later that month, Perot summoned representatives of both major-party tickets to Dallas, on a mission impossible: to persuade his volunteers that he should not get back in the race. Both sides dispatched delegations. The Bush team made only a token effort, and Clinton's negotiator, Mickey Kantor, argued behind the scenes that his man and Perot agreed on 90 percent of the issues. Kantor had correctly surmised that Perot held Clinton in higher regard than Bush. Even so, it was apparent that Perot meant to rejoin the race. He indicated this to Clinton during a lengthy telephone conversation that Clinton later described as "strange." See Goldman et al., *Quest for the Presidency, 1992*, 544–545. "Nothing about the Ross Perot presence hurts us," one "senior Bush aide" said to *Times* reporter Andrew Rosenthal. "Hey, we're the ones who are losing this election. Either he's going to help us, or we could end up where we are, losing. It simply can't hurt us." See Rosenthal, "Bush Campaign Welcomes Perot as Reconfiguring the Election," *NYT*, October 2, 1992, A10.

29. An unidentified source reportedly close to Perot told the *Times* that Perot had never expected to be attacked as a quitter: "And one reason I think he's back in is simply to prove this isn't true, to revive his name." See R. W. Apple, "Back in, without as Big a Splash," *NYT*, October 2, 1992, A1. There has been much speculation on whether Perot meant his July departure to be final. Aside from statements he made to close associates, it is notable that his July departure did not end the drive to put his name on the ballot in all fifty states.

30. Steven A. Holmes, "More Perot Hints on Renewed Race," *NYT*, September 23, 1992, A17.

31. Most accounts of the 1992 race agree that Bush's apparent surge resulted not from a genuine increase in support for him but from an increase in Perot support that cut into Clinton's polling numbers. According to a *Newsweek* team, "The only movement that mattered in the polls

was the division of the Not Bush vote. As Perot got more of it, Clinton got less, and Bush got closer simply by running in place, his share of the vote stuck where it had been all along." See Goldman et al., *Quest for the Presidency, 1992*, 604.

32. See Gerald M. Pomper, "The Presidential Election," in Pomper, ed., *The Election of 1992*; Paul J. Quirk and Jon K. Dalager, "The Election: A 'New Democrat' and a New Kind of Presidential Campaign," in Michael Nelson, ed., *The Elections of 1992* (Washington, DC: Congressional Quarterly Press, 1993), 57–88; Herb Asher, "The Perot Campaign," in Herbert F. Weisberg, ed., *Democracy's Feast: Elections in America* (Chatham, NJ: Chatham House, 1995), 153–178; and Herbert F. Weisberg and David C. Kimball, "Attitudinal Correlates of the 1992 Presidential Vote," in Weisberg, ed., *Democracy's Feast*, 72–111. Extrapolating from exit polls, Pomper ("The Presidential Election," 142) argued that Perot's vote would have split exactly even, 38 percent for Bush and 38 percent for Clinton. In an exhaustive analysis of 1992 National Election Study (NES) data, Asher found that 45 percent of all Perot voters had considered supporting Clinton at some point during the campaign, and 46 percent reported a similar inclination for Bush. He concluded that "Perot did not harm one candidate more than the other, although this still leaves open the possibility that his impact was more differential within particular states." Working with NES data, Weisberg and Kimball found that Perot peeled off more Bush than Clinton supporters. (Perot won 21 percent of all voters expressing positive affect for Bush, compared with 15 percent with a favorable view of Clinton.) Perot did more damage to Bush in that he reduced the president's already slim chances of holding on to all of his base and of stealing away Clinton supporters. Quirk and Dalager allowed that Perot's spring campaign helped Clinton by giving Democrats disgusted with their nominee apparent a halfway house; see their "Election: A 'New Democrat' and a New Kind of Presidential Campaign." No one denies that Perot's attacks on Bush supplemented Clinton's call for change. See also Goldman et al., *Quest for the Presidency, 1992*, 604.

33. Scott Keeter looked at other polls as well and reported an average lead of 12 percent. He also found merit in complaints that the polls had underestimated Republican support. Partly, this resulted from overestimating turnout and from missing a late Republican surge due to late-breaking news of a scandal over White House fund-raising. See Keeter's chapter, "Public Opinion and the Election," in Gerald M. Pomper, ed., *The Election of 1996: Reports and Interpretations* (Chatham, NJ: Chatham House, 1997), 129–131.

34. Michael Nelson, "The Election: Turbulence and Tranquility in Contemporary American Politics," in Michael Nelson, ed., *The Elections of 1996* (Washington, DC: Congressional Quarterly, 1997), 44–80; James W. Ceaser and Andrew E. Busch, *Losing to Win: The 1996 Elections and American Politics* (Lanham, MD: Rowman & Littlefield, 1997); Larry J. Sabato, "The November Vote: A Status Quo Election," in Larry J. Sabato, ed., *Toward the Millennium: The Elections of 1996* (Boston: Allyn and Bacon, 1997), 37–91.

35. *Presidential Elections, 1789–1996*, 75.

36. See Walter Dean Burnham, "Bill Clinton: Riding the Tiger," in Pomper, ed., *The Election of 1996*, 1–20; Ceaser and Busch, *Losing to Win*; Evan Thomas, Karen Breslau, Debra Rosenberg, Leslie Kaufman, and Andrew Murr, *Back from the Dead: How Clinton Survived the Republican Revolution* (New York: Atlantic Monthly Press, 1997).

37. The bank scandal was a bipartisan affair, but rightly or otherwise, Democrats received most of the blame, part of the burden of forty years as the House majority.

38. Dan Balz and Ronald Brownstein, *Storming the Gates: Protest Politics and the Republican Upheaval* (Boston: Little, Brown, 1996), 331–332; Gary Jacobson, "The 1994 Elections in Perspective," in Philip H. Klinkner, ed., *Midterm: Elections of 1994 in Context* (Boulder, CO: Westview Press, 1997), 1–20.

39. Ceaser and Busch, *Losing to Win*, 38. For example, not one House incumbent shared the stage with Clinton at a Michigan rally, and Speaker Tom Foley pointedly did not ask for his help in Washington State. Similarly, Representative Dave McCurdy, the Democratic candidate for an open Senate seat in Oklahoma, kept Clinton at arm's length. The Republicans, he said, were out "to wrap the president's unpopularity around my neck." McCurdy lost resoundingly to Republican James Inhofe. See Paul R. Abramson, John H. Aldrich, and David Rohde, *Change and Continuity in the 1992 Elections*, rev. ed., containing 1994 election analysis (Washington, DC: Congressional Quarterly Press, 1995), 324. This is not to discount other important influences working to Republican advantage in 1994, such as reapportionment favorable to the GOP; key Democratic retirements that left Republican-leaning districts open in House races; a strong crop of Republican challengers; Newt Gingrich's determined leadership; the Contract with America; a perception that the economy was still in recession; high levels of distrust of government; and disapproval of congressional job performance that rose from 54 percent when Clinton took office to 73 percent in October of 1994. See George Gallup Jr., *The Gallup Poll: Public Opinion in 1994* (Wilmington, DE: Scholarly Resources, 1995), 1957.

40. *Congressional Elections, 1946–1996* (Washington, DC: Congressional Quarterly Press, 1998), 53–56; Thad Beyle, "The State Elections of '96," in Larry Sabato, ed., *Toward the Millennium*, 193.

41. Leading election analysts have come to somewhat different conclusions about the importance of the "Clinton factor." Exit polls indicated that 52 percent of the voters did not mention Clinton as a reason for their vote, but the same polls showed that 72 percent of the voters who did mention Clinton voted Republican. The correlation between presidential job approval and vote choice was also very high: Among those approving of Clinton's performance, 84 percent voted Democratic; among those who disapproved, 82 percent voted Republican. Unfortunately for Democrats, more disapproved (49 percent) than approved (44 percent). Abramson, Aldrich, and Rohde conceded that Clinton's unpopularity may have dampened Democratic efforts to recruit good congressional candidates. See their *Change and Continuity in the 1992 Elections*, rev. ed., 324–325. Jacobson argued that Clinton helped drag down the Democratic vote by alienating swing voters. He also noted that white males voted 11 percent more Republican in 1994 than they had in 1992. Perot voters from 1992 supported Republican candidates by a two-to-one ratio. See Jacobson, "1994 Elections in Perspective," 5–7.

42. Emmett H. Buell Jr., "Some Things Are Predictable: Nominating Dole, Clinton, and Perot," in Harvey L. Schantz, ed., *Politics in an Era of Divided Government: Elections and Governance in the Second Clinton Administration* (New York: Routledge, 2001), 19.

43. George Stephanopoulos, *All Too Human: A Political Education* (Boston: Little, Brown, 1999), 412.

44. Buell, "Some Things Are Predictable," 21.

45. For an insider's account of how Clinton's early campaign depended on such money, see Dick Morris, *Behind the Oval Office: Getting Reelected against All Odds* (Los Angeles: Renaissance Books, 1999). See also Harvard Institute of Politics, *Campaign for President: The Managers Look at 1996* (Hollis, NH: Hollis Publishing, 1997).

46. Ceaser and Busch, *Losing to Win*; Elizabeth Drew, *Whatever It Takes: The Real Struggle for Power in America* (New York: Viking, 1997). October polls taken for the *New York Times*/CBS News as well as for the GOP found that most Americans wanted to retain Republican majorities in Congress if Clinton won the presidential election. See Adam Clymer, "G.O.P. Pushes Congress Strategy That Shuns Dole," *NYT*, October 23, 1996, A1. Immediately after the election, 53 percent of the sample in a Pew Research poll expressed satisfaction that Clinton had been reelected,

whereas 65 percent said they were happy that the Republicans still controlled Congress. See Gary Jacobson, "The 105th Congress: Unprecedented and Unsurprising," in Nelson, ed., *The Elections of 1996*, 161.

47. Richard L. Berke, "Dole Asks Perot to Quit Campaign and Endorse Him," *NYT*, October 24, 1996, A1.

48. Keeter, "Public Opinion and the Election."

49. Anthony Corrado, "Financing the 1996 Elections," in Pomper, ed., *The Election of 1996*, 135–171.

50. Nelson, "The Election: Turbulence and Tranquility," 70–72.

51. George Gallup Jr., *The Gallup Poll: Public Opinion, 1996* (Wilmington, DE: Scholarly Resources, 1997), 128–129. Perot's best showing was in Gallup's poll of March 15–17, 1996, when 44 percent viewed him favorably compared with a 46 percent unfavorable rating. By late August, Gallup found it was 32 percent favorable, 58 percent unfavorable. Perot's stock dropped in part due to the manner in which he wrested the Reform Party nomination from former Colorado governor Richard Lamm. For a detailed account of this poisonous affair, see Buell, "Some Things Are Predictable," 25–26.

52. This is not to deny that Perot had other reasons for becoming a candidate in 1992. Quirk and Dalager acknowledged that Perot "preferred Clinton to Bush and did not want to be responsible for a Bush victory," yet they concluded that his most important reasons for running were "to make a statement, draw attention to the deficit, and establish himself as a force in American politics." See their "Election: A 'New Democrat' and a New Kind of Presidential Campaign," 66. Parmet wrote that Perot entered the 1992 race "largely for his own ego and to fulfill his vendetta against Bush." See Parmet, *George Bush*, 501. Posner's extensive documentation of Perot's animosity toward Bush suggests that malice aforethought motivated Perot more than any other factor in 1992. See Posner, *Citizen Perot*, 191–217, and 245–322. Bush, his running mate, and his Texas campaign chairman unquestionably subscribed to this view as well. See Quayle, *Standing Firm*, 310; and Apple, "Back In, without as Big a Splash."

53. This paragraph relies chiefly on Posner, *Citizen Perot*, and Parmet, *George Bush*. Posner offered a particularly detailed account of Perot's difficulties with Bush, Reagan, and other top Republicans. Perot also demanded an FBI sting operation against the chairman of Bush's Texas campaign, charging illegal sabotage of his candidacy. The investigation ended abruptly when its indignant target threatened to refer the matter to federal authorities.

54. At a 1995 meeting of United We Stand, Perot laid down an impossible ultimatum to both parties: Unless they balanced the budget, fixed Social Security and Medicare problems, curbed the special interests, and imposed term limits on congressional service by Christmas, he might run again. He waited only until September before launching the Reform Party. See Buell, "Some Things Are Predictable," 25.

55. Germond and Witcover, *Mad as Hell*, 228.

56. Jane Gross, "Scholar Follows Perot into Heat of Campaign," *NYT*, October 4, 1992, A14.

57. Germond and Witcover, *Mad as Hell*, 477.

58. Julie Johnson, "On Stump, Reagan Makes It Personal," *NYT*, September 15, 1988, B11.

59. "In His Own Words," *NYT*, September 17, 1992, A10.

60. The best example of Perot ridiculing Clinton in 1992 appeared not in the *Times* but in the *Washington Post*. After noting that one of every five jobs created in Arkansas during Clinton's time as governor had been in the poultry industry, he exclaimed: "Now this is not an industry of tomorrow. . . . If we decide to take this level of business-creating capability nationwide, we'll all be plucking chickens for a living. So I guess you can just sum it up: The chickens keep on

clucking, and the people keep on plucking after twelve years of Governor Clinton's leadership." See Michael Isikoff, "Perot, in a Change of Tactics, Directs Fierce Attack at Front-Runner Clinton," *Washington Post*, November 2, 1992.

61. Robin Toner, "Dukakis in Levittown, Offers a Plan to Help Young Families Buy Homes," *NYT*, October 11, 1988, A28.

62. E. J. Dionne, "Bush and Dukakis Both Ready to Shift in the Campaign," *NYT*, October 16, 1988, A1.

63. Robin Toner, "Quayle Reflects Badly on Bush, Dukakis Asserts," *NYT*, October 7, 1988, B6.

64. Toner, "A Smiling Dukakis Renews His Offensive against Bush," *NYT*, September 27, 1988, B6.

65. Andrew Rosenthal, "Dukakis Says Standard of Living Is Deteriorating," *NYT*, October 4, 1988, D30.

66. "Excerpts from the Interview with Dukakis," *NYT*, October 9, 1988, A34.

67. "I Believe in an America That's in Command of Its Destiny," *NYT*, October 25, 1988, A26.

68. Robin Toner, "Dukakis, in Fiery Michigan Rally, Demands Atom Plant Safeguards," *NYT*, October 29, 1988, A10.

69. Andrew Rosenthal, "Dukakis Assails Corrupt Government," *NYT*, November 2, 1988, A20.

70. For an account of Quayle's Senate career, see Richard Fenno, *The Making of a Senator: Dan Quayle* (Washington, DC: Congressional Quarterly Press, 1989).

71. Larry J. Sabato cited Quayle's experience as a prime example of a press feeding frenzy and explored the dynamics that led to this explosion. See his *Feeding Frenzy: How Attack Journalism Has Transformed American Politics* (New York: Free Press, 1993).

72. Robin Toner, "Dukakis Starts New Round Slugging," *NYT*, September 14, 1988, A28.

73. Toner, "In Blur of Rallies, Dukakis Steps Up Attacks on Rival," *NYT*, November 7, 1988, B17.

74. Warren Weaver, "Bentsen Takes Up the Offensive, Assailing Bush's Choice of Quayle," *NYT*, September 16, 1988, B5; Weaver, "Bentsen, in Truman's Town, Turns Up the Heat on Quayle," *NYT*, September 19, 1988, D28.

75. E. J. Dionne, "Bentsen and Quayle Attack on Question of Competence to Serve in the Presidency," *NYT*, October 6, 1988, A1.

76. Robin Toner, "Quayle Reflects Badly on Bush, Dukakis Asserts."

77. Maureen Dowd, "Late and Loudly, Jackson Rejoins Fray," *NYT*, October 18, 1988, B7.

78. Andrew Rosenthal, "Invoking Kennedy Triumph, Dukakis Tours Connecticut," *NYT*, November 4, 1988, A19. At least two other Democratic television ads targeted Quayle. On the morning after the first presidential debate, the Democrats unveiled two television ads arguing that Bush had made a risky choice in Dan Quayle. One spot showed film of Truman, Johnson, and Ford being sworn in following the deaths of Roosevelt and Kennedy and Nixon's resignation. "Hopefully, we will never know how great a lapse of judgment that really was," the ad concluded in reference to Bush's selection of Quayle. The second ad showed a group of Republican handlers fretting about the possibility that their creation might become president. See Michael Oreskes, "Bush and Dukakis Try to Capitalize on Latest Debate," *NYT*, October 7, 1988, A1.

79. Robin Toner, "Dukakis Starts New Round Slugging"; Andrew Rosenthal, "Campaign Tactics Provoke New Charges," *NYT*, October 31, 1988, B6.

80. Toner, "Dukakis Starts New Round Slugging"; Rosenthal, "Dukakis Suggests Caution on U.S.S.R."; Rosenthal, "Campaign Tactics Provoke New Charges."

81. Warren Weaver, "Bentsen Tells Texans the Debate Was Turning Point in Election," *NYT*, October 8, 1988, A34; Weaver, "Bentsen Keeps Up Attack on Quayle," *NYT*, October 9, 1988, A32.

82. Maureen Dowd, "Bush Angrily Insisting He Fully Backs Quayle," *NYT*, October 9, 1988, A32.

83. Julie Johnson, "On a Campaign Swing, President Praises Quayle," *NYT*, October 8, 1988, A35.

84. E. J. Dionne, "Bush and Dukakis, With Anger, Debate Leadership and Issues from Abortion to Iran-Contra," *NYT*, September 26, 1988, A1.

85. Dionne, "Bush and Dukakis Quarrel on Pensions, Abortion, Arms and Campaign's Shrill Tone," *NYT*, October 1, 1988, A1.

86. Dionne, "Bush and Dukakis Claim Momentum in a Bitter Finale," *NYT*, November 7, 1988, A1.

87. Andrew Rosenthal, "More Mud Than Ever Slung Through the Mail," *NYT*, November 5, 1988, A8.

88. Michael Oreskes, "Dukakis and Bush Agree on the Rules for Debates on TV," *NYT*, September 15, 1988, A1.

89. Dukakis responded to the same question: "Should Governor Dukakis be held accountable for the failure of a prison furlough program he strongly supported for first-degree murderers?" He argued that the program had not failed, except in "one particular case, which was very unfortunate." He also noted that his Republican predecessor had started the program and that it had continued despite criticism. "And I am the first governor of three to stop it," Dukakis asserted. He also maintained that thirty-three states had furlough programs for "people convicted of a homicide," and that the federal government furloughed drug pushers and offenders. "A Reader's Digest Exclusive," *NYT*, September 16, 1988, A18.

90. Dowd, "Bush Angrily Insisting He Fully Backs Quayle."

91. This *Times* story also reprinted a 1987 quote from the *Boston Herald*, in which Dukakis refused to meet with Horton's victims: "I don't see any particular value in meeting with people. I'm satisfied we have the kind of furlough policy we should have." See Dowd, "Bush Portrays His Opponents as Sympathetic to Criminals," *NYT*, October 8, 1988, A35.

92. Ibid.

93. Dowd, "Bush Angrily Insisting."

94. Robin Toner, "As Bush Collects a Political Windfall, Dukakis Counterpunches in Boston," *NYT*, September 23, 1988, A22.

95. Gerald M. Boyd, "Bush's Attacks on Crime Appeals to the Emotions," *NYT*, October 11, 1988, A28.

96. Boyd, "Bush Cuts Fish and Baits His Opponent," *NYT*, September 6, 1988, D12.

97. Dionne, "Bush and Dukakis, With Anger, Debate Leadership and Issues."

98. Gerald M. Boyd, "Bush, in Michigan, Travels Two Roads on the Campaign Trail," *NYT*, October 20, 1988, B10; Boyd, "Bush Tries to Shift Emphasis off the Tone of His Campaign," *NYT*, October 26, 1988, A22.

99. Steven V. Roberts, "President Acts to Promote Conservative Issues Being Used by Bush," *NYT*, September 10, 1988, A7; Julie Johnson, "Reagan Calls Vote against Democrats Good Negative Campaigning," *NYT*, October 28, 1988, D24.

100. Frank Lynn, "Presidential Campaign Mail Inundating New York Voters," *NYT*, November 4, 1988, B2.

101. Robin Toner, "Dukakis Makes Strong Response to G.O.P.'s Ads," *NYT*, October 20, 1988, B11.

102. Rosenthal, "Campaign Tactics Provoke New Charges."

103. Robin Toner, "Dukakis Sees Heated 30 Days in Fight with a 'Bankrupt' Foe," *NYT*, October 9, 1988, A1.

104. Toner, "Dukakis Gets a Needed Boost for Campaign," *NYT*, October 19, 1988, B7.

105. Michael Oreskes, "Dukakis in TV Ads, Strikes Back in Kind," *NYT*, October 22, 1988, A8.

106. Rosenthal, "Campaign Tactics Provoke New Charges."

107. Maureen Dowd, "Bush Says Dukakis's Desperation Prompted Accusations of Racism," *NYT*, October 25, 1988, A1.

108. Gwen Ifill, "Bush and Clinton Go after Each Other on NBC," *NYT*, September 7, 1992, A9; Michael Wines, "Bush Again Vows No Tax Increase," *NYT*, September 10, 1992, A1.

109. Robin Toner, "A Tense Uncertainty Grows in the Campaign," *NYT*, September 27, 1992, A1.

110. Elizabeth Kolbert, "Bush Failed in Debate by Inviting Perot," October 13, 1992, *NYT*, A11.

111. Michael Kelly, "Encircling Arkansas, Bush Opens Harsh Attack on Clinton's Record," *NYT*, September 23, 1992, A1.

112. Michael Wines, "Bush Says Clinton Imperils Business," *NYT*, September 24, 1992, A1; "Bush Getting Tough with a Touch of Humor," *NYT*, September 24, 1992, A10.

113. Andrew Rosenthal, "The Ad Campaign: Bush Attacking Clinton's Tax Proposal," *NYT*, October 2, 1992, A10.

114. R. W. Apple, "In Texas, Three Neighbors Battle for a Vital Prize," *NYT*, October 4, 1992, A15.

115. Robin Toner, "Quayle and Gore Exchange Sharp Attacks in Debate," *NYT*, October 13, 1992, A1.

116. Michael Wines, "Clinton Painted as Taxer but Isn't Tarred," *NYT*, September 7, 1992, A8.

117. Karen DeWitt, "Quayle, Conceding 'Mistake,' Says Bush Won't Raise Taxes," *NYT*, September 9, 1992, A8.

118. Michael Wines, "Bush Again Vows No Tax Increase," *NYT*, September 10, 1992, A1.

119. Robin Toner, "Bush and Clinton Pull No Punches in Holiday Rallies," *NYT*, September 8, 1992, A1.

120. Joseph F. Sullivan, "Bush Finds Fertile Ground for Attacking Governors," *NYT*, September 10, 1992, A11.

121. Michael Wines, "Vowing a Revival, President Sets Out His Economic Plan," *NYT*, September 11, 1992, A1.

122. Wines, "Bush Paints Clinton as 'Social Engineer,'" *NYT*, September 18, 1992, A9.

123. "In Their Own Words: President Bush in a Speech Yesterday at a Rally in Marysville, Ohio," *NYT*, September 27, 1992, A18.

124. Steven A. Holmes, "Bold Perot Plan to Attack Deficit Thrusts Issue at Bush and Clinton," *NYT*, September 28, 1992, A1.

125. Robin Toner, "Bush Pushes Hard in 3d Debate but Foes Put Him on Defensive," *NYT*, October 20, 1992, A1.

126. "In Their Own Words: President Bush in a Speech to Kentucky Fried Chicken Owners Yesterday in Nashville," *NYT*, October 31, 1992, A7.

127. "In Their Own Words: President Bush in a Speech Yesterday at a Rally in Warren, Mich.," *NYT*, October 30, 1992, A10.

128. William Jennings Bryan introduced the concept of trickle down, if not its exact wording, while delivering his famous Cross of Gold speech at the 1896 Democratic convention. See William Safire, *Safire's Political Dictionary* (New York: Random House, 1978), 740.

129. Toner, "Bush and Clinton Pull No Punches in Holiday Rallies"; George Judson, "Clinton Tours Plant to Talk about the Issue: Jobs," *NYT*, September 6, 1992, A8; Wines, "Vowing a Revival"; "In His Own Words: Gov. Bill Clinton in a Speech Yesterday at the Maxine Waters Employment Preparation Center in South Central Los Angeles," *NYT*, September 17, 1992, A10; R. W. Apple, "Bush Stresses His Experience but 2 Rivals Cite Economic Lag," *NYT*, October 12, 1992, A1.

130. "In His Own Words: Gov. Bill Clinton in a Speech Yesterday."

131. Michael Kelly, "Clinton Says Bush Is Afraid of Debating 'Man to Man,'" *NYT*, September 19, 1992, A6.

132. Wines, "Bush Says Clinton Imperils Business."

133. Robin Toner, "2 Campaigns Begin Direct Discussion on Debate Format," *NYT*, October 1, 1992, A1; Apple, "Bush Stresses His Experience."

134. Robert Suro, "Gore and Clinton Share Language of Their Own," *NYT*, October 31, 1992, A6.

135. "The Ad Campaign: Clinton—Criticizing the President," *NYT*, September 21, 1992, A12.

136. Wines, "Bush Says Clinton Imperils Business."

137. Elizabeth Kolbert, "The Last Ads: The Tipoff to Endgame Strategies," *NYT*, October 20, 1992, A10.

138. Kolbert, "Bush and Clinton Customize Their TV and Radio Ads in the Swing States," *NYT*, October 22, 1992, A12.

139. Wines, "Bush Again Vows No Tax Increase."

140. Andrew Rosenthal, "Day of Brawling for Presidential Camps," *NYT*, September 21, 1992, A12.

141. Michael Kelly, "Clinton Again Faces Draft Issue as He Returns to New Hampshire," *NYT*, September 27, 1992, A17.

142. "The Ad Campaign: Clinton: Reminding the Voters of a Promise," *NYT*, October 3, 1992, A8.

143. John H. Cushman, "Fate of Tax Bill Is Far from Clear," *NYT*, October 5, 1992, A1.

144. "Honored to Accept: Excerpts from Perot's News Conference," *NYT*, October 2, 1992, A12.

145. Richard L. Berke, "Perot Says He Quit in July to Thwart G.O.P. 'Dirty Tricks,'" *NYT*, October 26, 1992, A1.

146. Ibid.

147. Barnes, the *Times* pointed out, was a former policeman and self-styled soldier of fortune, who claimed to have worked as an agent for foreign intelligence services and who had become notorious for having fabricated stories about undercover plots and dirty tricks. Moreover, Barnes had disconnected his phone, closed his office, and disappeared by the time of Perot's appearance on *60 Minutes*. See Berke, "Perot Says He Quit in July." See also Michael Kelly, "Perot Shows Penchant for Seeing Conspiracy," *NYT*, October 29, 1992, A10.

148. Kevin Sack, "Perot Assures the Faithful There Is Still Time to Win," *NYT*, October 26, 1992, A11.

149. Sack, "Perot Aides Try to End Story but President Keeps It Alive," *NYT*, October 28, 1992, A9.

150. Visited in Houston first by Barnes using a false name and later by "Cowboy Bob," an undercover FBI agent, Bush chairman Jim Oberwetter rebuffed both attempts to entice him into accepting materials supposedly harmful to Perot. See Posner, *Citizen Perot*, 307–322, for a detailed account of this bizarre episode.

151. "In Their Own Words: Ross Perot in a Speech at a Rally Wednesday Night in Denver," *NYT*, October 30, 1992, A10.

152. Berke, "Perot Says He Quit in July."

153. Steven A. Holmes, "Perot-Bush 'Dirty Tricks' Feud Persists," *NYT*, October 27, 1992, A1.

154. Ibid.

155. Sack, "Perot Aides Try to End Story."

156. Larry Rohter, "Unrepentant, Marilyn Quayle Stresses Family and Values," *NYT*, October 28, 1992, A10.

157. Gwen Ifill, "Despite Perot Surge, Clinton Keeps Sights on Bush," *NYT*, October 26, 1992, A12.

158. Michael Kelly, "As Race Looks Tighter, Theme Is Truth and Trust," *NYT*, October 29, 1992, A1.

159. "Honored to Accept: Excerpts from Perot's News Conference."

160. Richard L. Berke, "On Eve of Last Candidate Debate, Bush Aide Predicts 'Tough Race,'" *NYT*, October 19, 1992, A1; Kevin Sack, "Perot Scores in 3d Debate, Then Opens Fire on the Press," *NYT*, October 21, 1991, A12.

161. Toner, "Bush Pushes Hard in 3d Debate but Foes Put Him on Defensive."

162. Steven A. Holmes, "Perot Assails Rivals as Unfit to Run a Small Business," *NYT*, November 2, 1992, A12: Holmes, "Perot Wraps Up His Campaign Where He Mostly Ran It: On TV," *NYT*, November 3, 1992, A1.

163. In his memoir of life as a Clinton aide, George Stephanopoulos recalled that by June 1996, "damage control was a cottage industry in the White House. We had a team of lawyers, nicknamed the Masters of Disaster, whose sole job was to handle Whitewater and related inquiries—responding to grand jury subpoenas, preparing congressional testimony, answering questions from the press." He also described Filegate as a "bureaucratic screw-up," a "mess of our own making," when "two midlevel White House staffers mistakenly obtained the FBI files of nine hundred Republicans from previous administrations, including former Secretary of State James Baker." Still, "it had the potential to be our most serious scandal yet." See Stephanopoulos, *All Too Human*, 416.

164. David Johnston, "Clinton Attacked for Travel-Office Episode," *NYT*, September 14, 1996, A9.

165. Dole's use of abortion in his 1974 reelection bid for the Senate attracted national attention, as did his more prominent role as Gerald Ford's hatchet man during the 1976 presidential campaign. Critics still recalled his snarling reference to "Democrat wars," uttered during a vice-presidential debate with Mondale. Locked in a rough battle with Steve Forbes and Lamar Alexander for the Republican presidential nomination in 1996, Dole devastated Forbes in Iowa and stopped Alexander in New Hampshire with a lethal mix of attack ads and push polling. See Larry J. Sabato, "Presidential Nominations: The Front-Loaded Frenzy of '96," in Sabato, ed., *Toward the Millennium*, 37–91.

166. Adam Nagourney, "Dole Calls for Clinton to Release an F.B.I. Report on Drugs," *NYT*, October 3, 1996, A10; Katherine Q. Seeyle, "Changing Tactics, Dole Challenges Clinton's Ethics," *NYT*, October 9, 1996, A1.

167. "Excerpts from Debate between Vice President Gore and Jack Kemp," *NYT*, October 11, 1996, A14.

168. Katherine Q. Seeyle, "Dole Hints about a 'Surprise' for Clinton at the Next Debate," *NYT*, October 10, 1996, A14.

169. Adam Nagourney, "Dole Campaign in Discord over Attacking President," *NYT*, October 11, 1996, A1.

170. Ibid.; Jerry Gray, "Picking Up the Dole Refrain, Kemp Tries the Character Issue," *NYT*, October 13, 1996, A18.

171. Eric Schmitt, "Gingrich Vigorously Assails Democrats' Fund Raising," *NYT*, October 14, 1996, A11.

172. Adam Nagourney, "Shifting Tone of Campaign, Dole Presses the Ethics Issue," *NYT,* October 15, 1996, A1.

173. Nagourney, "Dole Accuses Clinton of Devaluing Presidency," *NYT,* October 16, 1996, A13.

174. Nagourney, "Dole, in California, Strikes Hard at Clinton on Illegal Immigrants," *NYT,* October 18, 1996, A1.

175. Katherine Q. Seeyle, "On Talk Radio, Bob Dole Just Took Off the Gloves," *NYT,* October 18, 1996, C21; Stephen Lebaton, "Democrats Curb Raising of Funds by a Top Official," *NYT,* October 19, 1996, A1.

176. Adam Nagourney, "Dole Warms to Task of Attacking Clinton," *NYT,* October 19, 1996, A8; Nagourney, "Dole Says Clinton Is Evading Questions on Campaign Money," *NYT,* October 20, 1996, A17.

177. Nagourney, "Dole Urges Action on Campaign Gifts," *NYT,* October 21, 1996, A1.

178. Richard L. Berke, "Aggressive Turn by Dole Appears to Be Backfiring," *NYT,* October 23, 1996, A1.

179. Katherine Q. Seeyle, "With Softer Tone, Dole Turns to the Economy," *NYT,* October 22, 1996, A12; Adam Clymer, "To Gingrich, Elections This Year Are Like 'Whitewater Canoeing,'" *NYT,* October 25, 1996, A1.

180. Seeyle, "Dole Shows High Spirits across Michigan," *NYT,* October 23, 1996, A13.

181. Seeyle, "A Frustrated Dole Asks Why Some Voters Aren't," *NYT,* October 25, 1996, A11.

182. Seeyle, "Dole Says the White House Is Now an 'Animal House,'" *NYT,* October 28, 1996, A10.

183. Adam Nagourney, "Dole Enlists Ford and Bush in Late Attack," *NYT,* November 2, 1996, A1.

184. Todd S. Purdum, "Clinton Urges Political Finance Overhaul," *NYT,* November 2, 1996, A1.

185. Ernest Tollerson, "Perot Demands That Clinton Unequivocally Rule Out Pardons," *NYT,* October 8, 1996, A12.

186. Tollerson, "Perot Sees Moral Problems for Clinton in '97," *NYT,* October 25, 1996, A10.

187. Tollerson, "Perot Says Whitewater Developments Will Hobble a Clinton Second Term," *NYT,* October 29, 1996, A12.

188. Tollerson, "Perot Keeps Up Attacks on Clinton's Integrity," *NYT,* November 5, 1996, A15.

189. Nagourney, "Dole Calls for Clinton to Release an F.B.I. Report on Drugs."

190. Schmitt, "Gingrich Vigorously Assails Democrats' Fund Raising."

191. Nagourney, "Dole Says Clinton Is Evading Questions on Campaign Money."

192. Leslie Wayne, "Foreign G.O.P. Donor Raised Dole Funds," *NYT,* October 21, 1996, A13.

193. Alison Mitchell, "Eye on Congress, Clinton Presses for Big Turnout in Eastern States," *NYT,* October 31, 1996, A1.

194. Mitchell, "Leaving Aides to Duel Dole, President Stresses Education," *NYT,* October 22, 1996, A13.

195. Ibid.

196. James Bennett, "Clinton Commercial Misleading, Election Finance Expert Says," *NYT,* October 23, 1996, A12.

197. Richard L. Berke, "Democrats Try to Defuse Fund-Raising Issue, Afraid It May Deny Clinton a Decisive Win," *NYT,* November 3, 1996, A20.

CHAPTER 4. THE COMEBACK RACES OF 1968 AND 1976

1. Gallup showed Humphrey five points ahead in June and trailing by two in July.

2. Carl Solberg, *Hubert Humphrey: A Biography* (New York: W. W. Norton, 1984), 372.

3. "Had the election been held in the first week of October," Stephan Lesher wrote, "Wallace would have collected more than 15,300,000 votes and, according to a *New York Times* survey published on October 6, seemed destined to win twice as many electoral votes as Humphrey." See Lesher, *George Wallace: American Populist* (Reading, MA: Addison-Wesley, 1994), 423.

4. For Nixon's account of this long night of election returns, see Richard M. Nixon, *RN: The Memoirs of Richard Nixon*, vol. 1 (New York: Warner Books, 1978), 409–412. Nixon based his campaign strategy on winning no fewer than three of the following states: New York, California, Illinois, Ohio, Pennsylvania, Texas, and Michigan. He conceded the Deep South to Wallace but not the Carolinas, Virginia, Florida, or any other state on the rim of the South. He also expected to win the Midwest, Great Plains, Rocky Mountains, and Far West. See Nixon, *RN*, 391. Lawrence O'Brien reported that the Humphrey camp "saw no hope of carrying the southern states and only faint hope of carrying two or three border states." Given these concessions, Humphrey had to prevail in big states such as Michigan, Ohio, California, Illinois, Texas, and New Jersey. See O'Brien, *No Final Victories: A Life in Politics, from John F. Kennedy to Watergate* (New York: Doubleday, 1974), 265. Dan T. Carter wrote that Wallace expected to carry all of the southern states that voted for Goldwater, as well as Arkansas and perhaps a border state or two: "In a very close three-way campaign, a candidate could throw the election into the House of Representatives with as few as 180 electoral votes." See Carter, *The Politics of Rage: George Wallace, the Origins of the New Conservatism, and the Transformation of American Politics* (Baton Rouge: Louisiana State University Press, 1995), 338.

5. *Presidential Elections, 1789–1996* (Washington, DC: Congressional Quarterly Press, 1997), 68 and 120. Ironically, Nixon had called on Humphrey to join him in a pledge that the winner of the popular vote should become president, regardless of the electoral vote. "The price America would have to pay for minority rule by Hubert Humphrey would be four years of division, dissension, and despair," he declared. See Robert B. Semple Jr., "Electoral Pact Pushed by Nixon," *NYT*, October 31, 1968, A1.

6. George Gallup lauded Ford's comeback as "the most dramatic in polling history," noting that it had surpassed Humphrey's surge in 1968 and Truman's in 1948. See George H. Gallup, ed., *The Gallup Poll: Public Opinion 1972–1977* (Wilmington, DE: Scholarly Resources, 1978), 879.

7. Philip E. Converse, Warren E. Miller, Jerrold G. Rusk, and Arthur G. Wolfe, "Continuity and Change in American Politics: Parties and Issues in the 1968 Election," *American Political Science Review* 63 (December 1969): 1083–1105, at 1087. Similarly, Jeremy D. Mayer wrote that the initial similarity of the candidates' stands on Vietnam lessened the war's potential as an issue in 1968. Accordingly, race became "easily the most important issue of the general election, implicated whenever the candidates talked about law and order, riots, or integration. Even Vietnam was in part a racial issue." See Mayer, *Running on Race: Racial Politics in Presidential Campaigns, 1960–2000* (New York: Random House, 2002), 70.

8. George H. Gallup, ed., *The Gallup Poll: Public Opinion 1935–1971* (New York: Random House, 1972), 2107, 2128, 2151, and 2158.

9. Ibid., 2128.

10. Hubert Humphrey, *The Education of a Public Man: My Life and Politics* (Garden City, NY: Doubleday, 1976), 354.

11. Clark Clifford, with Richard Holbrooke, *Counsel to the President: A Memoir* (New York: Random House, 1991), 562.

12. See Robert Caro, *Master of the Senate: The Years of Lyndon Johnson* (New York: Vintage, 2003), for a detailed account of their Senate relationship. Johnson also ran Humphrey through an emotional wringer before putting him on the ticket in 1964. Johnson summoned him to the

LBJ ranch right after the convention, dressed him in a western outfit, and saddled him out with a spirited horse. "Reporters grinned and cameras clicked as the critter reared," Humphrey's biographer later wrote, "and Humphrey in his ridiculous get-up hung on for dear life." See Solberg, *Hubert Humphrey*, 258.

13. Eventually, Johnson ordered FBI taps on Humphrey's phones. See Robert Dallek, *Flawed Giant: Lyndon Johnson and His Times, 1961–1973* (New York: Oxford University Press, 1998), 576.

14. Solberg, *Hubert Humphrey*, 327.

15. See Kenneth A. Bode and Carol F. Casey, "Party Reform: Revisionism Revised," reprinted in Emmett H. Buell Jr. and William G. Mayer, eds., *Enduring Controversies in Presidential Nominating Politics* (Pittsburgh, PA: University of Pittsburgh Press, 2004): 236–251.

16. For a good discussion of Humphrey's delegate count before the California primary, see Nelson W. Polsby, *Consequences of Party Reform* (New York: Oxford University Press, 1983), 23–24; Dallek, *Flawed Giant*, 570–573; see also Jules Witcover, *The Year the Dream Died: Revisiting 1968* (New York: Warner Books, 1997), 315.

17. Solberg, *Hubert Humphrey*, 340. See also Kent Sieg, "The 1968 Presidential Election and Peace in Vietnam," *Presidential Studies Quarterly* 26 (Fall 1996): 1062–1063.

18. W. Marvin Watson, with Sherwin Markman, *Chief of Staff: Lyndon Johnson and His Presidency* (New York: Thomas Dunne Books, 2004), 297–298.

19. O'Brien, *No Final Victories*, 251. Connally and other hawks had every reason to doubt Humphrey's resolve. Almost certainly, they knew of an effort by his inner circle to float a proposal to end U.S. bombing on North Vietnam in return for a halt to the Communist shelling of Saigon. As shown to Johnson, this plan also envisaged a phased replacement of American combat forces with South Vietnamese troops. Accounts differ on whether Humphrey met with Johnson to discuss this idea. O'Brien wrote that such a meeting had been scheduled but that it did not happen. See his *No Final Victories*, 248–249. However, Solberg wrote that the meeting took place and that Johnson had subjected Humphrey to a tongue-lashing. He quoted a conversation between Humphrey and Ted Van Dyk, in which Humphrey said: "Well, the truth is that Johnson said I would be jeopardizing the lives of his two sons-in-law and endangering the chances of peace. If I announced this, he'd destroy me for the presidency." See Solberg, *Hubert Humphrey*, 348. Humphrey made no mention of this episode in *Education of a Public Man*.

20. Approved by a 62-to-35 vote in the Platform Committee, the administration plank called for a bombing halt in North Vietnam only if American troops would not be placed in jeopardy. It held out no promise of a reduction in aggressive actions against Communist forces in South Vietnam, and it allowed for a change of the Saigon government only after the war had ended. The minority plank called for an unconditional end to the bombing of the North, reduction of offensive operations in South Vietnam, and the withdrawal of U.S. troops. It also called on the South Vietnamese to negotiate peace. See *National Party Conventions, 1831–2000* (Washington, DC: Congressional Quarterly Press, 2001), 128.

21. Humphrey, *Education of a Public Man*, 389. On pp. 299–300 in *Chief of Staff*, Watson wrote that, "as firmly as possible," he told Humphrey that the nomination turned on his stand on Vietnam. Watson ended this conversation unconvinced that Humphrey would stand by the president, and he accordingly related these misgivings to Johnson, who promptly called Humphrey (rather than the other way around). Speaking "more in sadness than in anger," LBJ supposedly asked Humphrey, "How can you change your position now? You have been with me regarding Vietnam for more than four years. You have agreed with every decision we have made, every step we have taken. Our policy is as much yours as mine. How can you not know that?" Humphrey promised not to abandon the president's position. Watson returned with a list of

possible vice-presidential picks approved by Johnson. What LBJ really wanted, Watson wrote, "was a Humphrey running mate who would shore up Humphrey and prevent him from wandering from his commitment to support the programs of the President, including especially Vietnam." Humphrey picked Senator Edmund Muskie of Maine, evidently not on the list but acceptable to Johnson.

22. *National Party Conventions*, 128.

23. For accounts of the 1968 convention and the consequences for Humphrey, see Clifford, *Counsel to the President*, 565; Theodore H. White, *The Making of the President 1968: A Narrative History of American Politics in Action* (New York: Atheneum Publishers, 1969), 257–313; and Witcover, *Year the Dream Died*, 320–345.

24. Solberg, *Hubert Humphrey*, 340 and 375.

25. George Christian, *The President Steps Down: A Personal Memoir of the Transfer of Power* (New York: Macmillan, 1970), 163–165.

26. Harry McPherson, *A Political Education: A Journal of Life with Senators, Generals, Cabinet Members and Presidents* (Boston: Little, Brown, 1972), 449.

27. Max Frankel, "Humphrey Says Doves' Plank Would Have Been Acceptable," *NYT,* September 10, 1968, A1; R. W. Apple Jr., "Humphrey Hails Unity on Vietnam," *NYT,* September 11, 1968, A1; Solberg, *Hubert Humphrey*, 376; "Rusk's View on Troops," *NYT,* September 10, 1968, A30.

28. Neil Sheehan, "Johnson Asserts Raids Will Go on until Hanoi Acts," *NYT,* September 11, 1968, A1; "Excerpts from the President's Address to the American Legion," *NYT,* September 11, 1968, A16 (emphasis added).

29. Solberg, *Hubert Humphrey*, 377.

30. Sheehan, "Johnson Asserts Raids Will Go On."

31. Solberg, *Hubert Humphrey*, 377–379.

32. Ibid., 381–385; Max Frankel, "Kennedy Hails Humphrey; Jeers Mar Rally in Boston," *NYT,* September 20, 1968, A1. Hecklers also hounded Muskie, Nixon, Agnew, Wallace, and LeMay, but they generally were not as effective.

33. Witcover, *Year the Dream Died*, 376–377.

34. Humphrey, *Education of a Public Man*, 403.

35. Walter R. Mears, *Deadlines Past: Forty Years of Presidential Campaigning* (Kansas City, MO: Andrews McMeel Publishing, 2003), 90. "The thing that really racked Johnson up," Harry McPherson recalled years later, "was Humphrey's attempts to go both ways. The Salt Lake City speech didn't seem to say that one side would stop the bombing independently of any action on the other side, but at Kansas City Humphrey said, 'I would stop the bombing *period*' [emphasis original]. Johnson got furious with that." See Merle Miller, *Lyndon: An Oral Biography* (New York: G. P. Putnam's Sons, 1980), 524–525.

36. Lyndon Baines Johnson, *The Vantage Point: Perspectives on the Presidency, 1963–1969* (New York: Holt, Rinehart, and Winston, 1971), 549. Interestingly, leaders in Hanoi swiftly denounced Humphrey's proposal as nothing new, "always the same demand for reciprocity which we reject." They also noted that Humphrey had previously tried to undercut Johnson's war policy. See Hedrick Smith, "Hanoi Aides Rejected Humphrey's Plan," *NYT,* October 2, 1968, A1.

37. R. W. Apple, "Humphrey Hecklers Less Vocal since Speech on Vietnam Policy," *NYT,* October 8, 1968, A35.

38. LeMay spoke at length about plant and animal life on Bikini atoll after a score of nuclear bombs had been detonated in the vicinity: "The fish are all back in the lagoons; the coconut trees are growing coconuts; the guava bushes have fruit on them; the birds are back. As a matter of fact, everything is about the same except the land crabs. They get minerals from the soil,

I guess, through their shells, and the land crabs were a little bit 'hot,' and there's a little question about whether you should eat a land crab or not." Still, one should not overlook the rats, which had gotten "bigger, fatter, and healthier than they ever were before." He also said that the world would not end "if we explode a nuclear weapon." See Walter Rugaber, "Gen. LeMay Joins Wallace's Ticket as Running Mate," *NYT,* October 4, 1968, A1.

39. Carter, *Politics of Rage,* 362, wrote that the LeMay press conference "helped to crystallize the misgivings of voters who had been cautiously leaning toward George Wallace." Lesher, in *George Wallace,* p. 426, wrote that the wasted-vote argument took a higher toll than the LeMay flap.

40. In August, Gallup showed 12 percent of union members backing Wallace in nonsouthern states, whereas Humphrey led Nixon by 43 to 36 percent. Wallace laid claim to fully half of all union members in the South, compared with 29 percent for Humphrey and 16 percent for Nixon. See Gallup, *Gallup Poll: Public Opinion 1935–1971,* 2159. Gallup polling in September showed Wallace winning 25 percent of "manual workers" in national samples; see "Gallup Poll Finds Many Traditionally Democratic Voters Are Switching to Nixon," *NYT,* October 2, 1968, A25. The general board of the AFL-CIO unanimously endorsed the Humphrey-Muskie ticket in a September 18 statement attacking both Wallace and Nixon. It described Wallace's "pretense to be the friend of the worker" as particularly galling, given Alabama's record of "low wages, poor working conditions, high crime rates, high illiteracy rates, anti-unionism, segregation and prejudice." See Damon Stetson, "Labor Federation Supports Humphrey and Warns against Wallace," *NYT,* September 19, 1968, A37. See also "Unions Plan Opposing Wallace among Members," *NYT,* September 21, 1968, A17. For details of the steps labor took on Humphrey's behalf, see Lewis Chester, Godfrey Hodgson, and Bruce Page, *An American Melodrama: The Presidential Campaign of 1968* (New York: Viking Press, 1969), 707–710; also see Solberg, *Hubert Humphrey,* 388–389.

41. "McCarthy Backers Shift to Humphrey," *NYT,* October 4, 1968, A53; "Humphrey Receives Koch Endorsement," *NYT,* October 28, 1968, A38; John Herbers, "McCarthy Backs Humphrey Race; His Plans Vague," *NYT,* October 30, 1968, A1. Some, such as Paul O'Dwyer, the Democratic candidate for the U.S. Senate in New York, remained unyielding to the bitter end. See Steven V. Roberts, "Sadness Touches McCarthy People," *NYT,* October 30, 1968, A26. See also Dominic Sandbrook, *Eugene McCarthy: The Rise and Fall of Postwar American Liberalism* (New York: Alfred A. Knopf, 2004), 214–215.

42. Neil Sheehan, "Johnson Cautions on G.O.P. Victory," *NYT,* October 27, 1968, A1.

43. R. W. Apple, "Humphrey Hails Decision as Wise," *NYT,* November 1, 1968, A1.

44. For detailed accounts of Johnson's disappointments as a House member and the questionable election that catapulted him into the Senate, see Robert Caro, *Means of Ascent: The Years of Lyndon Johnson* (New York: Alfred A. Knopf, 1990).

45. An acclaimed actress, the ultraliberal Helen Gahagan Douglas gave up Hollywood for a career in Congress. She served with both Nixon and Johnson in the House and, by some accounts, became Johnson's lover. Johnson bitterly resented Nixon's tactics against Douglas when the two fought for California's open Senate seat. See Caro, *Master of the Senate,* 142–145, and Greg Mitchell, *Tricky Dick and the Pink Lady: Richard Nixon vs. Helen Gahagan Douglas* (New York: Random House, 1998).

46. See Dallek, *Flawed Giant,* 460; Robert Mann, *The Walls of Jericho: Lyndon Johnson, Richard Russell, and the Struggle for Civil Rights* (New York: Harcourt, Brace, 1996); and Caro, *Master of the Senate.* We discuss the Nixon-Johnson clash over the 1957 civil rights bill in the next chapter.

47. This paragraph draws partly from Jeffrey Kimball, *Nixon's Vietnam War* (Lawrence: University Press of Kansas, 1998), 29–31.

48. See Nixon's extended account of this episode in his *RN,* 337–342.

49. Clifford, *Counsel to the President*, 595.

50. Nixon, *RN*, 380–381; Sieg, "1968 Presidential Election and Peace in Vietnam," 1064.

51. See, for example, Nixon, *RN*, 390–391.

52. Ibid., 183–184.

53. Johnson did go after Nixon in an October 10 radio address praising Humphrey. See "Text of Johnson Talk Backing Humphrey," *NYT*, October 11, 1968, A53; also Stephen E. Ambrose, *Nixon: The Triumph of a Politician, 1962–1972*, vol. 2 (New York: Simon & Schuster, 1989), 200.

54. William Safire, *Before the Fall: An Inside View of the Pre-Watergate White House* (Garden City, NY: Doubleday, 1975), 84.

55. "Johnson Aide Will Ignore Nixon Unless 'Aroused,'" *NYT*, September 14, 1968, A16.

56. Nixon, *RN*, 398–403.

57. Ibid., 402. According to Kent Sieg, Johnson had sent Senator George Smathers, a Florida Democrat and longtime political ally, to inform Nixon of an impending breakthrough on October 14. Nixon is said to have expressed outrage and accused Johnson of playing a "political trick." Smathers reported this accusation to Johnson the following day. Sieg based this account on documents viewed at the Johnson presidential library. See Sieg, "The 1968 Presidential Election and Peace in Vietnam," 1070.

58. R. W. Apple, "Nixon Again Backs a Bombing Pause If It Costs No Lives," *NYT*, October 17, 1968, A1.

59. Sylvan Fox, "Johnson Shares Dais Here with Nixon and Humphrey," *NYT*, October 17, 1968, A1.

60. Nixon, *RN*, 403.

61. Ambrose also wrote that Johnson had told the truth—that Hanoi was still insisting on an unconditional bombing halt at that point. see Ambrose, *Nixon*, 208–209.

62. Nixon, *RN*, 404.

63. Safire, *Before the Fall*, 86.

64. Ibid.; also see Nixon, *RN*, 404.

65. Neil Sheehan, "Johnson Calls Nixon 'Unfair' in Implying Cynical Peace Move," *NYT*, October 28, 1968, A1. See also Safire, *Before the Fall*, 86, and Ambrose, *Nixon*, 205, 210.

66. One cable later publicized by Ambassador Diem informed President Thieu that "many Republican friends" had urged him to resist a new round of talks and not to soften his position. Another cable sent on October 27 argued that the longer the status quo remained intact, "the more we are favored." In the same communiqué, Diem claimed to be in regular contact "with the Nixon entourage." See Clifford, *Counsel to the President*, 582.

67. Ibid., 583.

68. For varying insider accounts of Johnson's reasons for not exposing the Chennault channel, see Clifford, *Counsel to the President*, 583–584 and 589, and also Watson, *Chief of Staff*, 304–305.

69. Nixon, *RN*, 399, 406. Nixon concluded that Johnson's announcement "unquestionably resulted in a last-minute surge of support for Humphrey. The militant liberals came back into the fold. . . . The bombing halt also undercut one of my most effective issues—the inability of the Democratic leadership to win a permanent peace."

70. Solberg, *Hubert Humphrey*, 397.

71. White, *Making of the President 1968*, 380; Ambrose, *Nixon*, 212.

72. Safire, *Before the Fall*, 87–88.

73. Nixon, *RN*, 406–407; Ambrose, *Nixon*, 213; Clifford, *Counsel to the President*, 594.

74. See Witcover, *Year the Dream Died*, 425–426. Humphrey made no direct reference to this meeting in *Education of a Public Man*.

75. "1968 Elections and Peace in Vietnam," 1072.

76. Chester et al., *American Melodrama*, 657–658. Wallace reportedly obtained sworn affidavits from every one of his slated electors, promising to vote for him on December 16 or for the candidate of his choice. See Ben A. Franklin, "'Wallace Phenomenon' Appears Contained in South," *NYT*, November 6, 1968, A23. The Nixon camp may have approached Wallace electors at some point during the fall campaign. In any case, DNC chairman O'Brien maintained that such contacts had been made. See Warren Weaver Jr., "O'Brien Sees a Nixon-Wallace 'Deal,'" *NYT*, October 20, 1968, A76.

77. See Carter, *Politics of Rage*, 339; also Lawrence D. Longley and Neal R. Peirce, *The Electoral College Primer 2000* (New Haven, CT: Yale University Press, 1999), 62–63. After the 1968 election, Wallace told Peirce that he "probably" would have chosen Nixon over Humphrey on ideological and policy grounds but that support would demand such concessions as an end to federal enforcement of civil rights.

78. Nixon, *RN*, 391–392.

79. This is also the case when one averages Republican attack scores for the weeks preceding the Salt Lake City speech (44.6 percent) and afterward (43.5 percent).

80. For one account of how much control Wallace exercised over the AIP, see J. David Gillespie, *Politics at the Periphery: Third Parties in Two-Party America* (Columbia: University of South Carolina Press, 1993), 110–120.

81. Although stung by Humphrey's characterization of him as "Richard the Chicken-Hearted," Nixon refused the challenge. "I was determined not to be lured into a confrontation," he later wrote, "since Humphrey was still far behind me in the polls, and would therefore be the beneficiary of any debate. Besides, as Humphrey knew, there was no way that he and I could have a debate without including George Wallace. Wallace's candidacy was depriving me of a substantial number of votes, and anything I did to elevate Wallace would be self-destructive. It was not fear but self-interest that determined my decision on the debates. Naturally, my unwillingness to debate gave Humphrey a major campaign issue." See Nixon, *RN*, 395.

82. "Excerpts from Address by Humphrey," *NYT*, September 9, 1968, A42.

83. Benjamin Welles, "Politics: O'Brien Tells Voters Not to Back Humphrey Rivals on Basis of Bigotry," *NYT*, September 15, 1968, A40. The same story quoted Representative Melvin Laird, chairman of the House Republican Conference, who phoned in a condemnation of O'Brien: "To equate Richard Nixon with George Wallace and in the same breath to suggest that the election of Nixon would or might lead to apartheid is the most irresponsible statement I have ever heard uttered by a supposedly responsible spokesman of a responsible party." Nixon replied two days later that Humphrey should instruct O'Brien and "some of his real hatchetmen to be a little more responsible in their statements." He went on to argue that Democratic policies pushed blacks into a "separate colony" of federal dependency whereas he wanted to draw them into the social and economic mainstream. See Robert B. Semple Jr., "Nixon Sees a Plot by Rivals in South," *NYT*, September 18, 1968, A1.

84. Here is an example from Humphrey's speech to New York's Liberal Party: "George Corley Wallace simply does not want peace and reconciliation. He generates division and disunity. He tries to catch votes by playing on fear and hate. And I say he is playing a dangerous game—a game that could tear this country apart." See Max Frankel, "Humphrey Chides Nixon on Agnew," *NYT*, October 10, 1968, A1.

85. Tom Wicker, "Agnew Criticizes Humphrey Record as 'Soft' on Reds," *NYT,* September 11, 1968, A1. Under pressure from Republican congressional leaders, Agnew retracted the charge and issued a public apology. See Homer Bigart, "Agnew Retracts Charge Humphrey Is 'Soft' on Reds," *NYT,* September 13, 1968, A1. Asked about Agnew's retraction, Humphrey replied, "I don't think he ever believed it in the first place. I think he just got hold of one of Mr. Nixon's old speeches." See Frankel, "Humphrey Scores 'The Same Old Nixon,'" *NYT,* September 14, 1968, A1.

86. Frankel, "Nixon Says Rival Is Using Wallace," *NYT,* September 28, 1968, A1; Robert B. Semple Jr., "Nixon Denounces Rivals," *NYT,* October 16, 1968, A31; E. W. Kenworthy, "Nixon Bids Protest Voter Think Twice on Wallace," *NYT,* October 9, 1968, A1.

87. Homer Bigart, "Agnew Tells Montana Crowd Democrats Are Lax on Crime," *NYT,* September 19, 1968, A38; "Agnew Is Critical of Wallace Race," *NYT,* October 4, 1968, A53; Ben A. Franklin, "Agnew Makes Bid for 'Protest' Vote," *NYT,* October 8, 1968, A33.

88. Franklin, "Wallace Presses Voters to Enroll," *NYT,* September 4, 1968, A1.

89. Walter Rugaber, "Thurmond Promotes Nixon's Cause Deep in Wallace Country," *NYT,* October 13, A77.

90. R. W. Apple, "Underdog Role Buoys Humphrey," *NYT,* September 6, 1968, A32.

91. "Text of Johnson Talk Backing Humphrey."

92. R. W. Apple, "Humphrey Appeals for Prompt Action on Nuclear Treaty," *NYT,* September 19, 1968, A1.

93. For example, see Max Frankel, "Humphrey Scores Nixon Arms Stand as 'Irresponsible,'" *NYT,* October 26, 1968, A1. See also Frankel, "Humphrey Sees a Build-Up in Impetus," *NYT,* October 27, 1968, A71, and his "Humphrey Pleads for Key Ohio Vote in Push for Upset," *NYT,* October 29, 1968, A1.

94. Early in the fall campaign, Humphrey sought to diminish the war as a Republican issue. On September 1, he pointed up similarities in the platforms of both parties on Vietnam and called for a joint declaration of support for U.S. negotiators in Paris as well as a common message to Hanoi: "North Vietnam must understand that a political campaign in the United States will not result in our granting to North Vietnam concessions which it cannot obtain through the legitimate process of negotiations now underway in Paris. The time to negotiate is now, not later. The time to stop the killing is now, not later." See "Humphrey to Nixon: Show Unity to Hanoi on Talks in Paris," *NYT,* September 2, 1968, A2. Rebuffed, he tried again on September 10, calling on Nixon and Wallace to join him in a public declaration that Hanoi would gain nothing by waiting until after the election to settle. R. W. Apple, "Humphrey Hails Unity on Vietnam."

95. Steven V. Roberts, "Senator Presses Attack in Kansas," *NYT,* September 21, 1968, A16.

96. "Transcript of Speech by the Vice President on Foreign Policy."

97. Max Frankel, "Humphrey's Election Bet," *NYT,* September 23, 1968, A30.

98. Neil Sheehan, "Ball Quits U.N. to Aid Humphrey; Editor Is Named," *NYT,* September 27, 1968, A1.

99. Drew Middleton, "Ball Says Thant Is Naïve on War," *NYT,* September 28, 1968, A1.

100. "Transcript of Speech by the Vice President on Foreign Policy."

101. R. W. Apple, "Humphrey Visits West Virginia, Hoping to Reverse 1960 Defeat," *NYT,* October 4, 1968, A1. The same story pointed out that Nixon had frequently ruled out the use of nuclear weapons in Vietnam.

102. "Humphrey Scores Nixon Talk, Saying He's 'Distorted the Facts,'" *NYT,* October 28, 1968, A38.

103. R. W. Apple, "Humphrey Prods Thieu to Join Parley," *NYT,* November 4, 1968, A1.

104. "Humphrey Assails Nixon War Report in Remote 'Debate,'" *NYT,* November 5, 1968, A28.

105. R. W. Apple, "Democrats Are Elated," *NYT*, November 5, 1968, A1.

106. Robert B. Semple Jr., "Nixon's Policy of Silence," *NYT*, September 7, 1968, A20; Homer Bigart, "Agnew Says Republican Ticket Has No Plan for Ending War," *NYT*, September 22, 1968.

107. Kimball, *Nixon's Vietnam War*, 43.

108. Nixon's promise to go easy on Johnson evidently did not apply to Agnew, who took Johnson to task for not prosecuting the war with sufficient vigor. In Texas, he described Vietnam as "the most politically mismanaged" war in U.S. history, and he decried the draft evasion and acts of civil disobedience that this conflict had spawned. See Homer Bigart, "Agnew Declares Peace Is Top Aim," *NYT*, September 18, 1968, A39. In California, he accused the administration of lying about the costs of financing the war and promised that a Nixon-Agnew administration would abolish the "credibility gap" and adopt a policy of "the truth—the whole truth." See Bigart, "Governor Vows Policy of Truth," *NYT*, September 21, 1968, A16.

109. Martin Tolchin, "Humphrey Offer Spurned by Nixon," *NYT*, September 3, 1968, A1.

110. Tom Wicker, "Agnew Criticizes Humphrey Record as 'Soft' on Reds."

111. "Agnew Scores Humphrey," *NYT*, September 12, 1968, A36.

112. Robert B. Semple Jr., "Nixon Backs Nuclear Pact, but Asks Delay by Senate," *NYT*, September 12, 1968, A1.

113. "Laird Reports Troop Cut Plan," *NYT*, September 25, 1968, A1.

114. E. W. Kenworthy, "Nixon Says Humphrey Harms Efforts of U.S. in Paris Talks," *NYT*, September 26, 1968, A1.

115. Kenworthy, "Nixon Asks Clarifications Lest Foe Be Misled," *NYT*, October 2, 1968, A1.

116. Ben A. Franklin, "Agnew Deplores Humphrey's Talk," *NYT*, October 2, 1968, A24.

117. John W. Finney, "Senate G.O.P., Urged by Nixon, Attacks Humphrey's War Stand," *NYT*, October 4, 1968, A51.

118. Robert B. Semple Jr., "Nixon Asserts Humphrey Confuses Vietnam Talks," *NYT*, October 24, 1968, A1; E. W. Kenworthy, "Nixon Links Rival to 'Security Gap,'" *NYT*, November 2, 1968, A1.

119. James F. Clarity, "G.O.P. Cancels Commercial Showing Humphrey Grinning Amid Distress," *NYT*, October 30, 1968, A28.

120. Robert B. Semple Jr., "Nixon Hopes Johnson Step Will Aid the Talks in Paris," *NYT*, November 1, 1968, A1.

121. Warren Weaver Jr., "Democrats Fear Saigon's Boycott May Cost Votes," *NYT*, November 3, 1968, A1.

122. Robert B. Semple Jr., "Republican Stresses Paris," *NYT*, November 5, 1968, A1.

123. Senator Mike Mansfield launched a similar attack. See "LeMay's Remarks 'Shock' Humphrey," *NYT*, October 4, 1968, A51; "Mansfield Criticizes LeMay," *NYT*, October 4, 1968, A51.

124. Robert B. Semple Jr., "Humphrey Scorns Nixon as Furtive," *NYT*, October 8, 1968, A1.

125. John W. Finney, "Humphrey Taunts Nixon as 'Chicken,'" *NYT*, October 16, 1968, A1.

126. Warren Weaver, "Muskie Comes on Strong with Down East Candor Down East," *NYT*, October 13, 1968, A68.

127. Homer Bigart, "Nixon, Abandoning Silence on Wallace, Attacks," *NYT*, October 4, 1968, A50; E. W. Kenworthy, "Nixon Bids Protest Voter Think Twice on Wallace"; Ben A. Franklin, "Agnew 'Worried' by LeMay's Stand," *NYT*, October 5, 1968, A20.

128. Franklin, "Agnew in Alaska on One-Stop Visit," *NYT*, October 6, 1968, A77; for more Agnew attacks, see Thomas A. Johnson, "Agnew Cheered and Heckled in Maryland," *NYT*, October 12, 1968, A24; Thomas A. Johnson, "Agnew Solicits Wallace Votes," *NYT*, October 18, 1968, A28.

129. "Romney Assails the Wallace Ticket," *NYT*, October 5, 1968, A24; Irving Spiegel, "City Trades Council Endorse Javits," *NYT*, October 5, 1968, A22; Spiegel, "Javits Criticizes Wallace's Stand," *NYT*, October 6, 1968, A66.

130. Quotes from James T. Wooten, "Politics: 16,000 in Madison Square Garden Cheer Wallace," *NYT,* October 25, 1968, A32.

131. Roy Reed, "Wallace Taunts Nixon to Debate," *NYT,* September 19, 1968, A38.

132. Homer Bigart, "Politics: LeMay Blames 'Traitors' in U.S. for China's Entrance into Korean War," *NYT,* October 15, 1968, A34.

133. Bigart, "LeMay Says Bomb Curb Wastes American Lives," *NYT,* October 20, 1968, A1.

134. Jerry M. Flint, "LeMay Asserts Peace Gesture May Be a Trick," *NYT,* October 23, 1968, A17.

135. "Vietnam Peace Bid Is Worrying LeMay," *NYT,* October 27, 1968, A68.

136. On Ford's understanding of economics, see A. James Reichley, *Conservatives in an Age of Change: The Nixon and Ford Administrations* (Washington, DC: Brookings, 1981), 384. Reichley offers perhaps the most extensive discussion of Ford's economic policy published to date.

137. Accused of taking payoffs for much of his political career, including his vice presidency, Agnew at first professed innocence and vowed to fight. Behind this show of defiance, however, he negotiated a deal with the Justice Department that allowed a no-contest plea to a single charge of tax evasion, with a $10,000 fine and a suspended sentence of three years, subject to good behavior, in return for his resignation. Nixon approved in order to avoid impeachment proceedings that would affect his situation. The federal judge in Baltimore went along with the plea bargain because he deemed the national interest in this case "so great and compelling." See Jules Witcover, *Crapshoot: Rolling the Dice on the Vice Presidency* (New York: Crown, 1992), 213–263. Agnew protested his innocence in a book, *Go Quietly . . . Or Else* (New York: Morrow, 1980). On April 27, 1981, however, a Maryland judge ordered Agnew to pay $247,735 as compensation for bribes and kickbacks received while in high office. See Joseph Nathan Kane, *Presidential Fact Book* (New York: Random House, 1998), 251.

138. Nixon later wrote that he wanted to nominate Connally but became convinced that the Democrats in Congress would block his nomination. Connally in this account agreed with Nixon's judgment. Nixon picked Ford on grounds of his qualifications, ideological affinity, loyalty, and likelihood of prompt confirmation. See Nixon, *RN: The Memoirs of Richard Nixon,* vol. 2 (New York: Warner Books, 1978), 481–482.

139. The Senate confirmed Ford by a vote of 92 to 3 in November, and the House followed suit in December by a vote of 387 to 35. See William A. DeGregorio, *The Complete Book of U.S. Presidents: From George Washington to George W. Bush* (New York: Gramercy Books, 2001), 609. For Ford's account of the confirmation experience, see his *A Time to Heal* (New York: Berkley Books, 1980), 99–109.

140. This paragraph draws from Ford's account in *Time to Heal,* 109–120; Theodore H. White, *Breach of Faith: The Fall of Richard Nixon* (New York: Atheneum, 1975), 3–35; and John Robert Greene, *The Presidency of Gerald R. Ford* (Lawrence: University Press of Kansas, 1995), 13–17. Eleven days after becoming president, Ford nominated Nelson Rockefeller for vice president even though a White House poll showed leading Republicans favoring George Bush by a substantial margin. When questions arose about Bush's receipt of money from a Nixon slush fund during his unsuccessful Senate race against Lloyd Bentsen, Ford offered the job to Rockefeller. The choice outraged conservative Republicans, in and out of Congress, who viewed the liberal New Yorker as evil incarnate. Liberal Democrats also expressed reservations once the magnitude of Rockefeller's personal fortune was revealed. The fact that he also owed $1 million in back taxes added to his confirmation woes. Rockefeller appeared eight times before the Senate Rules Committee and nine times before the House Judiciary Committee between September 23 and December 5. Following their victories in the 1974 midterm elections, some Democrats wanted

to postpone a confirmation vote until the new Congress took office. After promising to put his finances in a blind trust and pay his taxes, Rockefeller finally won approval in both houses. He took the vice-presidential oath of office on December 19, 1974. See Greene, *Presidency of Gerald R. Ford*, 30–31; Reichley, *Conservatives in an Age of Change*, 300–301. Under pressure from Republican conservatives, Ford replaced Rockefeller with Senator Robert Dole as his 1976 running mate.

141. Ford, *Time to Heal*, 154–155.

142. Ibid., 155–175. See also John Herbers, "Ford Gives Pardon to Nixon, Who Regrets 'My Mistakes,'" *NYT*, September 9, 1974, A1.

143. Mark J. Rozell, *The Press and the Ford Presidency* (Ann Arbor: University of Michigan Press, 1992), 51–85. Greene, *Presidency of Gerald R. Ford*, 61; see also Jules Witcover, *Marathon: The Pursuit of the Presidency, 1972–1976* (New York: Viking Press, 1977), 44. For Ford's account of the initial reaction, see his *Time to Heal*, 174–177.

144. Gallup, *Gallup Poll: Public Opinion 1972–1977*. In the second prepardon poll, 66 percent approved of Ford's performance and 13 percent disapproved.

145. Ford, *Time to Heal*, 191–194; Greene, *Presidency of Gerald R. Ford*, 56–58.

146. Gary Orren, "Fall from Grace: The Public's Loss of Faith in Government," in Joseph S. Nye Jr., Philip D. Zelikow, and David C. King, eds., *Why People Don't Trust Government* (Cambridge, MA: Harvard University Press, 1997), 80. See also Charles Jones, *The Trusteeship Presidency: Jimmy Carter and the United States Congress* (Baton Rouge: Louisiana State University, 1988), 16–17.

147. In early 1975, Carter appeared as a contestant on the television show *What's My Line?* and came away a winner of sorts because none of the panelists could guess his identity or vocation. See Greene, *Presidency of Gerald R. Ford*, 175. Only a trace of support showed up for him in Gallup's earliest trial heat polls on contenders for the 1976 Democratic nomination. Starting at a fraction of a percentage point, he remained below 4 percent in Gallup's final poll before Iowa. See Emmett H. Buell Jr., "The Invisible Primary," in William G. Mayer, ed., *In Pursuit of the White House: How We Choose Our Presidential Nominees* (Chatham, NJ: Chatham House, 1996), 1–43.

148. Jimmy Carter, *Why Not the Best?* (Nashville, TN: Broadman Press, 1975).

149. Ibid., 154.

150. Witcover, *Marathon*, 198–199.

151. Michael Schudson, *Watergate in American Memory: How We Remember, Forget, and Reconstruct the Past* (New York: Basic Books, 1993), 74.

152. Carter unleashed the following attack on September 7: "When big and little people see Richard Nixon lying, cheating and leaving the highest office in disgrace and the previous attorney general violating the law and admitting it, when you see the head of the FBI break a little law and stay there, it gives everybody the sense that crime must be OK. If the big shots in Washington can get away with it, well so can I." See James Wooten, "Carter 'Would Have' Ousted Kelley, but Won't Say He Will If President," *NYT*, September 8, 1976, A1.

153. R. W. Apple, "Carter Seen Ending Erosion of His Lead by Taking Offensive," *NYT*, October 8, 1976, A1.

154. Ford, *Time to Heal*, 403–404, 412–413; Greene, *Presidency of Gerald R. Ford*, 179–181; Philip Shabecoff, "GOP Fund-Raising in Michigan Studied," *NYT*, September 22, 1976, A1; John M. Crewdson, "Ford Linked by Dean to '72 Fund Problem," *NYT*, September 23, 1976, A36; Christopher Lydon, "U.S. Steel Reports It Entertained Ford," *NYT*, September 24, 1976, A1; Nicholas M. Horrock, "Possible Covert Union Gifts to Ford from '64 to '74 Called Target of Inquiry by Watergate Prosecutor," *NYT*, September 26, 1976, A1; Shabecoff, "Ford Was a Corporate Golf Guest Numerous Times While in House," *NYT*, September 29, 1976, A22; Shabecoff, "Ford Disclaims

Diverting Funds to His Own Use," *NYT,* October 1, 1976, A1; Horrock, "Prosecutor Reports No Violation by Ford on Political Funds," *NYT,* October 15, 1976, A1; "Dole Denies Charge by Mondale," *NYT,* October 7, 1976, A30.

155. Nicholas M. Horrock, "Dole Is Reported Linked to '73 Gift by Gulf Oil Aide," *NYT,* September 6, 1976, A1; Horrock, "Ex-Lobbyist Recants on 1970 Gift to Dole," *NYT,* September 9, 1976, A1.

156. Gerald M. Pomper, "The Presidential Election," in Marlene M. Pomper, ed., *The Election of 1976: Reports and Interpretations* (New York: David McKay, 1977), 65. Democratic identifiers greatly outnumbered self-identified Republicans in Gallup Polls of 1975 and 1976. See Gallup, *Gallup Poll: Public Opinion 1972–1977.* A more elaborate breakdown provided by the 1976 American National Election Study (Center for Political Studies at the University of Michigan) also showed a decided Democratic advantage: Strong Democrats 15 percent, Weak Democrats 26 percent, Independent Democrats 11 percent, Independent Republicans 10 percent, Weak Republicans 14 percent, and Strong Republicans 9 percent. See Harold W. Stanley and Richard G. Niemi, *Vital Statistics on American Politics,* 4th ed. (Washington, DC: Congressional Quarterly Press, 1994), 158.

157. This paragraph draws on Reichley, *Conservatives in an Age of Change,* 390–406; Herbert Stein, *Presidential Economics,* 3rd ed. rev. (Washington, DC: American Enterprise Institute for Public Policy Research, 1994), 209; and Greene, *Presidency of Gerald R. Ford,* 67.

158. Greene, *Presidency of Gerald R. Ford,* 71–72; Reichley, *Conservatives in an Age of Change,* 390–391.

159. Gary C. Jacobson, *The Politics of Congressional Elections,* 6th ed. (New York: Pearson/ Longman, 2004), 154; Andrew E. Busch, *Horses in Midstream: U.S. Midterm Elections and Their Consequences, 1894–1998* (Pittsburgh, PA: University of Pittsburgh Press, 1999), 110. For varying perspectives on the relative importance of the pardon and other effects of Watergate versus economic problems on the 1974 elections, see Eric M. Uslaner, M. Margaret Conway, Gary C. Jacobson, and Samuel Kernell, "Interpreting the 1974 Congressional Election," *American Political Science Review* 80 (June 1986): 591–595.

160. Reichley, *Conservatives in an Age of Change,* 391–392.

161. Ibid., 392–394.

162. Ibid., 395–396.

163. Ibid., 397–398.

164. Ford, *Time to Heal,* 414–415; Reichley, *Conservatives in an Age of Change,* 401–404; see especially Marsh's statement on p. 403.

165. Martin Schram, *Running for President 1976: The Carter Campaign* (New York: Stein and Day, 1977), 269–270. See also James M. Naughton, "Ford to Aim at New York, New Jersey and 8 Other Key Industrial States," *NYT,* September 23, 1976, A1. Ultimately, Ford carried five of the battleground states (California, Illinois, Indiana, Michigan, and New Jersey), as well as fifteen states designated safely Republican, plus six more that Republican strategists categorized as swing states (Alaska, Connecticut, Montana, Oregon, Virginia, and Washington). New York would have put him over the top (Ford trailed there by roughly 289,000 votes out of more than 6.5 million cast); otherwise, a win in Pennsylvania, Texas, or Ohio would have fallen three to five electoral votes short of a majority, in which case Ford needed one more medium state such as Missouri, Kentucky, or Tennessee.

166. Witcover, *Marathon,* 528.

167. Schram, *Running for President,* 271.

168. Ibid., 253–261. Ford wrote that his pollster, Bob Teeter, "worked with his own figures

which projected that I could lose the election by 9,490,000 votes. There were seventy-three days left until November 2. All I had to do to win, Teeter pointed out, was convert 130,000 Carter supporters every day." See Ford, *Time to Heal*, 396.

169. Schram, *Running for President*, 263–268. See also Ford, *Time to Heal*, 398–399.

170. Greene, *Presidency of Gerald R. Ford*, 177.

171. Ford, *Time to Heal*, 398.

172. Witcover, *Marathon*, 553.

173. Ibid., 566–570; see also Charles Mohr, "Carter on Morals, Talks with Candor," *NYT*, September 21, 1976, A1.

174. Lee Dembart, "Carter's Comments on Sex Cause Concern," *NYT*, September 21, 1976, A1.

175. Schram, *Running for President*, 304.

176. Gallup, *Gallup Poll 1972–1977*, vol. 2, 889–892. Gallup asked about the *Playboy* interview in an October 8 poll.

177. Charles Mohr, "Carter in Texas, Says He's Sorry about His Criticism of Johnson," *NYT*, September 25, 1976, A14. See James Wooten, *Dasher: The Roots and Rising of Jimmy Carter* (New York: Summit Books, 1978), 34–35, for an account of Carter's effort to wiggle out of the Johnson condemnation. On another occasion, according to Wooten, Carter said of Nixon, "I despise the bastard but I pray that he will find peace."

178. Mohr, "Carter Assails Role of Lobbyists in 'Bloated Mess' of Government," *NYT*, September 28, 1976, A1.

179. Deidre Carmody, "Ford and Carter Forces Dispute G.O.P. Ad Showing Playboy Cover," *NYT*, October 22, 1976, A17.

180. Text of debate reprinted in Lloyd Bitzer and Theodore Rueter, *Carter vs. Ford: The Counterfeit Debates of 1976* (Madison: University of Wisconsin Press, 1980), 299–300.

181. Ibid.

182. See Witcover, *Marathon*, 594–608; Charles Mohr, "Ford Accuses Carter of 'Moral Conceit,' Admits Error in Remark on East Europe," *NYT*, October 13, 1976, A24.

183. James Wooten, "Carter Charges Ford and Nixon with Failure to Halt Rising Crime," *NYT*, October 16, 1976, A7.

184. Gallup, *Gallup Poll: Public Opinion 1972–1977*, vol. 2, 881–882. For one assessment of the importance of this effect on Ford's campaign, see James E. Campbell, *The American Campaign: U.S. Presidential Campaigns and the National Vote* (College Station: Texas A&M University Press, 2000), 181.

185. Aside from comments on the *Playboy* interview, we noted rumors of marital infidelity on Carter's part that allegedly came from Republican sources, according to columnist Jack Anderson. See Joseph Lelyveld's account, "Widespread Rumors Besmirching Carter Posed Problems in Ethics for News Media," *NYT*, October 16, 1976, A7.

186. These indicators bear a close resemblance to the variables comprising our combined leadership topic.

187. Greene, *Presidency of Gerald R. Ford*, 187.

188. Charles Mohr, "Carter Opens Drive by Denouncing Ford as Timid President," *NYT*, September 7, 1976, A1.

189. Mohr, "Carter Tries Out a Rougher Style in His Campaign," *NYT*, September 29, 1976, A1.

190. R. W. Apple, "Carter Attacks Ford, Ford Defends U.S. Foreign Stance in 2d Debate," *NYT*, October 7, 1976, A1.

191. Apple, "Ford and Carter, in Last Debate, Promise to Put Stress on Issues," *NYT,* October 24, 1976, A1.

192. Apple, "Ford and Carter Give Final Appeals in Race Still Viewed as Close," *NYT,* November 2, 1976, A1; Charles Mohr, "Carter Focuses on Two Key States," *NYT,* November 2, 1976, A1.

193. Mohr, "Carter's Style Is Mild but Far from Bland," *NYT,* September 11, 1976, A20.

194. The *Times* reported this argument in language better suited for an editorial than a news story: "Moreover, while Mr. Carter has been both confronting a probing press corps and crossing the nation with regularity, the President has made but three brief campaign journeys outside the White House in the six weeks since he won the Republican nomination. Instead, Mr. Ford has remained in the protective cocoon of the White House, producing a succession of bill-signing ceremonies, Rose Garden meetings and messages to Congress as news media events meant to underline his occupancy of the White House." James M. Naughton, "Incumbent Role a Boon to Ford," *NYT,* October 1, 1976, A1; Mohr, "Carter Assails Role of Lobbyists"; "Carter, in Comments on the Press, Asserts Accessibility Is Key Issue," *NYT,* September 30, 1976, A32.

195. Naughton, "Carter Assails Ford on 'Serious Blunder,'" *NYT,* October 8, 1976, A18.

196. Naughton, "Carter Turns to Biting Language in Effort to Capitalize on Debate," *NYT,* October 11, 1976, A1.

197. Joseph Lelyveld, "Focus in the Hall and on the TV Set Differed," *NYT,* September 25, 1976, A8.

198. Charles Mohr, "Carter Scores Ford on Missiles Sale," *NYT,* October 1, 1976, A19.

199. James M. Naughton, "Remark by Ford Is Aid to Carter at Rally in Ohio," *NYT,* October 10, 1976, A1.

200. Ibid.

201. James M. Naughton, "Carter Says He'd Never Increase Income Tax on Wages of Workers," *NYT,* October 15, 1976, B5.

202. James Wooten, "Carter Vows to End Boycott of Israel," *NYT,* October 20, 1976, A28.

203. William Robbins, "Butz Quits under Fire amid Rising Protests about Racist Remark," *NYT,* October 5, 1976, A1; see also Ford, *Time to Heal,* 406–407.

204. R. W. Apple, "Carter Emphasizing Mondale as An Asset," *NYT,* October 29, 1976, A1.

205. Linda Charlton, "Daley Welcomes Mondale at End of Whistle Stopping Train Trip," *NYT,* September 22, 1976, A24.

206. Charlton, "Mondale Marches in Two Parades, Sharing Spotlight with Republicans," *NYT,* October 11, 1976, A52.

207. Charlton, "Daley Welcomes Mondale."

208. Wayne King, "Rosalynn Carter, a Tough, Tireless Campaigner, Displays Same Driving Quality as Her Husband," *NYT,* October 18, 1976, A34.

209. Thomas P. Ronan, "Westchester Democrats, in Welcoming Mondale, Predict a Tough Battle," *NYT,* October 3, 1976, A31.

210. "Carey Is Host to Jimmy Carter's Son on Tour Upstate," *NYT,* October 22, 1976, A17.

211. Naughton, "Remark by Ford Is Aid to Carter."

212. Christopher Lydon, "Dole Makes Joking a Campaign Device," *NYT,* September 19, 1976, A38.

213. Douglas E. Kneeland, "Dole Charges Rivals Pose Peril to Texas," *NYT,* September 11, 1976, A26.

214. R. W. Apple, "Economy Is Stressed by Dole and Mondale during Sharp Debate," *NYT,* October 16, 1976, A1.

215. Douglas E. Kneeland, "Dole Is Stepping Up Attacks on Carter," *NYT,* September 29, 1976, A22.

216. Kneeland, "Dole, Stumping through the Midwest, Is Defending President's Farm Record and Sharply Attacking Carter," *NYT*, October 19, 1976, A29.

217. James M. Naughton, "Dole Sees G.O.P. Gain in Carter Campaign," *NYT*, October 2, 1976, A10.

218. Douglas E. Kneeland, "Dole, Campaigning in South Again, Sharpens Sallies against Rivals," *NYT*, October 7, 1976, A39.

219. Kneeland, "Dole Ends Campaign Cheered by Outlook," *NYT*, November 2, 1976, A18.

220. Liberal Democrats lost enthusiasm for Rockefeller as vice president upon discovering the magnitude of his personal fortune. The fact that he owed $1 million back taxes complicated matters further. Rockefeller appeared eight times before the Senate Rules Committee and testified nine times to the House Judiciary Committee. After their victories in the 1974 midterm elections, Democrats pondered a further delay until the new Congress in January 1975. Rockefeller overcame this resistance by promising to pay his back taxes and put his fortune in a blind trust. He was sworn in on December 19, 1974. See Greene, *Presidency of Gerald R. Ford*, 13–17; Reichley, *Conservatives in an Age of Change*, 300–301.

221. Richard Halloran, "Relaxed Rockefeller Enjoys Campaigning for Ford-Dole," *NYT*, September 25, 1976, A5.

222. R. W. Apple, "Debate Is Regarded as Draw by Experts within Both Parties," *NYT*, September 25, 1976, A1.

223. James M. Naughton, "Marked Contrast Cited by Connally," *NYT*, October 31, 1976, A34.

224. Naughton, "President in a Bid to 'Non-Republicans,'" *NYT*, October 7, 1976, A39.

225. Naughton, "Ford Says Remarks by Rival on Kelley Are 'Contradictory,'" *NYT*, September 9, 1976, A1.

226. "Ford Says Abortion Won't Be Exploited as Campaign Issue," *NYT*, September 12, 1976, A28.

227. James M. Naughton, "Ford Opens Drive, Pledging 'Specifics' Instead of 'Smiles,'" *NYT*, September 16, 1976, A1.

228. R. W. Apple, "Ford and Carter, in First Debate, Trade Charges on Economic Issue," *NYT*, September 24, 1976, A1.

229. Lelyveld, "Focus in the Hall and on the TV Set Differed."

230. Charles Mohr, "Ford, Trying to Bind Up Wound, Backs Freedom for East Europe," *NYT*, October 8, 1976, A18.

231. Mohr, "Ford Presses Drive to Gain Texas Votes," *NYT*, October 10, 1976, A1.

232. Mohr, "Ford Accuses Carter of 'Moral Conceit.'"

233. Mohr, "Ford Terms Carter Quick-Change Artist," *NYT*, October 16, 1976, A7.

234. Mohr, "President Asserts Carter Will Say 'Anything Anywhere' to Be Elected," *NYT*, October 17, 1976, A1.

235. Ibid.; see also James Wooten, "Carter Asks Ford to Stop Making 'Erroneous' Statements about Him," *NYT*, October 17, 1976, A1 (lead story).

236. R. W. Apple, "Campaign '76: Barren and Petty," *NYT*, October 20, 1976, A1.

237. James M. Naughton, "Ford Scores Carter over Boycott Stand," *NYT*, October 21, 1976, A44.

238. Bitzer and Rueter, *Carter vs. Ford*, 327.

239. Ibid., 327–328.

240. Ibid., 328–329.

241. Ibid., 350–353; see also R. W. Apple, "Ford and Carter, in Last Debate, Promise to Put Stress on Key Issues," *NYT*, October 22, 1976, A1, the source of this attack for our study.

242. Apple, "Ford Tactic: TV 'Documentary' Plus Chat with Sports Announcer," *NYT*, October 26, 1976, A29.

CHAPTER 5. THE DEAD HEAT RACE OF 1960

1. Richard N. Goodwin, *Remembering America: A Voice from the Sixties* (New York: Harper & Row, 1988), 103.

2. See George H. Gallup, ed., *The Gallup Poll: Public Opinion 1935–1971*, vol. 3 (New York: Random House, 1972).

3. Ibid.

4. Richard M. Nixon, *Six Crises*, Richard Nixon Library ed. (New York: Touchstone Books, 1990), 303 and 306.

5. Theodore H. White, *The Making of the President: A Narrative History of American Politics in Action*, Classic Bestseller ed. (New York: Barnes & Noble Books, 2004), 355–356. For a recent experimental study affirming the importance of television images in the first Kennedy-Nixon debate, see James N. Druckman, "The Power of Television Images: The First Kennedy-Nixon Debate Revisited," *Journal of Politics* 65 (May 2003): 559–571.

6. While he was still Kennedy's rival for the Democratic nomination, Majority Leader Johnson and his patron in the House, Speaker Sam Rayburn, hit upon the idea of holding a special session of Congress to promote Johnson, whom they expected to emerge as the eventual nominee in Los Angeles. Neither man anticipated Kennedy's first-ballot victory or the potential for the embarrassment that House and Senate Republicans would inflict on Kennedy and Johnson during the special session.

7. Nixon, *Six Crises*, 327.

8. Ibid., 375–376. Nixon traveled more than 65,000 miles after Labor Day; made 180 scheduled speeches; delivered at least as many impromptu speeches; and submitted to countless interviews, press conferences, radio and television appearances.

9. Richard Nixon, *RN: The Memoirs of Richard Nixon*, vol. 1 (New York: Warner Books, 1978), 269–270.

10. Robert Dallek discussed Kennedy's precarious health and drug use in detail. See Dallek, *An Unfinished Life: John F. Kennedy, 1917–1963* (Boston: Back Bay Books, 2003).

11. Theodore Sorensen, *Kennedy* (New York: Harper & Row, 1965), 179.

12. Ibid., 187.

13. Ibid., 179.

14. Goodwin, *Remembering America*, 130.

15. Nixon, *Six Crises*, 380.

16. In *Six Crises* (p. 320), Nixon wrote: "To balance our anticipated losses there [the big northeastern states], we needed every western, southern, and Midwestern state we could possibly win." He termed the Texas projection "our most discouraging news" (p. 382).

17. When Texas Democrats held their party convention on September 20, the delegates passed a resolution disavowing parts of the national party platform. They also booed at the mention of Johnson's bid for reelection to the Senate (at the same time he was running for vice president). Still, the convention voted to replace two Texas electors unwilling to vote for Kennedy. Johnson was not present for these festivities. See Gladwin Hill, "Texas Democrats Disown Party's National Platform," *NYT*, September 21, 1960, A1. More than a few conservative Democrats in Texas

accused LBJ of selling out on civil rights; anti-Catholic feelings also ran high. In mid-October, worried that Nixon would carry Texas, Johnson confided to his longtime ally John Connally that a Democratic victory without Texas would be terrible: "Imagine when we win how the next administration will look upon us." Jim Rowe, another aide, recalled Johnson being "wound up tight like a top" for constant fear of losing Texas. See Robert Dallek, *Lone Star Rising: Lyndon Johnson and His Times, 1908–1960* (New York: Oxford University Press, 1991), 586–588.

18. *Presidential Elections, 1789–1996* (Washington, DC: Congressional Quarterly Press, 1997), 118.

19. Ibid., 389–390.

20. Sorensen, *Kennedy*, 212.

21. Nixon, *Six Crises*, 388. The absentee vote put Nixon over the top in California by half a percentage point out of more than 6.5 million votes cast.

22. Nixon, *RN*, 276.

23. Dallek granted that "Daley's machine probably stole Illinois from Nixon," but he rightly noted that Kennedy would have won an electoral majority in any case. See Dallek, *Unfinished Life*, 295. Stephen E. Ambrose expressed a similar view in *Nixon: The Education of a Politician, 1913–1962* (New York: Simon & Schuster, 1997), 186. For an extended discussion of how Daley's machine managed it, see Adam Cohen and Elizabeth Taylor, *American Pharaoh: Mayor Richard Daley, His Battle for Chicago and the Nation* (Boston: Back Bay Books, 2000), 270–279. Andrew Gumbel challenged this analysis in *Steal This Vote: Dirty Elections and the Rotten History of Democracy in America* (New York: Nation Books, 2005), 161–169. Seymour M. Hersh argued that the Mafia assisted in the theft of Illinois per an agreement with Joe Kennedy, the candidate's father. See Hersh, *The Dark Side of Camelot* (Boston: Back Bay Books, 1997), 131–154.

24. Nixon, *RN*, 277.

25. Ibid., 278–279. Dick Tuck, a California Democrat, persecuted Nixon for more than two decades. He stung first when Nixon ran for the U.S. Senate seat in 1950. He struck again in 1956, when certain Republicans tried to remove Nixon from the ticket. Tuck appeared at the Republicans' San Francisco convention, and upon learning that city garbage trucks drove by the convention hall, he arranged to festoon each with "Dump Nixon" signs. In 1960, Tuck masqueraded as a fire marshal, which enabled him to mislead reporters about the size of crowds at Nixon rallies. Disguised as a Nixon campaign operative, he instructed a band to play "Mack the Knife" at one rally just as Nixon walked on stage. He also hired a middle-aged woman to embrace Nixon immediately after he returned to his hotel from the first debate. "That's all right," she loudly proclaimed with reporters looking on, "you'll do better next time." Reportedly, Tuck even bribed a fortune cookie company to insert the same message—"Kennedy will win"—in every cookie served at a Nixon dinner in San Francisco's Chinatown. Supposedly, during a reprise of the old-fashioned whistle-stop campaign, Tuck passed himself off as a train conductor and signaled the engineer to depart in the middle of a Nixon speech. He also played dirty tricks during Nixon's 1962 bid to become governor of California, and keying on the 1968 campaign slogan, "Nixon's the one," Tuck hired visibly pregnant women to appear at the candidate's rallies, holding up "Nixon's the one" signs. See Christopher Matthews, *Kennedy and Nixon: The Rivalry That Shaped Postwar America* (New York: Simon & Schuster, 1996); also see http://www.museumofhoaxes.com/tuck.html.

26. Nixon, *RN*, 279.

27. For the fifteen polls summarized in this paragraph, see Gallup, *Gallup Poll: Public Opinion 1935–1971*, vol. 3.

28. Emmet John Hughes, *The Ordeal of Power: A Political Memoir of the Eisenhower Years* (New York: Atheneum, 1963), 320.

29. For Ike's account of this meeting and his stated reasons for choosing Nixon, see Dwight D. Eisenhower, *Mandate for Change, 1953–1956* (Garden City, NY: Doubleday, 1963), 46.

30. Roger Morris, *Richard Milhous Nixon: The Rise of an American Politician* (New York: Henry Holt, 1990), 757–850. For Nixon, this episode was an emotional roller coaster of sufficient magnitude to qualify as the second of the momentous ordeals described in his *Six Crises* (see pp. 73–129). Eisenhower later described the fund flap as "the most troublesome problem of the entire campaign." For his version of events, see Eisenhower, *Mandate for Change*, 65–69.

31. Ambrose, *Nixon, Education of a Politician*, 384–408.

32. Fred I. Greenstein, *The Hidden-Hand Presidency: Eisenhower as Leader* (New York: Basic Books, 1982), 63. See Nixon, *Six Crises*, 152–167, for Nixon's account of the 1956 "dump Nixon" episode. Eisenhower concluded *Mandate for Change* with a lengthy discussion of how and why he decided to run in 1956 that makes no mention of Nixon (pp. 566–575).

33. For varying accounts of what transpired between Nixon and Rockefeller, see White, *Making of the President*, 234–252; Nixon, *Six Crises*, 313–316; Robert A. Divine, *Foreign Policy and U.S. Presidential Elections, 1952–1960* (New York: New Viewpoints, 1974), 221–226; Ambrose, *Nixon*, 550–553.

34. Divine, *Foreign Policy*, 227.

35. Ibid., 559–560 and 574. Ike belatedly tried to repair the damage when speaking via closed-circuit television to 38,000 Republicans attending four $100-a-plate dinners. "As a person ready to enter the duties of the presidential office," he declared, "Dick Nixon has the broadest and deepest preparation and experience of any man I know." See Felix Belair Jr., "Eisenhower Lauds Nixon Policy Role and 'Experience,'" *NYT,* September 30, 1960, A1.

36. No hint of Ike's unhappiness surfaced in the *Times* account of their October 31 meeting, and the front-page photograph accompanying this story showed a laughing Eisenhower as the two men clasped hands. See Belair, "Eisenhower Adds 2 Crucial States to Campaign Trip," *NYT,* November 1, 1960, A1.

37. Nixon, *RN*, 275.

38. Ibid., 206.

39. Gallup, *Gallup Poll, Public Opinion 1935–1971*, 1656, supplemented by information obtained from the Gallup Web site. Well over half (56 percent) of all responses corresponded to our "military/defense" topic, and another 19 percent matched our "foreign policy" category, leaving only 25 percent for domestic and other concerns.

40. Divine, *Foreign Policy*, 189.

41. Senate speech delivered August 14, 1958, and reprinted in John F. Kennedy, *The Strategy of Peace*, ed. Allan Nevins (New York: Harper & Brothers, 1960), 36.

42. Ibid., 194.

43. Nationalist troops had occupied the islands since 1949, using them as staging areas for CIA-assisted covert operations. Early efforts by PRC forces to storm Quemoy (actually, an archipelago consisting of Greater Quemoy, Lesser Quemoy, and some islets) failed disastrously. In August and September 1958, shortly after mainland forces began a new round of bombardment, American-trained pilots in the Nationalist air force inflicted catastrophic losses on the PRC air force in aerial combat over the islands. Accounts vary on when the Communist shelling of Quemoy and Matsu ended. James Lilley, a former CIA operative and eventually ambassador to the PRC, maintained that the bombardment went on for two decades, albeit at a reduced rate

of fire. See James Lilley, with Jeffrey Lilley, *China Hands: Nine Decades of Adventure, Espionage, and Diplomacy in Asia* (New York: Public Affairs, 2004), 92–93. Ultimately, the government of Taiwan withdrew its troops, and Quemoy became well known as a tourist destination. In 2002, direct travel opened between the island and the mainland, although it was suspended in 2003 because of the SARS epidemic.

44. Divine, *Foreign Policy*, 260.

45. Kennedy, *Strategy of Peace*, 103, emphasis original.

46. Divine, *Foreign Policy*, 191.

47. Gallup, *Gallup Poll, Public Opinion 1935–1971*, 1669–1671. Kennedy did much better on domestic economic issues.

48. Divine, *Foreign Policy*, 209–215. The efforts Eleanor Roosevelt and Truman made to deny the nomination to Kennedy were more than a little ironic. In 1948, Eleanor had worked behind the scenes to dump Truman and nominate Eisenhower. Illinois governor Adlai Stevenson joined in this effort, ostensibly led by Franklin D. Roosevelt Jr. See Steve Neal, *Harry and Ike: The Partnership That Remade the Postwar World* (New York: Touchstone, 2002), 128–130.

49. Divine, *Foreign Policy*, 234.

50. Gallup, *Gallup Poll, Public Opinion 1935–1971*, 1669–1670.

51. For "highly favorable" ratings of Lodge, Nixon, Kennedy, and Johnson, see Gallup, *Gallup Poll, Public Opinion 1935–1971*, 1681.

52. Divine, *Foreign Policy*, 228.

53. Ibid.

54. Andrew E. Busch, *Horses in Midstream: U.S. Midterm Elections and Their Consequences, 1894–1998* (Pittsburgh, PA: University of Pittsburgh Press, 1999), 94–95; Harold Stanley and Richard Niemi, *Vital Statistics on American Politics*, 4th ed. (Washington, DC: Congressional Quarterly Press, 1994), 36–40; Nixon, *Six Crises*, 302.

55. Nixon, *Six Crises*, 302. Nixon's view runs counter to Sorensen's statement that "by any historical test, even apart from his unprecedented religion and youth, Kennedy seemed likely to be defeated. . . . Nixon, on the other hand, was more popular than his party and more able and likable than his enemies portrayed him. . . . To lead his united and well-financed party, he had an efficient organization and personal staff and could draw on the entire Executive Branch for research and ideas. His running mate, Lodge, was far better known nationally than Johnson and may have been better known at that stage than Kennedy." See Theodore Sorensen, *Kennedy* (New York: Harper & Row, 1965), 169. Similarly, Fred Greenstein claimed that "the 1960 election was Nixon's to lose. He was second in command to one of the most admired presidents in American history. His eight years as vice president had given him extensive executive branch experience. His opponent . . . was a Roman Catholic at a time when anti-Catholic prejudice was common." See Greenstein, *The Presidential Difference: Leadership Style from FDR to George W. Bush*, 2nd ed. (Princeton, NJ: Princeton University Press, 2004), 97.

56. See http://www.brain.gallup.com/documents/questionnaires.aspx?STUDY=AIPO0633; Gallup Poll #507, Question 19a-b. The seven-category scale of party identification employed in the Survey Research Center's American National Election Studies of 1952–1960 provides breakdowns similar to Gallup's over the same period. Both sets of polls show that the Republican disadvantage in 1960 did not differ much from that in earlier election years. In 1952, for example, the National Election Study found that 45 percent of the sample were strong or weak Democrats, that 28 percent were strong or weak Republicans, and that independents of varying inclinations made up the remaining 27 percent. Similarly, in 1956, the breakdown was 44 percent strong and

weak Democrats, 29 percent strong and weak Republicans, and 27 percent independents. In 1960, the figures were 45 percent strong and weak Democrats, 30 percent strong and weak Republicans, and 25 percent independents. See Stanley and Niemi, *Vital Statistics*, 116.

57. Nixon, *Six Crises*, 310.

58. Theodore C. Sorensen, "The Election of 1960," in Arthur M. Schlesinger Jr., ed., *The Coming to Power: Critical Presidential Elections in American History* (New York: Chelsea House, 1972), 454.

59. For more on the 1928 campaign, see David Burner, *The Politics of Provincialism: The Democratic Party in Transition, 1918–1932* (New York: W. W. Norton, 1967); Allan J. Lichtman, *Prejudice and the Old Politics: The Presidential Election of 1928* (Chapel Hill: University of North Carolina Press, 1979); Robert A. Slayton, *Empire Statesman: The Rise and Redemption of Al Smith* (New York: Free Press, 2001). Election statistics cited in this paragraph are from *Presidential Elections 1789–1996*, 58, 110.

60. Carl N. Degler, "American Political Parties and the Rise of the City: An Interpretation," in Jerome M. Clubb and Howard W. Allen, eds., *Electoral Change and Stability in American Political History* (New York: Free Press, 1971), 124–147. See also William B. Prendergast, *The Catholic Voter in American Politics* (Washington, DC: Georgetown University Press, 1999), 96–103.

61. Louisiana was the most Catholic state in Dixie, and Smith's running mate, Joe Robinson, represented Arkansas in the U.S. Senate.

62. Walter Lippmann took the longer view, suggesting that the Massachusetts and Rhode Island victories marked the end of a party wholly dependent on the South and the West of William Jennings Bryan. See Richard O'Connor, *The First Hurrah: A Biography of Alfred E. Smith* (New York: G. P. Putnam's Sons, 1970), 226. V. O. Key, in the 1950s, argued that the demographic shifts in favor of the Democrats, including an influx of new voters, presaged the New Deal realignment even as he conceded that the Democrats might not have lasted without the Great Depression and the 1932 elections. See Key, "A Theory of Critical Elections," *Journal of Politics* 17 (February 1955): 3–18. See also Theodore Rosenof, *Realignment: The Theory That Changed the Way We Think about American Politics* (Lanham, MD: Rowman & Littlefield, 2003), esp. 45–61. David R. Mayhew challenged the notion of 1928 as a critical election in *Electoral Realignments: A Critique of an American Genre* (New Haven, CT: Yale University Press, 2002).

63. For an analysis of why so many Catholics voted for Eisenhower in 1952 and 1956, see Prendergast, *Catholic Voter*, 120–131.

64. Ibid., 138–139.

65. See http://brain.gallup.com/questionnaire.aspx?study=AIPO0602,0604,0622. Figures indicating reactions to a Jewish candidate for president closely resembled the Catholic figures, and more than 75 percent rejected the idea of voting for an atheist.

66. Prendergast, *Catholic Voter*, 136.

67. Sorensen, *Kennedy*, 108–109.

68. Ibid., 109.

69. Ibid., 110.

70. For one account of the role that Hoover supporters played in the religious assault on Smith, see Slayton, *Empire Statesman*, 305–308.

71. John Wicklein, "Vast Anti-Catholic Drive Is Slated before Election," *NYT*, October 15, 1960, A1.

72. Nixon, *Six Crises*, 327–329.

73. Prendergast, *Catholic Voter*, 140; Dallek, *Unfinished Life*, 283–284. One of the Democrats in need of persuasion was Truman, who had opposed Kennedy on religious grounds in 1959:

"The main difficulty with that situation [electing a Catholic as president] has been that the hierarchy of the Catholic Church always wants to control the political operation of government. When the Catholic Church gets to a point where it's in control, the government is always against the little people." Quoted in Neal, *Harry and Ike*, 311.

74. Sorensen, *Kennedy*, 193; Wicklein, "Vast Anti-Catholic Drive." Wicklein also reported that "not one piece of evidence has turned up to indicate that the Republican Party, nationally or locally, has anything to do with the planning or direction of the religious drive against Mr. Kennedy."

75. Sorensen, *Kennedy*, 194.

76. Tom Wicker, "Democrats Back Leaflet Charges," *NYT*, October 25, 1960, A29; "New Kennedy Charge," *NYT*, October 25, 1960, A29.

77. Anthony Lewis, "Johnson Receives Cheers in Virginia," *NYT*, October 7, 1960, A23.

78. Richard E. Mooney, "Morton Hits Foes on Religion Issue," *NYT*, September 16, 1960, A23.

79. Wicker, "Democrats Back Leaflet Charges."

80. Nixon, *Six Crises*, 366; Thomas C. Reeves, *A Question of Character: A Life of John F. Kennedy* (New York: Free Press, 1991), 181.

81. When asked about Powell's charge during the third debate with Nixon, Kennedy replied that it was "absurd." He added, "I don't suggest that, I don't support it. I would disagree with it." For the full text, go to the Commission on Presidential Debates Web site at http://www.debates.org/pages/trans600c.html.

82. Nixon, *Six Crises*, 366; Joseph C. Ingraham, "President Decries 'Evil Propaganda' in Election," *NYT*, October 18, 1960, A26. After Eisenhower denounced the UAW pamphlet, union president Walter Reuther issued a statement of regret.

83. Nixon, *Six Crises*, 366. Nixon let his resentment over these charges show during an interview with the *Times*. See Harrison F. Salisbury, "Nixon Confident Tide Had Turned; Opens Final Push," *NYT*, October 31, 1960, A1.

84. "Mrs. Luce Terms Religion an Issue," *NYT*, October 20, 1960, A32.

85. Mooney, "Morton Hits Foes."

86. "Playing Up Religion Laid to Democrats," *NYT*, October 21, 1960, A19.

87. Prendergast, *Catholic Voter*, 142.

88. Sorensen, *Kennedy*, 194.

89. Wicker, "Democrats Back Leaflet Charges."

90. Nixon, *Six Crises*, 367; also Nixon, *RN*, 27.

91. Philip E. Converse, Angus Campbell, Warren E. Miller, and Donald E. Stokes, "Stability and Change in 1960: A Reinstating Election," *American Political Science Review* 55 (June 1961): 269–280. See also Campbell, Converse, Miller, and Stokes, "Religion and Politics: The 1960 Election," in their *Elections and the Political Order* (New York: John Wiley and Sons, 1966), 96–124.

92. For one analysis of the relationship of Catholicism to the electoral vote in 1960, see George J. Marlin, *The American Catholic Voter: 200 Years of Political Impact* (South Bend, IN: St. Augustine's Press, 2004), 238–260.

93. See Nelson W. Polsby, *How Congress Evolves: Social Bases of Institutional Change* (New York: Oxford University Press, 2004).

94. Under Republican control, the House had passed an antilynching bill as early as 1921, but southern Democrats in the Senate killed it. See Steve Neal, *Happy Days Are Here Again: The 1932 Democratic Convention, the Emergence of FDR, and How America Was Changed Forever* (New York: William Morrow, 2004), 143.

95. James MacGregor Burns argued that these and other differences between the presidential and congressional wings of each party had transformed party politics into a four-party system. See Burns, *Deadlock of Democracy: Four-Party Politics in America* (Englewood Cliffs, NJ: Prentice-Hall, 1963).

96. Samuel Lubell, *The Future of American Politics*, 3rd ed. rev. (New York: Harper Colophon Books, 1965), 101. Lubell also noted (p. 102) that most black voters in California backed Nixon's opponent in the 1950 Senate race.

97. Stanley and Niemi, *Vital Statistics*, 122.

98. Jeremy D. Mayer, *Running on Race: Racial Politics in Presidential Campaigns, 1960–2000* (New York: Random House, 2002), 10.

99. *National Party Conventions 1831–2000* (Washington, DC: Congressional Quarterly Press, 2001), 120.

100. Mayer, *Running on Race*, 11–15.

101. Robert Caro, *Means of Ascent: The Years of Lyndon Johnson* (New York: Alfred A. Knopf, 1990), 125.

102. Caro, *Master of the Senate: The Years of Lyndon Johnson* (New York: Alfred A. Knopf, 2002), 213.

103. Ibid., 785–792.

104. During the 1960 campaign, Senator James Eastland of Mississippi, among America's most prominent segregationists, credited Johnson with having stripped "everything relating to integration" out of the 1957 bill. See Mayer, *Running on Race*, 37.

105. Caro, *Master of the Senate*, 1034.

106. Reeves, *Question of Character*, 208.

107. Mayer, *Running on Race*, 26–27.

108. Ibid., 27–28.

109. Warren Weaver Jr., "Nixon Renews Bid for South's Votes," *NYT*, October 4, 1960, A1.

110. Edward C. Burks, "Negro in Cabinet Pledge by Lodge," *NYT*, October 3, 1960, A1; Burks, "Pledge on Negro Diluted by Lodge," *NYT*, October 4, 1960, A1; W. H. Lawrence, "Nixon and Lodge Fail to Heal Rift on Naming Negro," *NYT*, October 17, 1960, A1. Four days later, RNC chairman Morton told a Cincinnati audience that Lodge had no basis for pledging that Nixon would appoint a Negro to the cabinet. Exhibiting a gift for understatement, Morton said that Lodge had placed the GOP in an "awkward position." See "Morton Chides Lodge," *NYT*, October 21, 1960, A24.

111. Reeves, *Question of Character*, 207–211.

112. Ibid.; see also Layhmond Robinson, "City Negroes Seen behind Kennedy," *NYT*, November 3, 1960, A28. Even so, no Republican candidate for president since has matched Nixon's share of the black vote in 1960.

113. White, *Making of the President*, 325.

114. Sorensen, *Kennedy*, 213–214.

115. Ambrose, *Nixon*, 560.

116. Sorensen, *Kennedy*, 214.

117. Leo Egan, "Kennedy to Shun Eisenhower Issue," *NYT*, October 3, 1960, A1.

118. See White, *Making of the President*, 330–331; Weaver, "Nixon Renews Bid for South's Votes."

119. W. H. Lawrence, "Nixon Vows Help in All GOP Races," *NYT*, October 6, 1960, A1; see also John W. Finney, "Nixon, in Final Plea, Asks Voters to Put U.S. First," *NYT*, November 8, 1960, A1.

120. Charles Grutzner, "Stevenson Calls Campaign Urgent," *NYT*, October 18, 1960, A1.

121. "Truman Suggests a Nixon Venture," *NYT,* October 29, 1960, A9.

122. Before running in 1952, Eisenhower had given considerable thought to the costs of foreign and military policy once the Korean War came to an end. Fred I. Greenstein cited a 1951 passage from Eisenhower's diary referring to the goal of achieving national security without national bankruptcy. See Greenstein, *Presidential Difference,* 50–52. Named after an advertising slogan for women's clothing after World War II, the "New Look" called for major reductions in military spending. The "massive-deterrence" corollary substituted the threat of annihilation with conventional or nuclear weapons for troops on the ground. Kennedy and other Democrats attacked cuts in defense spending and made an issue of the missile gap, which never existed, according to Greenstein and myriad other scholars.

123. Although seventy-six, Truman reportedly delivered more speeches for Kennedy than Eisenhower did for Nixon, according to Neal in *Harry and Ike,* 313. Measuring their efforts by campaign statements, we found that fewer issued from Truman than Eisenhower (80 to 114) but also that 90 percent of Truman's statements contained attacks, compared with only 37 percent of Eisenhower's.

124. Evidently, the makeup of Nixon's "truth squad" varied over time. The *Times* identified the following members: Senators Norris Cotton (New Hampshire), Kenneth Keating (New York), Roman Hruska (Nebraska), and Hugh Scott (Pennsylvania); Representatives Donald Jackson (California), Peter Frelinghuysen (New Jersey), and Charles Goodell (New York).

125. With respect to military and defense attacks in September, Kennedy and other Democrats unleashed a blistering and multifaceted assault on Eisenhower's New Look and massive-deterrence policies. Time and again, Kennedy assailed the administration as weak and irresponsible when confronting Soviet aggressiveness. At the same time, Kennedy blasted the alleged lack of preparation for disarmament talks with the Russians. With Khrushchev due to arrive in New York to attend sessions of the UN General Assembly, Nixon called for a moratorium on "weakness" talk until the Soviet leader departed. If anything, Kennedy stepped up the attack. One particularly harsh assault on Eisenhower, however, reminded JFK that negativity imposes costs as well as benefits on the assailant. Recalling Eisenhower's inaction during the Polish and Hungarian uprisings, Kennedy said: "We do not want to mislead the people of Poland and Hungary again that the United States is prepared to liberate them. We have no right—unless we are prepared to meet our commitments—to incite them to national suicide." See Leo Eagan, "Kennedy Outlines Program to Court East Europe Bloc," *NYT,* October 2, 1960, A1. Nixon countered with a demand that Kennedy lay off the president, an argument that evidently resonated with the public. In a statement so disingenuous that it strained the credulity of even his staunchest supporters, Kennedy insisted that he had no quarrel with Ike and that he was focused on the future, not the past. See Eagan, "Kennedy to Shun Eisenhower Issue," *NYT,* October 3, 1960, A1.

126. Russell Baker, "Nixon and Kennedy Clash on TV over Issue of Quemoy's Defense; U–2 'Regrets' and Rights Argued," *NYT,* October 8, 1960, A1.

127. Baker, "Nixon Risks War, Kennedy Charges," *NYT,* October 11, 1960, A51.

128. "Text of Kennedy's Speech to Democratic Dinner on the Offshore Chinese Islands," *NYT,* October 13, 1960, A24.

129. Literally, the fatigued Nixon described the policy as "war and surrender or both."

130. W. H. Lawrence, "Nixon Scores Foe on Quemoy Issue," *NYT,* October 12, 1960, A1. After quoting Nixon's vow never to surrender an inch of free territory, Lawrence inserted his view that Nixon had taken "a position beyond the Administration's. . . . President Eisenhower has never said flatly that the nation would or would not defend Quemoy and Matsu if they came under Communist attack."

131. Lawrence, "Nixon Is Pressing Issue of Islands," *NYT,* October 13, 1960, A25.

132. "Transcript of Nixon-Kennedy Debate," *NYT,* October 14, 1960, A20–21; Baker, "Nixon and Kennedy Renew Fight over Quemoy in Heated Debate; Also Clash on Labor Programs," *NYT,* October 14, 1960, A1. Transcripts of all presidential debates also can be obtained from the Commission on Presidential Debates, athttp://www.debates.org.

133. Ibid.

134. Baker, "Kennedy Steps Up Attacks on Nixon," *NYT,* October 16, 1960, A1.

135. Jack Raymond, "Eisenhower Says His Quemoy View Is Same as Nixon's," *NYT,* October 16, 1960, A1.

136. "Kennedy Sees Retreat," *NYT,* October 16, 1960, A51.

137. "Nixon Renews Attacks," *NYT,* October 16, 1960, A51.

138. Richard E. Mooney, "Kennedy Asserts Quemoy Question Should Be Closed," *NYT,* October 17, 1960, A1.

139. Baker, "Kennedy Assails 'Retreat' Charge," *NYT,* October 19, 1960, A1.

140. "Excerpts from Nixon Talk to the Legion," *NYT,* October 19, 1960, A39.

141. "Transcript of the Fourth Kennedy-Nixon Debate on the Issues of the Campaign," *NYT,* October 22, 1960, A8–9; Baker, "Nixon and Kennedy Debate Cuba; Also Clash over Quemoy Issue, Atom Testing and U.S. Prestige," *NYT,* October 22, 1960, A1.

142. "Transcript of the Fourth Kennedy-Nixon Debate."

CHAPTER 6. THE DEAD HEAT RACE OF 1980

1. Everett Carl Ladd, "The Brittle Mandate: Electoral Dealignment and the 1980 Presidential Election," *Political Science Quarterly* 96 (Spring 1981): 1–25.

2. Three years later, former Reagan campaign officials admitted that a "mole" in the Carter camp had given them a copy of Carter's briefing book for the debate. Carter cried foul, convinced that the debate had turned on the purloined book. He also maintained that columnist George Will, who had advised Reagan on how to debate him, had stolen the book. Carter repeated this charge on October 21, 2004, in an interview on National Public Radio. He further claimed that Will had written to him asking "forgiveness" for having stolen the book. Will emphatically denied having stolen the book or apologizing to Carter, in a column entitled "Briefing Book Baloney," *Washington Post,* August 11, 2005, A23.

3. Jack W. Germond and Jules Witcover, *Blue Smoke and Mirrors: How Reagan Won and Why Carter Lost the Election of 1980* (New York: Viking Press, 1981), 283–284 and 286–287.

4. Hamilton Jordan, *Crisis: The Last Year of the Carter Presidency* (New York: G. P. Putnam's Sons, 1982), 356–357.

5. Commission on Presidential Debates, available at http://www.debates.org/pages/trans 80bp.html.

6. See Andrew E. Busch, *Reagan's Victory: The Presidential Election of 1980 and the Rise of the Right* (Lawrence: University Press of Kansas, 2006), 121. At that point, Carter campaign manager Robert Strauss concluded that the race was lost; see Germond and Witcover, *Blue Smoke and Mirrors,* 294–295. See also Jordan, *Crisis,* 364–365. After the election, rumors circulated that the Republicans had secretly undermined Carter's efforts to free the hostages. See Gary Sick's *October Surprise: America's Hostages in Iran and the Election of Ronald Reagan* (New York: Times Books, 1991). This claim never reached the level of credibility accorded the Chennault affair in 1968 because of a thorough investigation conducted by special counsel Reid H. Weingarten; the

findings were released by the Senate Foreign Relations Committee as a report, *The "October Surprise" Allegations and the Circumstances Surrounding the Release of the American Hostages Held in Iran*, 102nd Cong., 2nd sess., November 1992. Addressing the question "Was there a secret agreement between the Reagan campaign and representatives of the Ayatollah Khomeini to delay the release of the American hostages until after the November 1980 election?" the report concluded: "In sum, the Special Counsel found that by any standard, the credible evidence now known falls far short of supporting the allegation of an agreement between the Reagan campaign and Iran to delay the release of the hostages" (p. 115). Yet the report did conclude that Reagan campaign manager William Casey likely "fished in troubled waters" by traveling abroad and gathering information on the hostage crisis. Casey's background as an operative with the Office of Strategic Services (OSS, forerunner of the CIA) lent credibility to this claim. Casey, however, seemingly wanted to expedite rather than delay the hostages' return. The report condemned his effort as "informal, clandestine, and potentially dangerous" (pp. 116–117).

7. See Germond and Witcover, *Blue Smoke and Mirrors*, 291–292.

8. Jimmy Carter, *Keeping Faith: Memoirs of a President* (New York: Bantam Books, 1982), 567–568; Jordan, *Crisis*, 364.

9. Accounts differ on the exact time when the polls closed; it may have been as early as 9:45 P.M. or as late as 9:52 eastern time.

10. *Presidential Elections 1789–1996* (Washington, DC: Congressional Quarterly Press, 1997), 71 and 123.

11. Gerald M. Pomper, "The Presidential Election," in Marlene Michels Pomper, ed., *The Election of 1980* (Chatham, NJ: Chatham House, 1981), 71–72. Stanley Kelley Jr. argued that such deviations assumed much less significance when one focused on the Republican candidate's share of the group's two-party vote minus his share of the two-party vote. Even by this measure, the deviations for Democrats, union families, Catholics, and male voters were high when compared to breakdowns of the vote for other Republicans. See table 9.2 in Stanley Kelley Jr., *Interpreting Elections* (Princeton, NJ: Princeton University Press, 1983), 178–179.

12. This paragraph draws heavily from William Schneider's account in "The November Vote for President: What Did It Mean?" in Austin Ranney, ed., *The American Elections of 1980* (Washington, DC: American Enterprise Institute of Public Policy Research, 1981), 225–226. See also Kathleen A. Frankovic, "Public Opinion Trends," in Pomper, ed., *Election of 1980*, 111–113.

13. In Massachusetts, where Carter lost to Reagan by 3,829 votes, Anderson garnered just over 382,000 votes, and in New York, where Carter lost by 165,459 votes out of 6.1 million cast, Anderson received nearly 468,000 votes. See *Presidential Elections 1789–1996*, 123.

14. For a careful analysis of the balance between retrospective and prospective judgments in 1972, 1976, and 1980 voting for president, see Paul R. Abramson, John H. Aldrich, and David W. Rohde, *Change and Continuity in the 1980 Elections* (Washington, DC: Congressional Quarterly Press, 1982), 141–157.

15. Frankovic, "Public Opinion Trends," 103.

16. In his previously cited chapter, "Presidential Election," Pomper argued that "the presidential outcome was predominantly a negative reaction to the leadership of Jimmy Carter, which yet provides an opportunity for building a Republican majority" (p. 65). Schneider, in "The November 4 Vote for President," saw 1980 as "a continuation of the long-term realignment that began in 1964 and was temporarily interrupted in the mid-1970s" (p. 258). He also argued that the partisan shift coincided with increased polarization of the parties along conservative-liberal lines. Kelley took a dim view of ideology's significance to the 1980 outcome; see his *Interpreting Elections*, 167–224. Abramson, Aldrich, and Rohde, in *Change and Continuity in the 1980 Elections*,

hedged on the realignment-dealignment issue. Ladd, in "Brittle Mandate," made a detailed case for dealignment.

17. This paragraph draws from Thomas E. Mann and Norman J. Ornstein, "The Republican Surge in Congress," in Ranney, ed., *American Elections of 1980*, 263–302; Busch, *Reagan's Victory*, 145–162; Charles E. Jacob, "The Congressional Elections," in Pomper, ed., *Election of 1980*, 1119–1141; Ranney, *American Elections of 1980*, appendixes G, H, and H-2, 376–379; and *Gubernatorial Elections 1787–1997* (Washington, DC: Congressional Quarterly Press, 1998), 4.

18. Busch, *Reagan's Victory*, 145–162.

19. Gary C. Jacobson and Samuel Kernell, *Strategy and Choice in Congressional Elections*, 2nd ed. (New Haven, CT: Yale University Press, 1983), 72–84.

20. Ibid. Jacobson and Kernell adduced data for House races that suggested a link between challenger quality and seniority of defeated incumbents. They found that strong challengers did better against incumbents representing previously noncompetitive districts than against incumbents from marginal districts in the House.

21. Abramson, Aldrich, and Rohde, *Change and Continuity in the 1980 Elections*, 222; Jacob, *Congressional Elections*, 124–126.

22. Carter, *Keeping Faith*, 127. Thomas P. "Tip" O'Neill later lauded the depth of Carter's knowledge on a broad range of topics but also observed that "he never really understood how the system worked and .... he didn't want to learn about it, either." See Tip O'Neill, with William Novak, *Man of the House: The Life and Political Memoirs of Speaker Tip O'Neill* (New York: St. Martin's Press, 1987), 355.

23. For a perceptive and surprisingly evenhanded discussion of the southern factor in Carter's presidency, see Joseph A. Califano, *Inside: A Public and Private Life* (New York: Public Affairs Press, 2004), 325–389.

24. Nelson W. Polsby, *Consequences of Party Reform* (New York: Oxford University Press, 1983), 129.

25. Quoted in Charles O. Jones, *The Trusteeship Presidency: Jimmy Carter and the United States Congress* (Baton Rouge: Louisiana State University, 1988), 5.

26. O'Neill, *Man of the House*, 361–362. "Hell, Mr. President," O'Neill supposedly responded, "you're making a big mistake. You don't mean to tell me that you're comparing the House and the Senate with the Georgia legislature?" O'Neill reminded Carter that he had run behind most of the congressional Democrats and added a warning: "Believe me, next time they won't hesitate to run *against* [emphasis original] you."

27. That representative was Andy Jacobs Jr. (D-IN).

28. Carter, *Keeping Faith*, 125.

29. For a good summary of the difficulties Carter faced and the concessions he made in getting his bills passed, see Richard S. Conley, *The Presidency, Congress, and Divided Government* (College Station: Texas A&M University Press, 2003), 190–202. Carter discussed many of these measures in *Keeping Faith*. See also W. Carl Biven, *Jimmy Carter's Economy: Policy in an Age of Limits* (Chapel Hill: University of North Carolina Press, 2002), 199–200.

30. Conley, *Presidency, Congress, and Divided Government*, 201.

31. In particular, the "Subcommittee Bill of Rights" had mandated a substantial increase in the number of subcommittees and thereby reduced the power of full committee chairs while dispersing power to relatively junior subcommittee chairs. The recently adopted procedure of multiple committee referral also undermined the old system and thereby complicated consideration of Carter's initiatives. For a good discussion of these and other changes in House procedures, see

Barbara Sinclair, *Unorthodox Lawmaking: New Legislative Processes in the U.S. Congress*, 2nd. ed. (Washington, DC: Congressional Quarterly Press, 2000), 11–14.

32. For a detailed discussion of the thinking and politics behind the stimulus bill, see Biven, *Jimmy Carter's Economy*, 61–93.

33. Michael J. Boskin, *Reagan and the Economy: The Successes, Failures, and Unfinished Agenda* (San Francisco: Institute for Contemporary Studies, 1987), 11–29.

34. Biven, *Jimmy Carter's Economy*, 254.

35. Murray Weidenbaum quoted in Boskin, *Reagan and the Economy*, 19.

36. Herbert Stein, *Presidential Economics: The Making of Economic Policy from Roosevelt to Clinton*, 3rd rev. ed. (Washington, DC: American Enterprise Institute for Public Policy, 1994), 221.

37. Boskin, *Reagan and the Economy*, 18; Stein, *Presidential Economics*, 220–221.

38. For conflicting views of tax revolts of the late seventies, see Howard Jarvis, *I'm Mad as Hell* (New York: Times Books, 1979); Robert Kutner, *Revolt of the Haves: Tax Rebellions and Hard Times* (New York: Simon & Schuster, 1980); and David O. Sears and Jack Citrin, *Tax Revolt: Something for Nothing in California* (Cambridge, MA: Harvard University Press, 1982).

39. Kutner, *Revolt of the Haves*, 8.

40. Steven M. Gillon, *The Democrats' Dilemma: Walter F. Mondale and the Liberal Legacy* (New York: Columbia University Press, 1992), 252.

41. Quoted in Biven, *Jimmy Carter's Economy*, 203.

42. Gillon, *Democrats' Dilemma*, 254.

43. Boskin, *Reagan and the Economy*, 23–24.

44. Biven, *Jimmy Carter's Economy*, 88–93.

45. Ibid., 140–143.

46. Daniel Yergin, *The Prize: The Epic Quest for Oil, Money, and Power* (New York: Simon & Schuster, 1991), 663.

47. Carter, *Keeping Faith*, 91–96.

48. Ibid., 103.

49. Yergin, *Prize*, 664.

50. Ibid., 91–106.

51. Biven, *Jimmy Carter's Economy*, 145–177.

52. Gillon, *Democrats' Dilemma*, 253.

53. Biven, *Jimmy Carter's Economy*, 191.

54. Gillon, *Democrats' Dilemma*, 255 and 260.

55. Carter, *Keeping Faith*, 114.

56. Ibid., 114–115.

57. Ibid., 115.

58. Germond and Witcover, *Blue Smoke and Mirrors*, 30.

59. All quotes in this paragraph come from Gillon's account, in *Democrats' Dilemma*, 261–263.

60. Carter, *Keeping Faith*, 116.

61. Gillon, *Democrats' Dilemma*, 262–263; see also Carter, *Keeping Faith*, 115–116.

62. Gillon, *Democrats' Dilemma*, 251–263. Hamilton Jordan, a Mondale ally, described the vice president's role in cabinet and other meetings with Carter as one of saving himself "for those occasions when he thought the president was making a mistake or wasn't getting good advice or didn't have all the facts." Jordan also noted that Mondale "fought hard for what he believed in on

the inside, yet would accept the president's decisions and go out and defend them publicly." See Jordan, *Crisis*, 68. Paul C. Light discussed Mondale's vice presidency at length in *Vice-Presidential Power: Advice and Influence in the White House* (Baltimore, MD: Johns Hopkins University Press, 1984).

63. This paragraph draws on Carter, *Keeping Faith*, 115–116.

64. Available at http://www.americanrhetoric.com/speeches/jimmycartercrisisofconfidence .htm.

65. For Califano's account, see his *Governing America: An Insider's Report from the White House and the Cabinet* (New York: Simon & Schuster, 1981), 427–448. Califano updated his account in his *Inside: A Public and Private Life*, 325–371.

66. Gillon, *Democrats' Dilemma*, 264–265; see also Germond and Witcover, *Blue Smoke and Mirrors*, 35–40.

67. James Mann, *About Face: A History of America's Curious Relationship with China, from Nixon to Clinton* (New York: Vintage, 2000), 95.

68. Ibid., 152–185.

69. Perhaps the fullest account of this episode appears in Douglas Brinkley, *The Unfinished Presidency: Jimmy Carter's Journey to the Nobel Peace Prize* (New York: Penguin Books, 1999), 388–391. Interestingly, Carter made no reference to this episode in his memoir.

70. Carter, *Keeping Faith*, 476.

71. Ibid., 265.

72. Germond and Witcover, *Blue Smoke and Mirrors*, 310. For other assessments of the harm done to Carter, see Zbigniew Brzezinski, *Power and Principle: Memoirs of a National Security Advisor, 1977–1981* (New York: Farrar, Straus, Giroux, 1983), 354; also Stephen Skowronek, *The Politics Presidents Make: Leadership from John Adams to George Bush* (Cambridge, MA: Belknap Press, 1993), 402–404. For a more nuanced analysis of polling data, see Frankovic, "Public Opinion Trends."

73. Carter, *Keeping Faith*, 436–437.

74. Kenneth M. Pollack, *The Persian Puzzle: The Conflict between Iran and America* (New York: Vintage, 2005*)*, 123–124.

75. Ibid., 129–140.

76. Ibid.

77. Most accounts agree on this point. See, for example, Charles Kurzman, *The Unthinkable Revolution in Iran* (Cambridge, MA: Harvard University Press, 2004), 104–124.

78. Some pegged the daily desertion rate at 1,000, but General Robert E. Huyser, a presidential emissary to Iran's top military leaders, maintained that the real figure was more like 100 or 200. See Huyser, *Mission to Tehran* (New York: Harper & Row, 1986).

79. Pollack, *Persian Puzzle*; Carter, *Keeping Faith*; Huyser, *Mission to Tehran*; Brzezinski, *Power and Principle*, esp. p. 396; see also Kurzman, *Unthinkable Revolution*.

80. Bernard Gwertzman, "U.S. Decision to Admit the Shah: Key Events in 8 Months of Debate," *NYT*, November 18, 1979, A1.

81. After receiving treatment at Columbia University Hospital, the shah decamped to Panama, an exile arranged by Hamilton Jordan. Unhappy there and spooked by rumors of Panama's willingness to extradite him, the shah accepted Anwar Sadat's invitation to relocate his family to Egypt. The shah died there on July 27, 1980.

82. At that point, roughly 200 Americans still lived and worked in Iran, many resisting pleas by their government to leave the country. American journalists in Iran added to the pool of replacement hostages. For the most extensive account of what the hostages experienced in

captivity, see Mark Bowden, *Guests of the Ayatollah: The First Battle in America's War with Militant Islam* (New York: Atlantic Monthly Press, 2006).

83. Gary Sick provided an exhaustive account of these efforts in *All Fall Down: America's Tragic Encounter with Iran* (New York: Random House, 1985), 205–296. Throughout, the White House regarded the Ayatollah Khomeini and his supporters as fanatics maddened by their hatred of the West. A White House aide at the time, Sick described Khomeini as "the archetype of the medieval prophet emerging from the desert with a fiery vision of absolute truth" (pp. 219–220). In *Keeping Faith*, Carter wrote that Khomeini was "insane," yet he sought to deal with him as if he were "a rational person" (p. 459). In the final hours of the crisis, Carter adviser Charles Kirbo exclaimed, "No wonder the Shah killed so many of those people, they're crazy!"; see Jordan, *Crisis*, 396. By some accounts, Khomeini and other haters of the Great Satan evidently felt that the seeds of the embassy crisis had been sown in 1953, when the CIA orchestrated a coup that overthrew Prime Minister Mohammed Mossadegh and returned a callow shah to power. According to some accounts, memories of Mossadegh's martyrdom colored Iranian perceptions of the embassy seizure, as did related fears that the CIA would engineer another coup, crush the Islamic revolution in Iran, and reinstate the fugitive shah a second time. For one work that makes this connection, see Stephen Kinzer, *All The King's Men: An American Coup and the Roots of Middle East Terror* (New York: John Wiley & Sons, 2003); see also Pollack, *The Persian Puzzle*.

84. Quoted in Sick, *All Fall Down*, 295.

85. Ibid.

86. For one account of the freezing of Iranian assets, see Mark Hulbert, *Interlock: The Untold Story of American Banks, Oil Interests, the Shah's Money, Debts and the Astounding Connections between Them* (New York: Richardson and Snyder, 1982).

87. See Carter, *Keeping Faith*, 461; also Paul B. Ryan, *The Iranian Rescue Mission: Why It Failed* (Annapolis, MD: Naval Institute Press, 1985).

88. See Ryan, *The Iranian Rescue Mission*, for an exhaustive account of mission planning, the high probabilities of failure, and the results of subsequent investigations.

89. George H. Gallup, *The Gallup Poll: Public Opinion 1980* (Wilmington, DE: Scholarly Resources, 1981), 96 and 128.

90. The following comparison of how a liberal group and a conservative group—Americans for Democratic Action (ADA) and Americans for Constitutional Action (ACA)—rated Anderson's voting record shows an increasingly liberal pattern:

Year	ADA (liberal)	ACA (conservative)
1968	17	67
1970	28	67
1972	44	43
1974	50	33
1976	50	29
1978	55	44

Sources: Michael Barone, Grant Ujifusa, and Douglas Matthews, *The Almanac of American Politics: The Senators, the Representatives—Their Records, States, and Districts 1972* (Boston: Gambit, 1972), 221–222; Barone, Ujifusa, and Matthews, *The Almanac of American Politics: The Senators, the Representatives—Their Records, States, and Districts 1976* (New York: E. P. Dutton, 1975), 248–250; Barone, Ujifusa, and Matthews, *The Almanac of American Politics: Their Records, States, and Districts 1980* (New York: E. P. Dutton, 1979), 264–266.

91. Lucey had played an important role in the Wisconsin Democratic Party and had briefly served as Carter's ambassador to Mexico. He broke with Carter, however, and resigned his position to support Ted Kennedy's bid to prevent Carter's renomination. He agreed to run with Anderson at the urging of his wife, who had been persuaded by Anderson's wife. See Leslie H. Southwick, *Presidential Also-Rans and Running Mates, 1788 through 1996*, 2nd ed. (Jefferson, NC: McFarland, 1998), 731–733.

92. Gallup, *The Gallup Poll: Public Opinion 1980*, 134. See also Germond and Witcover, *Blue Smoke and Mirrors*, 233–234, and Mark Bisnow, *Diary of a Dark Horse: The 1980 Anderson Presidential Campaign* (Carbondale: Southern Illinois University Press, 1983).

93. Gallup, *The Gallup Poll: Public Opinion 1980*, 139–140.

94. Germond and Witcover, *Blue Smoke and Mirrors*, 236–241.

95. Gallup, *The Gallup Poll: Public Opinion 1980*, 240–241.

96. Hedrick Smith, "Decision Day for Participation in the Presidential Debates," *NYT*, September 9, 1980, D18.

97. Germond and Witcover, *Blue Smoke and Mirrors*, 236–241.

98. "Democrats Press Efforts to Show Anderson Impact," *NYT*, September 12, 1980, D14.

99. Richard L. Madden, "Anderson Accuses 2 Foes of 'Low Level' Politics," *NYT*, October 8, 1980, B6. See also Steven J. Rosenstone, Roy L. Behr, and Edward H. Lazarus, *Third Parties in America*, 2nd ed. revised and expanded (Princeton, NJ: Princeton University Press, 1984), 44; see also J. David Gillespie, *Politics at the Periphery: Third Parties in Two-Party America* (Columbia: University of South Carolina Press, 1993), 126.

100. "Chip Carter Describes Anderson as a Spoiler," *NYT*, October 12, 1980, A34.

101. Steven R. Weisman, "President Sees Politics in Reagan Vow to Put Woman on High Court," *NYT*, October 16, 1980, A1.

102. Hedrick Smith, "Carter Declines to Debate after Anderson Is Invited," *NYT*, September 10, 1980, A1.

103. Warren Weaver, "Anderson Assails President for Implying Only He Can Keep World Peace," *NYT*, September 24, 1980, A26.

104. Leslie Bennetts, "Independent Candidate Encounters Some Difficulty Selling 'The Anderson Difference,'" *NYT*, September 12, 1980, D15.

105. Terrence Smith, "Anderson's Long Race against Long Odds," *NYT*, October 4, 1980, A9.

106. Gallup, *The Gallup Poll: Public Opinion 1980*. The combined percentages for inflation, high cost of living, and unemployment totaled 78 percent in April, 71 percent in August, and 76 percent in mid-September.

107. Ibid.

108. Richard L. Madden, "Anderson, in Manhattan, Says Rivals Flip-Flopped," *NYT*, October 10, 1980, D14.

109. Warren Weaver, "Anderson Charges Democratic 'Lie' for Black Vote," *NYT*, November 1, 1980, A8; "Campaign Report: 'An Angry Anderson,'" *NYT*, November 1, 1980, A8.

110. "Mondale Jabs at Reagan," *NYT*, September 20, 1980, A7.

111. Marjorie Hunter, "Mondale Stressing Reagan Flip-Flops," *NYT*, October 13, 1980, B6.

112. Warren Weaver, "Anderson Campaign Finishing with Upbeat Feeling," *NYT*, November 3, 1980, D13.

113. All quotes in this paragraph are from Adam Clymer, "Labor Day Symbols Vital to 3 Seeking Presidency," *NYT*, September 1, 1980, A1.

114. Ronald Reagan, *An American Life* (New York: Pocket Books, 1990), 220.

115. The long list of Reagan surrogates included Senator Howard Baker of Tennessee;

Governor James Rhodes of Ohio; RNC chairman Bill Brock; comedian Bob Hope; forties and fifties movie star Roy Rogers; and astronauts Walter Cunningham, James Lovell, and Eugene Cernan. Running mate George Bush made criticism of the economy a staple of his attacks on Carter and the administration. "At every stop the message was the same," Drummond Ayres Jr. wrote. "Mr. Bush charged that President Carter had egregiously mismanaged the economy and had failed to make good on 1976 campaign promises," despite a vow never to lie to the voters; see Ayres, "Bush, Confident of Winning, Is Satisfied in No. 2 Role," *NYT,* October 5, 1980, A37. For other accounts of Bush attacks on the Carter economy, see "Bush Stops at Carolina Stock-Car Race," *NYT,* September 2, 1980, B8; "Bush Campaigns in Midwest," *NYT,* September 10, 1980, B7; "Bush, in Iowa Visit, Pins G.O.P. Hopes on Economy," *NYT,* September 11, 1980, D18; Karen DeWitt, "Bush Predicts 20% Inflation with Carter," *NYT,* September 20, 1980, A7; "Attacks by Republicans Will Pay Off, Bush Says," *NYT,* September 23, 1980, B8; and "Bush, in Connecticut, Bids for Workers' Votes," *NYT,* October 11, 1980, A8. Ford also took the stump on Reagan's behalf. See Adam Clymer, "Ford Ranks as Reagan's Top Surrogate," *NYT,* October 26, 1980, A41. In that capacity, Ford repeatedly blasted Carter's record on the economy, telling reporters early in the fall campaign that his administration had "licked" the recession but "now the country's flat on its back." "I'm going to do everything I can to expose the failures of the Carter administration," he added. "If I can help elect a new president, it will be worth every ounce of energy I expend." In this initial foray, however, Ford balked at Reagan's proposal to cut taxes by 10 percent for each of the next three years; see "Ford Assails Disclosure of Secret Plane," *NYT,* September 9, 1980, D18. A week later, the former president was on the stump bewailing the "catastrophe, the disaster" that Carter had visited on the economy: "If you add an unemployment rate of 6.7 percent and an inflation rate of 13 percent, that comes to almost 21 percent. And if a misery index of 15.8 percent was enough to get rid of Jerry Ford, it's plenty good enough to get rid of Jimmy Carter": see "Ford Calls Economic Policy of Administration 'Disaster,'" *NYT,* September 17, 1980, B10. Ford also played a prominent role in the final days of the campaign; see Howell Raines, "Reagan Prepares an Attack on Carter If 52 Are Freed," *NYT,* November 2, 1980, A36; also see Raines, "Reagan Attacks President on Economy and Defense," *NYT,* November 4, 1980, B5.

116. Douglas Kneeland, "Reagan Accuses Carter of Breaking Faith with Israel," *NYT,* September 4, 1980, A1.

117. Kneeland, "Reagan, in Michigan, Focuses on Economy," *NYT,* October 16, 1980, B6.

118. Howell Raines, "Republican Stresses Economy," *NYT,* September 2, 1980, A1.

119. Douglas Kneeland, "Reagan Hits Chicago Streets with a Visit to Lithuanians," *NYT,* September 9, 1980, D18. By October, Reagan had made the depression claim a staple of his stump speech: "One day, I publicly declared that is a depression, and the president before the day was out went to the press to say, 'That shows how little he knows. This is a recession.' If the president wants a definition, I'll give him one. Recession is when your neighbor loses his job, depression is when you lose yours, and [pausing for laughter] recovery will be when Jimmy Carter loses his"; see Howell Raines, "Reagan in Speeches, Doesn't Let the Facts Spoil a Good Anecdote or Effective Symbol," *NYT,* October 19, 1980, A38.

120. "Transcript of Reagan Speech Outlining Five-Year Economic Program for U.S.," *NYT,* September 9, 1980, B4. See also Kneeland, "Reagan Offers Plan to Cut Taxes, Balance Budget, 'Restore Defenses,'" *NYT,* September 9, 1980, A2.

121. "Excerpts from Reagan Interview on Policies He Would Follow," *NYT,* October 2, 1980, B13.

122. Douglas Kneeland, "Reagan Declares Carter Is at 'a Point of Hysteria,'" *NYT,* October 8, 1980, B6.

123. "Excerpts from Reagan TV Address on the Economy," *NYT*, October 25, 1980, A10; Howell Raines, "Reagan Assails Carter on Economy," *NYT*, October 25, 1980, A1.

124. Raines, "Reagan Assails Carter on Economy." See also Joseph E. Sullivan, "Reagan, Campaigning in New Jersey, Receives an Unexpected Endorsement from a Mayor," *NYT*, October 7, 1980, A21, who quoted Reagan as claiming: "This creative use of statistics by the administration is a cruel hoax on the American people. Measured by the way this administration has used the 'Imperial Presidency' over the past year, I am not surprised at the recent 'jimmying' of official government statistics."

125. Adam Clymer, "Carter and Reagan Dispute Views or Arms Policy, Economy and Iran in a Broad Debate before Nation," *NYT*, October 29, 1980, A1.

126. Ibid.

127. Howell Raines, "Reagan Stresses Economic Issues Anew," *NYT*, October 30, 1980, B14.

128. Joseph E. Sullivan, "Reagan Is Endorsed by the Democratic Mayor of Lodi," *NYT*, October 31, 1980, A16.

129. Adam Clymer, "Carter and Reagan Make Final Appeals before Vote Today," *NYT*, November 4, 1980, A1.

130. Bernard Weinraub, "TV Battlefield Tests Presidential Strategies," *NYT*, October 8, 1980, B7.

131. Weinraub, "Carter and Reagan Go on Attack in Ads," *NYT*, October 19, 1980, A38.

132. Weinraub, "Mrs. Reagan, in Campaign Ad, Assails Statements by Carter on Her Husband," *NYT*, October 26, 1980, A41.

133. "Conservative Group Turns Carter '76 Ads against Him," *NYT*, September 25, 1980, B10.

134. Bernard Weinraub, "Independent Panels Press Campaign to Aid Reagan," *NYT*, October 5, 1980, A55.

135. Clyde H. Farnsworth, "Consumer Prices up by 1% in September and 12.7% in a Year," *NYT*, October 25, 1980, A1.

136. Steven V. Weisman, "President Denies Harming Security over Secret Plane," *NYT*, September 10, 1980, B5; Adam Clymer, "Lively, Loudly and at Long Distances: The Reagan-Carter Debate Has Begun," *NYT*, September 12, 1980, D14.

137. Terrence Smith, "Carter Aides Assail Reagan's Proposals," *NYT*, October 12, 1980, A34.

138. Steven Weisman, "Carter Says His Programs Can Lead U.S. to an 'Economic Renaissance,'" *NYT*, October 13, 1980, B5.

139. "Excerpts from the President's Remarks about Condition of Nation's Economy," *NYT*, October 15, 1980, A22; Terrence E. Smith, "Carter Challenges Foe on Economy," *NYT*, October 15, 1980, A1.

140. Frank Lynn, "Carter Hails Defense Record at 'Town Meeting' on L.I.," *NYT*, October 17, 1980, A1. Reportedly, Nassau County ranked at or near the top nationwide in property taxes.

141. Howell Raines, "President Urges Avoiding Tax Cuts," *NYT*, October 25, 1980, A1.

142. Carter's memoir gives the impression that the hostage crisis preoccupied his final days of campaigning; see his *Keeping Faith*, 554–571.

143. "Mondale Says Reagan Plan Perils Urban Redevelopment," *NYT*, October 17, 1980, A22.

144. Adam Clymer, "Carter Campaign Ad Attacked as a 'Smear,'" *NYT*, September 21, 1980, A34.

145. Clymer, "Carter's TV Ads Attack Reagan on Record as California Governor," *NYT*, October 1, 1980, B7; Wallace Turner, "Exaggerations Found in Comparing Reagan Ad with His Record as Governor," *NYT*, October 28, 1980, B17.

146. "Anderson Opens Campaign in Midwest," *NYT,* September 2, 1980, B8; Clymer, "TV News and the Campaign," *NYT,* September 3, 1980, B10.

147. Leslie Bennetts, "Anderson Attacks Rivals on Economics," *NYT,* September 13, 1980, A9.

148. Debate transcript, *NYT,* September 22, 1980, B6–B7, available at http://www.debates .org/pages/trans80a.html.

149. Warren Weaver, "Anderson Doubtful Reagan Would Make a Better President Than Carter," *NYT,* October 5, 1980, A35.

150. Weaver, "Anderson Tells What It Might Cost to Do the Things He Has Promised," *NYT,* October 15, 1980, A27.

151. "Excerpts from Anderson Responses to Questions after the Carter-Reagan Debate," *NYT,* October 29, 1980, A29. See also Weaver, "Anderson Sees Voters Shrugging Off Debate," *NYT,* October 30, 1980, B14.

152. Weaver, "Anderson Assails President for Implying Only He Can Keep World Peace."

153. See Schneider, "The November 4 Vote for President," 236–237.

CHAPTER 7. THE DEAD HEAT RACES OF 2000 AND 2004

1. Richard L. Berke and Frank Bruni, "G.O.P. Leaders Fret at Lapses in Bush's Race," *NYT,* September 7, 2000, A1.

2. For other late polls, see Janet Elder, "4 New Polls Show Bush with an Edge, with Nader a Factor," *NYT,* November 2, 2000, A19. Realpolitics.com offered a comprehensive summary of poll standings throughout the campaign.

3. Richard Johnston, Michael G. Hagen, and Kathleen Hall Jamieson, *The 2000 Presidential Election and the Foundation of Party Politics* (New York: Cambridge University Press, 2004).

4. Daron R. Shaw, *The Race to 270: The Electoral College and the Campaign Strategies of 2000 and 2004* (Chicago: University of Chicago Press, 2006), 125–128.

5. David W. Moore, "Presidential Race Remains Close: No Convention Bounce," Gallup Poll News Service, August 1, 2004, available at www.gallup.com. Worse for Kerry, McGovern had delivered his acceptance speech in the wee hours of the morning to a divided convention, whereas Kerry spoke in prime time to a party united in its antipathy toward Bush.

6. Jeffrey Jones, "Bush Gets Small Convention Bounce, Leads Kerry by Seven," Gallup Poll News Service, September 6, 2004, available at www.gallup.com. According to Democrat Ruy Teixeira, Bush's two-point bounce was the worst ever experienced by an incumbent president, as well as the worst ever for a Republican candidate. See his article "Public Opinion Watch," Center for American Progress, available at http://www.americanprogress.org/issues/2004/09/b183679.html.

7. For criticisms of the methodology of these polls, see Teixeira, "Public Opinion Watch," and John Zogby, "2004: It Is Not an 11 Point Race," available at http://www.zogby.com/news/ ReadNews.dbm?ID=859.

8. See Marjorie Connelly, "Other Polls Are Also Tight," *NYT,* November 1, 2004, A16. In Ohio, the final mail poll by the *Columbus Dispatch* showed a difference of eight likely voters in Kerry's favor out of 2,800 responding. See Darrel Rowland, "8 Votes Apart," *Columbus Dispatch,* October 31, 2004, A1. This was the tightest presidential race ever in the poll's history.

9. Shaw's running tally of likely electoral votes showed that Kerry never ran ahead of Bush in enough states to corral 270 but that Bush, who began in August with only 270, dipped below that minimum in mid-October before again commanding a majority. See Shaw, *Race to 270,* 127.

10. For state strategies in 2000, see Kathleen Hall Jamieson and Paul Waldman, eds., *Electing the President 2000: The Insiders' View* (Philadelphia: University of Pennsylvania Press, 2001). Similar information for the 2004 campaigns is presented in Institute of Politics (John F. Kennedy School of Government, Harvard University), ed., *Campaign for President: The Managers Look at 2004* (Lanham, MD: Rowman & Littlefield, 2006), 196–200. For information on candidate visits and ad buys in 2000, see Richard Johnston, Michael G. Hagen, and Kathleen Hall Jamieson, *The 2000 Presidential Election and the Foundation of Party Politics* (New York: Cambridge University Press, 2004), 66–77. On 2004 candidate visits, see Gerald M. Pomper, "The Presidential Election: The Ills of American Politics after 9/11," in Michael Nelson, ed., *The Elections of 2004* (Washington, DC: Congressional Quarterly Press, 2005), 54–56; also Susan A. MacManus, "Kerry in the Red States: Fighting an Uphill Battle from the Start," in Larry J. Sabato, ed., *Divided States of America: The Slash and Burn Politics of the 2004 Presidential Election* (New York: Pearson-Longman, 2006), 131–164.

11. For evidence of the Republicans' more "aggressive" battle plan, see Shaw, *Race to 270*, 71–109. Shaw's insider account offers the most informed analysis of how the two Bush campaigns targeted states and allocated advertising dollars to media markets, together with a well-documented study of Democratic strategy and advertising buys.

12. *Guide to U.S. Elections*, 5th ed., vol. 1 (Washington, DC: Congressional Quarterly Press, 2005), 718–719. Allegations of voting irregularities and illegalities dogged Wisconsin Democrats in both elections. The problem may have been more pronounced in 2000. See Andrew Nieland, "In Milwaukee, Activists Use New Tactics to Help Boost Voter Registration, Turnout," *Wall Street Journal*, December 18, 2000, A14. For a brief discussion of likely voter fraud in Connecticut, Florida, and Wisconsin, see James W. Ceaser and Andrew E. Busch, *The Perfect Tie: The True Story of the 2000 Presidential Election* (Lanham, MD: Rowman & Littlefield, 2001), 246–248.

13. Bush lost Michigan to Gore by 5.2 percent and to Kerry by 3.4 percent; he lost Pennsylvania by 4.2 percent in 2000, 2.5 percent in 2004. See *Guide to U.S. Elections*, 718–719.

14. Ibid., 712–719.

15. Ibid.

16. Ibid.

17. Ibid.

18. Alan Abramowitz, "Explaining Bush's Victory in 2004 (It's Terrorism, Stupid)," in Matthew R. Kerbel, ed., *Get This Party Started: How Progressives Can Fight Back and Win* (Lanham, MD: Rowman & Littlefield, 2006), 7–22.

19. See Pomper, "The Presidential Election," 42–43.

20. See http://www.cnn.com/ELECTION/2000/results/index.epolls.html.

21. See http://www.cnn.com/ELECTION/2004/pages/results/states/US/P/00/epolls.html.

22. Gallup data for the elections of 1960–2000 come from Harold W. Stanley and Richard G. Niemi, *Vital Statistics on American Politics, 2003–2004* (Washington, DC: Congressional Quarterly Press, 2003), 122–123. A higher percentage of Democrats voted for Clinton in 1996 than for Gore in 2000, and higher percentages of Republicans voted for Nixon in 1960 and 1972, Reagan in 1984 and 1988, and Bush's father in 1988 than for Bush in 2000. The 2004 figure of 93 percent was the highest for Democrats in the entire series, and Bush's 95 percent support among Republicans surpassed or equaled all others for the GOP except Reagan's vote in 1984.

23. John Kenneth White, "The Armageddon Election," in William Crotty, ed., *A Defining Moment: The Presidential Election of 2004* (Armonk, NY: M. E. Sharpe, 2005), 216.

24. Gary C. Jacobson, *A Divider, Not a Uniter: George W. Bush and the American People* (New York: Pearson-Longman, 2007), 189–190.

25. Ibid. See also Paul R. Abramson, John H. Aldrich, David W. Rohde, *Change and Continuity in the 2004 Elections* (Washington, DC: Congressional Quarterly Press, 2006), 194, and, by the same authors, *Change and Continuity in the 2000 and 2002 Elections* (Washington, DC: Congressional Quarterly Press, 2003), 176–178.

26. Unfortunately, the 2004 exit polls posted on cnn.com did not include a breakdown for white Protestants.

27. Stanley and Niemi, *Vital Statistics*, 124.

28. Exit polls for both elections are posted at http://www.cnn.com.

29. See http://www.cnn.com/ELECTION/2000/results/index.epolls.html. The 2004 exit poll omitted this question. On Rove, see Kevin J. McMahon, "A 'Moral Values' Election? The Culture War, the Supreme Court, and a Divided America," in Kevin J. McMahon, David M. Rankin, Donald W. Beachler, and John Kenneth White, *Winning the White House 2004: Region by Region, Vote by Vote* (New York: Palgrave-Macmillan, 2005), 24.

30. Russell Muirhead, Nancy L. Rosenblum, Daniel Schlozman, and Francis X. Shen, "Religion in the 2004 Presidential Election," in Sabato, ed., *Divided States of America*, 221–242.

31. McMahon, "A 'Moral Values' Election?" 24.

32. Barry C. Burden found that women figured critically in improving Bush's state-by-state vote as compared to the 2000 figures. See Burden, "An Alternative Account of the 2004 Presidential Election," *The Forum* 2, no. 4 (2004). See also Anna Greenberg, "Moving beyond the Gender Gap," in Kerbel, ed., *Get This Party Started*, 23–43.

33. Exit polls available at http://www.cnn.com.

34. Michael Nelson characterized the 2000 election as the closest witnessed by living Americans; James Ceaser and Andrew Busch concluded that it was the closest in American history when also taking account of the 50–50 split in Senate seats, the nearly even match-up in the House, and the number of split state legislatures. See Michael Nelson, ed., Preface, in *The Elections of 2000* (Washington, DC: Congressional Quarterly Press, 2001), ix, and Ceaser and Busch, *Perfect Tie*. As Ceaser and Busch also reported (pp. 213–219), the U.S. Senate divided exactly along party lines for only the third time in its history; House Republicans emerged with a majority of only nine seats (the fourth closest division of House seats ever) after winning 49 percent of the congressional vote nationwide to the Democrats' 48 percent; and when the dust cleared in the states, Republicans constituted a majority in seventeen legislatures, Democrats controlled another seventeen, and another fifteen legislatures ended up with split-party control. Moreover, senates in Arizona, Maine, Missouri, and South Carolina split exactly even along party lines, and just one seat marked the difference between majority and minority party status in the senates of Colorado, Texas, and Washington.

35. Bush trailed by 537,179 in the popular vote. See *CQ Press Guide to U.S. Elections*, 5th ed., vol. 1 (Washington, DC: Congressional Quarterly Press, 2005), 718.

36. *Guide to U.S. Elections*; Wilson garnered 277 electoral votes to Hughes's 254. This paragraph also drew on data summarized by Larry J. Sabato, "The Election That Broke the Rules," in his *Divided States of America*, 51–120.

37. Two recounts did not appreciably alter Bush's Ohio vote total.

38. Alec M. Gallup and Frank Newport, eds., *The Gallup Poll: Public Opinion 2004* (Lanham, MD: Rowman & Littlefield, 2006), 412–413.

39. Ibid., 407–408.

40. Sabato, "Election That Broke the Rules," 54–55; turnout figures were updated with data from *Guide to U.S. Elections*.

41. For detailed accounts of get-out-the-vote efforts by both sides in Ohio and other states,

see David M. Magleby, J. Quinn Monson, and Kelly D. Patterson, eds., *Dancing without Partners: How Candidates, Parties, and Interest Groups Interact in the Presidential Campaign* (Lanham, MD: Rowman & Littlefield, 2007).

42. Gallup and Newport, *The Gallup Poll: Public Opinion 2004*, 444. Truman stood at 39 percent approval in Gallup's last job approval rating before the 1948 election; Bush's final rating in 2004 was 48 percent, three points higher than Ford in 1976, eleven points higher than Carter in 1980, and fifteen points above his father's final figure in 1992.

43. "A Nation Transformed," available at http://clinton4.nara.gov/WH/Accomplishments.

44. Stock market data obtained from http://www.frwebgate.access.gpo.gov.

45. Daniel Gross, *Bull Run: Wall Street, the Democrats, and the New Politics of Personal Finance* (New York: Public Affairs Press, 2000), 4–5.

46. See Bill Turque, *Inventing Al Gore: A Biography* (Boston: Houghton Mifflin, 2000), 312–337; also see Bob Zelnick, *Gore: A Political Life* (Washington, DC: Regnery, 1999), 283–317. Bush made repeated use of "no controlling legal authority" throughout the campaign. Speaking in Pittsburgh on October 26, for example, he said: "In my administration, we will ask not only what is legal but also what is right, not just what the lawyers allow but what the public deserves. In my administration, we will make it clear there is the controlling legal authority of conscience." See James Dao, "Bush, Wooing Pennsylvania, Attacks Gore's Character," *NYT*, October 27, 2000, A26.

47. Turque, *Inventing Al Gore*, 356.

48. George Gallup Jr., *The Gallup Poll: Public Opinion 1988* (Wilmington, DE: Scholarly Resources, 1999), 122, 126, 130–131.

49. See Molly W. Andolina and Clyde Wilcox, "Public Opinion: The Paradoxes of Clinton's Popularity," in Mark J. Rozell and Clyde Wilcox, eds., *The Clinton Scandal and the Future of American Government* (Washington, DC: Georgetown University Press, 2000), 171–194; also see James L. Guth, "Clinton, Impeachment, and the Culture Wars," in Steven E. Schier, ed., *The Postmodern Presidency: Bill Clinton's Legacy in U.S. Politics* (Pittsburgh, PA: University of Pittsburgh Press, 2000), 203–222.

50. For an excellent analysis of why House Republicans decided to proceed with impeachment after their setback in the 1998 elections, see Nicol Rae and Colton C. Campbell, *Impeaching Clinton: Partisan Strife on Capitol Hill* (Lawrence: University Press of Kansas, 2004).

51. For an embittered account of how House impeachment managers felt about the Senate proceedings, see David P. Schippers, *Sellout: The Inside Story of President Clinton's Impeachment* (Washington, DC: Regnery, 2000). For the Senate Republican leader's perspective, see Trent Lott, *Herding Cats: A Life in Politics* (New York: Regan Books, 2005), 169–203.

52. Margaret Tseng, "The Clinton Effect: How a Lame-Duck President Impacted His Vice President's Election Prospects," in Stephen J. Wayne and Clyde Wilcox, eds., *The Election of the Century and What It Tells Us about the Future of American Politics* (Armonk, NY: M. E. Sharpe, 2002), 200–202.

53. Andolina and Wilcox, "Public Opinion," 192.

54. See http://archives.cnn.com/2000/ALLPOLITICS/stories/01/26/dem.debate/index.html.

55. Gallup findings were calculated by Tseng, in "The Clinton Effect," 204.

56. Ibid., 201.

57. "Richard B. Cheney Address Accepting the GOP Nomination for Vice President," available at http://www.cnn.com/ELECTION/2000/conventions/republican/transcripts/cheney.html.

58. Lieberman's September 3, 1998, speech condemning Clinton's behavior in the Lewinsky affair is reprinted in Stephen Singular, *Joe Lieberman: The Historic Choice* (New York: Pinnacle Books, 2000), 78–88.

59. Ceaser and Busch, *Perfect Tie*, 30–31.

60. "Albert Gore, Jr., Acceptance Speech, August 17th, 2000, Los Angeles, California," American Presidency Project, available at http://www.presidency.ucsb.edu.

61. Quoted by Marjorie Randon Hershey, "The Campaign and the Media," in Gerald M. Pomper, ed., *The Election of 2000* (New York: Chatham House/Seven Bridges, 2001), 55. After the dust of the Florida recount had settled, Clinton and Gore exchanged bitter recriminations in a one-on-one meeting. Reportedly, Clinton attributed Gore's loss to his refusal to run on the economic record of the previous eight years; Gore blamed his loss on Monica Lewinsky and other scandals. According to Tseng, "Gore's camp remained adamant to the end that Clinton was not the solution but the threat to his election victory." See Tseng, "The Clinton Effect," 210–211.

62. Melinda Henneberger and Don Van Natta Jr., "Once Close to Clinton, Gore Keeps a Distance," *NYT*, October 20, 2000, A1; Marc Lacey, "Gore Puts Limit on Politicking by the President," *NYT*, October 28, 2000, A1; see also Lacey, "Clinton Seeks to Help Candidates Where He Can Do No Harm," *NYT*, November 1, 2000, A26.

63. Katharine Q. Seeyle, "Gore Sharpens His Message in Campaign's Frenetic Closing Days," *NYT*, October 24, 2000, A18.

64. Katharine Q. Seeyle and Kevin Sack, "The 2000 Campaign: The Focus Is on Crucial States in Campaign's Final Hours," *NYT*, November 6, 2000, A1.

65. Tseng, "The Clinton Effect," 202.

66. This extensive record includes oft-published reports of exaggeration, distortion, dissembling, and/or wholesale invention on such matters as Gore and his future wife serving as models for the novel *Love Story*, Gore's recollection of his importance as a writer for the *Nashville Tennessean*, his early opposition to abortion while in Congress, and the famous Internet claim. His 1988 race for the Democratic nomination gave critics further ammunition, and his penchant for misrepresentation continued while he was vice president. Perhaps the most serious of these lapses occurred at the 1996 Democratic convention, when Gore spoke movingly about losing his sister, a heavy smoker, to lung cancer. This loss, he claimed, had transformed him into an ardent foe of tobacco. At a press conference the following day, reporters reminded Gore that he had continued taking campaign contributions from the tobacco industry years after his sister's death; that he had touted his experience as a tobacco farmer in 1988; and that he, along with other senators, pressured the first Bush administration to promote American tobacco products in foreign markets. (At roughly the same time, Gore became an advocate of warning labels on cigarette packages and a supporter of efforts to reduce teen smoking.) In response, Gore pleaded memory loss owing to grief-induced "psychological numbness." For an extensive discussion of such issues, see Turque, *Inventing Al Gore*, 151–164, and Zelnick, *Gore: A Political Life*, 276–280.

67. Walter V. Robinson and Ann Scales, "Gore Record Scrutinized for Veracity, *Boston Globe*, January 28, 2000, available at http://boston.com/news/politics/campaign2000.

68. Ibid.

69. Richard Berke, "Tendency to Embellish Fact Snags Gore," *NYT*, October 6, 2000, A24. Berke pointed up instances of Gore dissembling during the first presidential debate: denying that he had questioned Bush's qualifications to be president when the record showed otherwise; misrepresenting the lack of a desk for a Florida schoolgirl; wrongly crediting himself for enlisting a top Russian diplomat to help resolve the Kosovo conflict; and claiming that he accompanied the director of the Federal Emergency Management Agency (FEMA) to inspect fire and flood damage in Texas when, in fact, Gore had gone on his own.

70. Ibid. Also see Berke, "Candidates Meet in Restrained Debate," *NYT*, October 12, 2000, A1.

71. Cited in James E. Campbell, "The Curious and Close Presidential Campaign of 2000," in William Crotty, ed., *America's Choice* (Boulder, CO: Westview Press, 2001), 133.

72. Gerald M. Pomper, "The Presidential Election," in Pomper, ed., *The Election of 2000*, 146.

73. Shaw, *Race to 270*, 120.

74. According to Turque, Gore may have smoked marijuana regularly during his time in divinity school, while he was a writer for the *Nashville Tennessean*, and possibly as late as his 1976 campaign for election to the U.S. House. Hashish also figured in this account. See Turque, *Inventing Al Gore*, 101 and 125–126.

75. J. T. Hatfield, *Fortunate Son* (New York: St. Martin's Press, 1999). The *Dallas Morning News* revealed that Hatfield was a paroled felon, in jail for embezzlement as well as hiring a hit man to murder his former boss. St. Martin's recalled 70,000 copies of the book and impounded another 20,000. The book nonetheless came out under a different imprint. Hatfield died July 18, 2001, reportedly of a drug overdose. "Bush Denies Using Any Illegal Drug during the Past 25 Years," http://www.cnn.com/ALLPOLITICS/stories/1999/08/19/president.2000/bush/drug/.

76. "Bush Denies Using Any Illegal Drug."

77. Alison Mitchell, "Bush Acknowledges an Arrest for Drunken Driving in 1976," *NYT*, November 3, 2000, A23. Accounts differ on the magnitude of this effect on Bush's poll numbers. The Democrats attributed Gore's late surge to effective attack ads on Social Security.

78. On this point, see Justin Martin, *Nader: Crusader, Spoiler, Icon* (New York: Perseus Publishing, 2002), 254; see also James Dao, "Nader Fades in Polls but Draws Crowds," *NYT*, September 24, 2000, A26.

79. Peter Marks, "On Each Side, Accusing Fingers over Nasty Turn in Campaign," *NYT*, October 28, 2000, A1. A Nader spokeswoman criticized this ad for ignoring that Bush "also has an abysmal environmental record."

80. Katharine Seelye, "Barnstorming Nader Turf, Gore Draws 20,000," *NYT*, October 27, 2000, A27.

81. Adam Clymer, "The Ad Campaign: Trying to Sway Nader Voters," *NYT*, October 27, 2000, A29. The National Abortion and Reproductive Rights Action League (NARRAL) paid for this spot, which was aimed at progressives unhappy with Gore.

82. Nader ran as the candidate of the Association of State Green Parties, not to be confused with the Green Party USA, a mistake that nonetheless showed up in his media coverage. The members of this fringe group gathered in Denver on June 24–25, 2000, to choose Nader over Jello Biafra, formerly the lead singer of the Dead Kennedys and a fringe candidate for mayor of San Francisco in 1979, and Stephen Gaskin, the founder of a commune in Tennessee and an advocate for the legalization of marijuana. One observer of these proceedings wrote that the convention hotel had been chosen because of its willingness to prepare certain organic dishes, adding: "The Republican convention this was not: people beat tom-tom drums to call meetings to order and indulged in a custom called 'twinkling,' which involves silently wiggling one's fingers in lieu of applause." See Martin, *Nader: Crusader, Spoiler, Icon*, 234–238.

83. See http://www.pbs.org/newshour/election2000/demconvention/gore3.html.

84. Kevin Sack, "Political Memo: Gore's Calculated Risk in Taking on Big Business," *NYT*, September 24, 2000, A28.

85. Robin Toner, "The Issues: Health," *NYT*, November 5, 2000, A35.

86. Alison Mitchell, "Bush Spells Out Major Overhaul in Medicare Plan," *NYT*, September 6, 2000, A1.

87. Ibid.

88. Ibid.

89. Frank Bruni, "Bush Pushes Health Plan to Attract Older Voters," *NYT,* September 12, 2000, A15.

90. Alison Mitchell, "Shifting Tactics, Bush Uses Issues to Confront Gore," *NYT,* September 16, 2000, A1.

91. Sack, "Political Memo: Gore's Calculated Risk."

92. Robin Toner, "The Ad Campaign: Battle on Prescription Drugs," *NYT,* September 21, 2000, A20.

93. Kevin Sack, "Differences on Medicare Take Center Stage in Gore Campaign," *NYT,* September 25, 2000, 19.

94. Sack, "Bush Would Use Medicare for Tax Cuts, Gore Says," *NYT,* September 26, 2000, A18.

95. Ibid.

96. Sack, "Differences on Medicare Take Center Stage."

97. Richard Berke, "Bush and Gore Stake Out Differences in First Debate," *NYT,* October 4, 2000, A1.

98. Ibid.

99. Richard Perez-Pena, "Lieberman Stakes Claim to Basic Values," *NYT,* October 17, 2000, A20. Most of Lieberman's contribution to the debate over health consisted of attacks on Governor Bush's management of Children's Health Insurance Program (CHIP), as well as his alleged indifference to the pestilent conditions in which poor Latinos lived. Lieberman often appeared in Texas to utter these charges.

100. Alison Mitchell, "Gore and Bush, in Last Debate, Spar on Wide Variety of Issues," *NYT,* October 18, 2000, A1.

101. Ibid.

102. Robin Toner, "Gore and Bush Health Care Proposals Fall Well Short of Counterparts' Plans 8 Years Ago," *NYT,* October 15, 2000, A22.

103. Katharine Seeyle, "Seeking Wisconsin Votes, Gore Sounds Populist Note," *NYT,* October 31, 2000, A21.

104. "In Speech, Bush Says It's Time for Leader Who Will Do the People's Business," *NYT,* October 28, 2000, A8.

105. Jacobson, *A Divider, Not a Uniter,* 1.

106. Ibid., 2–9. Averaged over entire presidencies, the partisan gap on approval had widened since 1970. It rose to fifty-two points for Reagan, fifty-five for Clinton, and fifty-nine for George W. Bush.

107. Paraphrased in James W. Ceaser and Andrew E. Busch, *Red over Blue: The 2004 Elections* (Lanham, MD: Rowman & Littlefield, 2005), 136.

108. Edison Media Research and Mitofsky International exit polls, summarized by John Kenneth White, in McMahon et al., *Winning the White House 2004,* 17.

109. Gallup and Newport, *Gallup Poll: Public Opinion 2004,* 383. In all, 18 percent of Kerry voters chose "want/need change/get Bush out of office/dissatisfied with Bush," and another 9 percent chose "dislike Bush/poor character." In contrast, only 7 percent of Kerry voters cited "like Kerry/good character" as an important influence; 6 percent chose an honesty, integrity, and ethics category; and 4 percent put a lot of stock in "military experience." Conversely, 3 percent of Bush voters based their vote strongly on "dislike Kerry/poor character"; 1 percent chose "dissatisfied with Kerry's job performance."

110. Jacobson, *A Divider, Not a Uniter*, 60–67.

111. The bill came about after the 1998 murder of James Byrd, a black man in Jasper, Texas, who was killed by three white men, at least one of whom was an avowed white supremacist and an ex-convict. Two, including the tattooed supremacist, were given the death penalty in 1999, and the other assailant received a life sentence. The victim's daughter appeared in a 2000 attack ad aired by the NAACP claiming that Governor Bush had been indifferent (at best) to Byrd's murder. She reiterated this charge at a Gore rally with Gore looking on. On another occasion, Gore painted Bush as sympathetic to lynching, the Confederate flag, and the counting of each slave as three-fifths of a person. Jesse Jackson took a similar line as a Gore surrogate. See Jeremy D. Mayer, *Running on Race: Racial Politics in Presidential Campaigns, 1960–2000* (New York: Random House, 2002), 283–290.

112. Ceaser and Busch, *Perfect Tie*, 207.

113. Quoted in Juan Williams, *Enough: The Phony Leaders, Dead-End Movements, and Culture of Failure That Are Undermining Black America and What We Can Do about It* (New York: Crown, 2006), 57–58.

114. Jodi Wilgoren, "Kerry Invokes the Bible in Appeal for Black Votes," *NYT*, September 10, 2004, A18.

115. Sheryl Gay Stolberg and James Dao, "Congress Ratifies Bush Victory after a Rare Challenge," *NYT*, January 7, 2005, A15; Jonathan Riskind, "Electoral College Challenge Quashed," *Columbus Dispatch*, January 7, 2005, A1.

116. Jacobson, *A Divider, Not a Uniter*, 70.

117. Charles O. Jones, "Capitalizing on Position in a Perfect Tie," in Fred I. Greenstein, ed., *The George W. Bush Presidency: An Early Assessment* (Baltimore, MD: Johns Hopkins University Press, 2003), 181.

118. Quoted in Bob Woodward, *Plan of Attack* (New York: Simon & Schuster, 2004), 28.

119. This paragraph closely paraphrased the account by Ceaser and Busch in *Red over Blue*, 53.

120. In addition to Ceaser and Busch's account of the 2002 midterm campaigns, see Paul R. Abramson, John H. Aldrich, and David W. Rohde, *Change and Continuity in the 2000 and 2002 Elections* (Washington, DC: CQ Press, 2003), 252–281.

121. John Kenneth White, "Choosing the Candidates," in Kevin J. McMahon et al., *Winning the White House 2004*, 4.

122. Tom Daschle, *Like No Other Time: The Two Years That Changed America* (New York: Three Rivers Press, 2003), 3. Elected in 1996 to fill Sam Nunn's seat, Cleland became known as "a legislative moderate who steers clear of partisan disputes" and as one of the Senate's "New Democrats," a group trying to move the party closer to the middle. As a member of the Armed Services Committee, he figured importantly in steering defense contracts to Georgia. His ADA (liberal) score averaged over four years of Senate service was 82.5; the ACU (conservative) average was 8. See Brian Nutting and H. Amy Stern, eds., *Politics in America 2002: The 107th Congress* (Washington, DC: Congressional Quarterly Press, 2001), 256–257.

123. ABC News/*Washington Post* polls reported in Jacobson, *A Divider, Not a Uniter*, 150.

124. See p. 27 of report available at http://www.transatlantictrends.org/trends/index.cfm?year=2004.

125. Iraq Liberation Act of 1998 H.R. 4655, available at http://www.thomas.loc.gov.

126. Quoted in Norman Podhoretz, "Who Is Lying about Iraq?" *Wall Street Journal*, November 15, 2005, available at http://www.opinionjournal.com.

127. Kenneth M. Pollack, *The Threatening Storm: The Case for Invading Iraq* (New York: Random House, 2002).

128. Ibid., 168–173.

129. Ibid., 173–174.

130. Ibid., 174.

131. Ibid., 175.

132. Ibid., 155.

133. "Vice President Speaks at VFW 103rd National Convention," text available at http://www .whitehouse.gov/news/releases/2002/08/20020826.html.

134. George W. Bush, *We Will Prevail: President George W. Bush on War, Terrorism, and Freedom—Selected and Edited by the National Review* (New York: Continuum, 2003), 183–184.

135. Daschle, *Like No Other Time,* 243.

136. Ibid., 244.

137. See Robert C. Byrd, *Losing America: Confronting a Reckless and Arrogant Presidency* (New York: W. W. Norton, 2004), 160. According to Trent Lott, at that time the Senate minority leader, Daschle emphatically opposed the administration's war resolution at a White House breakfast meeting in early September. See Lott, *Herding Cats,* 239.

138. According to Lott, Senator Chuck Hagel, a Nebraska Republican, also played a part in framing the Biden-Lugar alternative. Lott further claimed that President Bush had commanded him to "derail" the Biden-Lugar alternative. See Lott, *Herding Cats,* 239–241.

139. Byrd, *Losing America,* 163.

140. Bush, *We Will Prevail,* 191–192.

141. Insiders gave Kerry the edge despite the fact that he never topped the list of aspirants in the Gallup Poll and that he trailed Lieberman in early polls of the invisible primary phase.

142. Todd S. Purdum, "2 Kerry Votes on War and Peace Underline a Political Evolution," *NYT,* October 27, 2004, A1.

143. See http://www.independentsforkerry.org/uploads/media/kerry-iraq.html.

144. Final Vote Results for Roll Call 455, H.J. Res. 114, October 10, 2002, available at http// clerk.house.gov/cgi-bin/vote.asp?year=2002&rollnumber=455.

145. U.S. Senate Roll Call Votes, 107th Congress, 2nd session, October 10–11, 2002, votes 232–237, available at http://www.senate.gov/legislative/LIE/roll_call_lists/roll_call_vote.

146. See Barry C. Burden, "The Nominations: Technology, Money, and Transferable Momentum," in Nelson, ed., *Elections of 2004,* 26–27. One polling firm found that Dean's standing soared from 19 percent in July 2003 to 45 percent in December, while at the same time, Kerry's dropped from 25 percent to 13 percent. In early January 2004, Kerry ran behind several others, with only 10 percent.

147. Ceaser and Busch, *Red over Blue,* 73.

148. David E. Rosenbaum, "Fact Check: A Closer Look at Statements from the Debate," *NYT,* October 2, 2004, A1; see also Rosenbaum, "Yes, He Said That, but What He Really Meant Was …" *NYT,* October 26, 2004, E8.

149. Ceaser and Busch, *Red over Blue,* 72.

150. For an excellent analysis of how Dean fell and Kerry rose, see ibid., 69–104; see also Burden, "The Nominations"; White, "Choosing the Candidates"; Brooke Brower, "Nominations and Conventions," in Sabato, ed., *Divided States of America,* 1–23, and, in the same collection, Claude R. Max, "The Rise and Fall of Howard Dean," 37–49.

151. U.S. Senate Roll Call Votes, 108th Congress, 1st session (2003), vote no. 373, October 2, available at www.senate.gov.

152. Pundit Joe Klein provided just such an interpretation. Kerry voted against final passage of the 2003 appropriations bill, Klein argued, to boost his chances against Dean in "the peaceable

kingdom of Iowa, where antiwar sentiment seemed to grow with the corn." Worse, Klein asserted, "Kerry had now cast three contradictory votes on Iraq—against the first Gulf War, for the second Gulf War, and against the money to fight the war for which he had voted. . . . He would no longer be able to run a credible national-security campaign against Bush. If he argued—as he later tried to do—that the administration was irresponsible because it hadn't provided the troops with sufficient body armor, the Bushies could respond that Kerry had voted against the money for the body armor. He had destroyed the original rationale, the moral and intellectual basis for his candidacy." See Klein, *Politics Lost: How American Democracy Was Trivialized by People Who Think You're Stupid* (New York: Doubleday, 2006), 201.

153. Table 7.7 omits two votes against the funding, one cast by Independent Jeffords (who also had voted against the 2002 authorization of force) and one cast by Frank Lautenberg, Democrat of New Jersey, not yet a senator when the 2002 vote occurred. Among Republicans, only Lincoln Chafee voted against the 2002 war resolution; along with every other Republican senator, he voted for the $87 billion supplemental.

154. In 1991, at the urging of Majority Leader George Mitchell and Armed Services Committee chairman Sam Nunn, Kerry had joined most other Senate Democrats in opposing the joint resolution authorizing President George H. W. Bush to eject Saddam's troops from Kuwait by force of arms. Providing similar authorization, UN Security Council Resolution 678 had already been passed, and a large American force already had been dispatched to Saudi Arabia. Economic sanctions had not diminished Saddam's defiance of previous UN resolutions. To drive him out before the onset of summer, coalition forces needed to strike sooner than the sanctions strategy allowed. Mitchell and Nunn moved this alternative in the form of S.J. Res. 1, the key provision of which stated, "The Congress believes that continued application of international sanctions and diplomatic efforts to pressure Iraq to leave Kuwait is the wisest course at this time and should be sustained, but it does not rule out declaring war or authorizing the use of force at a later time, should that be necessary to achieve the goal of forcing Iraqi troops from Kuwait." See S.J. Res. 1, 102nd Cong., 1st sess., January 10, 1991, available at http://www.thomas.loc.gov. The resolution lost, 46 to 53, in a January 12 vote. Several hours later, S.J. Res. 2, which authorized use of force at a time of the president's choosing, passed by a margin of 52 to 47. Gore was among the few Democrats who voted for S.J. Res. 2. Details on individual votes are available at http://www.senate.gov.

155. Michael A. Dimock, "Bush and Public Opinion," in Gary L. Gregg II and Mark J. Rozell, eds., *Considering the Bush Presidency* (New York: Oxford University Press, 2004), 75. Dimock relied on Pew Research Center polls.

156. Richard Brody, *Assessing the President: The Media, Elite Opinion, and Public Support* (Stanford, CA: Stanford University Press, 1991), 30–36.

157. Jacobson, *A Divider, Not a Uniter*, esp. 95–162.

158. This was not the case in Ohio, however, where Secretary of State Kenneth Blackwell and other Republican leaders took on the Democrats over provisional and absentee ballots, registration, and other issues of election administration.

159. FactCheck.org assessed these charges in several reports: "Bush a Military 'Deserter?' Calm Down, Michael," posted January 23, 2004, and modified February 11, 2004; "New Evidence Supports Bush Military Service (Mostly)," posted February 11, 2004, and modified February 15, 2004; and "Democratic Group's Ad Revives 'AWOL' Allegation against Bush," posted September 8, 2004, and modified September 10, 2004.

160. Richard W. Stevenson and David M. Halbfinger, "Bush and Kerry Step Up Attacks in Swing States," *NYT*, September 11, 2004, A1.

161. For an admiring account of Bush's reaction to the CBS report and a detailed criticism of how Mapes and Rather put it together, see Bill Sammon, *Stratergy: How George W. Bush Is Defeating Terrorists, Outwitting Democrats, and Confronting the Mainstream Media* (Washington, DC: Regnery, 2006); for Mapes's version, see her *Truth and Duty: The Press, the President, and the Privilege of Power* (New York: St. Martin's Press, 2005). See also Ceaser and Busch, *Red over Blue*, 123–124, and Vaughn Ververs, "A New Media," in Sabato, ed., *Divided States of America*, 184–185.

162. The *Times* covered the CBS affair extensively. See Katharine Seeyle and Ralph Blumenthal, "Documents Suggest Special Treatment for Bush in Guard," *NYT*, September 9, 2004, A1; Jim Rutenberg and Kate Zernike, "CBS Defends Its Report on Bush Military Record," *NYT*, September 11, 2004, A10; Rutenberg and Zernike, "CBS Offers New Experts to Support Guard Memos," *NYT*, September 14, 2004, A19; Maureen Balleza and Kate Zernike, "Memos on Bush Are Fake but Accurate, Typist Says," *NYT*, September 15, 2004, A20; Rutenberg and Zernike, "CBS Says It Will Check Questions on Bush Files," *NYT*, September 16, 2004, A16; Ralph Blumenthal, "Ex-guardsman Is Said to Be a CBS Source," *NYT*, September 16, 2004, A16; David R. Kirkpatrick and Rutenberg, "Texan Involved in CBS Report Tried to Help Kerry Campaign," *NYT*, September 18, 2004, A11; Richard W. Stevenson and Raymond Bonner, "Commander's Letter Praised Bush to Father," *NYT*, September 18, 2004, A11; Sara Rimer, "Portrait of George Bush in '72: Unanchored in Turbulent Time," *NYT*, September 20, 2004, A1; Rutenberg and Zernike, "CBS Apologizes for Report on Bush Guard Service," *NYT*, September 21, 2004, A1; Bill Carter and Jacques Steinberg, "CBS Quiet about Fallout, but Precedent Is Ominous," *NYT*, September 21, 2004, A22; Alessandra Stanley, "Even Humbled by Error, Dan Rather Has His Thorns," *NYT*, September 21, A22; Rutenberg and Carter, "CBS Producer Violated Policy by Putting Source in Touch with Kerry Aide," *NYT*, September 22, 2004, A14; Zernike, "Kerry Camp Describes Contacts with Source of CBS Papers," *NYT*, September 22, 2004, A14; and Rutenberg and Steinberg, "CBS Appoints 2-Man Panel to Investigate Guard Report," *NYT*, September 23, 2004, A22. See also "Report of the Independent Review Panel on the September 8, 2004, *60 Minutes* Segment for the Record, Concerning President Bush's Texas Air National Guard Service, January 5, 2005," available at http://www.image.cbsnews/com/htdocs/pdf/complete_report.

163. Elisabeth Bumiller, "Pentagon Releases Bush's Long-South Military Records," *NYT*, September 8, 2004, A21. Independent examiners later turned up twelve additional pages of Bush's service record as part of an agreement reached between the Associated Press and the Texas Air National Guard. This new material pertained to "physiological training" that Bush underwent to recognize the effects on his body from flying at high altitudes. One record established that Bush had been given a dental examination at his temporary base in Alabama. See "Professors Find More Papers on Bush's Guard Service," *NYT*, October 17, 2004, A19.

164. Zernike, "Kerry Camp Describes Contacts."

165. *Legislative Proposals Relating to the War in Southeast Asia*, Hearings before the Committee on Foreign Relations, U.S. Senate, 92nd Cong., 1st sess., April 20–22 and 28; May 3, 11–13, 25–27, 1971 (Washington, DC: Government Printing Office, 1971), 180–181.

166. See http://www.swiftvets.com/index.php.

167. Paul Freedman, "Swift Boats and Tax Hikes: Campaign Advertising in the 2004 Election," in Sabato, ed., *Divided States of America*, 169–170.

168. Ibid., 170; see p. 177 for text of first Swift Boat Vets ad.

169. *Legislative Proposals Relating to the War.*

170. For one assessment of the ad's effectiveness, see Freedman, "Swift Boats and Tax Hikes,"

171.

171. Reportedly, Kerry's account of what had been thrown away changed over time, from "giving back" upwards of nine of his medals to throwing away his ribbons but keeping the medals to throwing away the medals or ribbons awarded others. The initial report of seven to nine or perhaps more suggests that he may have tossed somebody else's decorations as well as his own.

172. As of September 2006, all of the ads were still accessible from the Swift Boat Vets Web site at http://www.swiftvets.com/index.php. FactCheck.org and some newspapers pointed up discrepancies between what some of Kerry's accusers earlier had said about his medals and their recent allegations. See "Republican-Funded Group Attacks Kerry's War Record: Ad Features Vets Who Claim Kerry 'Lied' to Get Vietnam Medals; But Other Witnesses Disagree—and So Do Navy Records," August 6, 2004, modified August 22, 2004. Another FactCheck report confirmed that American forces had indeed committed war crimes in Vietnam, but it stopped short of investigating whether Kerry had exaggerated the frequency of such atrocities or the numbers killed or brutalized. The report further suggested that Kerry since had claimed that his testimony applied to commanders rather than to the troops in the field. See "Swift Boat Veterans Anti-Kerry Ad: 'He Betrayed Us' with 1971 Anti-war Testimony: Group Quotes Kerry's Descriptions of Atrocities by U.S. Forces; In fact, Atrocities Did Happen," August 23, 2004, modified November 8, 2004, available at http://www.factcheck.org. FactCheck conducted no such investigation of Swift Boat Vets charges that Kerry had met with the enemy in Paris, that he had parroted its negotiating points, or that his 1971 testimony to the Senate Foreign Relations Committee had demoralized American POWs.

173. Numerous *Times* stories contended that Kerry had met with "both sides" in Paris. This language implied that he had conferred with the South Vietnamese as well as the North Vietnamese. In fact, he met with two Communist delegations under Hanoi's control. See Katharine Seeyle, "Both Sides' Commercials Create Brew of Negativity, at a Broil," *NYT,* September 23, 2004, A22. After writing that Swift Boat Vets charges had "frequently been unsubstantiated," Seeyle asserted that "Mr. Kerry testified shortly thereafter that he had met with both sides at the Vietnam peace talks to discuss the status of prisoners of war." Jodi Wilgoren perpetuated this error in "Truth Be Told, the Vietnam Crossfire Hurts Kerry More," *NYT,* September 24, 2004, A23: "Mr. Kerry's nemesis, Swift Boat Veterans for Truth, is spending $1.3 million in five swing states with a spot accusing him of meeting with the enemy in Paris—a reference to his trip to the Paris peace talks, where he met with both sides." Glen Justice and Jim Rutenberg reiterated the "both sides" claim in "Advocacy Groups Step Up Costly Battle of Political Ads," *NYT,* September 25, 2004, A10. For an accurate account on this point, see Michael Kranish and Patrick Healy, "Kerry Spoke of Meeting Negotiators on Vietnam," *Boston Globe,* March 25, 2004, A8, available at bostonglobe@newsbank.com.

174. *Legislative Proposals Relating to the War,* 186. The transcript quotes Kerry as follows: "I don't mean to sound pessimistic, but I do not believe that this Congress will, in fact, end the war as we would like to, which is immediately and unilaterally and, therefore, if I were to speak I would say we would set a date and the date obviously would be the earliest possible date. But I would like to say, in answering that, that I do not believe it is necessary to stall any longer. I have been to Paris. I have talked with both delegations of the peace talks, that is to say the Democratic Republic of Vietnam and the Provisional Revolutionary Government."

175. Adam Nagourney and David M. Halbfinger, "Kerry Enlisting Clinton Aides in Effort to Refocus Campaign," *NYT,* September 6, 2004, A1; Stevenson and Halbfinger, "Bush and Kerry Step Up Attacks." The latter article quoted an unnamed but high-placed member of the Kerry-Edwards organization, who maintained that the Swift Boat Vets had "damaged" Kerry's character and, further, that "the campaign failed to defend the guy. We're in a tough spot."

176. Halbfinger and David E. Sanger, "Bush and Kerry Clash over Iraq and a Timetable," *NYT*, September 7, 2004, A1.

177. Halbfinger, "Kerry Says Bush Broke His Word in Pursuing War on Iraq," *NYT*, September 9, 2004, A29.

178. David E. Sanger, "Kerry Says Bush Has Ignored North Korean Threat," *NYT*, September 13, 2004, A1.

179. Sanger, "In Guard Speech, Bush Says He Is Proud of His Service," *NYT*, September 15, 2004, A20.

180. Elizabeth Bumiller, "In Address to Guard, Kerry Says Bush Isn't Telling Truth on Iraq," *NYT*, September 17, 2004, A1.

181. Bumiller and David E. Sanger, "Kerry Sees Plan to Call Up New Reserves after Nov. 2," *NYT*, September 18, 2004, A11. Kerry's Halliburton claim rested on the $2 million that Cheney had received as part of a deferred separation package upon leaving the company in 2001.

182. Jodi Wilgoren and Bumiller, "In Harshest Critique Yet, Kerry Attacks Bush over War in Iraq," *NYT*, September 21, 2004, A1. See also David E. Rosenbaum, "Fact Check: A Closer Look at Cheney and Halliburton," *NYT*, September 28, 2004, A18.

183. David E. Sanger, "2 Iraq Views, 2 Campaigns," *NYT*, September 22, 2004, A1.

184. "Campaign Briefing," *NYT*, September 23, 2004, A22.

185. Elizabeth Bumiller, "Bush and Allawi Say Iraqi Voting Won't Be Put Off," *NYT*, September 24, 2004, A1. See also "In His Own Words," *NYT*, September 24, 2004, A21.

186. Robin Toner, "Kerry Promises to Refocus U.S. on Terror War," *NYT*, September 25, 2004, A1.

187. Adam Nagourney and Toner, "Strong Charges Set New Tone before Debate," *NYT*, September 27, 2004, A1.

188. Randal C. Archibold, "Edwards Says Bush Lead in Polls Is Temporary," *NYT*, September 13, 2004, A17.

189. Archibold, "Taking the Offensive, Edwards Says a Kerry Administration Would 'Crush' Al Qaeda," *NYT*, September 20, 2004, A16.

190. Richard W. Stevenson, "Kerry Maintains Domestic Focus, Turning to Social Security and Medicare," *NYT*, September 23, 2004, A23.

191. Randal C. Archibold, "Edwards Notes Cheney Warned of Getting 'Bogged Down' in Iraq," *NYT*, September 30, 2004, A20. Cheney maintained that 9/11 had changed his thinking.

192. Eric Schmitt and David E. Sanger, "U.S. Expects More Violence as Iraq Vote Draws Near," *NYT*, September 11, 2004, A5.

193. Michael Janofsky, "Kennedy Denounces Bush Policies as Endangering the World," *NYT*, September 28, 2004, A18.

194. Douglas Jehl, "U.S. Intelligence Shows Pessimism on Iraq's Future," *NYT*, September 16, 2004, A1.

195. David E. Sanger and David M. Halbfinger, "Cheney Warns of Terror Risk If Kerry Wins," *NYT*, September 8, 2004, A1.

196. Glen Justice, "Political Group's Antiwar Ad Draws Ire of the Bush Campaign," *NYT*, September 17, 2004, A13.

197. Archibold, "Taking the Offensive."

198. Seelye, "Both Sides' Commercials Create Brew."

199. Richard W. Stevenson, "Kerry Accuses President of Misleading U.S. on Iraq," September 24, 2004, A21.

200. Justice and Rutenberg, "Advocacy Groups Step Up Costly Battle."

201. Jodi Wilgoren and Robin Toner, "Trading Charges over Iraq While Preparing for Debate," *NYT*, September 28, 2004, A19.

202. See Evan Thomas, *Election 2004: How Bush Won and What You Can Expect in the Future* (New York: Public Affairs, 2004), 95–97.

203. Elizabeth Bumiller, "Kerry Mounts Fierce Attack on Bush's Economic Policies," *NYT*, September 16, 2004, A17.

204. As Kerry tacked back and forth in this ad to the strains of a Strauss waltz, the narrator said that the senator had "voted for the Iraq war, opposed it, supported it, and now opposes it again. John Kerry: Whichever way the wind blows." See Seeyle, "Both Sides' Commercials Create Brew."

205. Halbfinger and Sanger, "Bush and Kerry Clash."

206. Sanger and Halbfinger, "Cheney Warns of Terror Risk."

207. Stevenson and Halbfinger, "Bush and Kerry Step Up Attacks."

208. Sanger, "In Guard Speech."

209. Wilgoren and Bumiller, "In Harshest Critique Yet."

210. Raymond Hernandez, "Bush Carries His Attack against Kerry to Pennsylvania," *NYT*, September 23, 2004, A22.

211. Sanger, "In Guard Speech."

212. Bumiller, "Bush and Allawi."

213. Elizabeth Bumiller, "Bush Denounces Kerry for His Remark on Allawi," *NYT*, September 25, 2004, A11.

214. For insights into how local and regional newspapers reported Cheney speeches, see Joel Brinkley, "Cheney's Core Speech Seems Stale to Some in Local News," *NYT*, November 1, 2004, A19.

215. Sanger and Halbfinger, "Cheney Warns of Terror Risk."

216. Adam Nagourney, "When an Explosive Charge Is Not Handled with Care," *NYT*, September 9, 2004, A29; see also Rick Lyman, "Cheney Offers Explanation of Comment about Kerry," *NYT*, September 11, 2004, A10.

217. Halbfinger and Sanger, "Bush and Kerry Clash."

218. Bumiller, "In Address to Guard."

219. Sanger, "In Guard Speech."

220. Rick Lyman, "Cheney Calls Kerry Stance 'Incoherent,'" *NYT*, September 17, 2004, A14.

221. Stevenson, "Kerry Accuses Bush."

222. Halbfinger, "Kerry Says Bush Broke His Word."

223. Toner, "Kerry Promises to Refocus U.S."

224. Wilgoren and Bumiller, "In Harshest Critique Yet."

225. David M. Halbfinger, "Kerry Says Flip-Flop Image 'Doesn't Reflect the Truth,'" *NYT*, September 30, 2004, A21.

CHAPTER 8. SUMMARY AND SYNTHESIS: HAVE PRESIDENTIAL CAMPAIGNS BECOME MORE NEGATIVE?

1. John G. Geer, *In Defense of Negativity: Attack Ads in Presidential Campaigns* (Chicago: University of Chicago Press, 2006), 86.

2. Ibid., 25–29.

3. Thomas E. Patterson, *Out of Order* (New York: Vintage, 1994).

4. Ibid., 81–84.

5. Ibid., 116–117.

6. Ibid., 137.

7. For example, the Media Fund, directed by Harold Ickes, spent about $55 million on anti-Bush advertising, and the MoveOn.org Voter Fund spent another $21 million. Americans Coming Together (ACT) spent about $76 million on voter registration and get-out-the-vote (GOTV) activities. See Michael Toner, "The Impact of the New Campaign Finance Law on the 2004 Presidential Election," in Larry J. Sabato, ed., *Divided States of America: The Slash and Burn Politics of the 2004 Presidential Election* (New York: Pearson-Longman, 2006), 192.

8. Because Quayle and Cheney each relied heavily on the same speech on the campaign trail, it is likely that the *Times*'s record understated the frequency of their attacks.

9. "Between the end of the 1964 debacle and the beginning of the 1966 campaign," Nixon wrote in his memoirs, "I had logged 127,000 miles visiting forty states to speak before more than 400 groups. I helped to raise more than $4 million in contributions to the party." See his *RN: The Memoirs of Richard Nixon*, vol. 1 (New York: Warner Books, 1978), 335.

10. According to the *Times*, "a House candidate not helped by Nixon stood only a 45 percent chance of winning, while those for whom Nixon had stumped had a 70 percent chance of victory." Quoted in Stephen E. Ambrose, *Nixon: The Triumph of a Politician, 1962–1972*, vol. 2 (New York: Simon & Schuster, 1989), 100. Of course, Nixon carefully chose to stump in districts and states where he felt he could make a difference. See Nixon, *RN*, 337.

11. Anthony Downs, *An Economic Theory of Democracy* (New York: Harper & Row, 1957), esp. pt. 1.

INDEX

relative negativity among presidential
  candidates, 248
spoiler role of in 1992, 65, 92, 254, 263, 264,
  291n52
Perot, Susan, 86
Petrocik, John, 24–26, 283n53
Pew Research Center for the People and the
  Press, 2, 272n9
Pollack, Kenneth, 221–222
Pollard, Ramsey, 150
Polsby, Nelson, ix, 167, 275n44
Pomper, Gerald, 2, 3, 200, 289n32, 321n16,
  333n61
Powell, Adam Clayton, 150, 317n81
Powell, Colin, 221
Powell, Jody, 172 192
Pryce, Deborah, vii
Purdum, Todd S., 223

Quayle, James Danforth ("Dan"), 54, 55, 60,
  79, 80, 85, 93, 250, 260, 292n78
  attack on Perot, 59
  1988 attacks on Democrats, 82
  1992 attacks on Democrats, 68, 83
  relative negativity among vice-presidential
    candidates, 249, 259
Quayle, Marilyn, 87
Quemoy and Matsu, 145, 157–162, 267, 314n43,
  319n130

Rafshoon, Gerald, 172, 173
Rather, Dan, 231, 339n162
Rayburn, Sam, 149, 151–152, 312n6
Reagan, Ronald, viii, 15, 20, 37, 54, 65, 80, 169,
  170, 175, 178, 183, 191, 192, 193, 194, 195,
  218, 256, 259
  handling of Anderson in 1980, 179, 181
  1976 primary challenge to Ford, 119, 134
  1980 attacks on Democrats, 163, 181, 183,
    184, 186, 187, 188–190, 195, 260
  1980 "Capitol Compact," 166–167
  1980 poll standings of, 164, 179
  1980 popular and electoral votes of, 21, 163,
    164–165, 167
  1984 attacks on Democrats, 33, 35, 36, 41,
    44, 49, 50–51, 260
  1984 poll standings of, 32
  1984 popular and electoral votes of, 21, 196

1988 attacks on Democrats, 55, 74, 81
relative negativity among presidential
  candidates, 248
Republican National Committee (RNC), 45,
  90, 143, 147, 150, 158, 214, 215, 166–167
Ribicoff, Abraham, 98
Richardson, Glen W., 7
Rockefeller, David, 176
Rockefeller, Nelson A., 28–29, 46, 102, 134, 143,
  152, 158, 226, 257, 306n140, 307n140,
  311n220
Rodino, Peter, 121
Roe v. Wade, 209
Rohde, David, 165, 290n39, 290n41, 221n16
Romney, George, 28–29, 117, 280n4
Roosevelt, Eleanor, 146, 315n48
Roosevelt, Franklin D. (FDR), viii, 6, 7, 60, 62,
  131, 151, 255, 279n106, 292n78, 315n48,
  315n55
Roosevelt, Theodore, 56, 278n96
Rostenkowski, Dan, 61
Rostow, Walt, 98
Rove, Karl, 202, 215
Rowe, James, 104, 313n17
Ruff, Charles F. C., 122
Rumsfeld, Donald, 237
Rusk, Dean, 98
Rusk, Jerome, 94, 298n7
Russell, Richard B., 151, 152

Safire, William, 102
SALT II Treaty, 15, 175
Santorum, Rick, 219
Sasso, John, 77
Scalia, Antonin, 209
Schlesinger, James, 171
Schmidt, Steve, 243
Schultze, Charles, 171
Schwarzenegger, Arnold, vii
Scott, Hugh, 28, 49, 146, 319n124
Scranton, William, 28–29, 46, 257
Selective emphasis; issue ownership,
  avoidance, or convergence, 24–26,
  260–263, 264
  and comeback races, 107, 109, 110, 111, 118,
    128, 130, 137
  and dead heat race of 1960, 156, 157, 162
  and dead heat race of 1980, 183–185